WHERE THE HELL ARE THE GUNS?

Cloth edition 1997
Trade paperback edition 1999

Canadian Cataloguing in Publication Data

Blackburn, George G., 1917–
    Where the hell are the guns? : a soldier's eye view of the anxious years, 1939–44

Includes bibliographical references and index.
ISBN 0-7710-1504-6 (bound)   ISBN 0-7710-1506-2 (pbk.)

1. Blackburn, George G., 1917–   . 2. World War, 1939–1945 —
Regimental histories — Canada.   3. Canada. Canadian Army. Field Regiment,
4th — History.   4. Canada. Canadian Army. Field Regiment, 4th —
Biography.   5. World War, 1939–1945 — Personal narratives, Canadian.
6. World War, 1939–1945 — Artillery operations, Canadian.   I. Title.

D78.15.B57 1997   940.54'8171   C97-932028-3

Map by William Constable
Set in *Bembo* by Computer Composition of Canada Inc., Whitby

The publishers acknowledge the support of the Canada Council and the Ontario Arts Council for their publishing program.

Printed and bound in Canada

McClelland & Stewart Inc.
The Canadian Publishers
481 University Avenue
Toronto, Ontario
M5G 2E9

1 2 3 4 5   03 02 01 00 99

Where the Hell Are the Guns?

A Soldier's Eye View
of the Anxious Years, 1939-44

GEORGE G. BLACKBURN

CONTENTS

Introduction xi

PART ONE – MAY 1939–AUGUST 1940
TRANSFORMING CIVILIANS INTO SOLDIERS

1. The Faint Murmuring of Distant Guns 3
2. September 1, 1939 10
3. One Precious Last Sunny Day of Peace 15
4. War Doesn't Only Happen to Other People 19
5. *Blitzkrieg* 26
6. Riding on a Wave of Patriotism 30
7. An Officers' Mess in a Ladies' Washroom 35
8. A Turkey Neck Becomes a Legend 44
9. "Put Thine Hand into the Hand of God" 49
10. 4th Field to Petawawa as Nations Collapse 55
11. Roll Out the Barrel 61
12. Is It Possible We Have Lost the War? 66
13. Brave Children Hugging Teddy Bears 70
14. The Morale Booster 73
15. The First Canadian "Crash Action" 76

PART TWO – AUGUST 1940–JULY 1942
THE METAMORPHOSIS OF A REGIMENT

16. Aboard an Empress Built for an Emperor 87
17. Your Enthusiasm is Highly Commendable 96
18. The Guns of 1898 104
19. The Reformation of the Subalterns 108
20. Night Clouds Glow Red over London 114
21. "Snafu" Comes into Common Use 120

22. "We Shall Fight on the Beaches" 125
23. Back to the Coast and Hastings 132
24. Towards Becoming the Best 137

PART THREE – JUNE 1941–JUNE 1942
PRODUCING TRAINLOADS OF REINFORCEMENTS

25. Reinforcements 145
26. The Gospel According to Larkhill 154
27. Gunners Introduced to the Art of Skiing 162
28. Reluctant Gunners 167
29. Dental Visits Rate Wound Stripes 176
30. The Great Butter Theft Case 182
31. "Warned for Special Duty" 187
32. Footnote to the Battle of the Atlantic 190
33. Empress of Japan – Scotland 195

PART FOUR – AUGUST 1942–APRIL 1943
THE FAILURE OF DIEPPE SPURS MORE
INTENSIVE TRAINING FOR BATTLE

34. Royals Shot Down in Heaps on Blue Beach 205
35. Life at Barnham Junction 218
36. Bracketing by Puffs of Cigarette Smoke 228
37. "Leaning into the Barrage" 232
38. Map-Reading 236
39. Sennybridge 240
40. Paying Your Dues 244
41. Places of Warmth and Song and Laughter 250
42. Snafus Unlimited 254
43. Mike, Uncle, and Victor Targets 259
44. Waltzing Matilda and Yankee Doodle Dandy 267
45. Happiness Is a Child on a Gunner's Lap 272
46. No One Wishes Anybody a Happy New Year 278
47. More Days to Remember at Alfriston 283

48. A New Troop Commander Every Second Week 292
49. "Spartan" 299
50. Chicken au Diable 303

PART FIVE – APRIL 1943–JANUARY 1944
MORALE BECOMES THE BIG PROBLEM

51. Men Like Officers Who Try to Understand 311
52. "But No Damned Flowers" 316
53. Living with the Spectre of a Bowler Hat 323
54. Garnons 326
55. Back to 4th Field 331
56. Muddy Morale of Monks Common 335
57. The Regiment's Fourth Christmas Away from Home 345
58. Redesdale – The Last Training Camp 348

PART SIX – JANUARY 1944–JULY 1944
APPROACHING THE FINAL SHOWDOWN
ON THE CONTINENT

59. The Yanks Are Coming 357
60. A Continuous Drone Overhead 363
61. Unadulatered B.S., but Monty Impressive 368
62. Waldershare Park 375
63. This Blessed Plot 381
64. D-Day 389
65. Are You Really There? 393
66. Vergeltungswaffe-1 399

Appendix A – The Plunketts' Marching Song 405
Appendix B – How "Ham" Roberts Got His Guns Back to
   England 406
Appendix C – ". . . D'You Tell Me as You Didn't Know They
   Was There?" 407
Appendix D – The 25-Pounder: A Super Weapon 408

Appendix E – Artillery Board 410
Appendix F – Losses at Sea 411
Appendix G – A Grim Cavalcade of Defeats 413
Appendix H – Dieppe Reprisals 418
Appendix I – The Genius of Cardinal-Point Ranging 419
*Appendix J – The Destructive Power of the V-1s and the
   British–Canadian–American Proximity Fuse* 420
Appendix K – Officers of 4th Field Regiment RCA 421
Index 423

INTRODUCTION

———————— ✳ ————————

This is the first volume of a trilogy on World War II from the perspective of one regiment of 25-pounder guns, the last two volumes – *The Guns of Normandy* and *The Guns of Victory* – having been published in 1995 and 1996 respectively.

An odd way to offer a trilogy, you may say with justification, and the author hastens to place the blame squarely on his publisher, who believed he would have a warehouse full of unsold books if he attempted to offer a book by an unknown author on the subject of the growing pains of a regiment readying itself for action, but that he possibly might recoup the printing costs, at least, if he produced the volume on Normandy first, immediately after the high-profile ceremonies surrounding the fiftieth anniversary of D-Day had aroused interest in those far-off days.

And because of this unique approach to matters sequential by our market-wise publisher, Doug Gibson, we are in the unusual position of being able to report here on the reception of the last two books covering the final ten months of the war in Northwest Europe.

The generosity of reviewers and the warmth of the gratitude universally expressed by readers, impelled to phone or write, has been overwhelming – far beyond the wildest expectations of author or publisher. Some even go so far as to suggest the books could become important instruments for inciting pride in our heritage and, through such pride, a sense of national unity.

Veterans, regardless of whether they served on the Italian front or in Northwest Europe, and a significant number of veterans of the Navy and Airforce, almost without exception express their gratitude that "someone has finally told it like it was." And widows and sons and daughters of veterans who never spoke of the war to their families, or, if they did, recalled only humorous incidents, write in touching ways how grateful they are to learn with pride what their husbands or fathers endured in restoring freedom to Europe.

Middle-aged men whose fathers returned from the war as alcoholics have written that the books have changed their lives, letting them appreciate for the first time how frightened their fathers must have been in action, and that they can now extend tolerance to their fathers' distressing post-war behaviour.

Mindful of the admonition by our meticulous editor, Alex Schultz, who has worked with caring concern on all three books, to "keep it short," and conscious of having included in the introductions to the other two volumes most of what would be appropriate to an introduction to the trilogy, we will restrict ourselves to underlining the fact that apart from France, with her immediate concern for her own security, only Britain and four other British Commonwealth countries in all the world perceived the awful fate awaiting the globe if it was taken over piecemeal by fascist dictators and decided to draw the line when Hitler invaded Poland.

Of all the decisions of lasting importance taken by humankind through the ages, the one of greatest consequence to the cause of freedom may well have been made by this handful of nations who chose to risk everything in an all-out war to prevent democracy disappearing from Europe and eventually from the face of the earth, snuffed out by men subscribing to the savage principle that might is right, which Winston Churchill believed would, if not stopped, sink "all that we have known and cared for . . . into the abyss of a new Dark Age made more sinister, and perhaps more protracted, by the lights of perverted science."

Britain and France were at war with Germany the hour their ultimatum to Hitler to pull out of Poland ran out on September 3. Australia and New Zealand declared war at the same hour, South Africa three days later, and Canada on September 10. British colonies, including India and Burma, were automatically at war with Germany when Britain declared war, but the Commonwealth countries went to war of their own free choice, believing in a new concept of international brotherhood that subscribed to the notion of "the common weal" – not every man for himself or lofty isolation, but for the good and security of all.

And when France fell in June 1940, and Britain had to decide whether to accept Hitler's offer of peace, crucial to her decision to fight on was the support of those same "self-governing dominions . . . absolutely free to choose their own course," as Churchill put it in his memorable "their finest hour" speech to the British House of Commons. Emphasizing the independence of their decision, as he underlined the importance of their support, he said he had "fully consulted Prime Minister Mackenzie King of Canada, Mr. Menzies of Australia, Mr. Fraser of New Zealand, and General Smuts of South Africa, and received from these eminent men, who all have governments behind them elected on wide franchises, who are all there by the will of the people, messages couched in the most moving terms in which they endorse our decision to fight on, and declare themselves ready to share our fortunes and to persevere to the end. That is what we are going to do."

In recent days there has been much discussion on newscasts and in print about the "sun setting on the British Empire," inspired by Britain's returning of long-time colony Hong Kong to China. But little recognition has been given to the fact that as the Empire was shrinking the Commonwealth was growing, until now there are 49 member nations. Let future international bullies beware.

In view of the author's pride in his country's early decision to stand up and be counted, readers of the following pages could ask, Why did it take him so long to get into one of the services? The short answer is a certificate, still in his possession, dated August 7, 1940, from a Royal Canadian Navy medical officer rejecting him as "medically unfit for service." Receiving this notice the same day he was turned down by an RCAF recruitment officer for the same deficiency ("eyesight below requirements"), and scared the army would also turn him down for being near-sighted, he conspired to sneak in through the reserves. Enlisting in 51st Battery (reserve), he managed, after some months of weekend soldiering and a two-week summer camp at Connought Ranges, to get himself recommended for a commission. While taking training at the newly opened Brockville Officers' Training Centre in August 1941, he hitchhiked to Kingston one Saturday and enlisted in the "active force" as a gunner, using the medical exam given him eleven months before by a casual reserve-force medical officer who had awarded him 20-20 vision without testing his eyes. That he ended the war as a long-time forward observation officer – the very "eyes of the army" – has always seemed to him to be a delicious irony.

PART ONE: MAY 1939– AUGUST 1940

Transforming Civilians into Soldiers

I

THE FAINT MURMURING OF

DISTANT GUNS

---------------------- ✳ ----------------------

IN THE EARLY SUMMER OF 1939, LIFE IN CANADA IS DOMINATED by the daily progress of the royal train, carrying King George VI and Queen Elizabeth on the first tour ever by a reigning monarch of the senior dominion, igniting a joyous outburst of colourful exuberance after ten years of depression, with its drab images of breadlines, soup kitchens, dust-bowl storms, relief riots, and hundreds of unshaven, silent men staring at you with hollow eyes from open boxcar doors or hunched up on more precarious perches on the roofs of passing freight trains.

At every major centre, masses of men, women, and children assemble in sun-bathed, flag-lined streets and squares, caught up in a strange, happy unity – people of every social level and economic background, crushed together in good-natured, laughing, amorphous mobs, waving little Union Jacks or Red Ensigns with the Canadian crest in the fly, cheering each time the open limousine flying the royal standard rolls into view, and exploding with delight when they catch sight of the saucy tilt of a queenly chin and an upraised hand waving in a singularly gracious way. For those close enough to be bathed by her sunburst smile, with enough candle-power to make hearts sing a hundred yards away, the Queen is the topic of conversation for days on end.

The country has never seen anything like it. Undoubtedly, the threat of war hovering over Europe, the outcome of which no one can foretell, influences the intense feelings of loyalty to a throne that stands for decency, human dignity, and freedom of choice, in sharp contrast to the aims of the fascist dictators threatening to enslave the world.

In every province, the welcome is genuinely enthusiastic. But it is not until they are embarking on the *Empress of Britain* in Halifax on June 16 for their return to Britain and the real danger of becoming a target for German bombs, and a plaintive voice in the crowd sings out Caroline Nairne's venerable lyric composed for an earlier bonnie prince, "Will you no come back again," that the nation truly realizes the depth of the affection the royal couple has engendered and how much they will be missed if anything should happen to them.*

Your memories of these last sweet days of peace are associated with your work as a newspaper reporter, residing in the old Copeland Hotel in Pembroke, Ontario, whose "men's beverage room" is the favourite watering-hole of the gunners of A and B Batteries of the Royal Canadian Horse Artillery and a host of militia units attending summer camp at nearby Petawawa.

Last fall, around the time of the Munich crisis, you were sent up by the *Ottawa Journal* to take over the news-bureau job for the paper, regarded by the town and a large swatch of the Upper Ottawa Valley as "their daily paper" – and with some validity, for the bulldog edition is published especially for Pembroke breakfast tables, and an afternoon edition, featuring on its front page any story of consequence filed by you in the morning, is delivered to homes in the early evening.

Petawawa Military Camp and artillery ranges, embracing miles of scrubby pine trees and sandy tracks, only ten miles northwest of Pembroke along the Ottawa River, falls well within your news beat, and as August brings a deepening sense of impending war, you find yourself becoming more and more conscious of the faint,

---

* The *Empress of Britain* was sunk off Ireland by a submarine on October 26, 1940.

desultory, murmuring roars that come and go with the vagaries of the wind in the west.

For a few weeks the royal couple allowed you to look away from the war clouds over Europe – even as they welded the nation in loyalty and common cause with the Commonwealth about to face the gathering storm. But as the stories of their visit fade, and the front pages return to forbidding reality, it's clear the world is about to pay a heavy price for not having moved sooner to stop Hitler's wayward aggression.

As early as March 1936, when he ordered his élite guard regiment, SS-Leibstandarte, to carry out a symbolic occupation of the de-militarized Rhineland in defiance of the Treaty of Versailles, Hitler learned he could intimidate the democracies into restricting their actions to mere "strongly worded protests." And when the SS-Leibstandarte drove into Austria past cheering crowds in March 1938, and seven months later into Czechoslovakia's Sudetenland with the approval of France and Britain, the Führer could be for-given for concluding that no country, or combination of countries, was willing to go to war to oppose the annexation of a neighbour.*

Still, to pursue the course of action he now is threatening against Poland would be madness. The mood of the British public and their prime minister, Neville Chamberlain, has changed dramatically since he met Hitler in Munich last fall. To anyone scanning the stories from London, it is clear the trust Chamberlain showed in Hitler's word last September, when he traded away the freedom of the Czechs for "peace in our time," has long since gone.

In the second week of August, there are reports from Britain of "territorial army units engaging in mass manoeuvres," and of Lon-don and twenty-six counties running "blackout tests." Simulated

---

* Commanding the leading company of SS-Leibstandarte was Captain Kurt Meyer, who would become infamous in 1944 as the commander of a regiment of 12th SS that murdered unarmed Canadian prisoners. Though he was sentenced to death by a military tribunal, his sentence was commuted to life imprisonment.

air raids were "turned back," as "barrage balloons," tethered to long cables, floated on the London skyline to discourage hostile aircraft from flying low over the city. And the Air Ministry revealed the reassuring fact that Spitfire fighter-planes, now in service, are armed with eight machine-guns in their wings capable of delivering six hundred bullets in four seconds.

There are pictures of huge listening devices, shaped like ear-trumpets, pointing at the sky, "listening for aircraft." But a more intriguing story refers to "most secret spots reputed to spot planes at great distances, making surprise attacks impossible," which may account for the story on August 12: "After three days mimic warfare, our fighter planes more than match for any enemy."

Britain is clearly preoccupied with war arriving from the air. German Zeppelin raids on London in the 1914–18 war had introduced the bombing of civilian targets, and modern bombers are capable of carrying tons of bombs. How the people of Europe must dread the prospect of instant death showering down on their homes and places of work from unseen planes droning above them in the night sky – high-explosive bombs of awesome destructive capacity mixed with incendiary devices to set aflame unstoppable conflagrations in the subsequent chaos of broken water-lines and rubble-choked streets.

The depth of their fear for the safety of their children and other loved ones, and the intensity of their hopes and prayers that war not come to them, no one living on this side of the Atlantic could ever possibly imagine. But the feeling of security in Canada from trans-Atlantic bombing was shaken a bit with the inauguration this month of weekly air-mail flights from England, though clearly, even without the intervention of fighter planes, no bomber presently in service could carry a bomb load across the Atlantic, let alone make it home after dropping its cargo. The twenty-four-ton Imperial Airways flying-boat leaves England at 9:15 one morning and doesn't arrive until the next day at Botwood, Newfoundland, en route to Montreal, having made a maintenance stop in Foynes, Ireland, and having been refuelled in the air en route – the whole journey from Southhampton to Montreal taking thirty-three hours.

On August 14, Sir Percy Everett, of the Imperial Headquarters of the Boy Scouts – himself a journalist – speaking to the Ottawa Rotary Club, declared, "I'm convinced to a certainty there will be no war in Europe started by Hitler."

But next day, back to back with a report of Germany purchasing huge quantities of rubber, lead, and copper in London, is a report that German troops are dug in three hundred feet from the Polish border.

On the nineteenth, next to the front-page headline "Sir Malcolm Campbell Breaks Record on Water as Bluebird Goes 141.74 Miles per Hour over Lake Coniston" is the discouraging news "Hope for Danzig Settlement Fades – Nazi Accusation Same as One Hurled at Czechs."

Two days later, British and French cabinets repeat the warning that "Pledges to Poland Will Be Kept," and next day, August 22, the worst development yet. Germany and Russia sign a non-aggression pact, which, in effect, gives Germany a free hand to move into Poland without fear of interference by Russia. In response, "Poland Rushes Vast Defence Measures," and Britain begins "Calling Up More Men."

On the twenty-third, the War Measures Act is brought into effect in Canada as "Foreigners Flee Germany . . . Führer Insists Upon Proceeding Against Poland . . . 10,000,000 Men Under Arms in Europe."

These grim stories smother the pleasant news that Saskatchewan has at last "turned fertile again after years of drought," and that, only three days after Sir Malcolm Campbell set the world's water-speed record, another Britisher, John Cobb, has set a new land-speed record of 368.5 miles an hour on Bonneville Salt Flats, Utah.

Headlines of August 24 suggest events are rushing to a climax: "Imminent Peril of War . . . German Army Awaits Hitler's Zero Hour . . . Dictator Demands Free Hand in Eastern Europe . . .

British Prime Minister Seeks Broad Powers . . . Germans Moving Troops to Polish Borders . . . Britain Mobilizing Reserves – A Million Men Under Arms . . . Danzig Tense as Nazi Leader Takes Control . . . French Government Warns French to Leave Paris . . . All-Day Session of Canadian Cabinet . . . Führer in Berlin . . ."

On the twenty-fifth, there are pictures of Germany's Rhineland, showing the "dragon's teeth," rows and rows of concrete spurs protruding above the ground to prevent tanks from penetrating their Siegfried Line. And the next day there are even more ominous headlines: "Germany Cut Communications from the World for Seven Hours Last Night . . . Canadian Cabinet in Emergency Session . . . Hitler to Address Reichstag . . . Digging Trenches in Moscow . . ."

Finally recognizing that appeasement tactics are out of fashion, Canada announces that voluntary enlistments will be carried out by some militia units, naming, among others, Ottawa and district infantry regiments who will provide security guards on such installations as the St. Lawrence and Great Lakes canal systems. Within three days, ten thousand volunteer "civilian soldiers" sign up.

On August 28, the much-quoted playwright George Bernard Shaw offers one of his sillier comments: "Herr Hitler is under the powerful thumb of Stalin, whose interest in peace is overwhelming. And everyone except myself is frightened out of his wits. Why? Am I mad? If not, why?"

Adjoining this, and pointing up the shallowness of this distorted perception of events, is a picture of King George VI and two of his brothers on their way into Westminster Abbey to pray for peace. While on a preceding page, next to a graph showing Germany's airforce to be double Britain's and five times that of France, are pictures of mothers saying goodbye to a train loaded with little children being evacuated from London in anticipation of enemy bombs dropping from the skies.

The front page of the afternoon editions on Thursday, August 31, transmits the mounting tension in Europe: "War Censorship in London . . . Peace Hopes Fade . . . 370 Million Sand Bags Issued –

60 Million More on the Way . . . Germans Pause in Negotiations with Britain . . ."

But people are becoming blasé about scary headlines. After all, Hitler has been creating one crisis after another for Europe ever since the beginning of the Spanish Civil War three years ago, and they've all blown over. Used copies of the *Journal* left behind on the chairs in the lobby of the Cope tonight, where the travellers leafed through them after dinner, are turned to the sport pages, which, like the entertainment pages and syndicated boiler-plate features, continue to give no hint that a world conflict is on its way: "Jack Dempsey gives Nova the nod to beat Joe Louis . . . Big Four football teams begin practices . . ."

As it happens, the only story you were able to file at the CPR telegraph office tonight for the morning edition was a sports story about the team on which you've been a pitcher this summer: "Pembroke Senior Baseball Team, champions of the Upper Ottawa Valley League, have been ordered to pay Renfrew half of the gate from the final playoff game yesterday or be disqualified from meeting Madawaska Saturday . . ."

There is one crisis-related marketing story: "Rush for sugar starts in Ottawa, but prices remain at 10 pounds for 56 cents."

Big grocery ads offer "blade roasts" at nineteen cents a pound and "prime beef" at twenty-five cents. The paper is thick with back-to-school ads offering boys' wool sweaters at ninety-eight cents, boys' "all-wool tweed suits with vests" at $10.95, and youths' "broadcloth shirts" at seventy-nine cents. "Men's two-trouser suits of English worsted and tweeds" can be had from $17.50 to $22.50 (the weekly salary of one *Journal* reporter). Ladies' "Packard slippers" are on sale for eighty-five cents "regularly $1.45," and "muskrat coats that could easily be mistaken for mink" are $99.00.

2

SEPTEMBER 1, 1939

---------------------------------- ✳ ----------------------------------

YOU AWAKE TO A MUFFLED CACOPHONY OF SQUEAKING AND squawking voices of rapidly speaking newscasters coming in through the transom over your bedroom door. Radios all the way down the hall are cranked up to volume levels unusually high, even for early-morning in the "rams' pasture," the quaint name by which this wing of the Copeland Hotel – tucked away at the rear in the upper reaches of the rambling, old building and entirely filled with single males – is known.

Realizing at once it can mean only one thing, you turn on your own little Viking in time to catch an announcer quoting a message issued by Hitler's Chief-of-Staff to his legions as they were ordered to smash their way across the border into Poland in the predawn hours: "The time has come for us to prove we are men. . . . Under the supreme command of the Führer, we go to fight and conquer. . . . We know the power and the strength of the Reich's armed forces. We believe in the Führer, and may God be with us for Germany."

The morning *Journal* carries no mention of the German invasion, which occurred after the bulldog edition, printed for the Upper Ottawa Valley, was put to bed before midnight. But a commercial traveller, arriving at the Cope for lunch, carries with him the second of two "extras" put out by the *Journal* this morning.

And there it is – in deep, black, double-banner headlines:

BRITAIN AND FRANCE MOBILIZE, POLAND SEEKS AID
AGAINST FULL GERMAN ATTACK

The whole front page and much of the inside pages blaze with
grim headings and bulletins: "GERMANS SAY THEY ARE DEEP IN PO-
LAND . . . PLANES SWOOP LOW OVER WARSAW — SMASH CITY . . .
BRITAIN SENDS WARNING — HITLER MUST WITHDRAW OR FRANCE
AND ENGLAND ARE AT WAR . . . THE KING SIGNS ORDER FOR GENERAL
MOBILIZATION . . . FRANCE ORDERS MOBILIZATION . . . There's a
touch of sadness in busy London streets as more than a million
children are evacuated to the safety of the countryside . . . Prime
Minister King recalls Canadian parliament to ask the House for full
cooperation at the side of Britain . . . Canadian War Measures Act
of 1914 now in effect . . . Non-permanent Militia being ordered
on active service along with naval and air services."

Hitler's speech to the Reichstag, calling on the German people
to go to war, was heard by many over here with shortwave radios.
Der Führer promised to live "more than ever for Germany alone,"
and blatantly appealing to his countrymen's nationalism and sense
of the dramatic, he solemnly declared, "I am putting on the uniform,
and I shall take it off only in victory or in death!"

In the dark, early-morning stillness of Queen Street in Ottawa,
"crowds gathered quietly around the *Journal*'s bulletin boards after
the earliest radio news bulletin was heard during the night of hos-
tilities opening against Poland."

In Ottawa, a common reaction of a resigned populace awakening
to "the grim reality of war" seems to have been simply: "So, it's
come."

And this is also true of people up here in the Valley. Life is carrying
on as it has every day since you arrived up here late last September,
just in time to become embroiled in fierce arguments over dinner
in the Copeland about the Munich crisis. Already those days seem
of another era, when men, old enough to be your father, hotly
defended Chamberlain's appeasement of Hitler when you scoffed
at the spectacle of a British prime minister arriving back at London

airport waving a piece of paper, purportedly carrying the signature of the Führer, guaranteeing "peace in our time."

To these men, who'd lived through the Great War, nothing Hitler did was worth starting another war. But a few nights later, all sat in embarrassing silence when fellow hotel-resident Freddie Ritt, a Jew from Russia who runs a dress shop over the street, sat down for dinner and spread out on the table the paper displaying in pictures the horror of "crystal night," the night of breaking glass, when Hitler's bully-boys went on a rampage and smashed the windows in every Jewish shop and synagogue in Germany, beating up and arresting twenty thousand Jews.

Today, everywhere you go, people question you as though they think you have special access to the chattering teletypes on the sixth floor of the *Journal* building a hundred miles away in Ottawa: "What's the latest from Europe? Has Britain declared war yet? How are the Poles doing?"

Otherwise everything remains unchanged – at least until evening.

On your way to file some wire copy to the *Journal*, you spot Jack Dunlop, a young lawyer and a captain in the local militia (Lanark and Renfrew Scottish), looking very important and military, striding purposefully across Main Street, making for the telegraph office. It is only Friday, but he is in uniform, complete with highly polished Sam Browne belt and swagger stick.

It strikes you how different a man in uniform appears now the country is on its way to war. Even as late as last week – if you noticed him at all on his way to the armoury – he appeared quaint and anachronistic, as have all men over the years who, each Saturday night, attired themselves in old-fashioned uniforms and made their way to musty, poorly lit drill halls. But now, with war close at hand, these "Saturday-night soldiers" loom large in everyone's eyes.

Obviously, no militia unit could mobilize without a nucleus of men to provide leadership and training for the thousands of boobs like yourself who'll now be showing up as recruits, entirely devoid of useful military knowledge beyond what you picked up in public school and high school cadet corps. When you follow him into the office, he turns a very stern countenance on you, and you really don't expect to get any information out of him when you ask if he has any comment for publication on the status of his regiment. But to your astonishment, he lets you read the telegram he's received from Kingston, ordering full mobilization to war establishment of the Lanark and Renfrew Scottish, and tells you recruitment will begin tomorrow night at the armoury when the boys turn out for their regular Saturday-night parade.

You leave the telegraph office in a daze. Until this moment, preoccupied with the drama of Britain and France mobilizing for war, it all seemed real enough. But now that it's Canada – your own country – committing itself to war, the whole business takes on an aura of unreality.

And within the hour, you're provided with startling evidence that remarkable changes are taking place in the social attitudes of people facing imminent war. You receive a surprise phone call from your fiancée in Ottawa, telling you she is coming up on the mid-night train – alone! Until today, it would have been unthinkable that she'd come to visit you without your mother or her girlfriend Betty Beedie along as a chaperone. But tonight she tells you her parents not only approve, but have encouraged her to be with you this weekend when the inevitable news, that will drastically affect your lives, comes through.

Of course you are overjoyed. But even as the prospect of having her all to yourself for a whole weekend projects you into a state bordering on ecstasy, it raises the sobering thought that your enlistment (inevitable of course) will result in interminable separation, much more prolonged and harsh than the kind you've found so difficult to endure this past year. Facing such prospects, to postpone marriage any longer would be inhuman. To be denied some married life together, however short, before going overseas, is totally inconceivable. And yet there is no way you can get married. Under existing rules, your esteemed employer would immediately fire you, since you are not earning the magic figure of twenty-five dollars a week, which he considers a respectable salary for a married employee, and your betrothed would instantly be laid off if she became a married woman, because her employer (Metropolitan Life) has a rule, similar to the Depression-dictated rule of the Dominion Government, that married women must not be employed at the expense of married men.

That these conditions will prevail until you enlist and are swept away into training and a posting overseas, from which you may never return, is entirely probable. The thought arouses a maddening sense of frustration, though you know you are not alone. Thousands of young men and women of your generation are in the same boat or worse. Denied marriage by the condition of their pocketbooks and billfolds, pinched thin by ten years of depression, they now face separations extending into years – perhaps eternity – by the demands of war.

There's been an awful lot of talk, and much has been written about the so-called "lost generation" of the Roaring Twenties. Hell! They at least had the twenties. The young men of your generation have grown up in the Depression, have known nothing but the pinching and making-do of the Depression, and now they'll know nothing but war for years to come – a lifetime perhaps.

3

ONE PRECIOUS LAST SUNNY
DAY OF PEACE

——————————— ✳ ———————————

WHILE EVERYONE KNOWS THAT THE DAYS OF APPEASEMENT ARE past, and that it is now certain that Britain, along with France, will declare war, and Canada will promptly join them at their side, there still is a powerful inclination to postpone facing up to the awful implications until the official declarations.

You are determined to do your best to sustain the joy of having your beloved with you for at least this last weekend, even if it means living a lie and ignoring the news from abroad.

This is easy throughout most of the day. Though black headlines, suggesting Europe and the world is headed for another conflagration, crowd the pages of the *Journal* delivered to Pembroke breakfast tables on the morning of September 2, you're prevented from dwelling on them. Until noon you are too busy checking your beat – firehall, police station, municipal office, hospitals, and undertakers – to meet the earlier deadline of the Saturday noon edition. Then, throughout a truly glorious sunny afternoon, you are fully occupied helping Pembroke retain its Ottawa Valley Senior Baseball League title, turning back a challenge from Madawaska.

And a more pleasant, satisfying afternoon would be difficult to imagine. Had you been granted magical powers to arrange events in such a way as to allow you to appear as Superman in the eyes of your beloved, you could not have improved on real life this day. In the best traditions of a Frank Merriwell novel, the hero is the winning pitcher in a championship baseball game. Up in the grand-stand, sitting with Alice Roy, the owner of the Copeland, cheering you on, is your beautiful fiancée, who's never seen you pitch before, and while she may believe in you, she can't resist equating physical development with athletic ability. So when the lumbermen from Madawaska stride onto the field, her heart sinks. Those barrel-chested, bearded men, with bulging biceps and legs resembling maturing tree trunks, must surely massacre the slender lads from Pembroke who appear so puny by comparison. Ah, but then . . . surprise, surprise! As one of your more reflective team-mates so judiciously puts it, "Those guys couldn't hit a bull in the arse with a shovel."

And when it appears the game is in the bag, *she* gets so excited, she spills into her lap – from a cone that Alice has just handed her – a chocolate mello-roll, that melts considerably before she realizes it.

While this causes some temporary embarrassment, until she can get back to the hotel and change, it provides a wonderful story, sending everybody into gales of laughter that night when she re-counts it to the gang around the campfire at the corn-roast on the beach overlooking the wide, moonlit Ottawa River at Petawawa Point.

Throughout the evening, the delicious euphoria of the afternoon lingers on, completely banishing from mind the momentous hap-penings in Europe. And it isn't until you are being driven back to town by good friend Ramsey Garrow, and in the subdued quiet of the dark car Ramsey's girlfriend raises the question of what may happen in Europe tomorrow, that the chilling menace of impending war returns.

Back at the Cope, you pick up copies of the afternoon *Journal* and *Citizen* and take them up to her room at the head of the stairs. There, together, you stare at the first pictures of the Germans in Poland, and then at pictures of children boarding a train in Britain, the vanguard of three million children, the lame, and the infirm being evacuated from the cities. Pictures of sandbags, being piled high to form blast-walls around the entrances to hospitals and other vital buildings, tell their story without need for captions.

You try to find a comprehensive roundup of significant developments that might make the past twenty-four hours more understandable, but it seems the picture is too vast and things are moving too quickly for reporters and editors to develop such stories. Everything these days is reduced to a headline. Even the body-copy seems to be made up of a series of headings and subheadings, and only by scanning through all of them can you get any kind of picture:

"BRITAIN WITHHOLDS DECLARATION OF WAR . . . LONDON AND BERLIN BOTH BLACKED OUT LAST NIGHT . . . CHAMBERLAIN TO MAKE STATEMENT LATER . . . HITLER SAYS BRITISH-GERMAN WAR TO BE BLOODIER THAN 1914–18 . . . EXPECT JAPAN TO STAY NEUTRAL . . . In British restaurants and pubs, as 25 years ago, the arrival or departure of men in uniform is greeted with applause . . . Generally the British are saying, 'Well, it had to come. We might as well go ahead and get it over with' . . . Women join men in filling sandbags and digging trenches in London parks . . . Barrage balloons now float over the city . . ."

But not all stories are from overseas: "RECRUITING GOES ON APACE AT OTTAWA 1ST FIELD BRIGADE RCA . . . Two batteries are being mobilized, the 2nd Battery under Major G. E. Beament and the 51st under Major G. Hutchinson . . . Recruits are being given medicals, their names taken, and told to hold themselves in readiness for a day or two pending completion of recruiting arrangements. Age limits are 18 to 45; minimum height, five feet four inches; and minimum chest, 34 inches."

"Close to 1,000 World War I veterans register for guard duty of plants and oil depots outside the Capital . . . quite a number unemployed and anxious to get off relief . . . Average age of veterans is 50."

Buried among the jumble of stories on the forthcoming agonies of war in Europe is a bizarre report of a locked passenger train, guarded with fixed bayonets at Constanza Harbour, Rumania's chief oil port on the Black Sea, packed with Jewish refugees fleeing persecution in Europe. They have been waiting for ten days for a boat to Palestine.

It is very hard to concentrate on the printed word when you feel life as you've known and shared it with friends and loved ones is ebbing away. You want to hold on to it as long as you can, relishing every minute, securing it in memory forever.

You try to talk, but for some reason that, too, is difficult. So you turn on the little Viking radio and lie back with your arms around each other, listening to dance bands from far-off New York and Chicago, where life is carrying on as though no crisis exists – which indeed is the case in isolationist United States. However, your thoughts are on Europe and London, for you are certain that formal declarations of war by Britain and France are only hours away, there being no possibility that Hitler will heed their warnings to cease military action against Poland. And, of course, Canada's declaration will follow soon after.

You find yourself recalling the famous words of British Foreign Secretary Sir Edward Grey, spoken on the eve of the outbreak of the 1914 war as he stood at his Whitehall window in London, watching a lamplighter at work down on the street: "The lamps are going out all over Europe; we shall not see them lit again in our lifetime."

Tonight those despairing words are enough to crush the heart, for they epitomize with equal force the hour and the age you are entering.

4

WAR DOESN'T ONLY HAPPEN
TO OTHER PEOPLE

———————————— ✳ ————————————

SUNDAY, SEPTEMBER 3, 1939, PASSES LIKE A BAD DREAM FROM
which there is no escape. Shortly after the two-hour ultimatum
from Britain and France runs out at 11:00 A.M. (6:00 A.M. Ottawa
time), Prime Minister Chamberlain is on the air sadly announcing
that Britain is at war with Germany. And later the King – struggling
to control his emotions and his normal speech impediment, cruelly
underlined by the wavering hesitancy of short-wave radio that
swells and recedes like the stormy North Atlantic – broadcasts an
impressive message to his Empire and Commonwealth of Nations:

> We have been forced into a conflict . . . to meet the challenge of
> a principle, which if it were to prevail, would be fatal to any
> civilized order in the world. It . . . sanctions the use of force, or
> the threat of force, against the sovereignty and independence of
> other nations . . . the primitive doctrine that might is right. If this
> principle were established throughout the world, the freedom of
> our own country and the whole British Commonwealth of
> Nations would be in danger. But far more than this, the peoples
> of the world would be kept in the bondage of fear, and all hopes
> of peace and security, of justice and liberty among nations, would
> be ended. This is the ultimate issue that confronts us. For the
> sake of all we hold dear and of world order and peace, it is
> unthinkable that we should refuse to meet the challenge. . . .

The task will be hard. There may be dark days ahead, and war can no longer be confined to the battlefield, but we can only do the right as we see the right, and reverently commit our cause to God. If one and all we keep resolutely faithful to it, ready for whatever service or sacrifice it may demand, then with God's help we shall prevail.

May He bless and keep us all.

For a moment there is only the rustling sizzle of transocean static. Then there is a long roll of drums, and a band plays "God Save the King" in slow and reverent fashion. And for the first time, the full significance of this prayer for the safety of the monarch and state is borne in upon you.

Your beloved, sitting close at your side, squeezes your hand as though to reassure you, though she emits a vast, shuddering sigh. And when you turn to her, her eyes are so filled with heart-breaking distress, you have to fight back the tears welling up in your own.

Tonight you cannot sleep. Your mind insists on recalling those fateful broadcasts, wavering and crackling across the sea from London. The stark reality of Chamberlain's sorrowful announcement, and the King's sombre message have gradually sunk in: confrontation with the fascist dictators can be postponed no longer; your generation has been chosen to make the sacrifice.

War is no longer an academic subject, something that happens only in newsreels to the Ethiopians, the Chinese, or the Spaniards – or to past generations of Canadians like old Jack Campbell, red-chevron vet of the last war, who lost an eye on the Somme and has lived in that big corner-room with the fireplace across the hall, with his cigarette holder and his gin-and-gingers ever since being repatriated in 1917.

You and your friends will be expected to join up. Many will have to face death. Some will be maimed. And some will surely die.

You are filled with a sense of betrayal as bitter and inescapable as it must have been for another generation twenty-one years ago, so well set out in *All Quiet on the Western Front* by German author

Erich Maria Remarque, describing the disillusionment of the young soldiers with their elders who had preached nationalism and the glory of war – how such beliefs were shattered by the first deaths they saw, and how all their confidence, in what they'd assumed to be the greater insight and wisdom of those in authority, was blown away in the violence of their first bombardment.

Your generation's disenchantment, however, is significantly different in that it exists even before you put on a uniform, and springs from a perspective virtually one hundred and eighty degrees from the 1914 variety. No one could become unduly indoctrinated in unhealthy nationalism growing up in the 1930s in a democracy when pacifism was the "in thing"; when Britain's Prime Minister Ramsay MacDonald was making headlines calling for massive reductions in armies and navies; when fifty-nine leading countries kept discussions going for almost nine months at a 1932 Geneva disarmament conference; when Winston Churchill was labelled a "warmonger" for merely warning of the growing menace of the fascist dictators; and when Oxford University students were taking solemn vows never to fight for their country.

This universal spirit of pacifism – an understandable reaction to the still-vivid memories of the appalling bloodbath of the Great War, and in fashion for so long among the Western democracies – was reflected, as much as it was nurtured, by prominent figures. In Canada they included the first female member of parliament, Agnes McPhail, who wouldn't rest until cadet corps training was abolished from both primary and secondary schools, seeing something sinister and unhealthy in you and your schoolmates each spring putting on ill-fitting, wrinkled uniforms, smelling heavily of mothballs, to learn how to "form fours" and march in step while doing "eyes right" to an officer in uniform from the local militia unit who took the march-past salute standing beside the school principal.

No, your disillusionment with political leadership, and perhaps permanent loss of trust in elder statesmen, springs from a realization that they, like naive children, allowed themselves to be trapped by pacifism into what, until today, appeared to be terminal inertia, with the awful result that now no democracy is equipped to defend itself.

With some bitterness, you recall the arguments over dinner in the hotel last fall, when the patronising old men ridiculed your hot-headedness and inexperience for casting scorn on Chamberlain's inane statement "peace in our time" after selling-out Czechoslo-vakia. You had wanted so badly their approbation, but all you earned were smiles of amusement when you expounded the theme of your 1935 high-school essay that the secret of friendship among nations, as among individuals, is respect – that only strong nations are respected, and unilateral disarmament and appeasement serve only to encourage potential aggressors to become more aggressive.

And you curse the Ramsay MacDonalds, the Stanley Baldwins, the Neville Chamberlains, the Blums, the Daladiers, the Mackenzie Kings, the Herbert Hoovers, and the Roosevelts of the world, who could have stopped Hitler and Mussolini years ago with a maximum of will and a minimum of effort, but who either cringed at the thought of confronting the bombastic dictators or, in political in-dolence, simply sat back on their self-satisfied asses allowing them to arm and grow so strong that now only through sacrificing your generation will these arrogant monsters be brought to destruction.

Certainly no generation in history has ever gone to war with its eyes so wide open. Throughout the twenties and thirties, you have been exposed to a growing body of literature describing war, not in the traditional terms of glorious victories by gallant commanders, but in terms foul and realistic, as seen through the eyes of wretched lice-ridden men, gaunt with fear, surviving in rat-infested, sour-smelling dugouts.

And even more educational than books and plays themselves have been the motion pictures *based* on them, allowing you to see and hear what war can be like, in a way no previous generation could ever have imagined: dramatic works such as *The Big Parade*, the last major silent film taking its name from the stream of Red Cross ambulances moving to and from the front; the film *Journey's*

End, based on perhaps the most powerful play ever written, set in a dank and murky candlelit dugout in Flanders; and of course the classic film that Hollywood made of the most famous book on the war, *All Quiet on the Western Front*, a litany of pain, death, and disillusionment so grim and so damning of war and of those who start wars, that Hitler, on coming to power, forced its author, Erich Maria Remarque, to flee Germany.

And building on the cynicism induced by such dramatic works have been non-fiction bestsellers such as *Cry Havoc* by Beverly Nichols, promoting the suspicion that wars are the result of an international web of sinister plotting by munitions makers, and that only lunatics would oblige them by volunteering to fight. But despite all this, now that Hitler's legions have begun their unprovoked, brutal rampage across Europe, your generation will go to war as readily as did the youth of 1914–18.

Shortly after dawn, you go down to the lobby for the morning paper. The big story of the first day of the war is the loss of 118 lives (twenty-eight of them Americans) through the sinking of the liner *Athenia* off the west coast of Scotland by a torpedo from a German submarine. She'd been bound for Montreal with 1,400 passengers aboard, including 316 U.S. citizens.

Another story is headed "Winnie's Back," the signal passed by blinking lights from ship to ship yesterday throughout the British Fleet, indicating the navy is more than comfortable with the re-appointment of Winston Churchill as First Lord of the Admiralty, the post he held at the outset of the Great War. And he, in typical fashion, grasping the deepest meaning of this momentous day, wrapped its essence in his pungent prose: "Outside, the storms of war may blow and lands may be lashed with the fury of its gales, but in our own hearts this Sunday morning there is peace. Our hands may be active, but our consciences are clear."

Another reminder of how recently, in historical terms, the last war with Germany occurred, is a news item reporting that the much-hated German leader of that war, Kaiser Wilhelm, living in exile in Holland since 1918, will be following the course of this war on a "gigantic map of Europe."

Immediately after Britain declared war, there was an air-raid warning in London. It turned out to be a false alarm. However, an attack by Royal Airforce bombers on German naval bases at Wilhelms-haven and Brümsbutel was real, though it appeared to accomplish little by way of destroying enemy warships.*

According to the paper, in the past two days, since recruiting began Friday evening, the Canadian Militia has doubled in size to a hundred thousand. And already the sports pages are forced to recognize the war as they report the enlistment on Sunday of a good friend, Colin Ross: "Roughrider stalwart dons uniform of Ottawa Cameron Highlanders." Still, "Hefty" – as Colin will always be known to all who attended Glebe Collegiate with him – won't be moving very far, at least for the present, since the Camerons are mustering at Lansdowne Park, where he had been getting in shape for the Big Four football season.

---

* Of the 29 Blenheims and Wellington RAF bombers on the attack, 10 failed to locate the target and returned to England with their bomb loads intact; one plane bombed Esbjerg in neutral Denmark, 110 miles from the target; three decided to attack three men-of-war in the North Sea until they discovered they were British and returned home; seven were shot down by enemy ack-ack guns. Of the bombs actually dropped by the other eight aircraft who made it to their targets, three were duds landing on the battleship *Scheer*, and several hit the *Emden*, though the worst damage to the *Emden* was from a Blenheim that crashed into her forecastle. – According to the RAF Official History, Vol. I, *The Fight Against Odds*, by Denis Richards and Hillary St. George Saunders, published by His Majesty's Stationery Office, 1953, and so reported by Robert Goralski, page 92, *World War II Almanac*, Hamish Hamilton, London, 1981.

The same paper reports: "The Coliseum and its attached animal barns at Lansdowne Park have been taken over by 2nd (Ottawa) Battery and the 51st Battery for living and training accommodation."

5

BLITZKRIEG

———————————— ✳ ————————————

FOR THE FIRST FEW DAYS OF THE WAR, POLAND IS AT CENTRE
stage, and for a while the newspapers give the impression the Poles
are not only resisting bravely, but effectively. But soon the German
army is being referred to by correspondents as a "Juggernaut," and
a new and chilling word, *Blitzkrieg* (lightning war), begins to dominate their reports.

From mid-September, the word Warsaw becomes synonymous
with gallant resistance in the face of fearful bombing from the skies,
and you carry in your mind, wherever you go, a picture of a smashed
and doomed city under siege with its radio station repeating over
and over, after regular intervals of silence, a familiar musical phrase
from Chopin's Polonaise, assuring the outside world that Poland's
free heart is still beating. Everyone hopes they'll hold out, but deep
down you know the poor Poles, hastily mobilized and so ill-
equipped they have to resort to mounting a cavalry charge against
German tanks, cannot last long against the might of a modern
mechanized army.*

————————

* The perception of the German army as a highly mechanized force was
born at this time, and was reinforced by its *Blitzkrieg* through the Low
Countries and France in 1940. However, the German army had in use in
September 1939 more than 500,000 horses. Even their most highly mechanized divisions, with 394 cars and 615 trucks, still used 4,842 horses, and

When on September 17 Russia strikes at the beleaguered country from the east (with forty divisions), it's obvious Poland's fate is sealed. And when next day German and Russian troops join up in the interior of the country, the end of Poland as a nation is at hand.

Adding to this picture of treachery among neighbours, the same day, in sickening unison, Denmark, Finland, Norway, Sweden, and Iceland declare they intend to continue trading with all belligerents to protect their economic existence. By the twenty-fifth Warsaw is under savage bombardment as waves of Luftwaffe bombers fly at will over the defenceless city. And on the twenty-seventh, after twelve thousand have been killed (ten thousand of them civilians), the city capitulates, 140,000 laying down their arms.

During the whole of the fighting in Poland, France and Britain mount no ground attack to reduce the power of the German assault by drawing off some of their forces to defend their Western Front. And while it takes a few weeks, eventually it becomes clear that the Allies, with the full cooperation of Germany, are conducting what becomes known as the Twilight War or Phoney War.* This should have been clear from the outset, but was obscured by the combi-

---

their less-motorized divisions, 6,030 horses. By the time the war ended, 2,700,000 horses had seen service with the Wehrmacht, almost double the 1,400,000 used by the German army in World War I. Statistics are from Matthew Cooper's *The German Army, 1933–1945*, London, Macdonald and Jane's, 1978.

* Germany was not as reluctant as she appeared. Dissident elements in the German military hierarchy leaking Hitler's plan for invasion forced a postponement from November 12 to November 15. After missing assassination in the Munich Bürgerbrau cellar by only twenty minutes, Hitler postponed the attack until November 22. It was postponed again, by bad weather, to December 3. Further postponed until January 17, it was postponed once more, to spring, when a Luftwaffe major, carrying a copy of the maps and plans for the operation, was shot down over Allied territory, and an imminent thaw was predicted for Western Europe. (From details on pages 335 and 346 of *Monty – The Making of a General* by Nigel Hamilton, published by Fleet Books, Toronto, 1982.)

nation of horror and fascination with which the first days of the war in Poland were viewed. Even as the newspapers were printing pictures of Warsaw being devastated by Germans bombs, there appeared a story beginning, "British bomb Germany with propaganda leaflets for the third time." And no mention at all of any action by the French airforces, under orders not to bomb enemy territory and possibly incite bombing of French cities including Paris.

It seems Hitler is not ready for all-out war against the Allies, and the Allies are equally pleased to have breathing space to build up their forces and stocks of ammunition and equipment. And of course the most important fact on the Western Front, influencing the whole defensive strategy of the French general staff, is the existence of their great Maginot Line of vast underground forts, stretching from the Swiss border to Belgium. Spaced three to five miles apart and linked by underground railways, the forts are manned by thousands of troops content to wait to slaughter the Germans when they try to breach this impregnable line of pillboxes bristling with machine-guns, and concrete turrets ten feet thick housing big guns. Reached by elevators from living quarters and ammunition storage-dumps a hundred feet below ground, they are lit and air-conditioned by electric power generated by their own power plants.

Obviously, Canada is glad of the time to get on with the business of establishing temporary quarters for housing and training soldiers, sailors, and airmen, while building all-season training camps and setting up complex systems of manufacture and supply of everything from uniforms, guns, and ammunition, to military vehicles, ships, and planes, along with hundreds of items of special equipment for each branch of the service – not to mention an endless list of mundane items such as mess tins, knives, forks, spoons, enamelled mugs, shoe polish, shoe brushes, shaving brushes, and so on.

Just to equip 1st Canadian Infantry Division, scheduled for shipment overseas before Christmas, requires a gargantuan effort, and some things are simply not available this side of the Atlantic. Thus the divisional artillery regiments will sail without guns, there being

not a single 25-pounder in Canada, and as yet no factories tooled
up to produce any.*

Clearly, 2nd Canadian Infantry Division batteries have no prospect
whatsoever of getting 25-pounders in the foreseeable future, and
officers expect that they, too, will have to wait until they get to
England to be equipped. Currently, their concerns barely extend
beyond getting the men into proper uniforms so as to retain the
high state of morale these unusual recruits continue to exhibit in
spite of everything. All of them are bewildered and confused by a
way of life they'd never imagined they'd be living, and most of
them are trying to do the right thing and stay out of trouble as they
mimic the guy ahead of them, who often is equipped with two left
feet, or arms hinged in such a way as to swing back and forth in
disconcerting synchronization with leg closest at hand – right arm
with right leg, left arm with left leg.

Unquestionably, the batteries draw their strength in this important matter of morale from the fact that *all* are volunteers, though
it might be difficult to convince battery sergeant-majors of this, as
they struggle to pump a modicum of military order and discipline into their motley mobs, particularly at the moment still another put-
tee, unsupported at the ankle by the owner's low-cut civilian shoe,
starts unravelling from a leg trying to keep in step on morning drill.

---

* Britain, holding the patents, restricted their manufacture to the British
Isles. Only after horrendous losses in guns and vehicles at Dunkirk in May
1940 would the patents be released and Churchill make his plaintive appeal
to North America: "Give us the tools and we will finish the job."

6

RIDING ON A WAVE
OF PATRIOTISM

✳

CANADA BEGAN TO MOBILIZE FOR WAR THE SAME DAY
Germany attacked Poland, two days before Britain and France declared war on Germany, and nine days before Canada's parliament
officially got around to doing the same thing. Even before commanders of Non-Permanent Active Militia units got home from
their civilian places of work Friday evening and had a chance to
read the paper about the fighting in Poland, they were reading
telegrams from their military district headquarters ordering them to
mobilize their units for "active service."

Among the three hundred units so ordered were fifty-six artillery
batteries, fifty-one of them "reserve" batteries, including the 2nd
(Ottawa) Battery, the 14th (Cobourg), the 26th (Sarnia), and the
53rd (Toronto).*

From now until they come together in Petawawa months hence
to form the 4th Field Regiment, their stories will vary only in detail
from a common one: of enthusiasm persisting among officers and
men in spite of embarrassing deficiencies in equipment of all kinds,
sketchy training programs, makeshift living arrangements, and last,

---

* Battery commanders during the early months were: Major G. E. "Ted"
Beament (2nd), Captain F. V. M. Hinman followed by Major George
Arthur "Tiger" Welsh (14th), Major Eric Harris (26th), and Major Tom
Medland (53rd).

but not least, learning "to soldier" – to accommodate, adjust to, or circumvent a strange new set of rules and regulations designed to encourage them to think and act like soldiers, but restricting them, confining them, and controlling every facet of their lives twenty-four hours a day.

Immediately on receipt of the mobilization order, the opportunity is given to all members of the reserve batteries to enlist. Almost all officers and NCOs (non-commissioned officers), and a good percentage of the "Other Ranks," decide to enlist immediately, providing the core of a battery. After a few days, recruiting offices are set up and the public invited to join.

With Canada on the crest of a patriotic wave, each battery gets more applicants than it can take. In the first three days of public recruitment, the Toronto battery "interviews" three hundred and is up to strength in a week.* By September 6, 2nd (Ottawa) Battery recruitment is so advanced they become choosy and announce "only skilled truck-drivers of excellent physique, not under 5-feet 10-inches, will be considered."

Still, recruitment of skills is generally not very selective, since no one can say what the ultimate war-establishment of a field battery is likely to be. Thus, most of the men are selected merely on the basis of physical and educational standards.

The enlistment process for 2nd Battery is carried out at the old Regal Building in downtown Ottawa, within an open expanse of heavily waxed battleship linoleum, sparsely furnished with folding tables, folding chairs, wire file-baskets, and wire wastepaper baskets.

Besides eyecharts, the only decorations are poster-size stylized panoramas (as a talented gunner officer might paint) of patchwork English fields, hanging on folding screens, behind which men are

---

* The rush to enlist has sometimes been attributed to the Depression and widespread unemployment, but more than 80 per cent of the volunteers left jobs to enlist, according to military historian Terry Copp of Wilfrid Laurier University.

asked to strip, provide urine samples, and submit to chest-soundings and embarrassing "short-arm inspections" of dangling appendages by an MO (medical officer).

Among those clumping up the exceedingly worn and squeaky wooden stairs, in the old red-brick building redolent with dustbane, seeking to enlist as gunners with 2nd Battery, on Thursday, September 14, is Lloyd George Lavigne of Cornwall, Ontario,* and while it is entirely unlikely anyone makes any special note of the date, from this moment on, neither he nor His Majesty's Forces will ever be quite the same again.

In less time than it takes to describe the procedure, 2nd Battery signs up "Doc" – as he soon will be nicknamed, when, temporarily attached to the Medical Officer, he is taken in by some of his more conscienceless comrades and proceeds on his own initiative to generously dispense rubbing alcohol in little medicine bottles to the "strained-muscle" cases appearing in ever-expanding numbers on morning sick-parade, until his naivety is discovered by the MO.

Indoctrination into a new and coarse way of life, for which no recruit is ever really prepared, is best captured in Doc's own words, describing his first day in the service of His Majesty:

> After getting a medical in a dingy building, someone starts yelling,
> "Everybody outside!" (Interesting that the yelling only starts after
> you have signed the papers to serve anywhere in the world, under
> any arsehole they choose to put over you.) Outside a guy with
> three stripes on the sleeves of his tunic, standing by a truck, yells,
> "Hey, you. Get in!"

---

* In 1959, as Mayor of Cornwall, at the time of the opening of the great St. Lawrence Seaway, he and his wife, Myrtle (to whom he wrote every day of the five years he was overseas), were hosts at civic banquets for Queen Elizabeth and President Dwight Eisenhower, Supreme Commander of all Allied Forces on the Western Front in 1944–45.

We do, but already we don't like this guy. The bumpy ride on a bouncing steel shelf in the back of the truck out to the Coliseum in Lansdowne Park is as bruising as it is undignified, but we don't mind, for when we get there, we're going to get a uniform and a gun, and be on our way to becoming a real hero in the eyes of our family. But at the Coliseum, the guy with the stripes comes around to the back of the truck and starts yelling again: "Get out and line up."

Getting out doesn't require any special military training, but lining up is another matter. Guess no one is doing it right, because this guy with the stripes is yelling louder than ever:

"Hey, you! Move up! Hey, you! Move back!" and so forth and so on, while he gets redder and redder in the face.

At last we get it right, or maybe he gives up. Anyway, he roars, "Right Turn – Quick March!" and into the building we go.

"Wow," I say to the guy next to me, "this smells like a horse stable!"

"It should," says he. "This is where they hold the Winter Fair and Horse Show, and where they keep the horses and cows for the Central Canada Exhibition that only finished a week ago."

After marching around a ring of boards the shape of a hockey rink surrounded by bleachers, and up a concrete horse-ramp, lo and behold we're in a long concrete room with a lot of hey-yous armed with brooms, sweeping up after the last occupants – some horses – which, according to my new friend, were only removed a few hours ago. The odour is so strong that anyone who wanted to claim that horses have been stabled in here since prehistoric times would be believed.

Just then a guy with one stripe on his sleeve approaches. We take it he's some kind of straw-boss, since he has no broom in his hands. When he gets close, he yells, "Hey, you! Get yourself a broom and start sweepin'!"

Now, you aren't used to being yelled at, and are taking on an awful dislike for these characters' with stripes who assume everybody around here is deaf. But you think, Better play it cool, Lavigne, until you get to know the score.

After sweeping a while, you decide to light up a weed so as to enjoy the work better. But just as you get back to sweeping, in walks this guy who really seems to be somebody. He isn't wearing stripes, but has a round insignia sewn down near the cuff of his sleeve, which means something, for right away the guys with stripes run to him with shining eyes, and for a moment you think they are going to kneel down and kiss his ring.

Suddenly he is staring this way and talking. But you can't make out what he's saying. Then he starts walking this way, very stiff and military-like, with all the guys with stripes following him. By now he is talking very loud indeed, but still you can't understand him, until finally he gets through to you with a slow, deliberate, "Can't you understand English?"

"You'd better believe I do," says you.

"Well," says he, "you can't sweep and smoke at the same time."

To which you devote about three seconds of deep thought before agreeing, "You're right," and throw away the broom.

At this he turns seventeen different shades of red and roars:

"That will get you seven days CB, soldier."

Still, the day isn't completely lost. You learn not to trifle with battery sergeant-majors (particularly one named Arthur Wibe). You also learn "CB" means confined-to-barracks. Not bad for your first day in an army that doesn't even know your name.

7

AN OFFICERS' MESS
IN A LADIES' WASHROOM

---------------------- ✳ ----------------------

ENTHUSIASM, BORN OF THE EXCITEMENT OF RESPONDING TO the national emergency, alone keeps the early days of training from becoming totally ridiculous in the eyes of both men and officers.

Even uniforms, the most essential articles for the encouragement of a soldierly attitude, are lacking. And in all cases where men are outfitted with ill-fitting uniforms, they are of the outmoded 1914–18 vintage, with breeches, puttees, and brass buttons. Many recruits cannot be outfitted with army boots, which raises serious problems, since some don't even have decent civilian shoes in which to drill.*

----

* For infantry battalions mobilizing to form 4th Brigade (Essex Scottish, Royal Regiment of Canada, and Royal Hamilton Light Infantry), which one day the guns of the Regiment will be supporting in action, the lack of proper footwear is even more serious because of their emphasis on footdrill. Only a gift in early September of 130 pairs of boots and socks by a public-spirited Toronto lady (Mrs. F. H. Phippen) allows the Royal Regiment of Canada to march out of barracks. But as recruitment goes on, the problem returns, and when "a short march on wet pavements on 27 September left 30 virtually barefoot," the Royals' CO, Lt.-Col. Hedley Basher, arranges for "private purchase of boots and socks." (Page 356, *Battle Royal*, published in 1962 by Royal Regiment of Canada Association.)

Though the old uniform of puttees and brass buttons was officially replaced in the British army in March 1939 by the "battledress" – a loose-fitting blouse and baggy pants buckled in at the boot-tops by web anklets – it was not accepted as a Canadian uniform until the first week of October 1939, and only appeared late that month. Even then it was for 1st Division units only, which have priority for all fundamental equipment, since they are scheduled to go overseas before Christmas.

Issuing "breeches, cloth, drab" and "jackets, serge, drab" from the sparse supplies of 1914–18 uniforms available in battery stores is the least of the quartermaster's worries. To him it's enough that he gets every man into some kind of uniform. But for the gunner, who must wear breeches up under his armpits – the excess folds of "cloth, drab" protruding from his rear, lifting up the tail of his tunic like a rumble seat – it is quite something else.

And so during the fall, when the troops have to march out of the front gate of Lansdowne and display themselves to the public on such occasions as church parades, only their gallant effort to emulate a regiment of guards in the discipline and precision of their marching heads off the ridicule and disdain of observers along the route.

As it is, the men of 2nd Battery have to get used to people on the sidewalk tittering as they swing out onto Bank Street, since they, like all units training at Lansdowne, are followed each time by a retarded child wearing a Woolworth yachting cap and a chestful of tin medals, beating a tin drum, and periodically calling out throaty, unintelligible orders in an uncanny imitation of Sergeant-Major Wibe, whom he follows closely with exaggerated stride.*

---

* Five months later a "statement of clothing and necessaries" by 2nd Ottawa Field Battery, February 6, 1940, showed that while they had acquired enough boots, they had on charge only 12 battledress blouses and 12 battledress trousers, and were deficient 167 blouses and 167 trousers. And the 176 "breeches, cloth, drab," 156 "jackets, serge, drab," and 321 "drawers, woollen," drawn from mothballed 1914–18 stocks, were "old and in bad condition, or worn out."

Of course, makeshift arrangements apply to all four batteries. All acquire billets in buildings that happen to be empty in their communities. In Toronto, as in Ottawa, the Exhibition is over, and there are no horses in the Horse Palace in the CNE grounds. Nor is the elaborate and nobly proportioned Ladies' Washroom in use, so there is no objection to 53rd Battery establishing an officers' mess there.

At Sarnia, the tourist season is over, so 26th Battery is able to move into Lake Cabin Lodges at Crinnians Grove on Lake Huron. Men of Cobourg's 14th Battery "live out" in hotels and private houses until an addition to the local armoury to take care of an additional seventy-five men is completed. Their officers' mess is in the nearby Chateau Hotel.

In all current newspaper stories about the forces, reporters seem impelled to strike an upbeat note, and only by inference can the reader gain any insight into the discomforts endured by the early recruits. Typical is an *Ottawa Citizen* report on November 2, describing the conversion of Lansdowne Park into a military training camp:

The ring of the Coliseum [used in other times for animal judging and horse-jumping trials] is now used as a gun park where soldiers are drilled. The bases on which the guns (2nd Battery) are parked are concrete slabs from horse stalls. Two of the [cow] barns which run north from the Coliseum are now sleeping quarters. The ground floor of the Bate Barn contains showers and washrooms. The heavy-horse barn is a lecture room and drill shed. The old pigpens on the ground floor at the east end of the Coliseum have been changed into a dining room that takes care of 1,300 men. . . . The floor was washed with chemicals and then hosed down thoroughly. . . . Upstairs on the main floor are: the officers' mess, offices, some sleeping quarters, quartermaster's stores and a canteen. . . . In the poultry section, officers and men now sleep peacefully. The roof has been fixed and the broken windows repaired.

The same jolly heartiness is found in a *Journal* story, entitled "The Bugle At 6 A.M. Opens Busy Day for Soldiers at Lansdowne Park," studiously avoiding mentioning that soldiers, swathed in coarse, woollen army blankets, arise from lumpy, rustling denim bags stuffed with straw (which the army tries to dignify with the label "palliasse") resting on hundreds of iron double-bunks:

> There isn't any loitering between the sheets for the soldiers at Lansdowne Park. They have got to snap out of it and appear with shining faces for physical jerks at 6:30. . . . The half-hour physical drill that starts the day serves to limber up the muscles, brace the mind and sharpen the appetite for breakfast . . . prunes or porridge, beans and bacon, bread and butter and jam, tea or coffee. . . . The men sit at long double rows of tables. . . . At the far end of the room is the cookhouse well-equipped with gas and coal ranges which are generally diffusing a savoury odour that promises something good for the next meal.

The same day, October 19, a *Citizen* story, entitled "Troops Spend Interesting Day at Lansdowne Park in Training for War Service," has all the flavour of something out of a *Boy's Own* annual:

> Brass buttons are soon to be a thing of the past, Sam Browne belts may have been ordered to be tossed into storage, and "form fours" may be an order now unheard, but if anyone thinks that the training of the soldiers at Lansdowne Park is anything but the best is just dead wrong. Troops in the Ottawa area are getting a course of training that will result in their being able to take their place in the fight against Hitlerism along with the best in the Empire.
>
> There is nothing soft about the soldiers in Canada's army. They are a fine crowd and are taking to their mode of living with the spirit of true Canadians. They realize they have a job to do and are doing it with a will. Life at Lansdowne is not easy, but is

far from being unpleasant. If you have any doubts, just ask one of the soldiers stationed there.

If the reporter actually pursued his own suggestion, he chose not to let the reader in on the answers, and perhaps with good reason. Closer to the truth may be the recollections of Doc Lavigne, who, when asked later how on earth did they get rid of the animal odours, replied, "They didn't. They just moved the men in, some of them smelled worse than the horses." As for the kitchens "diffusing savoury odours," he could only snort, "More likely the smell of Catawba wine, which Bull Hunter's girlfriend, Trixie, regularly loads into a basket the Bull lets down on a string from a second-storey window overlooking Bank Street, right behind the sentry box. The only guy who likes the grub at Lansdowne Park is a guy just out of prison."

A *Journal* story of October 26 implies a notable consistency in the winning ways of 2nd Battery in weekly field-days:

> With Nick Ostapyk's brilliant victory in the discus throw, the gunners *again* captured aggregate honours in the weekly Soldiers Field Day yesterday with no fewer than seven units competing. Ostapyk, one of Ottawa's leading track and field athletes and crack swimmer, tossed the discus 112 feet seven inches. Keith McConnell, another gunner, won both the obstacle race and running broad-jump with a leap of seventeen feet and six inches. The 2nd Battery tug-of-war team came first as well.

Armistice Day this year takes on special meaning. Only twenty-one years have elapsed since the 1914–18 war ended, and many veterans of that conflict were among the first to line up at the recruiting offices for this one. For a couple of hours on the evening of November 11, at a memorial service in the Coliseum, the gap between the generations falls away as young recruits and veterans join in singing the old Great War songs – "It's a Long Way to Tipperary"

and "Pack Up Your Troubles in Your Old Kit Bag" – and periodically explode into roaring laughter and applause at the antics of
the famous Dumbbells of Flanders Fields, drawn out of retirement
once again to entertain the troops. (Some, including Al Plunkett
and his brother, had "toured" the vaudeville circuit for several years
after the Great War, where their talent had first blossomed in improvised entertainments for the weary troops just out of the
trenches. The Plunketts even composed a lively marching song,
"We're on Our Way . . . ," for the occasion, with a melody so
catchy that it was adopted overnight by 2nd Battery as their route-
marching song.*) Monday's *Citizen* claims it was "as enjoyable an
evening as this city has ever beheld. Three thousand veterans and
new recruits almost blew the roof off."

And this buoyant mood persists as winter closes in, despite the
serious lack of equipment for training. Apart from a couple of 4.5-
inch howitzers and a couple of wooden-wheeled 18-pounders, both
officially obsolete, almost no equipment is available. Even artillery
boards – drawing boards to carry gridded paper on which map
references of guns and targets can be plotted so that ranges (in yards)
and switches (in degrees) can be measured with "arm" and "arc" –
must be improvised. And artillery "directors" (survey instruments
for establishing precise bearings for laying the guns parallel on their
zero line, and providing their exact location on the face of the
globe) are "borrowed" from mysterious sources.

Each battery is able to scrounge a couple of civilian trucks to
transport essentials and to act as guinea pigs for blossoming motor-
mechanics. But for some time there are no trucks fitted to haul
guns, so on occasions when troop deployments are carried out, logs
are stuck in the ground to imitate guns, and gunners are required
to walk about carrying placards displaying the tactical names of
vehicles. Needless to say, this does little for the image of Canada's

---

* Fifty-eight years after that night, Brig. Ted Beament, Signaller Carl
Killeen, and Hervé Dupuis could still sing all the words of the Plunketts'
song. See Appendix A.

"fighting forces" among the civilian population. One day, Capt. McGregor Young, supervising a deployment of placard-carrying, two-legged "trucks" milling around outside the Horse Palace in Toronto, is accosted by an indignant civilian asking: "Why the hell is the army on strike?"

Battery schemes involving deployment of real guns become possible only after minor modifications to civilian trucks occasionally available for rent, and though a pink-and-blue truck advertising "Joe's Meat Market" may look incongruous pulling a gun and limber, when equipped with a proper hauling hook, it can do the job as effectively as one painted khaki.

A few gunners are chosen to be trained as signallers, but, there being no radio sets, the students learn how to send messages by hand-held flags, and in Morse code using buzzers and lamps.

Others, selected on the basis of their interest and level of education in high-school mathematics, start training as "surveyors," to become technical assistants to gun position officers and forward observation officers. A graduate of this course will be known by the odd-sounding title of "Ack" (being "A" in the military phonetic alphabet, standing for assistant), which, as time goes on and his training becomes more sophisticated, will earn him the utmost respect of all ranks, to the point that even when promoted to lance-bombardier or bombardier or sergeant, "Ack" will remain an honorable part of his title: "Bombardier Ack, Able Troop," or "Sergeant Command Post Ack, 2nd Battery."

There being plenty of large-scale maps available, and sufficient prismatic compasses, all ranks can be trained in map-reading through classroom study and field trips in the nearby countryside to test newly acquired knowledge.

Also, thanks to detailed pamphlets on the subject, all ranks are introduced to "gas training": the precautionary and defensive measures individuals must take to avoid injury during gas attacks, including recognition of the gases by smell and sight (some having distinctive vapour clouds that cling to the ground in low places). But when told how to neutralize their deadly effects by donning gas masks in the case of chlorine or phosgene, and oilskin "gas capes" to ward off searing splatters of mustard gas (that instructors claim will burn holes in skin that will never heal), the students must use their imagination, for as yet neither gas masks nor gas capes have been issued. Still, it all is taken very seriously, particularly the matter of decontamination of the victim and the immediate vicinity after an attack involving clinging oily mustard gas.*

Some instructors are from the Permanent Force and some are from the Royal Military College graduates among the officers in each battery, but in the main the load is carried by men like Sergeant-Major Wibe, who qualified as "a signaller first class" nine years ago and a "gun sergeant" seven years ago, who have until now been the so-called "Saturday-night soldiers," the officers and NCOs of the Non-Permanent Active Militia.†

For the officers, who must update and improve their knowledge, there is the stream of pamphlets from the British War Office now beginning to flow in earnest (and which will continue unabated to the end of the war), and certain nights are set aside for officer study

---

* Though the League of Nations, responding to worldwide revulsion at the use of poison gas by both sides in World War I, which left scores of men blinded or gasping for air for the rest of their lives, outlawed gas as a weapon of war, no one trusted Hitler (who broke treaties as casually as he crumbled biscuits in his soup) to abide by any clause in the Geneva Convention that didn't suit his purpose. Thus, training to meet and try to manage gas attacks, which began at the outset of the war, was carried on from time to time right up until D-Day in Normandy 1944, where both sides went into action carrying respirators – the Canadians and British in canvas bags on their chests, and the Germans in corrugated cans across the back of their hips. Also, tons of gas bombs were manufactured and stored openly along shady lanes in Britain throughout the war – a continuing warning to Hitler that should he be tempted to use gas, his Reich would be flooded with deadly fumes.

† Of the 58,337 men and women who enlisted in the Active Service Force in September 1939, 24,689 were from the Non-Permanent Active Militia.

groups. Such things as concealment from the air become questions to be argued at length.

Slowly, all four batteries are outfitted with uniforms (albeit of 1914–18 design), and with the outfitting come "spit and polish parades."

With the coming of cold weather, the 26th Battery discovers the Lake Cabin Lodges near Sarnia are not suitable for winter occupancy and moves to Guelph to the Winter Fair Building.

In Ottawa, deep snow prevents weekly field days at Lansdowne Park, but hockey and basketball teams play in forces' leagues, where competition sometimes turns ferocious. One game at the Auditorium between 2nd Battery and the Airforce turns into a riotous free-for-all both on and off the ice, bringing the wrath of the brass down on all concerned. Of course the matter is not pursued to any degree, for riotous battles between the services – for no reason other than loyalty to the colour of a uniform – are not uncommon throughout the fall and winter, especially across the Ottawa River in Hull, a location troops find peculiarly attractive because of a laissez-faire attitude by Quebec bars toward closing hours and other conventional niceties.

8

A TURKEY NECK
BECOMES A LEGEND

SINCE A MAXIMUM NUMBER ARE TO BE GRANTED LEAVE TO GO home for what will probably be their last Christmas in Canada for some time, all four batteries advance the date of their unit dinners. And according to witnesses, all are feasts of "huge proportions," served by the officers in splendidly decorated, if cavernous, mess halls, accompanied by some surprisingly good entertainment. Because of special connections with big retail establishments and the entertainment world, 53rd Battery's bash in Toronto is unquestionably the most spectacular. Their drab Horse Palace, transformed by decorations donated by Simpson's department store, provides a setting worthy of the entertainment supplied by Percy Faith's internationally famous orchestra.*

But if the other batteries have less famous names supporting their dinners, they are no less well done, with gifts supplied by service clubs or auxiliary organizations. All members of 26th Battery (now

---

* His "Music by Faith" show, carried by both the CBC and the Mutual Network, then ranked third among all America's musical radio shows. Faith also did the orchestral arrangements and conducted the "Woolworth Hour," the "Carnation Contented Hour," and the "Pause That Refreshes" hour. Postwar, he was in charge of the popular music division of Columbia Records, where he arranged and recorded some all-time classic albums.

in the Winter Fair Building in Guelph), at their dinner on the 21st, are presented with "royal artillery sweaters" by Major W. E. Harris.

According to the Ottawa-district army sheet, *The Tin Hat Chronicle* (even more inclined than the dailies to present unit news in a jolly fashion), the "Turkey Parade" at 2nd Battery was a very happy affair: "Never had a better Christmas dinner . . . The beam on Stan Godlewski's face registered utter satisfaction . . . Major Beament carving the turkey . . . Gunner Billings getting the first helping . . . Hearty (in the interests of accuracy, substitute rude) songs for the benefit of the sergeants . . . etc. etc."

But in none of the reports dealing with activities during the festive season are you likely to find any mention of a turkey neck that went missing from one of the 2nd Battery birds the night before their Battery dinner, though its disappearance, and the way it was utilized by one Gunner Tony Wilcox, seeking revenge against Lieut. Don Wilson, produced an undercurrent of unusual hilarity throughout the meal as the story was passed discreetly from one ear to another.

Fortunately the full flavour of the incident, which would become one of the great and lasting legends of 4th Field, has been captured in an account set down by Doc Lavigne:

It is only natural that two great soldiers like Tony Wilcox and Mr. Wilson won't have enough elbow room to operate in a small place like Lansdowne Park. Tony is a graduate of the 1914–18 fracas, wears a lot of coloured ribbons on his chest, and claims he came out of that conflict as a captain. Mr. Wilson is a product of the Royal Military College, with some service with some British outfit like the Bengal Lancers in India, and always makes like he's a real soldier – very strong on discipline and stiff as a ramrod on parade. (The only time he gets stiffer is when he and his pal, Lieut. George Brown, get into the grape in the officers' mess, but that's another story, or a lot of stories.)

Mr. Wilson doesn't have any ribbons on his chest, and maybe Tony's ribbons bother him. Whatever the reason, he chooses not to believe that Tony was an officer in the big war, and proceeds to give him the well-known works at every opportunity, but especially during footdrill. This may be aimed at Tony, but it gets all us hey-yous marching back and forth over that football field in front of the grandstand until it's tamped down about six inches. Around about then, Bull Hunter calls a council of war.

Some of us younger hey-yous are told, "You can attend, but keep your mouth shut." Actually everybody keeps his trap shut while the Bull points out that this I-don't-like-your-face situation between Tony and the Lieutenant is imposing altogether too much hardship on everybody – that something must be done about it, and he's decided Tony should work in the kitchen where he'll be out of sight. This should take the heat off all us hey-yous, and with cold weather coming, it will be better for Tony.

"Anybody disagree?" the Bull asks. Of course nobody disagrees with the Bull to his face, so he says, "Okay, it's unanimous."

For a while it seems the problem is solved. With Tony out of the way, Mr. Wilson's humour improves immensely, and Tony is happy as a lark in the kitchen with characters like Slim McGillis, Claff Gravelle, Bo Prud'homme, and about six others below the rank of gunner, looked after by Sgt. C. B. Price – not one to ever discourage his kitchen mechanics from maintaining their morale at a noticeably high level through having a gallon or two of Catawba stashed here and there about the place. For the most part Tony and his friends know what season it is only by what is brought in for them to cook. Thus they know Christmas is coming when the turkeys arrive.

Being fresh birds they have to be dressed for the oven. And the night before the big dinner, Tony is busy cleaning one of the birds – now and then having a sip of Catawba – when he gets his big idea. He's just cut the neck off one of them and is holding it in his hand. For a moment he hesitates, looking at that neck, all raw and bloody, and then he opens his fly and stuffs it into his shorts. Even while he's still buttoning up, he's heading straight for the Orderly Room where he knows Mr. Wilson is on duty

as the Orderly Officer. There he raps on the door and when the
Duty Bombardier calls "Come in," Tony enters announcing he's
come to see the Orderly Officer.

Naturally, Mr. Wilson is astonished, for he's been living with
the happy belief that Tony left the outfit long ago. And he turns
red with dislike when he sees him standing there:

"What the hell do you want, Wilcox?"

"Can I see you privately, sir – it's very important, sir?"

Impressed by Tony's respectful tone, Mr. Wilson steps out of
the office into the corridor with Tony: "Well, what is it?"

Now there happens to be a little alcove just a few feet away,
and Tony suggests very politely, "Can we step in here, sir, where
it's more private?" Again Mr. Wilson cooperates, and when they
are both in the alcove, Tony says, "I've got a big problem."

By now Mr. Wilson is losing his patience, which is never one
of his strong points: "Well, come on, Wilcox, out with it."

With seemly hesitation Tony unbuttons his pants, pulls out
one end of the bloody turkey neck: "What do you think of that?"

Now it's slightly dark in the alcove and to Mr. Wilson "that"
looks for all the world like something other than a bloody turkey
neck. Horrified, he yells: "My gawd, man, that should be shown
to the MO immediately!"

Tony sighs: "You're probably right, sir, but I'm kinda busy
working on Christmas dinner. Would you take it down for me?"
And with that he up and hands the bloody monstrosity to the
recoiling Lieutenant. As Tony makes a hasty retreat – and it has
to be hasty let me tell you, for Wilson won the fifty-yard dash at
the last Army Field Day – the waves of roaring that rise up behind
him are almost enough to blow the windows out of the building.*

---

* Subsequent disciplinary action of a more dignified nature, instigated by
Lieutenant Wilson, ostensibly aimed at reducing the alcoholic haze in the
battery kitchen, resulted in Gunner Wilcox and at least one other cook
being relieved of their kitchen duties, with the immediate result that Major

And if next morning people strolling past the Coliseum pause to wonder how a big bloody turkey neck managed to get flung out into the middle of Bank Street, you wouldn't be at all surprised.

Beament had to hire two civilian cooks and pay for them out of his own pocket because the government had just cut off all recruiting in Canada until accommodation and supplies of uniforms, boots, etc., caught up with requirements of those already on strength.

9

"PUT THINE HAND INTO THE HAND OF GOD"

---- ✳ ----

SINCE THE FALL OF POLAND, PRACTICALLY ALL THE ACTION HAS taken place at sea, with the Germans taking initiatives aimed at disrupting the movement of supplies to the Allies. As early as September 17, the British aircraft carrier *Courageous* was sunk by a torpedo off Ireland while on submarine patrol, with a loss of five hundred; and the battleship *Royal Oak* was sunk while at anchor in Scapa Flow by a sub that penetrated that supposedly safe anchorage, causing the death of 833 sailors.

Ships from both neutral and belligerent countries are being sunk by German submarines and magnetic mines sown by German planes in the Thames Estuary and along Britain's east coast – 60,000 tons sunk by mines alone in one week in November, including a Japanese passenger liner.

During this discouraging time, one heartening victory was achieved by the Allies. A British heavy cruiser, *Exeter*, and two light cruisers, *Ajax* (British) and *Achilles* (New Zealand), seriously outgunned by the German battleship *Admiral Graf Spee*, still managed to inflict such damaging blows to the giant surface raider as they harassed her off Uraguay that she was forced to seek shelter in the River Plate. There, on December 17, before thousands of Sunday strollers watching from Montevideo, her crew scuttled her as the free world – starved for a victory of any kind – huddled about their radios to listen and cheer.

Then three days before Christmas, the courageous Finns, with an army of only 150,000, launched a counter-attack with great success against three Russian armies of some 600,000 men that had invaded their country on the last day of November.

Still, on the Western Front the Phoney War continues, with only one skirmish disturbing the peace during all of fall, when some Germans drove some French back to the Maginot Line near Saarbrücken on October 16. British field guns, deployed in action in support of the British Expeditioriary Force (BEF) in France within a few days of the declaration of war, have not yet fired a shot. And RAF planes flying over Germany (over Berlin for the first time the night of October 1–2) continue to drop leaflets only.

However, recognizing that the twilight war cannot go on much longer – that planes must soon start carrying bombs in their bomb bays, and that 1940 is certain to witness battles that could decide the shape and security of the whole world for generations to come – the King in his quiet and hesitant way strikes a deep chord in hearts throughout the Commonwealth when he ends his broadcast Christmas Day with a moving quotation:

And I said to the man who stood at the gate of the year, "Give me a light that I may tread safely into the unknown." And he replied, "Go out into the darkness and put thine hand into the hand of God. That shall be to thee better than light and safer than a known way."

At first no one seems to know the origin of these inspiring words, which rather guarantees their fame and immortality when editorial-page writers throughout the world feel obliged to speculate. Eventually the poem is identified as "God Knows," by Minnie Louise Haskins, and the prescience of the advice becomes profoundly evident as the new year progresses.

On February 11, a Soviet force of 140,000 launches a decisive attack, resulting in Finland's capitulation and the surrender of 16,000 square miles of territory. While expected, it's sad news, for the Finns had captured the imagination of the world with images of troops on skiis ambushing invaders in snowy forests, and pelting their tanks with flaming glass bottles filled with gasoline.*

On April 9, Germany abruptly brings to an end their "Sitzkrieg War" by invading Denmark and Norway. Denmark offers practically no resistance, suffering only thirteen dead and twenty-three wounded, while inflicting only twenty casualties on the invaders before surrendering.

Norway is overwhelmed by paratroop landings on their airdromes and ten thousand German soldiers popping up out of the holds of merchant ships anchored in all their major ports. Taken by surprise, the Norwegian people put up a brave resistance. But the invaders are welcomed by a pro-Nazi faction led by ex-war minister Vidkun Quisling, who adds a new word for "traitor" to the language when he embraces the Germans and declares himself prime minister. Henceforth collaborators everywhere will be "quislings."

Soviet foreign secretary Vyacheslav Molotov tells the German ambassador in Moscow, "We wish Germany complete success in her defensive measures."

On April 18, signallers from all four batteries of 4th Field RCA gather in Barriefield Camp, Kingston, Ontario, for a six-week course provided by the Royal Canadian Corps of Signals. For the first time they learn how to lay line and operate radio transmitters

----

* First used in the Spanish Civil War, and perfected by the Finns, they later became known as "Molotov Cocktails" when the Russians took them into use against the Germans. The Finns threw at the enemy tanks some 70,000 glass bottles filled with a combination of petrol, kerosene, and tar, ignited by a rag wrapped around the neck and soaked in oil, or by a sulphuric acid pellet attached to the bottle. In four months of war, these fiery glass missiles, smashed against the sides or backs of Russian tanks, are reputed to have accounted for many if not most of the 1,600 tanks lost by the Soviets. The Finnish war cost Russia 68,000 killed, compared to Finland's 25,000 military deaths.

– albeit Number One Sets, the first primitive sets acquired by the army in the 1920s.*

Next day, even as Holland prepares for the worst and declares a state of siege, the Dutch reaffirm their desire to remain neutral, stating they "shun" all assistance, "whether offered or actually forced on us."

Early in May, certain captains, subalterns, and NCOs, selected from each battery, leave for England for courses at the Royal School of Artillery, Larkhill, given by their renowned IGs (Instructors In Gunnery), sometimes referred to as "the apostles of the gospel according to Larkhill." Then on May 10, Germany invades the Low Countries, Chamberlain resigns, and Winston Churchill becomes prime minister of Britain.

The party of 4th Field officers and NCOs from Canada arrives at Number One Canadian Artillery Reinforcement Unit, Bordon, Hants, just in time to hear a radio broadcast (on May 13) of the new prime minister's sobering, inaugural speech:

> . . . I have nothing to offer but blood, toil, tears, and sweat. We have before us an ordeal of the most grievous kind . . . many, many long months of struggle and of suffering. You ask, What is our policy? I will say, It is to wage war by sea, land, and air, with all the strength that God can give us; to wage war against a monstrous tyranny, never surpassed in the dark, lamentable cat-alogue of human crime. That is our policy. You ask, What is our aim? I can answer in one word, Victory – victory at all costs, victory in spite of all terror, victory, however long and hard the road may be – for without victory, there is no survival. Let that be realized . . . no survival for all that the British Empire has stood for, no survival for the urge and impulse of the ages, that mankind will move forward towards its goal. . . . I feel entitled to claim

---

* By then the British were using 11-sets, and by war's end were using 22-sets.

the aid of all, and I say, "Come, then, let us go forward together with our united strength."

Next day Holland surrenders after only four days' resistance. Four days later, the Germans break through Belgium to Antwerp and the coast. Now the gravity of the peril to France becomes clear in Churchill's "call and spur to the faithful servants of Truth and Justice."

While addressing the House of Commons in "a solemn hour for the life of our country, of our Empire, of our Allies, and, above all, of the cause of freedom," he clearly is sending a message to the desperate officers and men of the British Expeditionary Force on the continent:

A tremendous battle is raging in France and Flanders. The Germans, by a remarkable combination of air bombing and heavily armoured tanks, have broken through the French defences north of the Maginot Line, and strong columns of their armoured vehicles are ravaging the open country which for the first day or two was without defenders. They have penetrated deeply and spread alarm and confusion in their track. Behind them there are now appearing infantry in lorries, and behind them again, the large masses are moving forward. . . .

We must not allow ourselves to be intimidated by the presence of these armoured vehicles in unexpected places behind our lines. . . . If the French army, and our own army, are well handled, as I believe they will be; if the French retain that genius for recovery and counter-attack for which they have so long been famous; and the British Army shows the dogged endurance and solid fighting power of which there have been so many examples in the past – then a sudden transformation of the scene might spring into being.

It would be foolish, however, to disguise the gravity of the hour. It would be still more foolish to lose heart and courage or suppose that well-trained, well-equipped armies numbering three or four million of men can be overcome in the space of a few weeks, or even months, by a scoop, or raid of mechanized vehicles, however formidable. . . . The armies must cast away the idea of resisting behind concrete lines or natural obstacles, and must realize that mastery can only be regained by furious, unrelenting assault. And this spirit must not only animate the High Command, but must inspire every fighting man.

. . . We must expect that as soon as stability is reached on the Western Front, the bulk of that hideous apparatus of aggression, which gashed Holland into ruin and slavery in a few days, will be turned on us. I am sure I speak for all when I say we are ready to face it, to endure it, and to retaliate against it – to any extent that the unwritten laws of war permit. . . . One bond unites us all – to wage war until victory is won, and never surrender ourselves to servitude and shame, whatever the cost and the agony may be.

10

4TH FIELD TO PETAWAWA

AS NATIONS COLLAPSE

———————————— ✳ ————————————

ONLY EIGHT DAYS AFTER INVADING THE LOW COUNTRIES, THE
Germans have opened a fifty-mile gap in the French line, and
rampaging Panzer columns, like slashing sickle points, are spreading
chaos behind Allied lines. It takes just six more days for them to
reach Calais, far south of the Belgium–British sector. With French
resistance crumbling, some 380,000 Allied soldiers, two-thirds of
them British, are hemmed in on the coast at Dunkirk. As plans are
made to rescue as many as possible by sea, the officers and men of
the 4th Field advance party, now attached to #1 CARU (Canadian
Artillery Reinforcement Unit), Bordon, Hants, are organized to
receive the weary men.

In Canada this day (May 24), four batteries, destined to form 4th
Field Regiment under Lt.-Col. Frank Percival Lloyd, are ordered
to entrain for Petawawa. Since the current establishment calls for
only two batteries of twelve guns each, the batteries must be paired
up and amalgamated. Major Beament draws command of 2nd-14th
Battery and Major Harris 26th-53rd Battery. Major Medland becomes 2 IC (second-in-command) of the Regiment, and Major
Welsh assumes the duties of the adjutant, a position normally held
by a captain.

Two days later, on May 26, the evacuation from Dunkirk begins,
when, in answer to the navy's call for help, flotillas of little boats,
piloted by their civilian owners, swarm out of the Thames and the

mouth of every river emptying into the Channel, to join large naval vessels, chugging and burbling across to France – private motor-launches, river-excursion paddle-wheelers, river barges and tug-boats – some 861 vessels in all. No one expects more than a small percentage of the men will be taken off before the Germans overrun their rearguard. But with the seas barely swelling in miraculous calm, the like of which mariners can't recall having seen, evacuation goes on day after day, and night after night. At times they are aided by smoke drifting over the beaches from burning Dunkirk, obscuring the waiting men in their shallow holes in the dunes, and at other times screened by squadrons of RAF Hurricanes and Spitfires intercepting German planes bent on bombing and strafing the beaches and the long lines of vulnerable men wading out to the rescue boats.*

Even before the evacuation of those tortured beaches ended, the normally reserved *New York Times*, in a leading editorial on June 1, offered an emotionally charged tribute to both the rescued and the rescuers:

> As long as the English tongue survives, the word Dunkerque will be spoken in reverence. For in that harbour, in such a hell as never blazed on earth before at the end of a lost battle, the rags and blemishes that have hidden the soul of democracy, fell away. There, beaten but unconquered, in shining splendour she foiled the enemy.
>
> They sent away the wounded first. Men died so that others would escape. It was not so simple a thing as courage, which the Nazis had in plenty. It was not so simple a thing as discipline, which can be hammered into men by a drill sergeant. It was not the result of careful planning, for there could have been little. It

---

* In four days, May 27 to 30, RAF fighter planes shot down 179 of the Luftwaffe, while losing only 29 of their own. Still, by the time evacuation efforts ceased on June 4, 231 of the rescue vessels had been lost.

was the common man of the free countries, rising in all his glory out of mill, office, factory, mine and ship, applying lessons when he went down the shaft to bring trapped comrades, when he hurled the lifeboat through the surf, when he endured poverty and hard work for his children's sake.

This shining thing in the souls of free men Hitler cannot command, or attain, or conquer. He has crushed it where he could from German hearts.

It is the great tradition of democracy. It is the future. It is victory.

To the free world, awaiting news of the success or failure of this gallant rescue effort, the relief is so great you can almost hear a mighty, collective sigh when it is revealed that most of the British Expeditionary Force (224,585 officers and men) and half again as many French and Belgian soldiers (112,546) made it safely to England.

It is right to think of it as a tremendous accomplishment. But still it is a terrible defeat; Britain's best troops were driven cowering into the sea. Churchill hastens to rally the spirit of the nation with a rousing speech to the House of Commons, which strikes a confident, defiant note in his declaration: "We shall fight on the beaches, we shall fight on the landing grounds, we shall fight in the fields and in the streets, we shall fight in the hills; we shall never surrender . . ."*

Training suddenly takes on special urgency, but equipment is still a problem. All available guns have been brought to Petawawa and gun drill is stepped up, but drivers still have no transport of their

_____

* This memorable speech, sounding a ringing clarion to the nation and arousing the whole of the free world, was broadcast by BBC actor Norman Shelley imitating Churchill's manner of speech so perfectly no one ever suspected the great leader was too involved with other urgent matters, crucial to Britain's survival, to deliver it himself.

own, and have to rely on the limited supply of ancient Leylands and Marmon Harringtons, which wouldn't be out of place in a 1914–18 war movie.

When the signallers come back from Barriefield, they are given wire and out-of-date Don-3 field telephones with which to train. And as more technical equipment is acquired for training the gun position officers (GPOs), Battery command post officers (CPOs), and their many assistants (GPO Acks and CPO Acks), fancy deployments are held.

For the first time a troop of four guns is considered a separate fire unit, and troop exercises begin. This, however, raises competition for available transport to embarrassing levels. And on occasion a troop commander has difficulty keeping a straight face when his sergeant-major reports, "Troop ready, sir," and he must issue the order "Mount" to forty or fifty men standing "at detachment's rear" behind a single gun, drawn by a single truck. However, valuable lessons are learned even when logs are set up in pits to represent guns when a night deployment is scheduled and no transport is available.

Needless to say there is joy in the MT (Motor Transport) Section when in early June, a group of drivers under Major Medland goes off to Windsor and returns with shiny new "gun tractors." The distinctive humpbacked vehicles immediately become known to gunners as "quads" – short for quadrupeds, or four-legged beasts – in recognition of the fact they are equipped with four-wheel power drive. (Though a case could be made that the label springs from a nostalgic longing for a return to the horse-drawn-guns era that ended only nine years ago, when the harness for horses was withdrawn from militia units to the dismay of the gunners, who were left with no means of towing limbers and guns into action until funds could be found – very difficult as the Depression deepened – to modify the tongues of the limbers so they could be hooked to the back of rental trucks.)

For the drivers, the next couple of weeks are the most interesting so far, as they get to know these odd-looking, humpbacked vehicles. At first they are considered top-heavy, and it is suggested they never be driven at a slant up the side of a steep hill. But this worry proves unwarranted, and their power and general ruggedness so impress the drivers that it has to be pointed out that there are sufficient roads in camp and they needn't smash any more through the trees, even for the sake of the large number of newspaper cameramen now invading the camp.

In preparation for English blackouts, night-driving exercises are conducted without headlights – surprisingly, without mishap. Then come battery convoys to North Bay and other neighbouring towns, as well as real pukka deployments for battery shoots on the ranges, including a novel one when the guns are fired over "open sights" (telescopic sights) onto burlap-covered wooden frames shaped like tanks and towed across the front on a long rope.

On June 12, the existence of a second division is revealed in one of those our-boys-are-just-so-dang-healthy-and-keen newspaper stories – this one in the *Journal* by friend and fellow scribe Lance Connery, featuring the gunners at Petawawa under the dramatic heading, "CANADIANS OF 2ND DIVISION ARE BEING READIED FOR BATTLE":

> Canada's fighting forces are facing the prospect of *Blitzkrieg* warfare with a song of victory in their hearts and utterly unworried despite grave tidings from abroad. . . . Here, in this sylvan setting, is the perfect haven for those seeking sanctuary from the grim gossip of a people at war . . . thousands in camp . . . living the sort of life doctors prescribe. Good food, regular hours, sleeping under canvas, plenty of exercise . . .

Lance, a first-class newspaperman, and so recognized by the senior editors at the *Journal* as well as by his peers, must have been heavily into the "sauce" over a long lunch with Camp Commandant Lt.-Col. A. V. Tremaine in the RCHA mess, with its magnificent

hilltop view across the broad Ottawa River to the Laurentian hills.*
You can only imagine what the gunners must think, as they read
of their "perfect haven" in its "sylvan setting," while squatting in
their dusty tent lines that march on to infinity across an expanse of
sand and scrubby pines shimmering in the blazing sun.

To gunners and officers who served in the militia before the war
and attended "summer camps," Petawawa is an old story. But for
most members of 4th Field (and of 5th Field, now also in residence
in this same bell-tent neighbourhood), living under canvas and
route-marching, map-reading, and deploying guns sometimes deep
in this 150-square-mile bushland range, while plagued by mosquitoes at night and black flies in the daytime, it's a new and not very
pleasant experience.

At first there are no showers, and water for all purposes – including shaving at tin-covered "ablution stands" open to the sky in all
kinds of weather – is cold. The camp is in the throes of expansion,
but the reasonably comfortable accommodation and the recreational facilities, on which huge amounts of man-hours and money
are being lavished, will not be available until long after 4th Field
has left for overseas.

For the first part of the stay in Petawawa, morale is not good, for
several reasons: first, general living conditions are not nearly as good
as they were in the soldiers' home towns; second, the pairing-up of
the batteries, requiring modifications in policies and ways of doing
things to which they'd grown accustomed, raise petty nuisances;
and finally, evening visits to nearby Pembroke, bringing them into
contact for the first time with large numbers of soldiers from other
units competing for whatever there is to be had, frequently make
for unpleasant situations, for regardless of how tough a gunner may
think he is, there's always a guy across the room who thinks he's
tougher and is itching to prove it.

---

* Rejected when he tried to enlist in the navy, Connery was accepted for
aircrew in the RAF and ended up navigating Lancaster bombers over
Occupied Europe in 1944.

I I

ROLL OUT THE BARREL

———————————————— ✳ ————————————————

YOU FEEL SORRY FOR THE TRUCKLOADS OF SOLDIERS FROM
Petawawa who nightly invade Pembroke determined to have a
good time. For the most part, they spend their time "shifting their
cheeks" on hard wooden chairs in drab, noisy "beverage rooms,"
swilling down draught after draught, getting loaded out of sheer
boredom. They'll never know what a pleasant place this town was
before the war.

Gradually the tone and tempo of life in Pembroke have changed.
It began almost imperceptibly at first as construction of the "intern-
ment camp" to receive enemy aliens got underway near Chalk
River. Then came the conversion of Petawawa Military Camp into
a sprawling year-round facility for the "active force," complete with
all the attendant services needed to house and train thousands of
gunners and officers for overseas service. Even as roads were built,
sewers dug, and water, power, and telephone lines laid, pairs of
wooden buildings, linked together by enclosed walkways to form
"H huts," were rising to provide dormitories, mess halls, and canteens. While nearby, swarms of tradesmen rushed to complete lecture halls, gunsheds, and vast drill halls.

The immediate effect has been to absorb hundreds of men from
the unemployed relief rolls, and scandalous stories are circulating of
unskilled men being paid carpenter wages merely for showing up
at a construction site carrying a hammer or a saw to verify their

claim to being journeymen carpenters. Daily, now, you hear stories of shocking waste, of architectural monstrosities erected by counterfeit tradesmen that have to be rebuilt completely. Still, all this activity pours money into the town, and the sleepy afternoons along the main street have vanished. Merchants are friendly as ever but they have lost the ability to stand still and chat for more than half a minute. The only man left on the street with whom you can get a cribbage game going on a countertop (to decide who will buy a "mickey" before the liquor store closes) is Roy Deavitt, who runs the Malcolm Funeral Parlour. And these duels have become less and less frequent as Roy begins to show the strain of surging business from a rising number of fatal accidents on roads cluttered with military traffic. On a recent Sunday evening, he even had to enlist you to drive one of his two hearses to the midnight train, carrying the flag-draped caskets of two young officers killed when their motorcycle and sidecar collided head-on with a civilian truck loaded with barrels of apples passing an army convoy.

Few things have remained constant, unchanging like Russ, the town's best-known, wizened-up rubby-dub, who can still be seen each day walking up the main street, his feet spread a good yard apart as though navigating the deck of a ship in heavy seas, looking for a friend on whom he can put the touch for the means of purchasing his favourite diet. An institution, recognized by the soldiers as part of the scene, Russ doesn't bother them, preferring to follow his unique, lifetime rule of approaching only old friends from childhood, such as Crown Attorney H. B. Johnson, with whom he keeps in close touch through regular meetings in magistrate's court regarding his penchant for making a nuisance of himself when inebriated.

"Got a dime, H. B.? I promise never to pay you back," is not a line that would in most places in the world draw small change from the pockets of the crown attorney, the magistrate, the mayor, the town clerk, the editor of the weekly paper, prominent insurance brokers, and the like. But in Pembroke, where a sense of humour is ranked among the highest virtues of civilized man, and outrageous practical jokes are legendary, it draws the steady trickle of dimes required to keep Russ swaying down the main street on his way to the drugstore for another soothing bottle of rubbing alcohol.

But many things *have* changed, and from the perspective of some leading citizens, not always for the better. With the hotel beverage rooms restricted to serving beer, one could always get a stronger eye-opener with your coffee over at the Chinaman's restaurant across the street. Though still visited quite religiously, at least once each morning and afternoon by a handful of loyal regulars, including a couple of prominent lawyers and a main-street merchant, the clubman's privacy – the atmosphere of exclusivity (one could even say emptiness) so cherished by its discreet prewar clientele – has disappeared with the influx of military people, who, not knowing any better, actually go in and order meals listed in the fly-specked, faded menus.

And with each passing week, as more and more army vehicles crowd the roads into town, and more and more soldiers appear on the main street in the late afternoon and evening, Pembroke assumes the ambivalent character of all garrison towns: loving all the increased business the soldiers bring to stores, restaurants, and beer parlours, but detesting their raucous, rowdy ways after they've been into the suds a couple of hours. Remembering the last war, the older townsfolk – many of them veterans themselves – counsel tolerance, observing that most of the soldiers are very young and totally inexperienced at managing money and the alcohol it buys: "Why, many of them are only teenagers who ordinarily wouldn't even be allowed in a bar . . . and being away from parental guidance and other inhibiting, conventional influences of family and friends in Civvy Street and all . . ."

Still, their loud-mouthed, swaggering style – universally affected by soldiers in their early days in uniform – often stretches the tolerance of the townsfolk to the breaking point. Their behaviour is especially galling to those of military age but not yet in uniform, sitting at the next table in a restaurant or the beverage room of a hotel, the only real points of contact between soldiers and civilians.

There the loud, insensitive arrogance of a gang of soldiers can not only be irritating, but on occasion downright menacing.

Almost nightly now, outside your hotel window facing the darkened side street, there is at least one angry, thick-tongued, shouting argument well-larded with obscenities, leading up to the sickening sound of smacking fists, grunts, and scuffling feet, followed by sinister silence. And much too frequently you have to close the window to shut out the disgusting sounds of retching, as still another young soldier learns the hard way how disastrous it is to take on too many beers on an empty stomach, and then try to blotter them up with greasy French fries.

The fries are served in the restaurant across the corner on the main street, where a thumping jukebox sets the current mood and tone, not just for the street, but for the whole town. From mid-morning until well past midnight, hour after hour, day in and day out, that booming, gaudy machine blares out the jivey voices of the Andrews Sisters inviting the world to "roll out the barrel and have a barrel of fun" – over and over and over, with only brief respites of silence while another soldier locates more nickels to feed into the deep-throated, tireless monster.

Each night a military detachment (Pembroke Patrol) supplements the surveillance of the town police, collecting drunken trouble-makers in the cells at the police station, until around 11:30 P.M. they are dumped into trucks that will take them back to camp. One night, as you are passing the police station cells on your way from the firehall in back to the front office, you watch as they (military and civil policemen) knock senseless an insanely drunk soldier who is threatening to kick his cell-mate to death.

Combined, these images and insights into life in the military are not conducive to arousing enthusiasm for a career in khaki, though you do envy the young gunner officers, so damned impressive in their serge uniforms as they escort their ladies to their tables in the Cope's gracious dining room (particularly a dashing Lieut. Peter Carr-Harris, whose petite wife now resides in the hotel and has everyone under her spell since she agreed to exercise her well-trained voice at a Kiwanis Club luncheon with a charming rendition of the sprightly little song "Johann's Greeting"*). Like most of your friends who have yet to enlist, you picture yourself in navy or airforce blue – preferably the latter, with wings on your chest. However, until now there's been little urgency. After the first weeks of frantic enlistments, all recruiting was halted, except for some select categories of skills and know-how. The shortage of winter accommodation at the military camps and the general lack of things like greatcoats made recruitment during the winter months impractical.

And until the enemy went on the offensive in the Low Countries in May, both German and Allied forces meticulously avoided engaging in battle on the ground or in the air. So throughout the winter, the feeling your country urgently needed you faded as the "Phoney War" dragged on.†

---

* Based on Grieg's *Norwegian Dance.*
† British field artillery units deployed in action in France early in September 1939 did not fire for eight months.

12

IS IT POSSIBLE WE HAVE

LOST THE WAR?

———————————— ✳ ————————————

WHEN FRANCE SURRENDERS ON JUNE 21, 1940, YOU ARE BACK at the *Journal* in Ottawa. For days it has been perceived as inevitable, perhaps ever since Dunkirk seventeen days ago. Certainly, when the Germans entered Paris on June 14, and the next day French troops began abandoning their Maginot Line, the end was clearly at hand. Still, it's difficult to comprehend. A Europe without France is inconceivable.

Watching the clacking teletype machine industriously tapping out in its impersonal, routine fashion (as it would the day's Major League baseball scores), "THE AGREEMENT WAS SIGNED AT COMPIEGNE IN THE SAME RAILWAY CAR IN WHICH GER-MANY HAD SURRENDERED 22 YEARS BEFORE," it seems totally unreal, a nightmare from which you must surely awake.

It isn't until noon, when by chance you sit down beside E. Norman Smith, the white-haired vice-president of the paper, at the lunch counter in Lippet's drugstore across Bank Street, and find him crying, that your mind begins to grasp fully the dreadful im-plications to Britain, Canada, and the rest of the world.

It comes as a shock to find this most reserved and dignified man, normally of aloof demeanour, sitting with his head bowed over a bowl of soup, into which big tears from his eyes are plopping. At first he gives no sign he knows you've joined him. But when you remark it is a sad day for the world, he turns and asks:

"How can they be stopped, now they have defeated what we were told was the greatest army in all the world? Is it possible we have lost the war?"

Since Dunkirk, as much as it has been publicly acknowledged a miracle, people have had to accept the bitter fact that British arms suffered a defeat of awesome proportions. Anyone with a shred of common sense knows that the British Army is seriously disabled, and the possibility of Britain being invaded and overrun by irresistible Nazi legions, as all those continental nations have been, is very real, and perhaps imminent. France's army, dwarfing Britain's, was driven asunder in only a few days, and to total disaster in a few short weeks.

Churchill, speaking to the House right after Dunkirk, reported that the army had left on the continent a thousand guns along with all their transport and armoured vehicles: "They had the first fruits of all that our industry had to give, and that is gone." Realizing he must be putting the best possible face to the situation, the report of his speech makes for chilling reading:

Work is proceeding everywhere, night and day, Sundays and weekdays. . . . Already the flow of munitions has leapt forward. There is no reason why we should not in a few months overtake the sudden and severe loss that is come upon us, without retarding the development of our general programme. Nevertheless, our thankfulness at the escape of our army and so many men . . . must not blind us to the fact that what has happened in France and Belgium is a colossal military disaster.

And these awful words are uttered before it is clear the battle for France is irretrievably lost – before the newsreels in the movie houses show Hitler rolling around the Arc de Triomphe in an open car, and doing his high-stepping jig at Compiègne after accepting the French surrender in the same old railway car in which the defeated Germans signed the Armistice in 1918.

Hitler expects an early end to the war. And he isn't alone in such thinking. Important Americans advise President Roosevelt not to send any aid to Britain on the basis it will only be wasted, since Britain must lose the war. Not the least of these defeatists is Joseph Kennedy, American Ambassador to London.*

Senator Key Pitman, chairman of the U.S. Senate Foreign Relations Committee, in proposing Britain despatch its remaining ships to North America and then capitulate, wrote: "It's no secret that Great Britain is totally unprepared for defence and that nothing the United States has to give can do more than delay the result. . . . It is hoped that this plan will not be long delayed by futile encouragement to fight on."

But the people of Britain and the British Commonwealth, including Canada, refuse to recognize the war is lost, and are profoundly grateful when Churchill growls defiantly on their behalf.

Three days before France capitulates and the last ally on the continent is lost, Churchill, anticipating the necessity of pursuing the conflict alone, delivers a rallying cry of such tremendous power and noble purpose, it still rings on, and must surely continue to resound in the months and years ahead when things grow worse. Indeed, it may well continue to echo down through the ages, long after this crisis has passed, an inspiration to all people in adversity, determined to see freedom and justice prevail regardless of the odds: "Let us brace ourselves to our duties, and so bear ourselves that if the British Empire and its Commonwealth last for a thousand years, men will say, 'This was their finest hour.' "

Even as the newspapers carry pictures of a triumphant Führer, standing boldly on a headland in the Pas de Calais, studying England's white cliffs with powerful field-glasses in menacing fashion, supposedly planning his cross-Channel invasion, the news columns are remarkably free of defeatist material. Editors and correspondents choose to deal with the grim situation in the most optimistic terms, emphasizing the success of the Hurricanes and Spitfires in shooting

---

* Father of future U.S. President J. F. Kennedy.

down a few raiders each day, while playing down RAF losses. Of course, nobody mentions that the British Army is almost devoid of usable modern equipment, having been forced to smash and burn all they'd been issued before abandoning France.*

Still, the *New York Times* of July 17 editorially supports the very optimistic view that "so long as Britain retains command of the sea and is not overwhelmed in the air, the defeat of Germany is not only possible, it is probable."

Eminent journalists, who have earned a reputation for fearlessly ferreting out the truth, write as though they are paid propaganda agents for Britain. Drew Middleton, noted byline writer for Associated Press, following a conducted tour of the southwest coastal areas of England, declares under dateline London, July 19, "The mightiest army in Britain's history stands to its guns and positions each dawn and dusk fully confident of its ability to whip the German army in the field." Completely taken in by shadow over substance, he infers from the sight of a few squads of soldiers marching along the roads that many thousands are on the march. He waxes eloquent over concrete roadblocks and camouflaged gun emplacements, and is willing to explain the total absence of field artillery and tanks by the fact that "gun positions, redoubts and trenches are far more easy to conceal in foliage-covered hills than in the flat plain of Flanders."

It is as though no one wants to face the truth and its dreadful possibilities, perhaps because, as the famous American columnist Dorothy Thompson declares three days later on July 22, in a remarkable radio speech broadcast from Montreal, "Britain's fall would rock the earth . . . the British Empire is the only world-wide stabilizing force for law and order on the planet."†

---

* Left behind in smouldering, desolate masses on the perimeter of Dunkirk were 11,000 machine-guns, 1,200 field, medium, and heavy guns, 1,250 ack-ack and anti-tank guns, 6,400 anti-tank rifles, and 75,000 vehicles, including tanks, Bren carriers, gun quads, and lorries.
† She, as an American, would have believed she was including Canada and the other sovereign nations of the Commonwealth by using the word "empire."

13

BRAVE CHILDREN HUGGING

TEDDY BEARS

—————————— ✳ ——————————

YOU FIRST BECAME CONSCIOUS OF THE AWESOME DEMANDS imposed on the fragile courage of little children in war when pictures of families pushing baby carriages and wheelbarrows full of household essentials along refugee-clogged French and Belgian roads began to appear in newspapers and newsreels, along with heart-rending stories of children crying in anguish beside dead mothers killed with babes in their arms by strafing airplanes as they cringed in roadside ditches.

And there was the unforgettable story of a small boy carrying an even smaller boy on his back, trudging among the refugees, kilometre after kilometre, without a word of complaint. Impressed by this heroic effort, a man asked him how he could manage to carry such a heavy burden so far, and the boy replied, "He's not heavy; he's my brother."

Last night you were allowed to witness the courage of thirteen British children – some clutching teddy bears – as they arrived, without the support and comfort of their parents, in a strange city, among strange people, bound for a strange bed in a strange bedroom in some strange building somewhere. The thirteen youngsters were from a group of three hundred that landed at Quebec the night before, the first of many groups of children that will find safe haven in Canada in succeeding weeks.

The fascination of reporters and editors with the event, resulting in a page of pictures and stories in each paper, sprang both from a natural concern for the welfare of the young refugees, and from the ominous implications as to the future of their homeland, where clearly their parents believed the risk was greater than they would face on a ship sailing for several days through submarine-infested North Atlantic waters – a risk that had been underlined two nights ago by the sinking just off the coast of Ireland of the *Arandora Star* liner and the drowning of a thousand souls, eight hundred of them German and Italian prisoners.

The kids were remarkably calm and self-possessed, and if they were anxious, they didn't show it. On the contrary, they readily answered or did their best to answer every question, and provided every reporter with lots of "good copy." But it was friend Reg Hardy of the *Citizen* who did the truly unforgettable piece, expressing so well what all present felt that night. He did it as an "Open Letter to a Brave Little Miss," nine-year-old Daphne Carroll:

You stepped off the train at Union Station last night, Daphne, to find yourself, a little girl of 9, in a strange city in a new land, far, far removed from that lovely England you have learned to love so well. We know that in a very short while you will have learned to love this country too, and that as the days and weeks slip by you will come to think of it less and less as a strange land and more and more as "home." But last night you were lonely, and a little bewildered. You stood somewhat apart from the other children, and perhaps because you were older than most of your companions and could not find the same solace in the twisted grin of a teddy bear or hopes of seeing "real Indians," your expression was a trifle more serious and reserved than theirs.

But when we spoke to you your face lighted up and your little chin went out and we knew you were made of that stuff which has made the British people what they are – that although you might be lonely and a little afraid, you weren't going to wear your heart on your sleeve, or ask for sympathy, or do anything that would ill befit a young lady of your station.

And when you saw you had a part to play, that the reporters and cameramen expected you to "smile" and "talk about your trip," you rose to the occasion magnificently. You flashed us your nicest smile, listened with respectful attention to the questions that were flung at you, and did your best to find the "proper" answers. . . .

But most of all I think we were struck by your quiet, serene, unassuming courage.

We naturally expect a lot of bravery, Daphne, from a man such as your father, who, you gave us to understand, is in the army in India. But as we talked to you we wondered why poets and men who write books never seem to tell about the bravery of little girls like you. For we think, Daphne, that last night you exhibited a very particular kind of bravery, a kind that is a great deal higher and more worthy of notice than that which is exhibited by soldiers in battle, even.

For when we asked you about your Daddy and Mummy, and you explained that they were in faroff India, your little chin did not tremble even ever so slightly, and your blue eyes were as brave as any soldier. . . .

It was just the kind of reassurance, Daphne, that we in Canada need in these dark days – a reassurance born of the realization that if little English girls can show this kind of pluck, can be so brave this far from home, then English men and women are still made of the same dauntless stuff as Alfred the Great and Rich Coeur-de-Lion and Drake and Nelson and all the rest!

14

THE MORALE BOOSTER

---------------------- ✳ ----------------------

SHORTLY AFTER ARRIVAL IN PETAWAWA, ALL RANKS ARE informed that no more leaves will be granted until the Regiment arrives overseas.

At first this is accepted philosophically by the troops. The news from Europe is so grim, no one would be surprised if the Regiment is shipped overseas with little warning. But as days go by and the sense of crisis passes and the ban on leave is not lifted, there is a serious drop in morale. And the knowledge that some officers have their wives living within visiting distance in cottages in the civilian colony at Petawawa Point doesn't help matters. Many good men, who under normal conditions would never consider going "absent without leave," decide any punishment is worth suffering in the cause of seeing their folks before leaving Canada and join the "over-the-hill club." At last the number going AWL (absent without leave) becomes so serious that leaves are reinstituted.

However, regimental morale doesn't recover overnight. A good wet canteen (purveying beer) comes into being on a divisional basis, and movies and concert parties offer further relaxation. And as living conditions improve, training becomes more interesting, and week-end leaves offer opportunities to let off steam, morale gradually improves.

But there is another and, in a very special way, more important, reason for improved morale. Into all the business of building a

Regiment – lectures and drills, manoeuvres and convoys, trips home and trips to detention, promotions and demotions – the spirit of a ruddy-faced United Church minister from Toronto is slowly, but surely, injected. It is a spirit that will help sustain the morale of the Regiment through many long years in England, and through longer, terrible days in action.

"The Padre," Captain Ray McCleary. Can words capture a smile, a hearty laugh, the warmth of a handshake? Can anyone really describe the feelings of a man released from the hot detention barracks for an hour or so to swim with the Padre, under his surveillance, in the cool waters of the Ottawa River? Have words been invented to describe adequately the peace of mind countless men of the Regiment experience when they come with their problems and heartaches to this man, so young in spirit and so tolerant of the foibles and weaknesses of mankind that the lowliest bare their hearts to him, but so wise and persuasive a counsellor that the most rigid disciplinarians among the senior officers respect him and are proud to call him their friend.

Early in August, the first of what will later be popularly known as a "three-ring circus" is prepared for "a distinguished visitor," that in this case turns out to be the Governor General.

Preparations take the form of detailing intense if not spectacular employment for each and every man in the Regiment, including digging trenches, doing gun drill, carrying on anti-gas drill, etc., etc., with the grand finale "a shoot" carried out in front of a natural grandstand known as Jorgens Hill, where the spectators can observe both the guns firing and the fall of their shots on targets, in much the way it was in the Napoleonic Wars.

The most detailed preparations are made for the shoot. A "village" consisting of the fronts of several cardboard houses, destined for total destruction, is erected in the target area. Of course, there must be no slip-up, so not only are the guns surveyed-in, but the target as well. Special care is taken with the "meteor telegram" in working out the "correction of the moment" so as to adjust ranges and switches to allow for the effects of speed and direction of wind as well as the temperature and air pressure at various levels above the earth through which the shells will travel. All calculations are carried out as accurately as humanly possible, but just to make sure, each gun is "shot-in" on the target area before the cardboard houses are erected.

Preparation enough? Not for Major Medland. To make doubly sure the target will be destroyed and no one disappointed, he has dug in under the "village" a great charge of gunpowder, arranged so he can explode it by pushing a plunger in the safety of a nearby concrete OP (observation post).

The spectators arrive and the shoot begins. Capt. McGregor Young is detailed to handle a loudspeaker system to allow the spectators to overhear his orders to the guns. Of course, when he gives the order to fire, the shells start landing perfectly on and about the target, and he has no correction to make. For the sake of effect, however, he feels he should say something, so he orders, "Drop 25," which, to the gun-layers, means "reduce the range by twenty-five yards." And he mentally winks at Major Medland, hidden in his nearby OP.

Medland, taking his cue from the slight pause in the bombardment, waits until the shells start falling again on target, and then pushes the plunger on his detonator. To the amazement of the distinguished visitor, and the astonishment of the gunners, who are totally unaware of the gunpowder plot, the "village," with an unholy boom, disappears in a great cloud of black smoke.

15

THE FIRST CANADIAN
"CRASH ACTION"

———————————— ✳ ————————————

WITHIN THE MILITARY THERE PERSISTS AN UNWARRANTED optimism and confidence in the old ways of doing things, along with the belief that the British Expeditionery Force (BEF) was let down by the collapse of the Belgians on their left, and by the French on their right holed up in their outflanked Maginot Line.

That the swift defeat of all three armies might have been due to inadequate equipment and outmoded tactics is not prominent in the thinking of decision-makers ultimately responsible for such things as the design of tanks and their guns.*

But there are some at the lower levels of command who are able to accept the harsh realities of the resounding defeat of the best the British and French could muster: that the enemy, if not better equipped, at least employs superior tactics, so expressively suggested by their own word – *Blitzkrieg* – for the swift, flexible mobility of their assaulting forces. One of those willing to face the facts is professional soldier Lt.-Col. Frank Worthington, Commandant of the Armoured Fighting Vehicle Training Centre, Camp Borden,

————————

* The deficiency was obvious when the first monster Churchill tanks, designed to become the principal infantry tanks of British forces, came off the assembly lines in June 1941, equipped with a pea-shooter 2-pounder gun, which, though replaced a year or so later by a 6-pounder, never was modified to take the much-needed high-velocity 17-pounder gun.

Ontario. A veteran of 1914–18 who rose from the ranks, after *twice* winning the Military Medal, to win the Military Cross, *twice*, as an officer, he brings to bear on all tactical problems not just the broad perspective of the senior officer drenched in theory, but the sometimes narrow, but always highly concentrated, practical perspective of those lowly "odds and sods" who (he knows from having been one of them) must, in the end, make it all work.*

By nature a man always ready to re-examine old tactics hanging over from World War I, "Worthy," as he's widely known, has long held the belief that tanks could be a decisive factor in any new war. Now, fired up by stories filtering back across the Atlantic about lightning strikes of German columns, he decides to arrange an unusual experiment with a mobile column charging around the rural countryside of Western Ontario, from Orillia to high ground west of Barrie.

His "District Field Manoeuvres," scheduled for August 10, will involve a mobile column led by one company of medium tanks, followed by infantry in trucks, and field guns on wheels bringing up the rear. (In the event there will be a company of infantry and a troop of four guns following the tanks in what will one day be known by the British as a "jock column" when used as a small mobile striking force in the desert war in North Africa.) The artillery unit invited to take part is 4th Field, and Lieutenant-Colonel Lloyd and his senior officers are delighted with the prospect of the long 250-mile trip from Petawawa, which will provide a chance to develop training in convoy discipline.

---

* Major-General in 1942, he was in command of 4th Infantry Division when it converted to an armoured division and moved to Britain late that year. For a year and a half he readied it for battle, but just before the invasion of Normandy, 2nd Corps Commander Lt.-Gen. Guy Simonds replaced him with a younger man, Maj.-Gen. George Kitching (thirty-three), who'd been on Simonds's staff at 1st Division in Italy, and who had followed him to 5th Armoured Division as its infantry brigade commander.

It is so exciting, they can't wait to get started. And the night before they are to pull out for Camp Borden, it's decided to hold a night deployment out on the gun ranges and in the morning to take off for Borden from there. Later, in days of more experience, moving the guns to a designated area, putting them in action, and bedding down for the night will be done with such despatch that most of the night will be left for sleeping. But all ranks are so inexperienced in this sort of thing that instead of bedding down they busy themselves at one thing or another the entire night, and get no sleep at all. As a result, everyone is completely done in before the convoy even starts off.

No one, of course, has had any experience handling large convoys over long distances. So such crucial matters as "speed and interval," that later will be taken for granted even if they aren't specified, do not loom in importance this first morning. Still, it's obvious that a large number of vehicles cannot be led too quickly over congested highways. To the senior officers of the Regiment, thirty-five miles an hour seems like a nice accommodating speed for the leading vehicle, and so it is laid down.

However, no one foresees the "accordion" motion of a convoy, which, because of traffic, hills, and curves, stretches in and out like a giant caterpillar, until the tail-end vehicles are doubling, and sometimes trebling, the speed of the leading vehicle in an effort to keep up. And because of the drivers' inexperience in maintaining an interval between their vehicles and the ones ahead, this accordion motion is exaggerated beyond what will always afflict a seven-mile-long regimental convoy of guns and vehicles. Years after, sergeants will claim that for long periods their bouncing guns "touched the ground only every 200 yards." Fortunately just one gun rolls off its limber hook into the ditch; only its barrel is salvageable.

At Borden the night before the manoeuvres begin, when officers of 4th Field are informed of the role of the guns, Worthington's plan sounds so farfetched as to be utterly ridiculous. The instant the tanks meet any opposition from the "enemy," the guns will deploy without any reconnaissance or knowledge of the country, somehow get onto a zero line, and bring down fire on the opposition – all in a matter of minutes. What this irrepressible tankman demands is contrary to all training in the deployment of an artillery regiment, which, according to the drill in vogue, can take up to three hours, involving, as it does, bringing up the guns to a temporary "hide" (that may become the "wagon lines" for the quads after they've dropped their guns in position) while the Colonel and his battery commanders go forward to reconnoitre potential gun positions that can't be occupied until approved by the Brigadier CRA (Commander Royal Artillery) of the division.

However, after mulling over the problem most of the night, a solution is improvised: the guns will be put on line (pointed in the direction of the target) using a prismatic compass and an aiming point (any clearly identifiable point on the horizon), a procedure which, years later in England, will come to be known as "Crash Action." The idea is to just get a round down where the FOO (forward observation officer) can see it and can order corrections to bring the fire onto target. And while it doesn't work too well in practice, due mainly to the inability of radio transmitters to maintain proper communication between the guns and the FOO moving with the tanks, it starts everybody thinking. If a better radio became available . . . and with a little practice putting the guns on line with a compass . . . who knows . . . .

Worthington considers the results "extremely successful . . . much valuable experience gained by all elements participating . . . but all report the weak link in extended movements of mechanized forces is intercommunication – due partly to inexperience, but more largely due to lack of proper equipment."*

---

* It would take until 1942 to develop and bring into use mobile radio transmitters of sufficient strength and reliability to allow crash actions to come into their own; and, even more important, allow to develop a system of fire-control extending from a single radio transmitter of one FOO to

On the return journey to Petawawa, the Colonel takes his regiment by way of Cobourg to show it off. It is late in the afternoon when the vehicles pull into a central park in line, and a large crowd of spectators gather to see this display of military might and to welcome husbands, fathers, brothers, and friends.

Standing up in the rear of his car, the Colonel gives the order: "Dismount – Detachments Rear!" All jump smartly from the vehicles, and take up proper positions behind guns or vehicles. However, no one is prepared for the next order: "Gas alert!"

The Colonel is very proud of a recent issue of respirators, and it seems to him just the right time to try them out. As he gives the order, he pulls out his own from its case strapped on his chest up under his chin (as are all the others of this properly dressed regiment). Throwing back his steel helmet, he puts it on. And with the mask's elastic straps, stretched over and behind his head holding it tight to his face, he restores his helmet to its rightful place.

This is example enough for the rest of the Regiment, and all ranks pull on their respirators over their faces, transforming themselves into imitations of giant grasshoppers from Mars. Some female onlookers gasp. Children begin to cry, dogs to bark. It is a rather horrific sight.

But shortly things seem to settle down, until nothing can be heard but the gush of air through more than eight hundred facepieces. Now, thinks the Colonel, it is time for their natural faces to reappear. Unfortunately, no one has informed him how he's to issue an order to get everybody out of these cursed things, while he himself is muffled up in one (which, in the heat of this early August evening, is becoming damnably uncomfortable).

---

all radios in a division, or a corps or an army, allowing that FOO to bring down fire onto a single target from as many regiments as required, within minutes. Worthington's quotes are from his report written immediately following the exercise, on file with the National Archives of Canada in the war diary of A-8 Canadian Armoured Fighting Vehicle Training Centre, Camp Borden.

The Regiment stares at the civilians. The civilians stare at the Regiment. Seconds go by, then minutes. Finally the Colonel, with a vicious gesture, grabs the rubber tube and yanks the respirator off his face. The rest of the Regiment follows suit, and decorum is restored.

The town of Perth is next. The convoy is still led at thirty-five miles an hour, but now a new drill has been laid on. When the Colonel holds one finger out the side of his car, the vehicles are to travel at hundred-yard intervals; when he holds out two fingers, they are to close up to fifty yards; three fingers, to twenty-five yards – which is all very neat and tidy except for the fact that it occurs to no one that for a vehicle at the rear of the column, to accomplish this closing-up feat, it must attain speeds of up to eighty miles an hour, or better, on gravelled Highway No. 7.

No one taking part in their trip will ever forget the sight of Major Medland, standing on the running board of his roadster, rushing up and down the column, beating his officer's swagger stick on the hoods of vehicles, roaring, "Close up!" And now and then hacking away at hobnailed boots stuck out to cool from the sides of vehicles, yelling, "Take them in!"

When the dust-covered convoy finally reaches Petawawa, drivers are ready to fall asleep on their feet from driving almost steadily day and night. For years after, some will swear that their eyesight was so strained, they had to be led around by the hand for a couple of days.

The Regiment is back only a few days when, one evening, the Colonel stands up in the officers' mess and announces, "Gentlemen, you are warned for overseas service." While this announcement has been expected for weeks, it still strikes with dramatic force. And when the Other Ranks are told, a new enthusiasm takes hold. A few days of general tidying up, packing kit bags and getting rid of excess kit, and then, on the night of August 20, the Regiment, wearing "Canada" shoulder badges – the distinguishing mark of troops warned for overseas service – marches behind the RCHA

(Royal Canadian Horse Artillery) Band to a dimly lit train standing in the gloom on the camp's spur line.

In contrast to some other embarkations, 4th Field is very orderly. Even Gunner "Stan" Godlewski, the burly hard-rock miner and veteran of the Polish artillery in the Great War, though in the usual well-lubricated state he considers proper for such historic occasions, refrains from coming on parade for inspection with a huge Polish sausage under his arm, as he did last May in Ottawa prior to marching to the train for Petawawa.

Gunner "Buck" Saunders, who lined up near Godlewski in the Coliseum that night, will never forget "the look on the faces of Major Beament and Captain Steuart-Jones, as they came along inspecting every little thing so carefully, making sure everybody looked their best for the march down the driveway to the station. Their mouths dropped open when they saw that big thing sticking out from under Godlewski's arm. And Stan, who was in a jolly mood, pulled it out and said, 'Wanna piece of my baloney?' Of course, they tried to take it away from him. What a hope! Ten men couldn't have taken it away from him. He was bound he was going to march to the train with it so he could have a snack on the way to Petawawa. And he would have, too, if Lieut. Don Wilson hadn't been able to talk him out of it. He is the only man in the outfit Godlewski trusts, seeing him as a fellow hard-rock miner, because Wilson worked as a mining engineer with International Nickel before enlisting."

The train is hot and stuffy, crowded and boring. It's just another train ride in summer, except for one thing: they are on their way overseas, and although most resist thinking about it consciously, all realize they cannot be sure they will ever be coming back. A few are glad to be leaving domestic troubles behind, and some only think of the new places they'll be seeing. But others wonder about wives of only a few weeks, or of wives, parents, or children who are not too well. Some write letters feverishly, last minute "I love you so much" notes, to be mailed surreptitiously, against all security regulations, at stopping points along the way. Others sit with pencils poised, wondering what to say, and whether girlfriends really will wait for their return.

Still, it's the married men with children – like Gunner "Ed" Crosier, whose wife and three children (two boys, eight and seven, and a girl, three-and-a-half) will have to manage on seventy-nine dollars a month (his assigned pay and allowances*) – who have to work hardest at keeping up their spirits as the train rushes towards "an eastern Canadian port."

But to most people watching the troop train pass, it's just another trainload of carefree, noisy soldiers – rowdy and vulgar from drink – hooting and whistling at every girl along the way.

---

* At this time the government would pay allowances to three dependants only – a wife at $35 and two of the three children at $12 each – equalling $59. The gunner's assigned pay of $20, from his monthly pay of $39 (then at the rate of $1.30 a day) brought the figure to $79. In December 1940 pay for a private soldier was raised by twenty cents a day to $1.50.

PART TWO: AUGUST 1940– JULY 1942

The Metamorphosis of a Regiment

16

ABOARD AN EMPRESS BUILT
FOR AN EMPEROR

※

APART FROM A PLEASANT INTERLUDE AT QUEBEC CITY, WHERE they are allowed to stretch their legs marching up to the Château Frontenac "for fifteen minutes of cool beers," all are confined to train seats for thirty-six hours, including two long dreary nights. So there is a great feeling of relief when the train pulls into Halifax right out onto the dock, where they can march directly onto the ship. It's 3:00 P.M., August 22.

The ship, the *Empress of Australia*, reputed to have been built for the Kaiser to make a world cruise, and renamed when it was taken from the Germans in reparation after the Great War, brought the King and Queen to Canada a year ago last May 10. Most of the gunners, never having seen an ocean-going liner before, let alone been on board one, are totally fascinated, and during the first few hours no portion of the great ship is left unexplored. Even the sacred bridge is invaded until a few old salts with choice remarks put a stop to that.

A plan of the ship shows she is 600 feet long, 75 feet wide, and displaces 21,000 tons. She's yet to be converted to a drab troopship, and her furnishings and supplies are still of the same high quality her peacetime clients expected. Accommodation for officers, NCOs, and many of the gunners is excellent. Gunner Charles McEwen, who shares a double-bunk, third-class stateroom with Gunner Morley Stokes on E Deck, decides that "although it's not very big, it's very nice . . . we have a washbasin, and hot and cold running water."

But for a lot of 4th Field, the military caste system is brought home forcefully when they are crowded down the steel companionways towards the bottom of the ship, to a hold in no way entitled to the impressive title of F Deck. A barren, grey, steel-walled room with rusty stains where seawater has seeped in through eternally closed ports, it is lit day and night by stark electric lightbulbs hanging from a low-girdered ceiling. There are cockroaches, and the air – stuffy and humid – hums night and day from the throb of the engines. But there are bunks to sleep in, and the occupants of F Deck, fast becoming experienced in counting their blessings, thank the gods they've been spared the curse of troopships – hammocks. However, if the sleeping accommodation is not so good for some, the meals are excellent in the extreme for everyone, with all sorts of seafoods and meats on each meal's menu. A feature of the officers' table is caviar, which is available literally by the bucketful.

After three days at the dock – while a cargo of flour, fish, airplane parts, and four thousand bags of mail is loaded into holds not occupied by men – and another three days anchored in the North Arm basin waiting for the convoy to assemble, the *Empress* leads a parade of some thirty vessels, including five other troopships, out into the Atlantic past a submarine boom marked by floating steel drums. Soon, two destroyers are running zig-zag patterns on each side of the convoy, looking for lurking subs.

According to the crew, the *Empress* is a veteran of enemy action, having been on the disastrous British–French expedition that tried to prevent the German occupation of Norway. Though she wasn't hit, during the eighteen hours she and six other ships were under air attack in Narvik harbour, her stern on occasion lifted right out of the water from the blast of nearby bombs.

All members of 4th Field are assigned duties. Some stand "fire picquet" to ensure the fire-doors are closed against the spread of flames if a fire occurs. Others are to close the watertight bulkhead doors if the ship is torpedoed and in danger of sinking. Some serve in the kitchen as second cooks, potato peelers, and dish-washers. Others are assigned to carry up from a storage hold daily supplies of wine, beer, and soft drinks to an officers' mess, an NCOs' mess, and two canteens for the men.

Of this and other related matters, Gunner Charles McEwen will record in a letter home to his family:

> The cases are very heavy and we have to carry them up several flights of steps. However, it only takes about an hour and a half and then we are done for the day. The fellow in charge of the wine supplies tells us they've a six-month supply of alcoholic beverage on board. It must be a lot for they are carrying 2,000 men (1,700 of them soldiers). Everything on the ship is pretty reasonable: ginger ale, ginger beer, and lemonade in bottles are four cents; chocolate bars are five cents; and beer, 18 cents an English pint. Last night the padres held a concert on A Deck. One of our boys, Les Secord, played the piano, and there was a trumpet and a sax. Two padres and a Salvation Army officer sang a trio "My Bonnie Lies Over the Ocean." They had a treasure hunt at six o'clock for pieces of paper they'd hidden all over the ship. . . . We sang a lot of songs and a few hymns including "The Old Rugged Cross," "What a Friend We Have in Jesus," and "Abide with Me." One of the padres closed with a prayer and then we sang "The King."

One of the duties of the Regiment is to man some of the ack-ack defences. These consist of old, First War Lewis machine-guns issued in Halifax just before leaving, and on which hours must be spent cleaning out the rust. Practice is afforded the chosen Lewis gunners when they are allowed to fire at the black puffs of ack-ack airbursts put up by the three-inch guns at the stern of the ship.

The *Empress* is part of a convoy stretching across the seas to the horizon in all directions. Always floating nearby is the most important of the escort ships, the towering battleship *Revenge*, which is very reassuring, for enemy surface raiders as well as submarines are said to be currently quite active, and are the subject of much sober thinking. However, the great warship always rides far enough away from curious eyes that any movement on her cannot be discerned, inspiring the illusion that her entire company is sound asleep, and that she is as inoffensive as a sea turtle sleeping in the sun. But then one day this fancy is wiped out in a most decisive fashion.

It is mid-afternoon, and the *Revenge* is riding dead ahead of the *Empress*. Suddenly the quiet is shattered by the rattle of a Lewis gun as tracer bullets streak out from the troopship towards the *Revenge*. Someone has fired by mistake. Instantly the great battleship bristles like an angry porcupine; all her aft guns are seen to nod and converge on the *Empress*. Onlookers on deck feel ridiculously like the bull's-eye of a target as they look down the muzzles of the *Revenge*'s 16-inch guns and wonder, "What the hell??!"

After a few minutes' tension, the *Revenge* and the *Empress* relax – the battleship first.

Rumours are circulated each day about subs sinking ships in the convoy, and there is much speculation as to the ultimate destination, for there has been no official information as to where they are bound. Sailors who claim the ship visited Iceland on their last trip add weight to one rumour that that is where they are headed. However, most persist in the belief they are going to England.

Only once during the voyage does a dangerous situation arise. This is during a foggy afternoon when the convoy comes face to face with another big convoy going in the opposite direction. But though foghorns hoot their most ominous notes all around, and some ships pass very close to each other, there are no collisions. Unquestionably, it is a most trying time for those on the bridges of those ships, and undoubtedly they have to execute brilliant feats of seamanship to prevent collisions, but to most of the 4th Field men on board the *Empress*, it is only vaguely exciting, and the games of chance go merrily on below.

Lifeboat drills are instituted, and a variety of signals are explained, including the thought-provoking order "Abandon Ship":

Abandon Ship Stations: In the event of the above order being given (6 short blasts and one long on the klaxons) 2 occupants of this cabin will proceed to boat No. 13 starboard side, the re-mainder to rafts on Boat Deck at nearest point. The occupants of this cabin must decide amongst themselves who are to be in boats and who on rafts, and the decision reached will be strictly adhered to. All occupants of this cabin are responsible for making themselves thoroughly acquainted with the shortest way to their boat and boat deck.

Heard for the first time is the klaxon, a horn that sounds as if it might have graced the hood of a 1920 McLaughlin-Buick. No one is allowed to forget the possibility of being sunk; every man must at all times carry his life preserver, either a cork belt or two over-stuffed pillows dangling on tapes which can be tied securely fore and aft.

Daily BBC broadcasts tell of heavy air raids on Britain. No one doubts these are the prelude to Hitler's invasion. Churchill under-lined this the day 4th Field left Petawawa, when, in reference to the British, Canadian, and other Commonwealth pilots fighting the Battle of Britain he concluded that "never before in the field of human conflict was so much owed by so many to so few."

And as the convoy steams on, all on board the *Empress* carry images of a storm of swirling aircraft in desperate battle over bomb-cratered airfields of England by day, and of droning bombers by night attacking the Channel ports and industrial centres as far north as Liverpool and Birmingham. While the *Empress* is still two days out, neutral U.S. correspondents on September 1 are reporting the joy of Berliners on hearing their soldiers predict that "Operation Sea-lion" (the code name for the German cross-Channel operation) will be launched "in the next four days."*

---

* August 15, 1940, Reich Marshal Göring stood on a headland at Calais and watched his bombers escorted by swarms of fighters sweep over the

At 12:30 P.M., September 3, six Royal Navy ships join the *Revenge* and the two destroyers shepherding the convoy. Obviously, the six troopships carrying some twelve thousand soldiers would be a prize for the German subs, and the Royal Navy is taking no chances during the final run to the Clyde, now the obvious destination since the convoy passed Ailsa Craig, the towering rock island, with its crest enshrouded in clouds, sitting alone in the sea off Scotland. But while disturbing rumours abound, and sub-chasers scurry about dropping depth charges, nothing happens. And on the afternoon of September 4, workmen lining the sunny banks of the Clyde cheer the 1,700 soldiers from Canada packing the open decks of the *Empress* as she steams slowly up to Greenock. Men of 4th Field have never been cheered before, anywhere, and this spontaneous tribute is the crowning touch to happy emotions aroused by the magnificent scene around them.

After a week of nothing but sea and plodding grey ships, this colourful, animated scene is truly a sight for sore eyes. Long red-brick row-houses, topped by stubby rows of chimney-pots, shelving down the smooth green hills, are reflected in the water. Several destroyers and corvettes, some flying the flags of other nations, ride at anchor among liners and merchant ships, while tenders and tugs and other smaller harbour craft scurry about in industrious fashion. All wear a common coat of wartime grey, but all are still worthy of an artist's pleasure.

Low over the water and ships glide the whitest of white gulls, now and then descending in squawking clutters on a tidbit tossed overboard by a gunner. And high in the distant sky towards Glasgow

---

Channel initiating Operation "Adler" (Eagle) meant to destroy RAF airfields and fighters in sufficient numbers to achieve air supremacy over the Channel, a necessary condition for Hitler's invasion scheduled the first week of September. On "Eagle Day" the Germans made 1,786 sorties, losing 75 planes compared to 32 by the RAF, setting the pattern for the next two weeks.

ride countless silver barrage balloons, hanging absolutely still as though painted there in the blue sky, like clouds on a windless summer day.

The hours pass quickly, with river and shore providing a continual source of diversion throughout the daylight hours, extended by double daylight-saving time. Such things as "goods trains" (freight trains) – their dumpy little cars, primitively joined together with three chain links and pulled by open-cab locomotives emitting shrill toots like a peanut-vendor's whistle – are the source of great amusement to men accustomed to the deep-throated wail of Canadian monsters.

Officers with experience in England, some during the First War, take the opportunity to warn all ranks that a great many things will appear strange over here, but they must be on their guard not to give offence by laughing. As time goes on, they'll learn there's method in their madness; for instance, English locomotives, such as the one pulling the Royal Scott, with a funny whistle just like the goods trains', have set world speed records.

It is midnight, in the blackout, when 4th Field disembarks. Total darkness is something most have never known before, for in North America (or any other part of the world free of total blackouts), even on cloudy nights, far out in the country, there is always reflected light from the surrounding towns and villages. The British blackout is so complete that on cloudy, starless nights like this, when it's not possible for a man to see the ground around his feet, even the low curbs along both sides of a street can be real hazards.*

---

* The inky density of the British blackout during a pea-souper fog on occasion even defeated London bus drivers, if they were given an unfamiliar route, as happened to the driver of a bus carrying the first draft of CWACs (Canadian Women's Army Corps) the first night they were in England. They were on their way, early in the evening, to a formal welcoming reception arranged for them in the West End of London, when the driver became lost. Leaving them on the bus, he went off on

Fortunately the special troop train is not far away, waiting on the docks. Somehow, in the inky blackness, they jam aboard, six to a compartment with all their kit, including a "bag lunch," a going-away present as they left the darkened ship. For those who have difficulty falling asleep sitting up, it is a long night, for the train is also in darkness except for a slight hint of pale, bluish light at the end of the corridor next to the toilet. There is no drinking water on the train, and so the hot tea, served with cold, glutinous pork pies on the station platforms at Leicester and Banbury, is exceedingly welcome.

It's a tedious trip, with frequent long pauses and diversions onto sidings to accommodate through-trains and unusual scheduling due to bomb-damage repairs. Even when daylight comes and they can see quaint villages flashing by, and can study the ever-changing scene of patchwork fields outlined by dark-green hedges, and distant tall church spires, the hours pass slowly. By evening, when the train finally pulls into North Camp Station in Aldershot, all are weary and spirits are low. It does no one any good to have a soldier from a Canadian Scottish regiment yell at them from the platform, "Go back home. This is a helluva place to be stuck in!"

But, thinking anything is better than being jammed on a train for hours without end, they pile off and heave their kit bags onto lorries. When they are lined up on the platform in "full marching order," they are told by the Colonel it will be a long march to camp and it'll have grown dark before they get there. During the rest break there will be no smoking, and "Anyone striking a match or showing a light will be shot." With this grim warning ringing in their ears, officers and men of 4th Field move off towards Leipzig Barracks, six miles away on the most hateful route march ever conducted by the unit.

---

foot to try to get his bearings. On the way back to them he lost his way and didn't show up at the bus until dawn, accompanied by a bobby with a soothing voice urging him not to get hysterical.

The shipbuilders and dock workers along the Clyde had cheered, but the civilians of Aldershot hardly give more than a passing glance at the soldiers marching by. Too long has Aldershot been a garrison town for its citizens to pay any attention to a column of soldiers clumping by. After a two-day train-trip in Canada, six days on ship waiting to sail, nine days at sea, and almost twenty-four hours on a crowded English train, the men are in no condition or spirit for such a march, even without the "full marching order" feature. Moreover, it is an unusually hot evening for England, and the sun beats down unmercifully for the first part of the march. And to cap it all, during the after-dark break, innumerable civilians go by with brightly glowing cigarettes and pipes, their tantalizing smoke wafting past the noses of the gunners dying for a drag.

17

YOUR ENTHUSIASM IS HIGHLY COMMENDABLE

———————————— ✳ ————————————

SETTLING INTO THE RAMSHACKLE LEIPZIG BARRACKS, AND into the ways of this country, where so much is strange and new, takes many days. The batteries spend the time conducting courses in small arms, anti-gas procedures, "smartening-up" footdrills, and route marches as they wait to be equipped with 25-pounders and quads.

That the Regiment will not see a 25-pounder for months is not something anyone foresees until the CO returns from a meeting at 2nd Division Headquarters with the bizarre story that 1st Field RCHA, the only regiment in England equipped with 25-pounders, is being used as a sort of "travelling circus," crossing and recrossing the country to give the impression there is unlimited artillery still available to repel invaders.

It seems this odd business was brought into being by orders from the highest authority immediately following 1st Field Regiment's return from a three-day junket into the heart of France – twenty-five miles southwest of Le Mans – ten days after the British Expeditionary Force abandoned France via Dunkirk. For a time, the British War Office thought it might still be possible to establish a redoubt in the Brittany Peninsula. But before the guns of 1st Field fired a round, they were ordered back to Brest, their point of entry, where they were ordered to burn their vehicles and spike their guns.*

First Field CO, Lt.-Col. "Ham" Roberts, managed, however, to talk the British port authority into allowing them to take their guns on board, a remarkable feat in the face of the stern orders from London that only men should occupy space in the returning vessels, though the holds would have been almost empty had they left their guns behind.† Back in England, they were issued unlimited petrol and ordered to haul their precious guns hither and yon across the southern counties, in highly visible fashion from dawn to dusk, providing any irresolute citizen or lurking spy with clear evidence that the rumour the nation has been rendered weaponless by Dunkirk is pure nonsense.

Other Canadian gunners, armed at this time with effective weapons, but too large (21 tons) to be trundled about, are those manning four 9.2-inch guns of the Super-Heavy Railway Group RA, composed of some twenty railway guns (9.2-inch guns and 12-inch howitzers) just hauled out of storage depots and obscure corners of railway rolling-stock yards, and an 18-inch monster "lurking in a tunnel near Canterbury," to meet the expected invasion. In activating the super-heavy batteries, dormant since 1918, the prime problem – once the weapons themselves are located†† – is to find enough gunners in Britain with some training or experience on big guns to be able to learn how to fire them in time to be of any use in countering the expected invasion. When a call went out to

---

* Normally accomplished by loading a shell in the breech and another pointing backwards down the muzzle, and pulling the firing lever from the safety of a distant slit trench with the aid of a couple of drag ropes spliced together.

† For more details, see Appendix B.

†† For the amusing story of how two of the 9.2-inch guns were found in startling fashion see Appendix C.

Canadian artillery holding or reinforcement units, the first week of September 1940, enough men with training on medium, heavy, or coastal equipment were found to man X and Y Superheavy Batteries RA of two guns each. After brief training on a 9.2-inch gun at Hythe, they manned their pair until February 1941, when they reluctantly turned them over to British gunners and returned to their holding units.*

At any rate, the only thing now available to 4th Field in plenty is *time*, which every officer and NCO knows must never be left unfilled. Every waking hour must be taken up with some form of activity, even if it is no more than calling snap kit inspections. Thus, simple regimental muster parades each morning are very formal and drawn out, with everyone, from sergeants up through troop sergeant-majors, battery sergeant-majors, the subalterns and the captains to the battery commanders (majors), taking turns giving every man the once-over before the Colonel strides down between the perfectly "dressed" lines, looking for an undone button, a little brass strip on a web belt unpolished, an anklet needing blanco, or some wisps of hair on a neck needing a trim.

At first the meals, even by army standards, are atrocious, as the harassed cooks struggle with the British scale and quality of rations. For the first time the word "rations" takes on its full meaning and becomes more than just army slang for food. In the early days of mobilization last year in Canada, the scale of issue of meat was a pound per man per day. Now it's four and a half ounces of fresh meat and an ounce and a half of bacon per day. Fatty, strong-smelling, and even stronger-tasting, mutton comes on the menu. And a pressed-meat full of little pieces of bone and gristle (immediately given a most uncomplimentary appellation suggestive of a protruding portion of a stallion's anatomy) appears in mess tins and is promptly ignored – so thoroughly and consistently that it eventually disappears from rations.

---

* These Canadian gunners are not to be confused with the gunners of the 57th and 59th Newfoundland Heavy Regiments in the Royal Artillery.

But one food appears that can't be ignored, even by those with the most underdeveloped sense of smell: "Herrings in Tomato Sauce." Once the cans are open, no one within a sixty-foot radius of the kitchen can disregard the stench, but like the greasy, malodorous mutton, they are on the menu for the duration.

However, in spite of unappetizing meals, the clammy old barracks, and the cold aloofness of the civilians of Aldershot, morale is high among all ranks. They are *here*, right next to London, on the main stage at one of the most dramatic hours in the story of humankind.

On September 11, some bomb damage is sustained by Buckingham Palace and St. Paul's Cathedral as the Germans swing their raids from fighter airfields to cities, especially London, reputedly in retaliation for RAF raids on Berlin. On September 15, a day of massive daylight raids on London, when RAF Hurricanes and Spitfires shoot down sixty German planes while losing only twenty-six, one pilot is singled out for special recognition in the press. For shooting down the German bomber that chose the Palace as its target, Canadian Pilot Officer Keith "Skeets" Ogilvie (a friend from Glebe Collegiate days) receives the warm personal commendation from Queen Wilhelmina of the Netherlands, currently a guest at the Palace.

The Battle of Britain seems to be reaching a decisive phase, and all day long from up in the blue skies come faint dronings and whinings and stutterings in the vicinity of senseless scrawls of vapour trails left by "The Few." On the ground, there is continuing anxiety as all able-bodied men not in the forces or engaged in ARP (air-raid precautions) work are earmarked for anti-invasion roles, even though most of these "home guard" men (too old or physically unfit for regular military service) can be armed only with iron pikes manufactured by local blacksmiths.

To overcome the dire deficiency in firearms, legends of ingenuity are being created by commanders of Home Guard units. But none is more bizarre than the use of overturned soup plates on the western beach of Anglesey Island, off Wales, initiated by ex-Canadian

F. N. Carpenter, a veteran of both the Boer War (British Army) and the Great War (Canadian Army).*

Now a major in the 1st Anglesey Battalion Royal Welsh Fusiliers, responsible for the defence of miles of beaches, Carpenter can arm only six of his men with rifles and hand them five bullets each (allotted him from a supply of 75,000 1914-18 Canadian Ross rifles and sixty million bullets rushed to Britain by Canada in May 1940). Undaunted, he collects all the soup plates he can beg from neigh-bouring farms and places them upside down on the sand along the beach in a symmetrical pattern suggestive of anti-personnel devices accidentally exposed by tidal action. His hope is that the sinister menace of these gleaming white objects will slow the Germans' rush ashore and inspire them to avoid that stretch of beach, thus funnelling them towards his handful of armed snipers.

The Regiment, lacking guns, is organized into "infa-artillery units." Batteries are split into three sections: a PAD Section (person-nel anti-gas decontamination); a Molotov Cocktail Section, for tossing gasoline-filled bottles at tanks; and a Rifle Section, for searching out and destroying parachutists. Safely stored in each battery quarter stores are forty rifles and fifteen cartridges for each rifle, to be issued to those on duty when the enemy paratroopers start dropping.

---

* Between the wars, Major Carpenter had been a master at Upper Canada College, responsible for its cadet corps, from which came several officers for the Royal Regiment of Canada, a battalion of 4th Brigade that 4th Field will support in action. Before the start of World War II, he and his wife and the youngest five of their eight children returned to Britain to take over the family estate on Anglesey. All eight children volunteered for service in the war: Squadron Leader Tom, RCAF; Group Captain (and postwar Air Vice-Marshal) Fred, RCAF; Captain Alan, MC, a FOO with the RCA in Italy; Naval Lieutenant Jack, of the Fleet Air Arm, who was killed flying an RAF Hurricane in the Battle of Britain; Wren Barbara, Royal Navy; WAAF Betty, RCAF; Squadron-Leader Craig, of No. 6, Bomber Command; and Officer Cadet David, at Sandhurst at war's end.

Thus some five hundred will be weaponless and forced into the uncomfortable state of "lurking" when the enemy arrives, at least until casualties present the opportunity to obtain a weapon with a round or two left in its magazine.

From September 15 to 21 the German invasion is expected by the British high command, and all units in Britain "stand-to" each morning in readiness. The war diary of 4th Field of the fifteenth reports: "Warning was received that reveille would be at 0500 hours with the possibility of operations starting at 0700 hours." Next day the entry is even more ominous: "Possibility of actual operations imminent. All ordinary camp operations frozen."*

However, September 21 comes and goes without anything developing, and morning stand-to's are replaced by a state-of-readiness, described in orders as "ready to move on an hour's notice from 7:30 A.M."

On September 25, the unit is visited by His Royal Highness the Duke of Gloucester, who shows a keen interest in how an artillery regiment carries on without guns, and is especially curious about the contribution to the defence of the realm expected of one captain occupying an observation post in a tree.

In the months that follow, there are many inspections, including one by King George and Queen Elizabeth, who seem truly fascinated in the use of a "ground-anchor" that allows a truck to attain a steady purchase for winching itself from the mud. There are also visits by the Honourable Anthony Eden, secretary for war, and Field Marshal Sir John Dill, chief of the imperial staff.

In most cases, these inspections are not of the Regiment drawn up in close ranks in a field in traditional fashion, but are in the form of a "three-ring circus," with troops engaged in various tasks indicating intense activity, but which for the most part are simply repetitive gestures suggesting frantic maintenance of equipment.

---

* On September 3, Hitler did set the invasion for the twenty-first, but he later postponed it.

The idea is not really to accomplish anything, but to create the impression of keenness.

Of these peculiar displays of energy, the most memorable is that presented for inspection by Canada's minister of defence, Hon. J. L. Ralston. For the visit by "Colonel Ralston" (as he prefers to be known, being a veteran of the First War), one battery will give a display of vehicle maintenance. Six men are assigned to each of the vehicles lined up around the square, and when the distinguished visitor arrives, men are swarming over the trucks with wrenches of one kind or another, loosening or tightening nuts and bolts – all of them playing their roles with gusto, except for the poor drivers, who technically are supervising this mayhem to their beloved vehicles.

Colonel Ralston, having suffered a slight accident a few days ago, is on crutches and forced to survey the scene from a distance. Thus, he doesn't get close enough to hear the drivers grinding their teeth and muttering curses under their breath. And when he calls a halt to the affair so he can address the Regiment, he's able to say in all honesty, "I'm not quite sure I know what you're doing, but your enthusiasm is highly commendable!"

On the night of September 27, about 11:00 P.M., someone dashes through the barracks yelling, "Parachutists have landed! All those in rifle sections fall out on the parade square!"

With intense excitement, those so designated go dashing about to arm themselves with a rifle and the precious fifteen rounds of ammunition, so precious that Sergeant Coats in charge of 26 Battery quarter stores will not issue rifle or shells until he receives a signature from each man. German paratroopers be hanged, he is not going to be stuck paying for any rifle or ammunition lost by careless gunners!

When the paperwork is all in order, the section is divided into ten-man patrols, each under a lieutenant, and off they go into the foggy heath. It is very dark and quiet, and at first very spooky. But as bodies begin to perspire from exertion, clothes become clammy and wet from the dripping gorse, and eyes, now accustomed to the dark, can see nothing of the alleged parachutists, it all becomes a great bore. And after about two hours thrashing about the country-side, the patrols return to barracks and to bed. Thus ends the first "paratrooper scare."

But there is a postscript. In the morning, when the rifles are examined in daylight, they are found to be chock-full of mineral jelly, just as they'd come from the factory. Had they been fired that way, the results would have been dire indeed.

18

THE GUNS OF 1898

--- ✳ ---

ONE DAY, AT THE BEGINNING OF OCTOBER 1940, A STORY IS circulated that "the guns are coming." This, to the gun sergeants, can mean only one thing – spanking new 25-pounders.

Because the Regiment has no quads, regular 30-hundredweight trucks are sent to fetch them. Of course, everyone is waiting expectantly when the convoy returns, and there is great disappointment when they see no guns rolling behind the trucks. But as they watch them turn in the gate, one onlooker catches sight of an ancient field piece riding in the rear of a truck. All the trucks, it turns out, are carting French 75-mm guns with wooden wheels so shaky-looking it was considered best not to pull them behind the trucks. On examining his gun, one sergeant finds it was accepted by the French government in the year 1898. And the allotment of ammunition is just seven rounds of high-explosive per gun.

The sighting arrangement may have been ingenious in its sim-plicity in 1898, consisting of a straight piece of half-inch pipe with a black glass aperture on which a white cross is superimposed, but it is almost impossible to see the aiming-point through it. All graduations on the guns are in metric and when gun drill is undertaken, sergeants work out the conversion in chalk on the trails of their guns – for example, converting 3,000 yards, ordered by the GPO, to 2,700 metres, for application to the guns.

The actual drill for preparing the gun for firing, taught by IGs from Larkhill, is strenuous and complicated. On the order from the gun sergeant to "Anchor," the detachment raises the trail of the gun until the muzzle strikes the ground in front, at which moment a pin is pulled, releasing a pair of "shoes" that drop, one behind each wheel. Now the detachment jumps up and pulls the trail down in firing position. After loading, the order "Stand Clear" is given, for the gun jumps about a foot in the air and back about three feet upon firing.

Actually, the only time the guns are fired is one round each for calibration at Larkhill. Each detachment, after loading and aiming its gun, is marched back to slit trenches some fifty yards away, from whence the firing lever is pulled with a lanyard made by hooking together several drag ropes.* Needless to say the shoot takes some time. With the calibration of each gun riding on one round, calculations have to be checked and rechecked. And before the order to fire is given, many eyes check the lay of the gun, starting with the gun sergeant, then the troop leader, then the GPO, then the troop commander, then the battery commander, and finally the 2 IC (second-in-command) of the Regiment. Still, when the whole thing is complete, the results don't seem quite reasonable, and on further checking, the initial surveying-in of the guns is found to be in error!

The signallers acquire new Don 5 telephones and some cable with which to practise cable laying. And most important, they get some new No. 11 wireless sets. To the signallers it's like learning wireless all over again, as they take instruction from the signal NCOs who came over in advance to England for courses on the subject.

From the outset in Aldershot, the Regiment has two 60-hundredweight trucks and two 30-hundredweight trucks for each

---

* Sturdy hemp ropes with hooks designed to fit into steel eyes on the hubs of the gun wheels, used for dragging the guns when only manpower is available.

battery to take care of essential transport of supplies and personnel. This allows most of the drivers to take turns becoming accustomed to driving on the left side of the road and changing gears with their left hands. Steering wheels placed on the right side of the cab make the transition much easier than expected for most drivers, and by the time the gun tractors arrive, they're ready to do convoy duty.

Also received late in September are a few 15-hundredweight trucks, and some little 8-hundredweight trucks that ride very comfortably and drive almost like a car on metalled roads – making them very useful for junkets over to Maidenhead or up to London, but not really practical for cross-country work on rough artillery ranges. Still, they are the vehicle of choice for FOOs until they get their armoured tracked-vehicles known as Bren Gun Carriers – lowslung, open, steel boxes of 12-mm armour plate designed to provide four-man carrier crews with some protection when moving with the infantry and exposed to small-arms fire.

Automatic weapons – tommy-guns and Bren guns – arrive in dribs and drabs over a long period. As fast as the Brens arrive, men are chosen for ack-ack (anti-aircraft) duties, and set up in posts around camp where they have a clear field of fire skyward. The first casualty in 4th Field from enemy action occurs on October 9, when one of these gunners, C. W. Carlisle, suffers a superficial cut from flying debris blown by a bomb landing near his post.

On other nights, bombs land very close to the camp, but the Regiment suffers no other casualties to men or equipment while billeted in and around Aldershot, though air raids are frequent. And in a surprisingly short time, the wail of the air-raid siren in the night becomes so familiar as to cause only the most restless sleepers to roll over in their bunks, in contrast to the Regiment's first air-raid alert that occurred the second night after they arrived here. That night there had been a bedlam of noise and flashing "lamps-electric"* as

---

* Issue flashlights of peculiar rectangular design, with unstable metal hoods to shade the light.

all ranks sought shelter below ground in trenches outside the barracks with the first sound of the siren rising and falling.

19

THE REFORMATION OF
THE SUBALTERNS

✳

ON THE FIRST DAY OF DECEMBER 1940, THE REGIMENT MOVES
into Salamanca Barracks in Aldershot for what is generally considered to be "a better go." Living quarters are newer, and the cooks
begin to produce more palatable meals, having acquired some tricks
to cope with rationing, such as squirrelling away sugar to produce
extra desserts – a matter of no small consequence to morale at this
stage of 4th Field's British experience.

Aldershot being within South-Eastern Command, 4th Field,
along with the rest of 2nd Division, is under a feisty British general
named Bernard Montgomery. As part of a line of defence designed
to block enemy forces moving on London, the Regiment recon-
noitres several gun positions as plans change for countering the
expected invasion. It seems Montgomery favours manning the
coastline itself with light forces only, freeing the bulk of his troops
to form mobile reserves, with emphasis on mobility, so they may
be concentrated rapidly on invading spearheads once it is established
where the main enemy thrusts are being made. (To increase mobility, Monty arranges for civilian buses to be seconded for transporting the infantry if and when the need arises.) And responding
to the perceived need to be able to deploy the guns anywhere along
this wide stretch of coast guarded by 2nd Division, as many as
possible widely spaced, pre-reconnoitred gun positions are estab-

lished; though, to save wear and tear on the old guns, none of the positions is ever occupied.

In December – on the basis of the brief experience of the British with mobile warfare in Belgium and France (lasting only ten days from when the German Panzers sliced through Belgium on May 16 until they began their escape by sea at Dunkirk on May 26) – the organization of a field regiment is changed to make it more manoeuvrable: from two batteries of twelve guns each to three batteries with eight guns each – four per troop. The three batteries of 4th Field are: 2nd, 14th, and 26th.*

More reorganization, however, cannot improve the mobility of batteries towing guns of 1898 vintage, and when troop or battery schemes are held, they still proceed at a snail's pace to prevent the ancient, wooden wheels collapsing on the road.

Mobility of personnel, however, increases significantly with the addition of more trucks, and officers and men take to the business of learning their way around the south of England in earnest. Surprisingly, petrol poses no problem, and map-reading junkets hither and yon become the most popular form of training.

Far from discouraging this extravagant use of petrol, senior officers seem clearly in favour, suggesting this "toodling about" has the blessing of upper echelons, originating in the same high-level policy that, right after Dunkirk, sent convoys of 1st Field guns parading back and forth across the southern counties of Britain from dawn to dusk to convey the impression the island was crawling with guns and vehicles, when in fact, apart from two tank battalions and light armoured units, Gen. Andy McNaughton possessed the only mobile force of consequence in Britain.

---

* Major Beament commands 2nd Battery, Major Medland the 14th, and Major Harris the 26th. Four officers (Capt. G. E. Woodrow and Lieuts. J. R. Pepall, C. R. Osler, and C. W. Couch) and one hundred Other Ranks, mostly from the 53rd Battery, leave to form the nucleus of the new 3rd Light Anti-Aircraft Regiment.

While this highly visible display of war machines, trundling about on the highways and byways, may raise civilian morale, it seems not to confuse enemy intelligence. The British traitor known as "Lord Haw-Haw," in one of his nightly taunting "Jarmany Calling" radio broadcasts, designed to arouse despair and hopelessness among the British waiting to confront a German invasion, predicts an issue of peanuts is about to be made to "the monkeys in McNaughton's travelling circus." And a few days later every "monkey" does indeed receive a bag of peanuts, a commodity now rarely seen in England.*

Still, "junketing about" by 4th Field is encouraged, and in a most curious way by Major Medland in collaboration with Major Harris. They thumbtack to a wall of RHQ (regimental headquarters) a large-scale map of the Aldershot area and issue instructions that anyone discovering a new pub shall mark on the map its position and a rating of its quality: "first, second, or third class."

Officers' weekend "map-reading expeditions" now extend to some distant destinations, including Bournemouth and its Norfolk Hotel, but most officers seem drawn to testing their skill at finding their way to the heart of London. Trucks marked with a white "42" on a square of artillery colours (red on top and blue on the bottom) can be seen most weekends moving along Piccadilly to the Park Lane Hotel, or parked outside the Grovesnor House, where each Sunday afternoon scores of charming young hostesses (chosen by a committee of élite ladies) attend a mammoth "tea-dance" in what is reputed to be the largest hotel ballroom in Europe.

Some officers even indulge in midweek evening visits to London, in what they have come to consider their personal vehicles – the lively little 8-hundredweight trucks – until these sorties start producing headaches beyond what even the most indulgent deserve. For instance, about 2:00 A.M. on a wet and slippery morning, one such vehicle fails to make a sharp turn in Guilford and enters a store

---

* Lord Haw-Haw, the British fascist William Joyce, would be captured at Flensburg, Germany, May 28, 1945, brought back to the Tower of London, tried as a traitor, and hanged.

through its front window, allowing the officer in charge to step out into the lingerie department. Ultimately he receives a bill for eighty-five "quid" – the equivalent of about four hundred and twenty-five Canadian dollars.*

Less costly, but no less memorable, is a lonely hike of many hours over many miles of unfamiliar, blacked-out suburban London streets by Capt. McGregor Young.† Loaded by a fellow officer into the back of a vehicle as it pulls away from a West End hotel late one night, Mac dozes off, secure in the knowledge his pal up front will see he gets home. Since debarkation has always been at a corner in Aldershot where stoplights glow, it is natural enough that Mac should believe he is home when he wakes up, finds the truck stopped, and stoplights glowing. Only when he climbs out and the truck pulls away, leaving him standing alone watching its tail-light disappear, does he realize he is still in a suburb of London.

Such experiences – combined with the continuing hazards of the blitz in which more than 1,500 civilians are being killed each week, the majority in London – dampen enthusiasm for trips up to the West End, and the Queen's Bar in Aldershot becomes a favoured spot for an evening out. Also, when troop recreational trips are laid on over weekends, they head far away from targets for German air raids, up to fifty miles distant, including the Vale of the White Horse.

One memorable weekend is spent in Wantage, where the villagers, who have not seen Canadian soldiers since 1915, provide billets and heartwarming hospitality, including a Saturday-night dance attended by the prettiest girls in town. But some gunners behaved very badly. To quote the regimental diary: "Shameful it is to relate, some of the boys became rowdy and windows were broken. Sunday morning they all marched off to church to hear the pastor tell them what fine fellows they were."

---

* A staggering $4,250 in terms of 1990 dollars.
† He would be the commanding officer of the Regiment for the last nine months of the war on the Western Front.

While the memories of this period at Aldershot will always be dominated by all this exploration of winding country lanes with charming tearooms, and picture-postcard villages with Dickensian pubs – all so different and refreshing to a new arrival from Canada – the most remarkable event of the Aldershot era, with long-term implications to the capacity of the Regiment to meet the enemy, is the phenomenon known as the "reformation of the subalterns."

The fact that no subaltern can recall where the initial meeting was held that spawned this startling development suggests the inspiration derived from a night of "elbow-bending." Still, the revolutionary idea was conceived in utter sincerity, survived the grey light of dawn, and is being carried out with complete seriousness. At that historic meeting of subalterns, it was decided unanimously the Regiment was "going to the devil," and that the fault lay with them. So a campaign in self-discipline and self-instruction was mapped out calling for: firmer parades; getting up each morning at 0615 hours and going for a three-mile run before breakfast; devoting three nights a week to lectures on such subjects as "fire control discipline"; and practice in the use of directors, slide-rules, and artillery boards. All classes are purely for subalterns and are handled by the subalterns themselves. And the most impressive part of it all is that weeks after the decision was made, the syllabus is still being strictly adhered to.

The first Christmas away from Canada is marked by a tremendous deluge of parcels and letters from home, not likely to be duplicated any year in the future. As might be expected, Ray McCleary is active in all the festive arrangements, scrounging decorations and arranging a party for 140 children (evacuees from London) attended by the Mayor of Aldershot and his wife "fully robed in their official dress."

Due to the abundance of seasonal cheer, persisting until New Year's Day – the day officers traditionally hold an "at home" and let their hair down (unlike Christmas Day, when the officers are expected to serve the dinner to the Other Ranks) – details of adult parties will always remain a bit hazy. However, rumours will persist for years that when Capt. Mac Young, well into the spirit of things on New Year's Eve, decided to throw a party for his troop and organized a "patrol," he netted a roast turkey and several bottles of refreshment from what he considered to be an excessively large stock of goodies accumulated in the officers' mess for the "at home" next day.

The blitz on London is now in full swing, and for hours it seems each night, the sky is filled with the long, drawn-out quavering roars of the Luftwaffe bombers passing overhead, followed by the distant rumble and *crump* of tons of bombs landing on the heart of the last active resistance on Earth to the mad Führer. Each morning, barrack windows, left up the night before, have jiggled down, and doors left closed have sprung ajar from the shuddering vibrations. Still, no bombs land on the barrack blocks, and the windows remain intact. Clearly, Aldershot is not on the current list of places to be flattened, and the gunners continue to go to bed in their bunks.*

---

* British civilian casualties the first seven months of the Blitz:

	1940			1941	
	Killed	Injured		Killed	Injured
Sept.	6,954	10,615	Jan.-Feb.	2,289	3,080
Oct.	6,334	8,695	Mar.	4,259	5,557
Nov.	4,588	6,202			
Dec.	3,793	5,244			
			Totals:	28,217	39,391

(Figures are from Robert Goralski, pages 133 to 151, *World War II Almanac*, Hamish Hamilton, London: 1981.)

20

NIGHT CLOUDS GLOW RED
OVER LONDON

※

FOR MEN ON LEAVE IN CENTRES TARGETED BY THE LUFTWAFFE for heavy bombing, it's quite a different story from Aldershot, as Gunners George Bracken, John Dunsmore, and "Slim" E. McGillis find out on the first night of their weekend pass to Portsmouth. Caught in a pub as an air raid begins, with no place to go and no useful knowledge of the city, having arrived in the blackout, they decide to "ride it out right there," with the approval of the sympathetic publican, who locks them in as he departs.

With an unlimited supply of "mild" and "bitter" on tap, they approach the night with creditable optimism. But soon they are down under the sturdy bar on their hands and knees in the foetal position as bombs whistle and scream down, crashing closer and closer with thunderous, shuddering concussions that set all the glasses above their heads and the bottles in cases beside them rattling and clashing. When morning comes and the publican returns and unlocks the door, he suggests they go outside and have a look. Their pub is the only building still standing along the entire street.

London, of course, is the chief target of the Luftwaffe, and though the worst bombing is in the dock areas of the East End, the West End – of famous historic buildings, posh hotels and restaurants, theatres, and Dickensian pubs – receives its share, and it's hardly a healthy place to visit. However, it is so close and is served by so many trains, it is irresistible to the officers and men of 4th Field.

A sentry paces in front of the entrance to the Coliseum at Lansdowne Park in Ottawa, where the Ottawa units were mobilized in September 1939. The horse and cow stables, where the men of 2nd Battery were billeted all that fall and winter, were just to the left rear of the Coliseum. (*Recruits Wanted*, by Orville Norman Fisher, cat. no. 12584, copyright Canadian War Museum)

Looking very smart in their new battledress uniforms, 2nd Ottawa
Field Battery, with A Troop in front, led by Battery Commander Major
Ted Beamont, leave Parliament Hill after a garrison parade, April 28,
1940. (Public Archives RG 24, vol. 14545)

Second Battery crew firing a sombre salute in Ottawa, April 1940, on their wooden-wheeled 18-pounder guns on the occasion of the funeral of Major-General H. H. Matthews, CMG, DSO. (Public Archives RG 24, vol. 14545)

Firing an 18-pounder with pneumatic-tired wheels in Petawawa, August 1940. (National Archives of Canada, PA-197865)

Petawawa Military Camp during the summer of 1940 – lines of bell tents sheltering almost three thousand officers and men of 2nd Division artillery preparing to go overseas. (National Archives of Canada, PA-197866)

Having little equipment, signallers resort to training with signal flags, learning how to transmit the alphabet visually. Lamps were also used for the same purpose at night. (National Archives of Canada, PA-197867)

25-pounders deploying at Petawawa. (Painting by Joan Wanklyn, courtesy 2nd RCHA and its CO, Lt.-Col. Stu Beare)

A Gun Position Officer (GPO) puts his guns on line using a field artillery survey instrument known as an artillery director. (National Archives of Canada, PA-197874)

Another subaltern checks the work of a Sergeant Ack (technical assistant) at a battery command post. The senior Ack at the troop command post is a bombardier (two stripes). (National Archives of Canada, PA-197873)

The *Empress of Japan*, newly re-named the *Empress of Scotland*, steaming up the Clyde to Gourock, June 24, 1942, with 4,500 on board (most of whom are service personnel, including the 3rd Canadian Medium Regiment). (National Archives of Canada, PA-197861)

Photo taken in mid-Atlantic from a porthole of the *Empress*. The *Letitia*, another troop carrier, is close by. The distant aircraft carrier is a converted banana boat, with a total compliment at the outset of the voyage of three Swordfish biplanes. (Photo courtesy Ray Irwin)

St. Lucia Officers' Mess, which, like Quebec Mess (below), saw hundreds of young Canadian officers pass through #1 Canadian Artillery Reinforcement Unit on their way to regiments in Britain. (Photo courtesy Ray Irwin)

Wives of officers (on staff), who had married in England, and other guests, were often invited to garden parties. This one occurred the first Sunday the author arrived at Quebec Mess, #1 Canadian Artillery Reinforcement Unit Bordon, Hampshire. (Photo courtesy Ray Irwin)

Inevitably, at least two 4th Field types are in London as the mournful wail of the air-raid sirens begin to rise and fall Sunday night, December, 29, as the Luftwaffe begins its massive incendiary raid that sets off fifteen hundred fires, many growing into raging conflagrations in the heart of the city.

Gunner Charles McEwen of 26 Battery is there to witness it all with his buddy Warren McParland on a weekend pass, and sends home such a vivid account, the paper in Petrolia, Ontario, carries it in full:

We got on the train at Aldershot and were in Waterloo Station about 2:30 P.M. We took a tube to Trafalgar Square and from there to the Beaver Club where we got a ticket that would let us ride on buses, trams, and tubes [underground] all day Sunday for a shilling [25 cents]. We went to St. Paul's Cathedral and spent about an hour there. We saw where the time-bomb had been dug out, and while we were poking around, a man offered to show us around. The cathedral had one bomb come through the roof over the altar. The altar was destroyed, but otherwise little damage was done. There were very few people around the last Sunday of 1940, and everything was quiet and peaceful. The cathedral is in the centre of the street. The Strand passes each side of it. None of the buildings had been hit, and there were very few signs of war around that part of the city.

But then we took a bus to Oxford Street where quite a few stores have been hit. Lewis's is a very large department store, in fact two stores each about the size of Eaton's in Toronto. The Huns dropped a landmine on each store and completely destroyed them. Nothing stands but the walls. It is indeed a terrible sight. We saw huge steel girders twisted like match sticks.

We went to see the Chaplin film *The Great Dictator* at the Palladium that afternoon and back to the Beaver Club for supper. We started out again about 6:00 P.M. Just as we were leaving the air-raid siren blew. We had heard it so often at camp we didn't pay much attention to it. We were walking across Trafalgar

Square in front of Nelson's statue, when we heard the planes overhead.

This didn't mean much; we'd had them overhead hundreds of times. Suddenly we heard whistling in the air, and we flattened down on the sidewalk. Two H.E.'s [high explosive bombs] landed about a block away and two incendiaries lit up the street about fifty yards away.

In about twenty seconds shrapnel started tinkling down in the streets and we crouched beside a wall. I didn't feel at all brave. In fact I was thoroughly frightened. The raid lasted only a few minutes, but the Jerries dropped a terrible amount of incendiaries and H.E.'s. In minutes a large fire was blazing a block or two away, and others starting up everywhere we looked. We ran to an underground station. The civilians didn't seem half as frightened as we were, but I guess they've got used to bombs.

We didn't have to be in Aldershot until 6:00 A.M. Monday, and had planned on catching a 4:00 A.M. train at Waterloo, but decided we'd better try to get out Sunday night. We tried to take a tube to Waterloo, but the trains had stopped. They run under the river from Trafalgar Square and during an attack they shut flood-gates in case of a direct hit. We came up to the street and started walking when we met some soldiers who told us Waterloo was closed.

There seemed to be fires everywhere. One of tremendous size was right around St. Paul's. The dome of the cathedral stood out like a great ball against the reflection of the fire. It was a sight I will never forget. The clouds were fairly low and were lit up a bright red. And we could see the barrage balloons overhead very plainly.

While we were standing there, we heard the planes coming back, and started for the Underground. We noticed the guns had stopped firing and soon we heard the RAF fighters going up and their machine-guns barking. They drove the Huns away.

The steady, all-clear signal blew about 10:00 P.M. and they did not come back. The night would have been very dark, but the city was lit up like day. You can't possibly imagine the extent of the fires. They could be seen plainly in Aldershot forty miles away.

We started looking for a bed. Westminster Y was full. We started up to Trafalgar Square again and asked a bobby on guard in front of a building [the Home Office] if London Bridge Station might be open. We were standing right in front of the Cenotaph which figures in so many newsreels. Suddenly a taxi pulled up and a rather small man jumped out. The bobby held the door and the man went in. We asked who it was? The bobby said, "Herbert Morrison." [The Home Secretary and Minister of Home Security responsible for Civil Defence and the safety of the civilian population.]

As we walked down the Strand gradually getting closer to the fires, we started going by buildings where the fires were almost out. They were still playing water on the tower of St. Bride's Church, one of the famous ones burned that night. The firemen had literally dozens of units working in those few blocks. They have many pumps that can be pulled by automobiles. We saw very few fire engines like ours at home. However, small as they were, they were doing a marvellous job. We went down past the Old Bailey, quiet at this time. A large office building was just starting to burn through the roof.

A lot of firemen were AFS [Auxiliary Fire Service] made up of office and factory fellows who work all day and volunteer for firefighting at night. They were handicapped by lack of pressure in the lines due to so many fires. We were going to walk past the burning buildings, but the smoke was so thick, we decided to go back and try to get an air-raid shelter for some sleep.

You can't imagine the quiet manner in which everyone took this great fire. We saw firemen and AFS men crowding around a YMCA truck at the height of the fire for a cup of tea. When we started back for Trafalgar Square, St. Paul's Cathedral was completely surrounded by burning buildings. As we walked back we could see a whole square of buildings burning very fiercely [Fleet

Street]. A number of printers' buildings and a lot of printers' ink, paper, etc., was going up in smoke, the sparks blowing a hundred feet in the air like a snowstorm.

All the time these firemen were working they expected more raids. In fact they were very surprised more bombs hadn't dropped.

You really have to hand it to these English civilians for the spirit they show in the face of all this sudden death . . . still living in the tubes in terrible circumstances.*

Some of the firemen had been fighting fires the night before in Manchester. Also some Brighton firemen had been called in. From what we heard the fires were bigger than any before. . . . Some very old buildings went up in smoke including the Guild-hall and five churches.

We went back to an air-raid shelter across from Big Ben, a few feet from Abraham Lincoln's statue. We lay down at 3:00 A.M. and awakened at 4:00 A.M. almost frozen. It was drizzling

---

* From August 1 to December 31, 1940, the Germans (according to Luft-waffe diaries) dropped 31,626 tons of bombs on Britain. Each night, for fifty-seven consecutive nights, beginning September 1, an average of 200 German bombers attacked London. In the first two weeks they caused more than 10,000 civilian casualties. From September 1 to December 31, 21,669 British civilians were killed and 30,756 were injured by bombs. During the period July 10 to October 31, when domination of the sky over the Channel and the southern counties of England was sought by Göring's Luftwaffe, a total of 1,733 German planes of all types were destroyed (at the time the RAF claimed 2,698); and the British lost 915 planes of all types (the Germans claimed 3,058). At the outset of this battle, which became known as the "Battle of Britain," the RAF possessed 609 fighter planes; the Luftwaffe 809 fighters and 280 fighter-bombers. His-torians appear to agree that the Luftwaffe, in spite of heavier losses, was on the point of putting all the fighter airfields out of action and winning the Battle of Britain, when Göring, with Hitler's blessing, turned to bombing London and Birmingham and other industrial cities, allowing the fighter airdromes to be brought back into action.

rain outside so we stayed there until 6:00 A.M. when we took a tube from Trafalgar to Waterloo. It had been burnt somewhat as we could see the water on the floor and could smell burned wood. The station was still closed down as far as trains were concerned, so we took a bus to Clapham Junction where we caught a train for Aldershot.

21

"SNAFU" COMES INTO

COMMON USE

——————————— ✳ ———————————

BLITZ OR NO BLITZ, TRAINING MUST GO ON. THE OLD FRENCH 75-mm guns having been gradually replaced late in December by British 75s with pneumatic tires, troops and batteries can now take to the roads to practise convoy discipline and deployments at a more respectable pace than was possible with the wooden-wheeled guns.

Finally, in April, the first eight 25-pounders and sixteen ammunition trailers arrive.* By tossing a coin it is decided that 26 Battery should have the lot. Those receiving the guns are so excited, the eight gun crews work until ten o'clock the first night, cleaning the packing jellies and grease out of their weapons.

Enthusiasm for gun drill and the desire to get acquainted with the equipment soars, and the handbooks explaining the internal workings of the gun and proper methods of maintenance are at a premium for after-parade study. With this enthusiasm, there comes into being a new desire to excel in all areas, and troop deployments in the gorse and sand of Cocked Hat Woods reach a new high point in efficiency.

However, large-scale manoeuvres are something else. Though the Regiment has been wearing the dark-blue shoulder patch of 2nd Division for months, it is not until the second week of June that it takes part in a divisional scheme called "Waterloo." The

———————

* See Appendix D on the 25-pounder.

gunners consider it appropriately named, for it rains every day for four days until called off in such a complete and utter shambles it may well have caused the birth of the highly useful expression "snafu" (short for "Situation normal, all fucked up") now in common use by everyone from the Chief of the Imperial General Staff (it is said) down to the lowliest gunner. Inexperience in map-reading the tortuous maze of English roads, from which all signs have been removed that might help an invader, is seemingly the cause.

At one point the CRA of 2nd Division, Brig. R. A. Fraser, conspicuous in his red-banded forage cap, is seen directing traffic at a confused and cluttered crossroads. While elsewhere, the CO of 6th Field, Lt.-Col. P. C. Tees, then acting CRA, is being captured by the "enemy." The wretched exercise ends at about 6:00 P.M., but it is midnight before anyone covers the few miles back to Salamanca. One 4th Field battery is well on its way to London before it gets turned around. And one troop commander arrives home with one of his own guns and seven belonging to 6th Field.

And such foul-ups are not restricted to 2nd Division. Back in February, the complacency of 1st Division in its level of training was badly shaken during "Fox," their first full divisional scheme near Dover. Before noon of the first day, every road in the area was "hopelessly jammed with vehicles and guns" – so hopelessly that when Maj.-Gen. J. R. Pearkes, VC, arrived at one crossroads, his division was approaching him from all four directions. When he personally took over traffic control and sorted things out, he ordered everyone back to their billets without completing the exercise.

Around this time, Prime Minister Churchill is reported to have said, "If you Canadians were to leave Britain, I would not sleep at night." He must surely have been paying tribute to the high reputation Canadian soldiers earned in World War I as courageous, dependable comrades-in-arms, not to the level of their training and potential effectiveness in early 1941.

It is unlikely the people of Britain will ever properly appreciate how lucky they are that Hitler decides to attack Russia in June 1941, instead of mounting a cross-Channel effort against this section of the English coast defended by the guns of 2nd Division. The very day the Führer launches, without warning by way of an ultimatum or declaration of war,* his massive attack of three million men and 3,580 tanks towards the East, on June 22, 4th Field takes part in its first-ever divisional creeping barrage at Larkhill – an event that turns into a snafu of embarrassing proportions.

With everyone of consequence "from General Andy McNaughton down" on hand to watch the affair, the division offers an exhibition of gunnery so miserable the furious CRA has every artillery officer under his command in 2nd Division paraded before him in an attempt to place the blame.

Actually, this snafu is readily traceable to the fact that the "meteor telegram," containing atmospheric data affecting the flight of the shells, arrived at the guns only ten minutes before zero hour – not enough time for inexperienced command post crews to convert accurately the meteorological data into tables of adjustments for the guns to compensate for air pressures, air temperatures, and speed and direction of the winds at various levels above the earth through which the shells must loop from lift to lift throughout the barrage.

Received at regular intervals throughout the day from the Meteorological Section of the Survey Regiment, the figures in the telegram are calculated from information gained from releasing a red gas-filled balloon and following the speed and direction of its rise and drift with instruments. While command post staffs are now accustomed to receiving these telegrams, and have had some practice in converting the information to terms applicable to the guns, this is the first time they ever applied the result to barrage forms in an actual shoot with live ammunition. And with so little time to do the work, panic developed and foul-ups occurred in applying the adjustments to the gun programs. Hence the strange pattern of shell distribution from lift to lift throughout the course of the barrage.

And this shaky state of training in gunner regiments could be matched or even surpassed by most, if not all, of the infantry bat-

---

* Hitler did not even notify his ally Mussolini.

talions. Illustrative (if not entirely typical) of the unstructured, inconsistent, and sometimes non-existent training for battle conducted by infantry battalions in late 1940 and early 1941, when the risk of invasion was highest, is the experience of Lieut. John Edmondson* on being posted as a platoon commander to the South Saskatchewan Regiment of 6th Brigade, 2nd Division. Dug-in along the cliff-edge of a golf course on the headland at Seaford, staring out over the misty Channel waiting for the Germans, the twenty-two-year-old Edmondson, a permanent force soldier since 1938, and recently commissioned, is very conscious of the need for upgrading the expertise of his men. But when he inquires if there is a program of training he should be following with his platoon, his company commander tells him airily, "No. Write your own."

At this time, according to Edmondson, "no one in the battalion seems even to have heard of the March 1940 British War Office pamphlet 'Training in Fieldcraft and Elementary Tactics,'" though by mid-1941 it will be inspiring imaginative training in field tactics and a high degree of fitness within units, which quickly will lead to the establishment of sophisticated "battle-drill" training, first for officers and NCOs, and later for the men.†

————

* Edmondson in August 1942 will go with the SSRs on the Dieppe Raid to fight on the Pourville beach, make it back to England, and in 1944 lead a company of SSRs in the awesome battles south of Caen in Normandy.

† This concentration on infantry training, with emphasis on toughening men physically and mentally for combat, clearly was influenced by Lt.-Gen. Bernard Montgomery, OC of 12th Corps in Kent. And it really swung into high gear in December 1941, when he was put in charge of South-Eastern Command Army, responsible for the defence of the "invasion corner" of Surrey, Sussex, and Kent, where, he recognized, "The whole future of England, and indeed civilization, was at stake." Drenched in the subject of infantry training to a degree, perhaps, no other officer of high command had ever been, having written the 1929-30 British War Office *Infantry Training Manual*, Monty insisted every man under his command, regardless of his rank or job, get in top shape.

And this vital training will become available to all ranks when battalions open up their own battle-drill courses, utilizing as instructors officers and NCOs as they return from battle school as self-confident, aggressively oriented soldiers equipped with the necessary knowledge and attitude for ruthless close-combat in small groups operating as a team.

By the summer of 1941, the first Canadian Training School, or "battle-school" as it will be known, is concentrating on matters totally relevant to preparing men for battle, including: unarmed combat; how to assault *over* nasty obstacles and *under* even nastier obstacles (sometimes cluttered with broken glass and putrid refuse of dead animals and the like); how to avoid booby traps; and, the ultimate "innoculation" to the strains and anxieties of battle, exposure to "live fire" of real bullets zipping just overhead as they crawl and cut their way through barbed wire and resist befuddlement by heart-stopping "thunder flashes" (69-grenades*) and buried bundles of gun cotton (electrically set off) exploding about them as will shells and mortar bombs one day.

---

* Bakelite grenades designed to produce great blast effect, but little or no damaging fragmentation.

22

"WE SHALL FIGHT ON THE BEACHES"

✳

CHURCHILL'S DEFIANT WORDS, AS HE CALLED ON HIS NATION to stand-to in anticipation of imminent invasion, still ring in the ears of officers and men of the Regiment on July 5, 1941, as they deploy their guns in camouflaged pits behind the very beaches to which he referred, close by the white cliffs that have become a symbol of hope and freedom for the world.

Three hundred yards from the muzzles of some guns is the Channel, and along the beach, between the guns and the restless sea, stretch tangled coils of concertina barbed wire and concrete anti-tank blocks, so close together they almost touch. And under the sand are mines. This is the front line of this bastion of resistance to dictatorship.

Across the Channel – in French, Belgian, and Dutch ports, and in canals and rivers leading to these ports – fleets of motorized barges lie awaiting Hitler's order to take aboard assaulting forces for an attack on this shore. And though, for the present, he is fully occupied with his invasion of Russia, this may not be the case for long, if the speed of advance of his Panzers is any indication. They appear to be pushing through Russian territory even faster than they swept through the Low Countries and France last summer. After only six days, they captured Minsk, 200 miles inside Russia, and only eleven days later surrounded and captured 290,000 men, 2,500 tanks, and

1,500 pieces of artillery. Then, a week later, Smolensk, 150 miles farther on, fell, trapping 600,000 more Russians.

And even before Russia has been subdued completely, Hitler may turn his attention back to his implacable island enemy, knowing that ultimately he must defeat her or lose the war, and that with each passing day, the RAF and Allied squadrons grow stronger. Overhead, Hurricanes and Spitfires (for the first time seen in numbers) now fly unchallenged, visible proof that Göring's bold promise to wipe the skies clean of British aircraft has not been fulfilled.

Everyone goes about their duties in a remarkably earnest way, as though they have taken their cue from the man in charge, General Montgomery, who said, "No German must live to say he has been an invader of English soil."

At the guns, half the personnel stand-to at all times, day and night, and officers take turns staring out over the Channel from OPs (observation posts). Some are in Martello towers – round stone structures built long ago for that very purpose when Napoleon was contemplating emulating a Norman conqueror who successfully made it ashore right here at Hastings in 1066. But most OPs are in seafront buildings, such as the white Marine Court Hotel, where Lieut. Lloyd Fromow, GPO of Charley Troop, 14th Battery, peers from the penthouse, ready to call out his guns from a parking garage under the beachfront road to fire over open sights at enemy landing craft.

Five or six miles separate the three batteries, and their four-gun troops are so widely dispersed (a mile between the troop gun positions of 2nd Battery) that shells, from at least part of the Regiment, can be brought down anywhere along a thirty-mile stretch of coastline. One troop of 2nd Battery is at Rye and the other at Camber, and 26th Battery is around Hastings. Charley Troop of 14th Battery is in a fixed position at Winchelsea, but because the artillery is so obviously thin on the ground, Don Troop has been designated a mobile force and held "on wheels" at Sedlescombe, six miles north of Hastings, ready to move at a moment's notice wherever required by 4th Brigade.

Commanded by Capt. Don Wilson, Don Troop is the first troop in the Regiment trained to move in "jock column" with a mobile infantry reserve, ready to deploy instantly using "crash action" to get the guns on target – now an accepted and well-developed system of deployment, its worth well-proven in the fluid battle conditions of North Africa.

To enhance Don Troop's effectiveness, innumerable positions have been reconnoitred, some to provide a good broad field for firing over open sights in an anti-tank role, and other hidden positions for their normal role of providing indirect fire on all points of the compass.

The whole section of coast for which 4th Field Regiment is responsible has been divided into targets, and the line, range, and angle of sight have been worked out by each troop command post for each target, thus making it easy for a FOO (forward observation officer) in an O Pip (observation post) to call down "fire for effect" without having to waste time ranging.

Four times a day, battery command post staffs are reminded their work is for real and not a training scheme when, with each meteor telegram, they receive a report on tides and weather along the coast, pointing out areas where conditions are most favourable for enemy invasion. Another sobering matter is the after-dark curfew for both soldiers and civilians that goes into effect each night all along the waterfront. Anyone moving on the beachfront after dark is to be challenged, and if he offers any resistance, he is to be shot.[*]

However, despite the seriousness of the times, now and then absurd incidents occur to challenge the earnest dignity that all men-at-arms tend to assume when standing-to in these grave and dangerous days.

One incident develops on the blackest of nights in a hillside underground garage for 14th Battery vehicles, which can be entered

---

[*] From 5:00 P.M. to 5:00 A.M. as laid down by Lieutenant-General Montgomery.

from a roadway at the top of the hill and exited onto a seafront road at the bottom of the hill. It seems only sensible to mount a guard here, and each night gunners, armed with rifles, patrol this inky dark hole. When, on the second night, infantrymen on patrol on bicycles decide to use this shortcut, they are stopped by clicking rifle bolts and a stern challenge from the gunner guards:

"Halt! Who goes there?"

"What do you mean, '*Who goes there?*'" replies an indignant voice from the dark. "Who are you?"

"Never mind who we are," retorts the gunner. "Who are you?"

"Look here," yells the infantryman, losing patience, "*who the hell are you?*"

"We are guards," replies the gunner haughtily, "and you are coming with us. We have loaded rifles pointed at you!"

"Well," says the infantryman, "*we* are guards, and *we* have loaded tommy-guns pointed at *you*!"

"Okay," says the gunner, "we'll go with you!"

Though things are quickly sorted out by an exchange of telephone calls between the guard room of the Royal Hamilton Light Infantry and the regimental headquarters of 4th Field, passwords will be in vogue from now on.

Because the guns cannot be taken "off line," and all personnel are either on duty or resting before going on duty, no training can be carried out. Billets are requisitioned houses devoid of all furniture, including beds, and being in most cases small, they are somewhat crowded. Morale, however, is high, all ranks believing they are engaged in a useful role, which at any hour could turn into something vital to the defence of freedom and democracy.

At first the people of Sussex are aloof and coldly polite, having been told that Canadians are nothing short of barbarians. Later, they will confess that at night they bolted their doors carefully, and the regimental war diary will record that "an old lady in Winchelsea, on hearing the Canadians were coming, bolted all windows and doors and got down a revolver she'd been saving for the invasion."

If the troops are aware of this, they don't let it bother them. They're so happy to be out of the dingy barracks of troop-crowded Aldershot, doing a job with an obvious point to it and living in small groups away from the spit-and-polish atmosphere of RHQ, to let anything depress them.

So from the very first they act like Canadians, without reference to guidebook etiquette – simply and naturally, without putting up a false front that some officers feel they must assume to get along over here. If a man likes to sing and be noisy as he drinks, he sings and is noisy as he drinks. If he is homesick, he says so, and tells the buxom woman behind the bar all about his wife and shows her pictures of his kids. Sometimes he's so frank as to be naive; at other times he is very blunt in his criticisms of England, the army, and himself. But always he is basically kind, and his criticisms are usually directed towards bettering the lot of the underdog, whether this happens to be himself or some vague class of Englishmen oppressed by an equally vague bunch of "dukes and lords." And in an unbelievably short time, the good people of Sussex become aware that they like these open-faced "Caw-nigh-dians" and their joy of living, and take them to their hearts and hearths, adopting them as sons, and some, as time goes on, as sons-in-law.

Perhaps the most interesting of the billets is Brick Wall House where regimental headquarters personnel reside at Northiam, some eight miles as the crow flies north of Hastings. It is a large and venerable house, parts of which were built in the seventeenth century. The brick wall that girdles the house and obviously gives it its odd name, is green with moss and lichen. Outside the wall is a park filled with great oak trees, among which deer can be seen in the early morning, moving along bridle paths cut through the ancient turf.

Although the house is devoid of all furniture except a grand piano, it takes little imagination to picture beautifully gowned, regally poised women moving about its splendid rooms with handsome escorts, some of them in dress uniform, beneath the great crystal chandeliers still hanging from the high, ornately moulded ceiling.

However, each night, as darkness descends in Brick Wall House, reality introduces a sour note, or, more accurately, an abundance of sour notes: rats – huge rats, dozens of rats – squealing and scuttling about in the gloom. It seems the house stood empty for some time before 4th Field came, and the rodents took possession and now are very reluctant to leave. In fact they never do leave, and in time soldiers and rats learn to tolerate the others' presence to an extraordinary degree.

By the end of July 1941, the threat of invasion has cooled off (Russia not having collapsed as expected), and orders that have kept guns in action and personnel in a permanent state of readiness are relaxed, allowing training to be started again.

The first scheme in which the Regiment takes part shows just how badly training has suffered from inactivity. Held in Ashdown Forest, it calls for a simple regimental deployment. Though orders are given to the battery commanders at 8:30 A.M., no battery is yet in position at noon!

One complete battery is lost through poor map-reading. One battery sends its cooks off to prepare a meal and then spends almost two hours looking for the cooks to get said meal. And when in a spirit of utter desperation the scheme is called off, a bevy of vehicles is discovered parked along the main street of Tunbridge Wells.

After six weeks, the Regiment moves in September to requisitioned houses along the Hog's Back at Runfold. Here, training begins again in earnest, for now both 2nd and 14th batteries get their 25-pounders – second-hand training guns for 2nd Battery and brand-new guns for the 14th. At first, only a few of the guns have dial-sights, making it necessary to put them on line with borrowed sights, and applying switches as necessary using zero-line markers and open sights.

Despite these obstacles, training begins to show results, and when a battery fire-and-movement exercise is held at Larkhill in September, the Regiment puts on a really good show, A Troop of 2nd Battery setting a regimental record by deploying their guns and getting a round on the ground three minutes after an infantry officer points out a target to their forward observation officer. Clearly, the skills of all ranks in the Regiment are beginning to gel.

But now a sense of uneasiness ripples through the unit as a general turnover begins of all the senior officers (except the Colonel) who came over with the Regiment. It is the first of an endless round of changes in the officers of the Regiment that will continue over the months and years ahead – mostly through promotions, but some through postings of older officers to less strenuous jobs at holding units or back to Canada on "adverse reports." So many officers will come and go that NCOs will come to believe the Regiment is being used as a training unit for officers, inciting Regimental Sgt.-Major A. C. Hanks (who himself will one day be posted to a less demanding job because of his age) to grumble, "Nothing but a damned game of musical chairs!"*

---

* The departures and changes began in January 1941, when Major Ted Beament, who had recruited 2nd Battery and brought it to England, left for a staff course that earmarked him for important postings which one day would lead to the distinguished level of Brigadier General Staff 1st Canadian Army in the final crucial operations in Northwest Europe. Now Major Medland left to take command of 1st Anti-Tank. Major Welsh went with him as his 2 IC. (Two and a half years later Welsh would be awarded the first DSO awarded a Canadian artillery officer in the Italian campaign, for gallant action during the taking of Leonforte, Sicily, the first of two DSOs he would earn – a feat duplicated by only one other Canadian artillery officer, another 4th Field original, McGregor Young.) Major Harris became 2 IC, and was replaced as CO of 26th Battery by Major William Fleury from 11th Army Field. Captains McGregor Young and E. W. Steuart-Jones were promoted, to command 14th and 2nd Batteries respectively. Capt. Harry Berry was promoted to major and left for 6th Field; Major Harris was again promoted, to command 11th Army Field Regiment; Major N. E. Smith joined 4RCA as 2 IC and Lieut. John Harrison was promoted to captain and appointed adjutant.

23

BACK TO THE COAST
AND HASTINGS

THE FIRST REALLY BIG SCHEME IN WHICH 4TH FIELD participates is called Exercise "Bumper." A quarter of a million men, most of them Brits, are involved for several days in a mock war ranging from the South Coast to Bedford, forty miles north of London.

Primarily designed to provide staff officers of two armies, four corps, and twelve divisions with experience in deploying and supplying large formations in mobile warfare, it also allows all ranks at the regimental level to sharpen their skills in convoy movement over roads cluttered with tanks, guns, marching troops, and trucks of all kinds – made more difficult by "umpires" denying formations the use of bridges designated "blown" by opposing strategists.

While the weather is benevolent, the whole thing becomes a bore for the gunners since they never engage in any actual firing. However, all ranks learn, shortly after the start of the manoeuvres, that feeding troops during a fast-moving campaign presents problems. Cooks lose track of the Regiment or vice versa for hours on end. Still, no one suffers much, for the brass neglected to declare tearooms and pubs out of bounds.

On returning to barracks, joy spreads among all ranks when they learn they are returning to the South Coast for a real tour of duty, not, as was the case the first time, a temporary tour just to relieve a

Limey division in need of training after being held on guard duty from Dunkirk days.

Unlike the last time, the guns will be available for training every day. With Germany more preoccupied than ever with Russia, the only possibility of enemy action along here now, in mid-October, would be a night raid. And so guns are put on line in their pits only at night. Only half the Regiment is confined to barracks, and a single OP per battery is manned round the clock by officers taking turns.

Troop deployment competitions, started at Runfold, are intensified, and this pays dividends when Charley Troop of 14th Battery, with GPO Lieut. Lloyd Fromow in charge, wins top honours in a competition in which all eighteen troops of 2nd Division are judged by Larkhill IGs on the basis of speed, accuracy, and correctness of drill.

No one relishes this achievement more than 14th Battery Commander Major "Mac" McGregor Young, who remembers his own troop's first fumbling attempt at crash action, improvised overnight at the request of Worthington, a year ago at Camp Borden, Ontario.

Now arriving at the Regiment one or two at a time, (like the dial-sights for the guns) with weeks between deliveries, are lightly armoured tracked vehicles. Officially called Universal Carriers Mark II, they will continue to be known by most soldiers as Bren Gun Carriers in deference to the original purpose of the first models of these squat, steel boxes on tracks – to provide transport for infantry Bren gunners while offering them some protection from small-arms fire and shell fragments as they go into the attack.

Someone at a high level of command, after watching one of these low-profiled vehicles rock and dip across rough terrain at the brisk pace of more than thirty miles an hour, concluded that this would be the ideal conveyance for FOOs and their crews, readily accommodating the troop commander and his driver-ack riding in the uncluttered front cockpit, and two signaller-acks riding, surrounded by a great clutter of equipment in the rear compartments, one on each side of the engine amidships.

A few new portable radio transmitter-receivers are also taken on strength. They are back-packing 18-sets, which will allow FOOs, when they must leave their carriers hidden and proceed forward on foot to gain better observation of the enemy zone, to still have communication with their carrier and thus the guns.

IGs from the Larkhill School of Artillery now start showing up at batteries to assess levels of training, offer advice on new developments, and conduct courses in all aspects of modern gunnery procedures, including signal procedures, command post procedures, and gun drill. The presence of the IGs makes everybody a bit uneasy, especially the officers, for IG reports can make or break an officer or NCO.

Acks, however, seek their advice hungrily, regardless of their seniority – from battery command-post sergeants down to acks without stripes (into which category most of them fall). Acks are aware that the more they know about their jobs, the more there is to know. Though battery command-post officers and gun position officers supervise the work of their acks, and take responsibility for every fire-order they issue to their guns, the acks actually *do* the technical work, including the production under pressure of supremely accurate and complicated gun programs for creeping barrages with many timed-lifts. Thus their continuing desire to equip themselves with whatever information they can gain from these highly experienced men from Larkhill who seem to have the answer to every problem.

In November – two years and two months after mobilizing – 4th Field fires their new 25-pounders for the first time. This event occurs on a newly opened artillery range with a postage-stamp target area of just five hundred yards square, about five miles northeast of Seaford on the rolling gorse-covered hills known as the South Downs, near the charming ancient village of Alfriston that will lend its name to the range.

Early in December, 2nd Battery joins regimental headquarters at Burwash about twenty miles north of Hastings, to become a mobile reserve replacing the one-troop arrangement previously taken care of by Capt. Don Wilson's troop. Seven miles now separate the troops billeted in large houses, the more striking being Southover Hall, housing B Troop and battery HQ. The Sergeant-Major draws a bedroom with bathroom ensuite, its ceiling and walls covered with mirrors. In the face of such ostentatious luxury, the officers' mess garden, with its fishpond, replete with goldfish, is hardly worth mentioning.

The weather is particularly wet, even for bally old England, and fields where deployments are practised are exceptionally soggy. So many complaints come from farmers about ruts in their mowing meadows, troops are forced to improvise, and they discover that 25-pounders, with their wonderful attached gun-platforms negating the need for trail-spades to dig-in, can be deployed quite satisfactorily along the verges of roads, and on the roads themselves if necessary.

After December 7 everyone is talking about the attack by Japanese bombers on an American naval base at some place in the Pacific called Pearl Harbor. At last the reluctant Yanks have been forced into the war. But at what cost! Much of their Pacific fleet was destroyed.*

With the coming of the Christmas season, 4th Field is able to reciprocate in a small way for the continuing hospitality of the people of Sussex. Batteries hold parties for the children in their areas, providing some form of entertainment, an abundance of

---

* A total of 2,334 American servicemen were killed and another 1,347 wounded. U.S. ships sunk were four battleships, one mine-layer, and a target ship. Seriously damaged were four more battleships, three light cruisers, three destroyers, a seaplane tender, and a repair ship. Also destroyed were 92 navy planes and 96 army planes. The Japanese lost only 28 aircraft and fewer than 100 men.

candy (much of it contributed from parcels from home), and a gift for each child (either purchased here or sent from Canada), all of which is handed out by a white-whiskered, genial old chap in a red suit. In all some five hundred kids are so entertained. And on the Sunday before Christmas, the famous play company of St. Martin-in-the-Fields church on Trafalgar Square in London is brought down to Hastings by the padre to put on a performance of its Nativity play for the Regiment. Some intrepid gunners, along with a few residents of Hastings, succumb to a request for volunteers to thicken up the crowd scenes on stage.

On January 18, 1942, Lieutenant-Colonel Lloyd leaves 4th Field to take over a training wing of the reinforcement depot at Bordon, Hants. The war diary makes note of the fact he has seen the Regiment through its most difficult period of recruitment and training, and is leaving behind a well-knit unit.[*] However, when Lt.-Col. P. A. Stanley Todd (brigade major at 2nd Division Artillery Headquarters) assumes command, he discovers a shortage of trained signallers, and immediately arranges for many men to be sent on course. This turns out to be the start of a three-point training plan introduced by the new CO to address perceived deficiencies in "signalling, discipline, and anti-tank shooting."

---

[*] A veteran of the Great War, Lloyd had become a medical doctor on returning to Canada, but went back to soldiering when World War II broke out in 1939.

24

TOWARDS BECOMING THE BEST

---- ✳ ----

A TRULY SPECIAL ERA, WHICH WILL ALWAYS BE REFERRED TO with a tinge of nostalgia as "when we were at Hastings," comes to an end on April 30, 1942, when the Regiment moves to Possing-worth and then to Green Street, near Horsham. Only now do officers and men fully realize how much they have been made to feel at home by the people of Hastings, and the degree of affection this has engendered in them for the town.

During these months here, the men of 4th Field have become part of England, taking on the habits and tastes of the people among whom they have been living – sharing their experiences, tightening their belts for "total war," and learning to live with increasingly strict rationing as U-boat sinkings of Allied shipping in the North Atlantic become more and more serious. For the first time in their lives, the men of 4th Field learn the value of a "real egg," as opposed to the crumbly, dried variety. And some gunners discover that even the lowly onion can be a prized possession, when they are ordered to pay compensation of "three ha'pennies" each for onions "borrowed" from the nearby garden of an Englishman who complained to their troop commander that when he counted his that morning he found only fifty-seven where there should have been seventy-six.

Memories of happy times in friendly off-duty spots* loom so large in everyone's recall there is a danger these weeks at Hastings will be written off as simply a time of pleasant pursuits. But in a very real sense, 4th Field grew up in this picturesque town. All have been treated so well by the civilian population, morale in the unit has shot up, a new enthusiasm for training has taken hold, and a new pride in themselves and the Regiment has developed.

Though strict restrictions on petrol consumption have appeared in orders, and certain days are now set aside as "vehicle holidays," when no vehicle can be moved without permission, "crash actions" have been raised to an art form by 4th Field troops practising deployments in nearby farmers' fields every chance they get. The interest in crash actions is consistent with the current emphasis on using single troops as separate fire units. (Thought is even being given to leapfrogging the right and left two-gun "sections" of a troop.)

Still, regimental training is not totally neglected. In March, 2nd Division artillery regiments – 4th, 5th, and 6th Field – are ordered to Sennybridge Camp in mid-Wales for a week of shooting.

At this vast camp in the Welsh mountains continually swept with dramatic, black clouds roiling in from the Irish Sea, dropping water or ice pellets on guns and gunners when they are not enshrouding them with fog, OP officers (captains) are allowed periodically to practise ranging guns on targets, and subalterns at the gun positions to conduct technical shoots, including "predicted" smokescreens, airburst ranging, and chemical shoots using tear-gas shells. Gun crews get the chance to fire over open sights at moving burlap tanks, and of course everyone is very much involved in the frantic moves and deployments during battery fire and movement and regimental fire and movement.

While rain, fog, hail, and snow flurries succeed in inhibiting perfect shooting, the Regiment is deemed to have done quite well

---

* Peggy's Teashop, The Cave, Queens' Bar, Crown and Thistle, Six Bells, The Red Lion.

by the IGs, who are always in attendance in OPs, and by Ack IGs, who haunt the gun positions, making notes of criticisms for delivery to the officers of the Regiment assembled for that purpose each night before dinner.

Beyond the weather, the most detested feature of Sennybridge, as far as the gunners are concerned, is the road-building detail which camp authorities require each time a regiment turns up for a week of shooting. A detail of a hundred men and an officer is made responsible for building a stretch of road across the barren hills, regardless of weather conditions.*

Infantry officers and sergeants, on loan to the Regiment, conduct classes in small-arms training, including the correct way to arm and throw grenades, and how to handle the recently issued "sticky bomb," an ingenious invention, consisting of a yellow ball of explosive, encased in a gummy substance resembling pitch, contained within a glass beakerlike ball until someone chooses to smash it against the side of an enemy tank, where it will stick and blow a hole.

And all the while the "paper war" continues. Arriving in rapid succession are several amendments to instructions on how an anti-gas cape should be folded, rolled, and held in place by its tapes above the shoulder-pack of each man. (Is it possible the brass are unaware how extensively these oilskin capes are used as slickers to enshroud the water-absorbent greatcoats of men huddled at the guns in drenching rain during schemes and all-day shoots?)

Possingworth is not, by any standard, a "good go." Living in mouldering tents pitched under trees, on ground always wet and muddy, with no running water until the Regiment lays a pipeline, is not conducive to high morale. Fortunately, the stay is only two weeks.

---

* So extensive was the road-building conducted by Canadians, it would be memorialized in the name "Canada Corner" given to one of the principal crossroads on postwar maps of Sennybridge ranges.

Next stop is Green Street, near Horsham, again under canvass among trees for almost three months, but a drier more wholesome camp. Here, in the early summer of 1942, rumours that invasion of the continent is imminent hit something of a peak with the "Cages at Croyden" myth, believed by everyone in the Regiment with the possible exception of the Colonel. According to the rumour, "the cages" are places where a regiment drives in at one end with their old equipment, and drives out the other end with brand-new stuff, ready to proceed onto the boats bound for France and "action."

Whether it is the thought of getting into action, or simply that training has peaked, an exhibition of fire and movement put on at Larkhill during the first week of June earns the Regiment the reputation of being "the best field artillery regiment in Britain."

Carried out under the critical eyes of officers from the War Office sent to Larkhill to judge the current level of training of artillery regiments in Britain, the display takes the form of battery fire and movement for the first few days, each battery deploying in three or four positions as quickly as possible and getting off a few rounds from each.

Then comes the final show: "regimental fire and movement."

Everyone is keyed up for this, the most enjoyable and demanding form of training, and they push their trucks and quads to the limit over rolling Salisbury Plain with guns bouncing wildly behind them. At such breakneck speed, errors are almost inevitable, and one ranging round lands on the rising ground behind where Commanding Officer Todd has chosen to observe proceedings, bringing forth, over the full wireless network, the memorable comment, "That round landed twenty yards from my ass! Add 1,000! Repeat!" But with the emphasis on speed, this one error is not considered serious enough to alter the judges' opinion that this regiment is good – in fact, the best.

When the Regiment returns to Green Street, the Colonel declares next day, June 9, Todd's Holiday, "when no man shall have any duties of any sort whatsoever." Most take him at his word, but when meal times come around, to the relief of all, especially those who haven't recently received parcels of goodies from home, some cooks, with admirable judgement and a highly developed sense of duty, have remained on the job.

Not surprisingly, during a couple of minor schemes, a certain degree of slackness begins to show up in the unit as smugness at being "the best" is relished by all ranks.* By July 28 this slackness has settled in to the point where the Colonel decides the subalterns are to blame and must be sharpened up. This is hardly unusual, but the procedure invoked to improve matters certainly is (some blame the idea on Adjutant John Harrison): all subalterns must take gun drill under Larkhill IG Major H. S. Borton. Resentment is so high at what they consider an indignity, that when the officers' mess burns down, there is some suspicion it was arson.

And when shortly thereafter, to counter boredom and lethargy, perceived to be threatening to take over the unit, Captain Harrison exhorts the subalterns to devise make-work projects – "If you haven't anything else to do, round up ten men and a bombardier and dig a ditch!" – they threaten to take him at his word and trench the whole camp from beginning to end. Fortunately, as with all ambitious schemes concocted late at night after many trips to the bar, the threats are not carried to fruition.

---

* During this period, 26th Battery gets a new commander, Major Don Cooper, replacing Major Fleury, who leaves to become 2 IC of 6th Field.

PART THREE: JUNE 1941–

JUNE 1942

Producing Trainloads of Reinforcements

25

REINFORCEMENTS

———————————————— ✳ ————————————————

WHILE THE MEN WHO ENLISTED IN SEPTEMBER 1939 WILL remain the core of the Regiment, the regional character of batteries is changing as a remarkable number of officers and Other Ranks are replaced by what they call "reinforcements" from all parts of the Dominion – from Nova Scotia to British Columbia, and even a smattering of Americans who come up to Canada to enlist. Of course the turnover is most noticeable among the officers, who are vulnerable to postings-out to other units through promotions based on artillery seniority lists kept by division and by corps.[*]

Replacement of captains and up is usually by promotion from other units. But reinforcement subalterns and gunners are largely the products of the two artillery training camps in Canada – Peta-wawa, in Ontario, and Shilo, in Manitoba. The two camps have grown into huge, all-season facilities offering well-organized courses for officers and gunners, turning out reinforcements in numbers equivalent to several regiments each year.

And since June 1941, Officers' Training Centres at Brockville and Gordon Head, near Victoria, B.C., have ensured a supply of junior officers by providing the first three months of basic training and physical hardening for officer cadets from all branches of the

———————

[*] By September 1942, only seven of the original officers were still with the Regiment.

army.* After one month of "common-to-all-arms" training, the cadets are split up into their specialized training courses as infantry, engineers, artillery, and so on. On passing their exams at the end of another two months, they are awarded commissions and allowed to put up one "pip" on their epaulettes, signifying "second lieutenant." They are then sent on to their respective training camps. For gunner officers, it's Petawawa in the East and Shilo in the West.

Until training was formalized at Brockville and Petawawa, junior officers who had not benefited from training at Royal Military College gained their knowledge in a hit-and-miss fashion – as much from their own initiative in studying pamphlets issued by the British War Office as from the loosely structured courses set up by their units.

Lieut. S. G. M. "Sammy" Grange, who joined 2nd Battery on July 21, 1941, in England, passed through the old Canadian system (if it can be called that) before Brockville OTC came into being and when Petawawa Camp was still in the midst of its growing pains. To illustrate the unique way some training was organized at the time, he tells how, after completing the course for officers at Petawawa (A-1 RCA Training Centre), he was given the job of instructing gunners how to drive and maintain trucks, though he himself had never received any instruction whatsoever in the subject – in fact, had never learned to drive a car, let alone a truck. Still, the appointment may have been admirably suited to the situation as it then existed, and certainly didn't prove as embarrassing as it might have, had there been any trucks available for instructional purposes. As it was, unencumbered by trucks, he was able to parade before his students a torrent of impressive facts (culled from an unusually fulsome army pamphlet), and, using pantomime, illustrate

---

* Early in 1942, a special French-speaking wing was opened at Brockville OTC. And in September 1943, Gordon Head was closed down, and all basic officer training was at Brockville.

the technique of changing gears – double-clutching and steering a monster vehicle with great flourish – while seated on a folding chair at the front of the classroom.

(Actually, Grange's lack of driving experience was eventually turned to advantage when, sent on a course to learn to drive a tank in England – when it looked as though tanks might become the normal vehicles for forward observation officers – the tank instructor offered him this advice: "The only way to learn how to drive a tank successfully is to forget everything you've ever learned about driving wheeled vehicles." Thus, Lieutenant Grange learned to drive a tank before he learned to drive a car. And among those who have risked driving with him, there are some who claim it shows.)

Whether or not this remarkable story ever reached the ears of those planning the training of junior officers, from the outset at Brockville OTC considerable emphasis has been placed on teaching officer cadets to drive trucks. And now the piercing sounds of scraping and clashing gears can be heard from the vehicle compound at any hour of the day as novice drivers learn to "gear up" and "gear down" their big, sluggish vehicles – most particularly those cadets who go on failing their driving tests day after day, not knowing they should be taking their tests in a Chevy truck, where the gas pedal (crucial to double-clutching), is sensibly placed on the floor, not suspended from above and skittishly sensitive to a hobnailed boot, as in a Ford truck.

If previously the training was sparse and confined to bare essentials, now everything the Commandant, Col. R. G. Whitelaw, thinks might conceivably be useful or beneficial to the moulding of a junior officer is packed into a three-month course, including learning to pot clay pigeons with a shotgun in the off chance you may one day be invited by the British gentry to do some grouse-shooting in Scotland. The day begins with bayonet drill and PT before breakfast, carrying on through foot drill at 140 paces to the minute, to periods of small-arms training, infantry tactics, gun drill, lectures and written examinations on gunnery, and regular ten-mile route marches. After supper there are driving lessons, track-and-field trials, voice-control discipline, and the aforementioned skeet-shooting. Then, as technical courses in gunnery become more sophisticated, there is enough homework to occupy you until lights out.

And overlaying the whole highly compressed mixture of physical and mental testing, and the demanding, hour-to-hour training schedules that begin before dawn with a roll call starting precisely as the last note of the reveille bugle ends, is the taut personality of the Commandant, spreading anxiety and tension of the kind that must have pervaded the quarterdeck of HMS *Bounty*. His speech at Sunday church parade (August 3, 1941), the day after you arrive, setting the tone for your three-month stay, would have warmed Captain Bligh's heart.

When your group of newly arrived cadets is told to stand fast while the parade marches off, it is clear you are to be recognized with a few perfunctory remarks from a red-faced man with chubby, sunburned knees, who appears at the microphone on the far side of the square. Though dressed like everybody else, in khaki denim shorts and woollen puttees, he is readily identifiable as "The Colonel" by virtue of the red tabs on the collar of his shirt and two spotted coach-dogs hovering near him. (You weren't in camp an hour, yesterday, before you were told that, fortunately for all concerned, the Colonel's unexpected arrivals around the corners of buildings will always be announced by those dogs preceding him.) While all of you realize a welcoming address by the CO is only fitting, you hope he'll keep it short, for you already have been too long standing in the blazing sun and the simmering heat rising from the rolled gravel. But every last hobnailed boot has to crunch off around the corner of an H-hut, before a snarling voice comes through the loudspeakers:

"Most of you come here with little or no training of consequence, and this applies not only to military matters, but in the matter of manners and conduct becoming a gentleman in polite company.

"I have no right to expect that you are any better than those who

have preceded you, and most of them have arrived here with manners and social graces no better than those of pigs. But before you
leave here, you will have learned to conduct yourself as an officer
and gentleman, fit to be accepted as a guest in an English gentleman's
home, or you shall not leave here as an officer.

"And a start will be made immediately to teach you correct table
manners. I have issued instructions that tablecloths in mess halls will
not be changed for laundering more than once a week. Therefore,
any cadet who drops anything on the tablecloth at his place will be
relegated to another table set aside for sloppy eaters, which will be
known as 'The Pig Table,' where he will remain until he is judged
fit to return to eat with civilized people at his regular place. To
ensure this is strictly enforced, your name has been pasted on the
back of your chair, and after each meal a staff officer will check each
tablecloth."

When one of the cadets, overcome by the sun, collapses in a dead
faint with his face in the gravel, and a couple of nearby cadets bend
over him in concern, the voice in the loudspeaker quickly brings
them upright with the snarling order, "Leave him lie! Leave him
lie! Just cover his head!"

And the lecture continues, on and on, point by point. He explains
that a spot on the tablecloth beside your plate will not only send
you to the "pig table," but will constitute a black mark on your
record. And that other black marks will be earned by failing a test
of any kind – written exams, physical-agility tests, or endurance
tests, such as dropping out of a regular ten-mile route march or
failing for any reason whatsoever to complete a four-day exercise
of marching and skirmishing covering some eighty miles just before
graduation. And of course, such simple things as being late for
parade, leaving your bed or kit untidy, or being deficient in dress
or personal maintenance on or off parade, will automatically mean
more black marks.

He concludes his talk with the chilling thought that any cadet
unfortunate enough to accumulate three black marks will be returned forthwith to his unit as "unsuitable officer material," and

you are all left wondering how on earth anyone can expect to survive such an obstacle course.

It is reasonably certain that no cadet could ever make it through the hazards of Brockville OTC without the advice and watchful guidance of the training staff, including the sergeants. These conscientious men, each of them determined to bring their squad of cadets to a high level of competence in their specialty, often seem as much the leaders of a general conspiracy to outwit the outer limits of the Commandant's policies, as they are the guardians of high standards of training.

The best example of their concern would be the advice given to each cadet invited for his one and only mess dinner with the Colonel in the staff-officers' mess. Each cadet is the guest of a member of the training staff, and the night before the dinner, the staff officer visits his guest to warn of the pitfalls that lie in the path of the unwary, and to offer advice on conduct that could please the Colonel while avoiding those things that could earn a black mark. Under no condition, for instance, must you take your fork in your right hand, the Colonel being of the opinion that the best English etiquette calls for the fork to be always in the left hand and the knife in the right hand. He cannot abide what he calls "fork shifters," and at these mess dinners he always makes sure that green peas are served. Therefore, if you have not learned to eat peas with your fork in your left hand, it would be best to leave them on your plate as though you don't like peas.

Needless to say, knocking over your water glass or wine glass, or spilling the gravy or your coffee, would be a social disaster. But you must be sure that you don't go through the meal just concentrating on not making a goof; the Colonel insists that members of his mess and their guests engage in "animated conversation" with their neighbours throughout dinner. And because of the heavy pressures that must devolve on those three or four who draw the seats immediately opposite or on each side of the Colonel at his place halfway along the very long mess table, you should ensure that you join the lineup proceeding from the ante-room into the dining room in such a way as to end up as far away as possible, preferably one end of the table or the other.

But perhaps the worst hazard of the night will be the "passing of the port." The Colonel loves a game, and the passing of two decanters of port, one on each side of the table, starting together at one end and racing to see which one will arrive first at the other end of the table, delights him – particularly if the decanter passing along on his side of the table wins, since he inevitably places a small wager with the cadet sitting directly opposite him. Needless to say, you must be prepared to feel the pressure.

Receiving a heavy, tall, crystal decanter from the person on your right in a rush, tipping it over a spindly wine glass and filling it without spilling a drop, then passing it on to the next person on your left as quickly as possible, opens up all sorts of possibilities for accidents. But your adviser suggests you don't contemplate substituting caution for speed; merely going through the motions would be noted and considered bad form by the Colonel and might earn you a black mark.

In some ways the affair turns out to be worse than you imagined. Even before going in to dinner, the tension is raised to the cracking point as far as you are concerned when the Colonel draws the full attention of everyone in the ante-room to your particular host, a most pleasant, erudite, highly cultured gentleman from Quebec City.

You and he are sitting together on a chesterfield at the far end of the room quietly talking. He's just poured out the last of a quart of beer you are sharing, and has placed the empty bottle down on the floor at the end of the chesterfield – there being no coffee-table or end-table anywhere nearby – when over the hum of conversation filling the room, comes a snarling roar bringing the room to an embarrassing silence: "Pick up that bottle! Where do you think you are – at home?"

The whole thing disturbs you and your host so much that, a few minutes later, when joining the lineup going in to the dining room, you both forget to calculate the right position to place you at the far end of the table, and you end up almost directly opposite the Colonel.

But thanks to your host, who has a marvellous ability to converse about nothing, and the Colonel, who prefers speaking to listening, it never becomes obvious that you are contributing nothing in the way of "animated conversation."

You'll not remember a single word uttered at the table by anyone. But you'll retain forever the image of all those plates going back to the kitchen adorned by mounds of green peas. And the astonishing weight of that damned big decanter, so heavy you almost drop it as you try to pour with one hand while steadying your glass with the other.

At last it is over, and you gratefully retire to the ante-room, where you intend to relax. But no sooner are you there, settled on your chesterfield, than another instructor, the inevitable mess piano player, comes over and recruits you and some others for a sing-song, informing you quietly, "The Colonel likes to see the officers gathered around the piano, singing and enjoying themselves."

"Dizzy" Dean, one of the staff instructors, tells you that one day, when he was orderly officer, he received a telegram from a family doctor requesting compassionate leave for one of the cadets, whose mother was dying. The Colonel wrote a big "NO" across the telegram, and, handing it back to Dean, asked rhetorically, "What possible military information can a man pick up watching his mother die?"

The fear of failing – not just failing the course, but failing to measure up in the smallest way – overlays life in the camp and breeds a ferocious determination in every cadet, that come hell or high-water, he'll not be beaten!

The feeling that there is an unforgiving tribunal, watching over your every move, is so ingrained after a few weeks, it causes the death of Cadet Joseph E. Messick. He'd complained of severe stomach cramps the morning he was to graduate, and his fellow classmen tried to get him to report to the medical officer. But he was determined to go through the final "marching-out parade," afraid they might still find an excuse to fail him. And he made it through the whole, long, tedious business of ceremonial drill, including the final, strenuous "slow march" to "Auld Lang Syne" off the parade square, before collapsing among the cheering cadets as they are broken off. He died two days later from peritonitis from a burst appendix, which, the MO reported, had burst long before he'd gone on parade.

On August 29, 1941, the final night of your common-to-all-arms course (the night before you are to be married), there's an all-night scheme involving among other things a compass march by syndicates: so many hundred yards on this bearing, and so many on that, hither and yon across cow pastures, creeks and swamps, to reach a rendezvous around midnight where each of you is given a pick and shovel and told to dig a weapon pit. This done, the whole course falls in as a troop on the road and marches ten miles back to camp, arriving just as the sun is rising.

It being Saturday you are only kept on parade in the morning. For your wedding and honeymoon you've been allowed leave from noon until reveille at dawn Monday. There being no public transportation to get you to Ottawa in time for the wedding scheduled for 3:00 P.M., you have to hitch a ride, still wearing the same battledress you wore last night.

You arrive at St. Matthew's Church with five minutes to spare to await the arrival of your bride, who has been up most of the night helping her family get their new house ready for the reception – having moved only yesterday from another house to accommodate its new owners who otherwise would have been out on the street. *C'est la guerre!*

26

THE GOSPEL ACCORDING

TO LARKHILL

✳

LIKE ALL "ONE-PIPPERS" ARRIVING AT PETAWAWA FRESH FROM Brockville, which was strong on physical conditioning and light on the technical-training side, you are, at the outset of the course, snowed-under and bewildered by the amount and complexity of the data on gunnery, ballistics, maintenance of equipment, and artillery tactics thrown at you by instructors.

And when you try to find the answer to a vexing question, the stacks of pamphlets, obviously meant to clarify technical matters, cluttering your tiny desk in the room you share with another trainee, usually have the opposite effect. If not written in a foreign language, some of them might as well be. Very ordinary words are used in a syntax foreign to your experience, and even where definitions are provided as a foreword to a subject such as "airburst ranging," they can be confusing:

"Quadrant elevation – The angle between the horizontal plane and the breech clinometer plane, measured before firing."

"Tangent elevation – The angle between the line of sight and the breech clinometer plane, measured before firing."

"Angle of departure – the angle between the horizontal plane and the direction of flight of the shell as it leaves the muzzle."

"Angle of projection – The angle between the line of sight and the direction of flight of the shell as it leaves the muzzle."

If your sanity has remained intact during the first weeks here, it's only because of one Sgt.-Major "Dusty" Miller, an instructor in gunnery at A-1 Training Wing, who daily assures all of you that if you just take it one day at a time and don't worry about trying to relate the lessons learned today with the principles you learned yesterday, suddenly, at some point down the road, all the parts of the jigsaw will come together in a completely understandable arrangement.

Dusty downgrades most of the pamphlets, referring to them as "so much War Office bumpf" that you'll seldom if ever refer to again after the course ends. He does, however, recommend you give full attention and study to the one entitled "Artillery Training, Volume II, 1934," which he refers to as "The Gospel According to Larkhill," the full significance of which you'll not understand until you arrive in England and come in contact for the first time with an apostle from Larkhill, the exalted home of the British School of Artillery.

There are several excellent instructors at A-1, each of them an obvious specialist in his field, but only Dusty qualifies as an unforgettable character, representing the very heart and soul of artillery. A sergeant-major of the permanent force (as the regular forces were known between the wars), he is a veritable walking encyclopedia of guns, gunnery, ballistics, and entertaining artillery lore. His lectures are always presented in the light-hearted, offhand manner you tend to associate with a man who is completely sure of himself and his subject. And lending tremendous authenticity to his unlimited store of anecdotes, on the development of artillery pieces and their tactical use, is his unique appearance. Black hair parted in the middle, arching over each of his laughing, blue eyes, and a long, black, carefully groomed moustache, sweeping across his face and curling up along his cheekbones, combine to give the impression (in spite of his modern battledress) that he has just stepped out of the sepia pages of an old issue of *London Illustrated* recalling the Boer War, or the Northwest Frontier of India at the turn of the century.

You find yourself looking forward to his lectures as you have never looked forward to classroom instruction before. Even on a subject requiring the most serious attention and concentration, he rarely allows more than a few minutes to elapse without tossing in a crazy, offhand remark or offering a ridiculous illustration. These, of course, incite roaring, convulsive laughter, which must on occasion bewilder the visiting civilian dignitaries from Ottawa, who seem to be forever floating around these days, poking their heads in gunsheds and dropping in at the back of lecture halls, wearing the fixed and serious expressions men wear when they want you to believe they know what's going on.

To Dusty, no subject connected with gunnery is so dull, no problem so tedious, no concept so complex or esoteric that it can't be reduced to simple understandable components with vulgar new labels so appropriate they seem to have been concocted on the spot – driving home the salient point with a risqué one-liner as pungent with meaning as it is hilarious.

Characteristically, one morning early in the course, he claims to teach the class in less than one minute all the technical knowledge required of artillery officers from the invention of gunpowder until guns ceased engaging the enemy by open sights at the beginning of the 1914–18 war, when, striking a Napoleonic pose, he barks out orders to an imaginary battery lined up at Waterloo: "Take post – target enemy attacking – range one thousand yards – fire when ready – see you Tuesday."

However, he warns, it could take an hour or two to teach you all you need to know to point guns in the right direction with the proper elevation to hit a target many miles away out of sight – the fundamental problem confronting every gun position officer every time his guns are dropped helter-skelter in a field here, and he is expected to loop some shells onto a target spotted by a FOO (forward observation officer) beyond the horizon over there.

The key, of course, is a military map over-printed with a "grid," consisting of vertical lines (a thousand yards apart) pointing to "grid north," numbered from left to right (west to east), and horizontal lines (a thousand yards apart) numbered from the bottom to the top (south to north), which allows you to read off a precise map reference for any identifiable point on the ground. Thus, when you mark on the map the position of your "pivot gun" (the right-hand gun of a troop of four guns) and the position of the target (the map reference supplied by a FOO), you are able to measure the "range" in yards from gun to target, and to establish the precise direction to the target in relation to "grid north."

Now, if the actual barrel of your pivot gun could in some way be oriented to "grid north," it would be possible to get it pointed along that same bearing to the target. The answer, of course, is your artillery "director," a survey instrument set up on a tripod out in front of the guns before they arrive.

Using the instrument's own built-in compass (adjusted to show grid north when its magnetic needle points magnetic north), the instrument is oriented and locked-in on a distant aiming-point, so that, when the guns arrive, you can sight it on each of their "dial-sights" and pass precise reverse bearings to "put them on line" – bringing their barrels parallel to a "zero line" (a designated bearing running through the middle of the target-zone along the axis of advance). Then, when each gun-layer locks his dial-sight on a distant aiming-point, guns can be "switched" so many degrees right of the zero line to a target, or so many degrees left of zero line to another target.

Ranges and switches to new targets could continue to be measured to targets plotted on a gridded map, but obviously this would result in a confusing clutter of lines and dots mixed in with, and disappearing among, the normal clutter of details printed on all maps. So the "artillery board" was born. This is simply a drawing board to carry a blank sheet of gridded paper – the vertical and the horizontal lines of which can be numbered to duplicate the numbering of the vertical and horizontal grid lines of the map – and an arm and arc to simplify measuring switches from zero line and yards to targets.*

And so, in a painless fashion – almost without knowing it, thanks to Dusty – concepts are absorbed and the language of gunnery becomes second nature as you pass endless tests, leading up to conducting an actual shoot with live ammunition, on the road from "One-Pip Wonder" to "First Looie" entitled to two pips on your epaulettes.

During the fall and winter of 1941–42, the only shells available in Petawawa for practice shoots are shrapnel shells left over from the last war. And these are used sparingly, for the grassed-over ammunition bunkers are fast emptying, and no new shells are arriving.†

"Shrapnel" is probably the most misused word in the language – so consistently misused that even gunners, who should know better, often surrender to common usage and refer to any fragment of a bursting high-explosive shell as "shrapnel." But in Petawawa in 1941, they truly are shrapnel shells, which, according to Dusty, are named after one Lt.-Gen. Henry Shrapnel of the Royal Artillery, who invented the shell some time around the siege of Dunkerque in 1783, while serving with the Duke of York's army in Flanders, and for which he received a handsome government pension as royalty in addition to his pay.

The shrapnel shell, instead of being filled with high explosive, is filled with lead pellets the size of marbles, with an explosive-charge

---

* See Appendix E.

† The supply of shrapnel shells by then must have been meagre, for seven years before, in May 1935, Gen. Andy McNaughton reported in a secret paper circulated among cabinet ministers: "The stocks of field ammunition on hand represent 90 minutes' firing at normal rates for the field guns inherited from the Great War and which are now obsolescent." In 1937 new batteries, formed by the 1936 expansion, were allotted no ammunition whatsoever, and instructing officers at summer camp found themselves teaching the principles of "bracketing" targets by tossing pebbles at a tin can floating in the Petawawa River.

in behind them in the base of the shell to blow them out the nose in a shower when it arrives above the heads of the enemy.

Rumour has it, the British continued long after the Great War's end to turn out tons of 18-pounder shrapnel shells simply because no one thought to shut down production, which accounts for supplies still extant here in Petawawa. Though shrapnel shells are designed to be exploded by time-fuse high above the ground, these Petawawa shells are allowed to strike the ground and explode in the target area so that normal ranging can be practised. And while these explosions are pale imitations of the cataclasmic bursts of real high-explosive shells, they allow officers to gain experience ranging on targets, while giving gunners the chance to participate in an actual shoot.

During "course shoots" – when all jobs at the OP (observation post) directing the shoot and at the gun position are conducted entirely by the officers in training – you gain a variety of experience, not only laying and firing the guns, but filling one of the GPO ack (assistant) positions, normally filled by highly skilled Other Ranks trained as surveyors and equipped to carry out, under supervision, all the technical work required to point guns in the right direction to loop shells precisely onto targets. And as you function as an ack, you participate in matters that can only be learned and practised during actual deployment and firing of guns.

You quickly learn that a GPO (gun position officer) must never cease following on his map his progress across the landscape. He must know at all times, within twenty-five yards (the permissable length and breadth of error allowed a gun), precisely where he is on the globe, so that when his pivot gun drops its trail at the marker he has planted, he can immediately provide an eight-figure map reference to his ack to plot on his artillery board. And this keeping track of where he is on the map calls for intense concentration during both reconnaissance and deployment as he directs his driver here and there along a confusing network of tracks over the ranges to an allotted area. A serious error here in map-reading and the precision of subsequent calculations will be for nothing.

You'll eventually have to accommodate the arrival in succession of "regimental grid," "divisional grid," and "corps grid," each fixing the line and position of your guns more accurately until the ultimate grid, "theatre grid," brings all the guns in the theatre of operations into alignment with each other to an accuracy possible only when the source of the survey is a bronze benchmark imbedded in rock on a hill by the topographical service of the country in which you are operating.

Instructors constantly checking your work never cease impressing on you that accuracy is paramount in the world of the gunner – that some day there will be men out there pinned down, waiting for your shells to neutralize the enemy fire, or following close behind your barrage, trusting your shells will continue landing just in front of them as they follow the advice of their leaders to "lean into the barrage and get to the enemy before he can get his head up again."

And while there are no infantrymen to worry about during these training shoots, everyone is conscious that the Trans-Canada Highway runs right through the camp, cutting it in two; and though the ranges cover a hundred square miles, target areas are never far from civilian habitations. So when you are required to work as an ack at the Troop Command Post artillery board, you find yourself panting and the palms of your hands sweating as you plot your pivot gun and targets with a needle-sharp pencil, reading off ranges and switches from zero line with great care. And when gun-laying, you see to it that all the bubbles are precisely level and the cross-hairs in your dial-sight are just so on your aiming-point, before pulling the firing lever and sending a shell hurtling over the pine trees to a distant, unseen target.

All of which is leading up to the ultimate in a gunner officer's training, the day you'll be asked to take charge of a troop of four guns as a GPO, who, as Dusty Miller explains it, outranks everybody on his gun position, even the Brigadier CRA (Commander Royal Artillery). The only way a senior officer can interfere with a GPO is to take over command of the gun position himself. And Dusty in his inimitable style drives home his point: "You may be only a one-pip wonder – the lowliest, limpest pecker in the whole pecking-order around here – but when you're the GPO on that gun position, you stand up straight and tall, for you're in charge, and don't you ever forget it!"

And while you dread it, you can't wait for the day when you'll take charge of a troop command post and guns firing live ammunition, experiencing for the first time the awesome weight of responsibility every gunner officer must learn to live with: the crucial need to ensure absolute accuracy, knowing anything less could spell disaster.

Regardless of what experience life has provided before this, regardless of how exalted a man's position may have been – what power he has wielded, how many persons may have been at his beck and call, and how consequential his decisions – none of it can prepare him for this moment when he becomes ultimately responsible for the work of a large team of men, any one of whom could make an error with terrible consequences within seconds of his yelling "Fire"!

However, although you get to act as GPO during "dry-firing" exercises (when firing pins click on empty breeches), others are chosen to act as GPOs during the two training shoots with live ammunition in which your class participates, and you have to wait until you have a training troop of your own for your first experience.

27

GUNNERS INTRODUCED TO
THE ART OF SKIING

---- ✳ ----

FOR THE TRAINING OF GUNNERS ARRIVING IN MONTHLY
batches from basic-training centres, the camp at Petawawa is divided
into two wings, each containing several training batteries. Senior
administrative staff, including the battery commanders, are mostly
Great War veterans. But responsibility for day-to-day training following a rigid syllabus – gun-laying, map-reading, small-arms and
gas training, foot drill, and route marches – devolves largely on the
newly graduated 1st Lieutenants. This arrangement is designed to
round out the new subalterns' training by providing some experience in man-management before being posted to a regiment
overseas.

There is a brief breaking-in period, when you are attached to a
subaltern of some months' experience who is now nearing the end
of his tour of duty as commander of a training troop. Your duties
consist mainly of observing how he and his NCOs (two sergeants
and a bombardier) conduct themselves as they carry on lectures,
gun drill, muster parades, kit inspections, and the like, taking special
note of their transparent, but effective, tricks in manipulating fifty
men, drawn from every strata of society, through long days that
could easily become tedious and boring. During this breaking-in
period, you are seconded to help the newly designated camp skiing
instructor, fellow subaltern A. A. Paré, a real expert in the subject,
having practically grown up (you are told) on the snowy slopes of

Mount Tremblant, north of Montreal. Somehow, he persuaded you to help him introduce the officers of your course to downhill and cross-country skiing, and mysteriously gained the totally erroneous impression you are an experienced skier. Now nothing you can say will dissuade him, and there being a dearth of skiers among the officers, senior staffers make it very clear you must cooperate fully.

Fortunately, the course is introductory only, calling for recruits to be led shuffling along well-broken trails through the snowy bush, learning, by illustration, to "fishtail" up the fairly steep slope of the only sizeable hill in camp next to the Camp Commandant's cottage, and then, with luck, keeping their balance as they slide down, knees bent and leaning forward, following the example of their instructors.

Among your first victims are men of the Sportsmen's Battery (30th Battery, 6th Light Ack-Ack) recruited by Major Connie Smythe, MC, veteran of both artillery and Royal Flying Corps in the Great War, and more recently founder of Maple Leaf Gardens.

Included among the sports figures enticed by Smythe to join his battery as ordinary gunners is Ted Reeve, *Toronto Telegram* sports columnist. And within days of his arrival by train – chugging up the spur line into camp through the moonlit, snow-laden pines – sporadic columns by the "Moaner," as Reeve styles himself, begin appearing on the sports pages of the *Telegram*. Sometimes his "Sporting Extras" actually deal with sport, but it is his columns about army life that are devoured by all having access to copies of the *Telegram*.*

For instance, terse though it is, there has never been a better description of soldiers arriving anxious and uncomfortable at a new camp in the middle of a winter night, than that which appeared in his first column from Petawawa, January 15:

---

* For the serviceman, interest in professional sporting events was almost nil. With the front pages carrying stories of awesome contests on land and sea and in the air – struggles of the gravest consequence to the world – who won or lost a game played with a ball or a stick couldn't matter less.

. . . A siding is reached and we line up outside, cheered by the news it is only 34 below zero [Fahrenheit]. A quick march through big, dark trees, and a moon shining on the snow creaking and screaming under boots. Line up for muster in a big, warm hall. Another queue outside the stores for blankets. A gallop to our new quarters, a scramble to get beds sorted out so various groups of pals can be close together. It is good to hit the mattress. Reveillé before you can roll over more than once, and everybody gets up braced for the worst. Here we are five days later almost as much at home as if we were at the Beaches.

Of course, January 16, the day you and Paré have him and the rest of Smythe's battery for skiing, is suitably immortalized:

. . . It is 12 years since we resigned from the Faith and Hope Ski Club, and we found that old specialty of going downhill backwards is no longer with us. It used to be that without the least effort or premeditation on our part, we would start from the top, revolve slowly till we faced the people we had just left, and shoot swiftly downward to our doom, as though, like the Wiff-Wiff bird, we cared not where we were going, but only wanted to see where we had been. Now we fall before we have time to turn. Of course this is on the wide hills. On narrow trails, especially the steep ones, we were alarmed to find we still retain our almost uncanny habit of crossing the toes of our skiis, which causes us to stop suddenly . . . straight forward head down. The very first hill on a dash through the pine woods found us up to our old sensational act.

A gent in front of us (who until this week had never been on anything faster than galoshes) hit a fir tree and rebounded. We swung spectacularly past the body, crossed our wooden runners and crashed, prow forward with our feet locked behind up in the air as though caught in a bear trap. We couldn't holler much with our neck up against a tree, and couldn't hear very well with the snow in our ears, but there was nothing wrong with the ski harness they issue in the army. It held so tight our boots were bent back in a beautiful bow. And today we are walking around with only our toes and heels touching the ground, like a ballet dancer going after a high note. Flat feet? Doc Locke [the famous foot specialist from Williamsburg, Ontario] never figured out a better treatment than that. We now have a three-inch instep in Technicolor. . . . So the ski patrol with all their white capes and Ku Klux cowls and their "ghosting across the wintry wastes to strike silently, etc." can get along without Gnr. McGruffey. If they want to fight in Russia they can jolly well send us a toboggan. Or the old snowshoes. What was good enough for Radisson, is good enough for us.

Too bad Reeve isn't doing "profiles" on individuals. You'd love to read one on Lieut. Hymie Ginsberg, the best-natured, best-liked, most unforgettable character on course with you since your first days at Brockville. He has just been posted back to Brockville as an instructor! Blessed with a tremendous sense of humour, which can even extend to thoughts on Hitler ("Hard to believe he's just a man who has to wipe his own ass like everybody else"), he's going to need it to survive at Brockville.

Hymie will be much missed here, but will be a tremendous asset to Brockville, where he may restore a sense of humour among the staff extending to the Commandant Colonel himself. Could anyone in that officer-cadet sleeping hut in Brockville ever forget that night last summer when a fellow cadet, returning from downtown after "lights out," ran into an obstruction in the dark and began cursing, "Jesus . . . Jesus . . . son of a bitch . . . Jesus!" until from the darkness there arose a deep and resonant voice that would have done justice to a "voice of wrath" in the Old Testament: "Here now! That's enough of that! He was one of our boys!"

The upper echelons owe an enormous debt, which they'll never understand or repay, to guys like Ginsberg and Reeve, who, by regularly exercising a profound sense of humour, reduce wastage among officers and men who might otherwise go off the deep end, roaring, "Oh, to hell with it!"

28

RELUCTANT GUNNERS

※

ONE MORNING, WHEN YOU REPORT TO THE FROSTY PARADE square to take up your position in front of the troop, blowing out white clouds of vapour as they shuffle "eyes right" up and back, following the shouted instructions of a sergeant lining them up to his satisfaction ready for inspection, you discover your troop commander is not there. Nor will he be there again. Overnight, the names of officers on the next overseas draft were posted, and already he has taken off on embarkation leave. When the Major arrives, the names of those gunners "warned for overseas duty" are read to the assembled battery, and by afternoon embarkation leaves have emptied the troop huts of all but a few men who are being held back because they failed their map-reading and gun-drill tests through being unable to read or write, unable to distinguish numerals, let alone understand what degrees and minutes on a dial-sight mean.

When a few days later, the new crop of recruits arrive from a basic training centre, you are placed in charge of a troop of fifty of them.

Just to march them off for their first lecture, knowing that from now on you are totally responsible for bringing them to a level where they can pass all required tests to qualify as field gunners, is a sobering experience. Until now you were not aware just how accustomed you'd become to the cocoonlike atmosphere of your officers' course – living within the security of a privileged group, sheltered from any responsibility except to pass your tests. Now, as the saying goes, you are "out on the ice alone." And to complicate matters, you are handed the most demoralized, mutinous gang ever to arrive in Petawawa.

Some officer at a basic training depot, under pressure to increase enlistments from among the conscripts for service in Canada only, promised them they could choose whatever "trades training" they wished (including the glamorous radar mechanic course) if they enlisted. He even issued those who enlisted Ordnance Corps cap badges before they boarded the train. Understandably their outrage went off the scale when they woke up this morning in Petawawa artillery camp.*

Not having been forewarned, you are halfway through the required reading aloud to them of the specified sections of "K. R. Can" (Kings Regulations Canada) concerning matters of good order and discipline, before their total disinterest becomes evident from a rising hum of conversation in the mess hall. When you seek the cause and learn of the incredible hoax perpetuated on them, you charge over to the Battery Office.

------

* Canada had conscription, officially known as "compulsory service" for men between the ages of twenty-one and twenty-four, from October 9, 1940, but only for service within Canada. At first it was only for thirty days' training, but on March 20, 1941, it was extended to four months for twenty-one-year-old "call-ups." Then in April it was announced they would be kept in service in Canada to take over coastal defence duties to allow regular active force personnel to go overseas. In July 1941 those who had been called up previously for thirty-day training were recalled to finish their training and serve for an indefinite period in Canada. Many of these call-ups chose to enlist in the active force for service anywhere: 7,868 in 1941, 18,273 in 1942, but only 6,561 in 1943. In November 1944, because of the lack of volunteers to replace the heavy casualties in Northwest Europe, the Canadian Government decided to send conscripted men into action as every other country involved in the war (on either side) had been doing since entering the war.

But you receive no sympathy there. Major G. S. Browne, DSO, a First War vet, instructs you to tell them the truth: that when they enlisted, they gave up their freedom of choice in most matters for the duration, including freedom of movement. They can be placed wherever needed; they have no choice in the matter. And you have no choice but to go back and expose them to this harsh reality, advising them to accept their lot and not even consider entering into a feud with the army by going AWL (absent without leave).

You hope that in a few days, when they cool down, their common sense will prevail. But there is much truth in the old adage about leading a horse to water. Their resistance takes the form of feigning ignorance and stupidity. In the gunshed, for instance, when you try to evoke their curiosity about the dial-sight of a gun, though most are high-school graduates, they ask with such an enraging air of affected innocence: "What's a degree, sir?" And then, "What's a minute, sir?"

Having just read two entertaining and instructive books about British gunners embroiled in trying to halt the German *Blitzkrieg* in May last year – by a British officer, writing under the pseudonym "Gunbuster," and entitled *Return Via Dunkirk* and *Battledress* – it occurs to you they might enjoy them too, and in the process accept the idea of belonging to an artillery unit. Getting the major's blessing to set aside the training syllabus (his precise benediction is, "Do whatever you want, so long as you get the buggers trained"), you assemble them each morning in a lecture hut and read to them all day long. It takes more than a week, for shortly after you start reading, they begin to ask questions on how you get a shell to land on a target miles away, out of sight.

This means you have to go to the blackboard to explain all sorts of things: how a compass bearing, based on magnetic north, is converted to "grid north" so the guns can be laid on a grid bearing related to the map and the zero line; how the position of the guns in some bleak field, far from any distinguishable landmarks such as a crossroads, can be precisely fixed in relation to the map by a survey carried from a distant point that is identifiable and whose map coordinates can be established; and even how the GPOs calculate the necessary adjustments to the guns' elevation and line to compensate for the temperature of the propellant charge, the speed and direction of the wind, and the pressure and temperature of the air at various levels above the earth through which the shells will loop. These last calculations are based on data in the meteorological telegram. And who produces the telegram? Why, the quick-witted, dexterous men of the Meteorological Section of the Survey Regiment, who, using a cunning instrument, follow the course of a red, gas-filled balloon set adrift in the sky, tracing and recording the speed and direction of its ascent to oblivion.

And their curiosity is compounded when they learn the weapons themselves – carriages and sights – are designed to compensate for the "droop" of the barrel (particularly long barrels), the "jump" of the muzzle each time it fires, and the "drift" of a shell at various "charges" from the spinning motion (essential for stabilization during flight) imparted to it by the rifling (spiral grooves within the barrel) biting into the copper driving-band imbedded near the base of the shell, the soft copper serving as a lubricant as well as a seal to retain the expanding propellant-gases behind the shell until it is driven out of the muzzle.

By the time you finish the book, they can hardly wait to get down to the gunsheds to the old 4.5-inch howitzers and 18-pounders, to set the dials, including the "sight clinometer," which compensates for the difference in height between gun and target. (Obviously, if the gun is at a higher level than the target, the muzzle must be lowered a bit or the shell will land beyond the target when set for the correct range.)

As soon as they become proficient in laying the old guns, they question why they aren't being taught to fire the weapon in current use – the 25-pounder. You, in turn, pass on their frustration in the officers' mess, expressing the opinion that the four 25-pounders, on which officers are taught gun drill, are being wasted most days, just sitting there unused in a dark gunshed.

A few nights later, Lieutenant-Colonel van Steenburgh, Chief Training Officer of A-1 CATC (Canadian Artillery Training Centre), seeks you out: "I hear you have been beefing about your gunners not being given training on 25-pounders?"

Expecting your answer will trigger a blast on the temerity of a newly hatched officer to question the judgement of his superiors, but feeling you must stick to your opinion, you confirm the rumour.

"Well, here's your chance," says he. "We've been asked to test a new fuse for 25-pounder shells before some VIPs from Ottawa a week from today. Do you think you can get your troop up for it?"

One week? You think quickly . . . with that enthusiastic "Gunbuster gang" anything is possible.

"If we can have the guns all day long," you reply.

"Impossible. The guns are in use for officers' training every day except Saturday and Sunday. You'll have to do your training at night."

You are tempted to tell him to shove the fuses up the ass of whoever is responsible for not having gunners already training on the 25-pounders. And he knows it.

"I understand," says he, looking down into his drink, "there'll be a lot of firing involving all four guns. So make sure they know how to get off troop fire [guns firing in rotation at specified intervals] and salvoes [all guns firing at the same instant]."

Put that way, the proposition is irresistible. When you leave him, however, you start worrying. After all, it is the gunners who'll decide if they want to give up their evenings and weekend leisure time. But when they hear they'll be the first gunners to fire 25-pounders in Canada, they look at each other and shrug, What the hell . . . why not? The wet canteen is pretty boring, and Pembroke isn't that much better.

From the outset it is clear that at a shoot of such importance – before all the senior officers of the camp and the VIPs from Ottawa – it will be impossible to arrange for all fifty gunners in the troop to lay a gun and pull the firing lever the day of the shoot. So you propose they all get equal training at all positions on the gun until

Saturday afternoon, at which time gun-laying tests for speed and accuracy will be held. Their marks on the test will establish what position on the crews they'll assume at the shoot; the top four will be Numbers One (normally gun sergeants), the second four will be Numbers Two, and so on. Thus established, these crews will have all day Sunday to practise. And during the shoot, you will rotate them so that numbers one, two, and three will get a chance on the layer's seat to pull the firing lever.

For four six-man gun crews, you need only twenty-four gunners, but you assume that only slightly more than half the troop will show up for the extra-curricular night training. The first night, however, almost all show up after dinner at the 25-pounder gunshed. During the week, a few book out on sick parade or decide that an evening junket down to Pembroke is more entertaining. Still, on Saturday afternoon, under the critical eyes of staff NCOs and officers with stopwatches, there are more than three dozen intensely competitive men taking gun-laying tests.

Just how competitive is illustrated by the conduct of one thin young boy wearing glasses, who goes about turning the knobs of his dial-sight, setting the correct number of degrees and minutes, with blood running down his wrist. Seemingly oblivious to the nasty gash he's torn in a finger on the sharp edge of a brass sight-clinometer (still raw and unburnished as from the factory), he continues to whirl gears and level bubbles while peering through his dial-sight, until he finishes his lay and flings his bloody hand in the air to report ready.

So, Saturday night, when you belly-up to the bar alongside Colonel van Steenburgh, smug in the knowledge you will be ready Monday morning, you wait impatiently for him to inquire how things are going. Instead, he hits you with the incredible news that the Monday shoot is off. No, he doesn't know why; they simply sent word from Ottawa to cancel it.

But, sir, you protest, those gunners have given up their off-duty hours every night to get themselves ready. Furthermore, they're the same boys who were lied to by the recruiting officers at the basic training depot and arrived here wearing Ordnance hat badges. They've only just begun believing they might trust an artillery officer. Now this!

He is completely unperturbed, and assures you that's the way things work in the army, and that you and your men simply have to get used to it.

Maybe, you think, as he walks away from you. But *he* doesn't have to face those guys down at the gunshed tomorrow morning. All night you worry. But when you tell them that they are free for the day – that there will be no gun drill training, that the shoot has been cancelled by Ottawa – they take it so well and are so damned decent about it, your heart aches for them.

At four o'clock on Monday morning, you are awakened and handed a message from Colonel van Steenburgh instructing you to get your troop and the four 25-pounders out on the ranges in firing position at such and such map reference by 0800 hours. Dress: webbing, small packs, respirators, and steel helmets. You will arrange for early breakfast and haversack lunches for all ranks.

For the next three hours, when you aren't cursing the whimsical, thoughtless clots in Ottawa who cheated you and your men out of a day's crucial gun-laying practice, you are: searching for the transport officer's sleeping quarters to get him to lay on trucks and drivers; locating sergeants and bombardiers in the gloom of one of dozens of identical H-huts so they may organize the men; and waking cooks to get them started on breakfast and bully beef sandwiches for haversack lunches. You seem to be walking miles, and for the first time since arriving here, you really become aware of how vast and complicated the camp has become since 1940.

One advantage of all this is you don't have any time to worry about how the gunners will fare on the guns with live ammunition. When you get to the position and get the guns on line, you find you are counting heavily on Russ Everett, a fellow lieutenant, who is acting as your troop leader (assistant GPO), and on two sergeant-instructors and a bombardier-instructor, each of whom is made responsible for the safety of one gun, ensuring that the gun under his surveillance doesn't apply an incorrect line or range and send a shell where it isn't meant to go.

The show gets underway right on time, and to your surprise the whole thing proceeds as smoothly as though you are still practising in the gunshed.

The deafening *wham* of the muzzle blast of the Charge III, which you are ordered to use for purposes of accuracy, and the jarring shock of the recoil for the rookie layers on the firing seats, which you thought might put them off their concentration, is apparently not affecting them in the least. They carry on as though they are old hands at this. And you're astonished at how perfectly at home you feel.

For a while the OP orders one round at a time, first with the safety fuse-cap off each shell in the normal way to obtain minimum cratering and maximum blast and fragmentation, then with cap on to let the round dig-in a split second before blowing, as if you were shelling a building or a bunker.

Then they ask for "troop fire," with each gun in the troop firing in turn from right to left, leaving a designated number of seconds between each round. Athough there are only twenty-four rounds per gun, the shoot continues for a respectable period. Finally, they order salvoes – which call for the Numbers One reporting "Ready" by holding up their arms – and when all are ready, the GPO drops his arm signalling "Fire." Simultaneously, the Numbers One yell "Fire" and all equally alert four gun-layers pull their firing levers and all guns blast as one gun.

One of your safety sergeants was overseas with the RCHA until recently, when he was sent back to Canada because of a stiff knee injured last May in a motorcycle accident in France, when the gunners were retreating to the boats waiting at Brest to evacuate them as France fell.* This morning you could have hugged him

---

* Capt. "Teddy" McNaughton, General McNaughton's son, who, the Sergeant claims, was riding pillion on his motorbike, was also injured in the accident.

when, after your four guns have blasted away as a single gun, salvo after salvo called for by the OP, he yells to you so all on the gun position can hear, "Terrific, sir! The RCHA couldn't do any better!"

And before you know it, the shoot is over and the troop can "stand easy." The lunches of bully beef sandwiches are broken out, along with mugs of hot coffee, and suddenly there is a happy, picniclike atmosphere on the position, now so warm and sunny in contrast to the frosty and forbidding early hours this morning. Everybody is proud of what has been accomplished, and you are able to pass on the complimentary message from the OP that comes down with the order to limber up and return to camp: "The first firing of 25-pounders by gunners in Canada was carried off in a most commendable manner. All are to be congratulated. These sentiments are echoed by our important visitors from Ottawa."

And you think, Well, here's one draft of gunners who'll arrive in England knowing how to lay and fire a 25-pounder.*

---

* The brass in charge of distributing reinforcements in England were quite indifferent to the gunners' level of training on 25-pounders. When the author met some of these gunners on a scheme over there in 1943, they reported that as far as they knew not one of their number had been posted to a field regiment.

29

DENTAL VISITS RATE
WOUND STRIPES

✳

IN PETAWAWA ALL RANKS LEARN THERE ARE TWO KINDS OF army dentists: mature men who appear to know what they are doing and have developed all the necessary skills to do it well, and very young men, fresh out of dental school, picking up their experience as they go. And the odds are in favour of drawing one of the latter, for they seem to be in the majority. While full of breezy confidence, most of them, you suspect, are grateful for the endless supply of fresh mouths appearing before them in which they can practise their bloody art, and which conveniently disappear from their orbit on a regular basis, as their transitory gunner clientele moves on to other theatres of operations, taking their dental errors, major and minor, with them.

Before being placed on draft for overseas, all ranks, in addition to receiving shots for tetanus and so on, must have their dental work brought up to date. In due course, you are told to report for a routine dental checkup at the camp clinic, where a long line of dentists, working side by side like barbers in an oversized barbershop, get through a remarkable number of soldiers each day. If only you'd kept your mouth shut – or perhaps, more accurately, kept your tongue from wagging – you would not have incited action that would lead to you being booked into hospital with a crater in your jawbone big enough to arouse curiosity for years to come in every dentist peering inside your mouth. But bravado set your tongue wagging.

From your first experience as a little boy, with a village dentist grinding into a sensitive tooth with a drill powered by a foot-treadle similar to that on a Singer sewing machine, you have hated – with all your body and soul – visits to the dentist. As they gently prod your teeth looking for cavities, you are left breathless, hands clenched until your fingernails bite into your palms, sweat flowing freely from all pores. So it's with the greatest relief you receive the news from the young dentist, on one end of the row of dentists, that you have no cavities. The happiness on learning this is so intoxicating that, with the false courage of a drunk, you inquire if that wisdom tooth back there is all right, explaining that now and then it seems to want to push up through the gum. You know of course there is nothing the matter with it, your civilian dentist having told you to leave it alone. Your cool inquiry is sheer bravado.

However, no weird potion supplied by a Dr. Jekyll could possibly have produced more startling results on this young man's personality than your innocent inquiry. A wild gleam appears in his eyes, and he almost slobbers as he breathes: "An impacted wisdom tooth!"

After a perfunctory examination, mostly with his index finger, he informs you that it must come out – without delay – tomorrow, Saturday morning, at ten o'clock. In the meantime, an X-ray is needed, and this is duly taken in a room adjacent to his dental chair.

At 10:05 A.M. the next morning he freezes your jaw with needles. By 10:30 a circular, revolving, porcelain tray, slightly to the right of your eyes, has disappeared under a layer of bloody forceps and prys of every size and shape imaginable. As he adds more freezing to your jaw, you momentarily catch sight of his perspiring, anxious face before you close your eyes and concentrate on trying to keep your lower jaw from being pushed out of its socket, as more instruments grind into it with all the force of his muscular young frame behind them.

By 11:00 the mound of discarded instruments has grown into a small mountain, and he is borrowing more from an older dentist at the far end of the line of dental chairs. At about 11:30, he adds more freezing to your jaw, but perhaps you are starting to turn pale, because instead of carrying on, he helps you out of the chair and into the adjoining room to a couch where he has you lie down.

When again he brings you out to his dental chair, he has with him the older dentist from down the far end of the line, studying what you assume is an X-ray of your reluctant tooth. While grateful a more experienced hand has been called in, a feeling of despair settles over you. It is now noon. After two hours of outrage to your mouth and jaw, they are starting back at square one!

Turning over the operation to the older man, the young dentist straddles you and the chair, and with his full weight resting on your lap, grips your head and jaw tightly in his two hands. You shut your eyes so as not to see the older man go to work with the mallet and chisel he has just produced. But you feel the banging – not as pain, but as a grisly, crunching sound in your skull. After it is over, and he is filling the cavity with some form of wadding, he explains he had to cut a hole in the jawbone and push the stubborn tooth sideways.

Back at the officers' mess luncheon table, with the freezing still intact, you attempt to consume some soup knowing that once the anaesthetic wears off you won't want to eat anything. But you discover that the muscles at the hinges of your jaws are taking their revenge for the outrage they suffered for more than two and a half hours. Try as you will, you cannot open your jaws to insert a spoonful of anything. And within an hour, you are almost running down across the valley to the low-slung, white building housing the camp hospital to book yourself in for some painkiller.

The doctor who pries open your mouth and withdraws the packing from its bloody crater involuntarily lets out a series of terrible oaths, and then the question, "Who in the name of God did that to you?" What he does with the information you give him, you can only guess, but he books you into hospital with a poultice tied around your jaw and a diet of extremely strong pain-killing tablets.

As the days pass, the discomfort reduces dramatically, and on the sixth day, Thursday morning, remembering your turn for a forty-eight-hour pass is coming up this weekend, you ask the doctor if he will discharge you so you can get home to see your wife. He says it is entirely up to you; all he needs is a report from the nurses on your ward that you have been able to exist without a painkiller for twenty-four hours.

While this doesn't sound like something you can accomplish, you are determined to try, for you are very concerned that your wife will really start to worry if you don't arrive home on leave, because of the shocking and uncanny way she learned you were in hospital. The same night they booked you in, she'd gone to bed early, but was no sooner asleep than she woke again with a terrible sense of dread that something had happened to you. So powerful was the feeling, she felt obliged to try to reach you by phone in Petawawa Camp, something she'd never tried before. But with the helpful persistence of a switchboard operator and some luck in drawing someone to a phone in the midst of a noisy Saturday-night party in the officers' mess, she located you.

All of this you had learned at a phone hanging on the wall of your ward, where, through locked teeth and a hypo-induced fog, you were able to communicate only the fact you had had a tooth removed. Now if you fail to arrive home on your scheduled leave, she is bound to conclude something more serious is the matter.

So mentally gritting your teeth, you hold out against all pain-killing tablets all day and through the evening until around 11:00 P.M., when it becomes too much for you. Putting on a dressing gown that must have been designed for a midget, you paddle down the hall in your bare feet towards a glass enclosure at the far end where there is a nurses' sitting room.

There you find a nurse, talking to a couple of well-turned-out subalterns in their serge uniforms, complete with well-polished Sam Brownes, who have obviously been at large this evening. Not only do forage caps, gloves, and swagger sticks lie on their laps, but they wear that excessively healthy glow usually induced by several enlivening cups of good cheer. All conversation ceases as you arrive, and you notice the jaws of the subalterns go slack as they stare at you.

The smiling nurse asks if she can help you. You explain your dilemma: you can't go any longer without a painkiller, but if she tells the doctor, he won't allow you to go home to your wife for the weekend. It turns out she's a gal with an understanding heart, and winking broadly, goes to get you a pill.

The two subalterns look at each other and then back at you. One of them, wagging his head, snorts, "My gawd! Here we are, well over a bout with pneumonia – even to the point of being allowed to go down to Pembroke for the evening – but still we aren't considered ready for discharge. And you are going home on leave tomorrow? Oh, my gawd!" And they go into gales of laughter.

Glaring at them does nothing towards restoring dignity to your situation. If anything, they laugh the harder. At last one of them, realizing you are not really seeing any humour in the situation, says, "Sorry, Mac, but have you looked at yourself in a mirror recently?" And he jerks a thumb over his shoulder at a wall mirror.

Even if the thought had occurred to you, there was no mirror in the ward, and with your jaw covered with the poultice, you hadn't been able to wash or shave your face for the past week. So when you look, you see what they mean.

First there's the bulky, sling-type bandage holding the poultice on your chin, tied on the top of your head in a way that forms a ridiculous set of bunny's ears. Then that wayward knot – forever sliding too far back or too far forward on your skull, continually forcing you to restore it to a central position – has tortured your hair over the course of the week into a mass of unbelievable tangles. What facial skin is visible is covered in shaggy beard, suggestive of Bathless Groggins, and strange sunken, red-rimmed, wild, black eyes stare back at you from the mirror. You most certainly are a mess, and as you retreat down the hall to your ward, clutching your precious pill, you don't blame those splendid young men protesting to the nurse the unfairness of the medical world that would keep them in hospital while that wretched hulk shuffling down the hall will be discharged in the morning.

30

THE GREAT BUTTER THEFT CASE

---------------------------- ✳ ----------------------------

SINCE LAWYERS, FOR SOME REASON, SEEM UNDULY ATTRACTED to taking commissions in the artillery, the one duty you least expected to have to perform is defend a man in a court-martial. However, Gunner Leonard Kiely, C-1352, accused of purloining two pounds of butter from the Crown, remembering you from recent newspaper days, decides (very sensibly as it turns out) you might be more helpful than a stranger.

When they let you take him for a walk outside the compound in which he has been incarcerated for the past month awaiting trial, he freely admits he took the butter from the cookhouse, where he was working as a cook. He could hardly deny it, having been caught carrying the stuff in a small pack slung over his shoulder by no less than Sgt. E. V. "Mac" McNeil of the provincial police and the provost marshal of Petawawa Military Camp, who were looking for a suspect in a jewellery store break-in the night before.

According to their written report, they piled out of the police car and descended on the startled Kiely as he crossed the bridge over the Petawawa River, demanding to know what he was carrying in that pack.

"Butter – I stole it from the kitchen where I work," was his reply, according to the eminent witnesses.

Kiely thinks that because you knew him in Civvy Street, you can speak up for him, tell them he is not a thief, and get him a light sentence. However, from the advice offered by Lieut. J. J. Mc-Kenna, the camp prosecutor (a practising lawyer in Ottawa before enlisting) as he handed you the case, mercy will not be on the table when the court assembles on May 20: "All you can do is produce character witnesses, if any, and ask for leniency – though there isn't much hope of that, for we have been instructed to make an example of him because of the large amount of theft that's been going on in camp."

You could have told him the "leakages" have been running at more than eighteen thousand dollars a month* and are removed from camp by the truckload with official "work tickets" signed by officers. You learned this as a reporter some months ago when covering the trial of a Pembroke butcher charged with "receiving." The crime was witnessed by the Pembroke chief of police himself when by chance he looked out the rear window of his main-street flat – over a store next door to the butcher's – and saw barrels of coffee and such being carried into the shop by soldiers from an army truck backed up to the rear door. That the butcher and the soldiers would be found guilty had seemed a certainty.

But when a sergeant under cross-examination began to reveal facts that clearly showed officers of higher rank had to have known, and that a real can of worms was opening up, the Crown seemed to falter and the magistrate abruptly threw out the case.

That the powers-that-be should now decide to make an example of the first gunner they catch "borrowing" a couple of pounds of butter one Saturday afternoon to raise the price of a few draughts of beer, is so hypocritical as to almost make you puke.

You decide there'll be no begging for mercy – you'll go for an acquittal. And you know you have a good chance, for over endless days spent covering criminal court cases as a reporter, you learned that it's the lawyer who knows the rules of evidence and how to use them who gets his clients off, guilty or not. And you know the

---

* Amounting to $216,000 a year – in excess of $2,160,000 a year in 1990 dollars.

rules – at least those that lawyers most commonly abuse and ma-
nipulate – better than a lot of lawyers, and certainly better than the
prosecutor in this case, who has had limited courtroom experience.

First the court must throw out Kiely's damning confession
blurted out on the bridge when the two high-ranking policemen
piled out of the car and rushed at him, obviously intending to
prevent him casting his small pack, suspected of containing stolen
jewellery, over the rail and into the fast-flowing Petawawa River
below. Was Kiely "warned," in the formal manner laid down by
law, that he need not make a statement, but that if he did, it might
be taken down and used in evidence at his trial? No, of course not,
not then or at any time later on. Could a statement be obtained
from an accused man under more intimidating circumstances, with
two burly policemen leaping out of a car and rushing at him? And
when you draw the attention of the court to the size of burly OPP
Sgt. "Mac" McNeil, compared to your pint-sized client, the judges
(lawyers all) are bound to agree.

As for the butter, it no longer exists as evidence. Only two greasy
pieces of paper remain, dated and initialled by the provost marshal,
who took them into custody. That the butter – crucial evidence,
surely – has not been kept locked up in refrigeration, for the month
or so of unusually hot weather since Kiely's arrest, must be made a
source of embarrassment to the prosecution, even to the point of
there being no evidence of a theft of butter.

Still, the policemen cannot be prevented from introducing his
small pack and testifying that when they took it from him just
outside the gate of Petawawa Camp they found it contained two
pounds of ice-cold butter.

But what if Kiely were to testify that, when he picked the small
pack off a nail on the wall of the cookhouse, he thought it was his
own, containing laundry that he wanted to take to his laundry lady
across the bridge in Petawawa village, and that just before passing
out the camp gate he discovered, on opening up the straps to see
what made the pack so lumpy, not laundry but two pounds of butter
– obviously placed there by someone else awaiting an appropriate

moment of departure. Then, not relishing the long walk back to the cookhouse in the hot sun, Kiely continued out the gate to that unexpected and awkward confrontation with the police. In those circumstances, would it not then make sense for him to reply to the policeman's challenge as to what was in his pack with: "Butter . . . it was stolen from the cookhouse where I work."

Obviously, the real thief picked up the wrong bag – the one with Kiely's laundry in it – and left the butter bag hanging on its nail.

Kiely, entering into the spirit of the thing, volunteers crucial information which could support this. It seems he was not the original owner of the pack they seized, and when the prosecutor is requested to read the regimental number inscribed in indelible ink under its closing flap, the court will learn it is not Kiely's.

Only one thing more is needed to guarantee an acquittal: Kiely's mild stutter, which can be quite pronounced under stress, as when accosted by two burly policemen while in possession of stolen goods, or when placed on the witness stand.

And an unqualified acquittal he gets. Your old friend "Mac" McNeil, the Crown's first witness, can hardly believe it when the court, after long deliberation behind closed doors, agrees with your contention that Kiely's statement was obtained under intimidating circumstances, and therefore is not admissible. However, though you deride the pitiful pieces of rancid, greasy paper as exhibits of stolen butter, and the prosecutor is thoroughly embarrassed by the small pack with the wrong regimental number tattooed under its flap (which he admits was not kept under lock and key awaiting the trial), the court is reluctant to bow to your request for a dismissal until they have heard from the accused.

Never mind – Kiely turns out to be a great witness. His stutter is so atrocious, particularly at the outset, you can hardly keep from laughing and you are constantly forced to calm him down so his words may be understood, reassuring him that the court only wants to know the truth of the matter.

Of course the words, "Butter . . . I stole it from the cookhouse where I work," when they can finally be understood, become,

"Butter . . . it was stolen from the cookhouse where I work" –
presumably by somebody else.

Declared not guilty as charged, Kiely is so grateful he wants you
to have half the back pay that will be coming to him, and is greatly
disappointed when you turn him down.

And as you are leaving the building, threading your way through
the members of the court dispersing in all directions, the frustrated
Kiely calls to you from some distance, without the trace of a stutter,
"Well, anyway, sir, any time you're going on leave and want a nice
pie or a cake to take home to the wife, just drop over to the kitchen."

As you scurry away as unobtrusively as possible, you hear
a murmur of comments being exchanged, and then explosive
laughter.

3 1

"WARNED FOR SPECIAL DUTY"

———————————— ✳ ————————————

EACH MONTH ANOTHER "DRAFT" OF MEN AND OFFICERS assemble in the dark on the parade square, totally unattended except for Lieutenant-Colonel van Steenburgh, Chief Instructor CATC A-1 (Canadian Artillery Training Centre), and his adjutant, who at the last moment hands the subaltern designated "draft commander" a large sealed brown envelope with the records of all the bodies who are to be shipped out. Then, without ceremony, the parade moves off for a darkened train on the camp siding that will take them to "an Eastern Canadian port."

The whole business is carried off in a most matter-of-fact way, starting with a mimeographed list of names appearing on the bulletin board under the heading "Warned for Special Duty." Your name appears on an officers' list in April, and although you have been expecting it, training for it, desiring it, and mentally preparing for it since the day war broke out, life – which has been thoroughly enjoyable with your improved status at Camp Petawawa – suddenly takes on a bleakness that grows steadily worse during the week at home on your "embarkation leave." It reaches an indescribable low during those last moments when your wife is packing in your kit everything she can think of that you might need "for the duration," including many bars of soap, a shameful number of oversized chocolate bars, and scores of razor blades.

There's so much to say, but the words won't come. And as you wait for the taxi to take you to the station to catch the midnight train for Pembroke and Petawawa, you become almost inarticulate.

But when you get back to camp, you discover your name has been stroked off the draft list, leaving you struggling with conflicting emotions. While truly grateful that fate has intervened to allow you to have another embarkation leave with your beloved when you are listed on the next draft, you dread having to go through those last, painful, bittersweet hours of parting again.

However, when it comes about, it turns out to be not as bad as the first time, since she, the eternal optimist, almost has you believing you won't be going this time either, that when you get back to Petawawa your name again will have been stroked off the list.

Incredibly, she turns out to be right; once again there is a pen-stroke through your name on the list hanging on the bulletin board in the mess. Smelling a rat, you confront Major Browne of your training battery, demanding to know why you are being removed from drafts after being warned and allowed to go on embarkation leave.

Evincing the forthright pragmatism you've come to expect from World War I veterans – who, having lived through that horrible business, are forever oriented towards survival in comfort – he readily admits he's responsible. Knowing you were only recently married, he's been using the device of listing you on overseas drafts to get you embarkation leaves at home with your bride. Far from being apologetic, he proceeds to lecture you in a most forceful, but kindly, manner:

"You should be grateful, dammit. Why this rush to get overseas? This war is going to last years. Surely you're better off here in Canada than puttering around England, waiting for action – which won't be for a hell of a long time, if I'm any judge of matters – when you could be of real use here. We want to get you on staff. You're a good instructor—especially good at handling new recruits."

For a moment you're tempted to take the advice of this considerate man who, judging from the string of Great War ribbons on his chest, knows how to approach war in honourable fashion. What he says makes sense, and the prospect of being able to bring your wife up from Ottawa to live in the Copeland Hotel in Pembroke, only twenty minutes away, is tremendously attractive. But something inside you says, No, don't do it. If you do, you'll always regret it.

You elicit a promise he will not intervene the next time your name comes up for overseas posting. Thus, when your name appears on a warning list late in May, you and she know it will still be there when you join the draft on the dark parade square one week hence. To make it a little easier on the rest of the family, you and she spend your last weekend in the Copeland, surrounded by old friends Jim and Ruth Findlay, Jack Campbell, Freddy Ritt and all, and spoiled rotten by Alice Roy, the proprietress, and her cook, Mrs. Chaput, whose steaks fill an entire dinner plate, and who will strip an entire pork roast to provide you with "outside cuts, well-done."

Your predawn last farewell before the taxi comes to take you to camp on "the day" is strangely passive. It's as though your emotional mechanisms are finally exhausted. But then, with only hours to go, you are granted permission to visit Pembroke one last time. And just after supper you say your final goodbye, clinging to each other desperately out in the street, in front of a taxi-stand at the west end of the town.

As the taxi pulls away and you peer through the rear window, straining to maintain sight of her fast-disappearing image until the last possible moment, you know you shall never feel as sorry for anyone in your life as you do for that gallant lady, standing alone on the curb waving at the departing cab, for you are convinced you won't be coming back – that this is the last time you will ever look into her eyes on this earth – and she is carrying your child in her womb.

32

FOOTNOTE TO THE BATTLE
OF THE ATLANTIC

※

DURING 1942, EIGHT MILLION TONS OF ALLIED SHIPPING WILL be sunk, and imports to Britain – essentials for her survival and prosecution of the war – will drop to two-thirds of what she imported in 1939. In June 1942 the chances of a ship being sunk on its way from Halifax to Britain are very high. Sinkings of Allied ships throughout the world will hit 830,000 tons for this, the worst month of the entire war – 90 per cent of them sent to the bottom of the Atlantic. Of the 173 ships sunk, 144 will be victims of U-boats, averaging one every five hours.*

And the Germans are not paying the price. With 212 U-boats, Admiral Dönitz will have twice as many submarines operating at the end of 1942 as when the year began. Only twenty-one U-boats are sunk during the first half of 1942, while in the Gulf of St. Lawrence alone – where few escort ships can be made available from the overstressed ships involved in the Battle of the Atlantic – twenty-three ships are sunk during five months starting in May.

Not until May 1943 – when thirty-eight U-boats will be sunk (twenty-eight of them mid-Atlantic) – will the tide turn against the wolfpacks of submarines through new Allied strategies and tactics. The Allies begin using: more long-range aircraft such as the Sutherland Flying Boat, as well as aircraft concentrating on subs coming

---

* See Appendix F.

and going from French ports on the Bay of Biscay (their movements revealed by the Brits decoding their messages); more and better detection equipment installed on ships (particularly crucial to the effectiveness of Canadian corvettes); and more search-and-kill ships not tied down to riding herd on convoys. And though U-boats will go on sinking Allied ships until the end of the war, the tonnages they sink will never rise beyond a hundred thousand tons a month, and they will suffer awesome losses.*

Of the U-boats' losing battle after May 1943, United States Coast Guard Captain John M. Waters, Jr., will be impelled to write: "The Battle of the Atlantic, as a decisive influence on the outcome of the war, ended May 1943, but the U-boats fought a holding operation to the bitter end and paid a horrible price. Allied ships and aircraft roamed the oceans, striking the U-boats wherever they showed themselves. Yet the U-boat men continued to sail in the face of forbidding odds, and their morale remained, for the most part, unimpaired."†

But even as Waters perceived "the bravery, the fighting spirit, and the dedication" of the men in U-boats, serving a government of "evil design," he recognized the awful menace they presented to the survival of the free world: the Allies had to win the Battle of the Atlantic or lose the war. And the American captain pays tribute to the Royal Navy, which escorted convoys from mid-Atlantic to Britain, and the Royal Canadian Navy, which by 1942 had thirteen destroyers and seventy corvettes escorting convoys from Halifax to a midway point:

> The immensity of the Battle of the Atlantic dwarfed all other sea battles in history, and its pivotal effects in many respects exceeded

---

* Of 1,150 German U-boats operational during the war, 791 were sunk. Of 39,000 U-boat personnel, 28,000 died and 5,000 were taken prisoner.
† Page 236, John M. Waters, *Bloody Winter*, Princeton, N.J.: D. Van Nostrand Co., 1967. The quotes on the following pages are also from *Bloody Winter*, pages 237–38 and page 24 respectively.

Waterloo, Trafalgar, Gettysburg, or the Marne. Not only in its broad strategic implications, but in the number of ships involved, it was gigantic: 85,775 ships in 2,889 escorted convoys ran to and from the United Kingdom across transocean routes.

Of those lost (1,232), 654 were sunk with convoys and 578 were sunk while sailing independently – a total of almost 12 million tons on the North Atlantic run alone. Over half were British ships and 30,248 British seamen gave their lives that Britain might continue to fight.

Credit for the victory must be largely given to the Royal Navy and the Royal Canadian Navy,* which for the most part of 45 months, before the Spring of 1943, fought alone, with support coming from the Americans in the last third of the crisis.†

. . . A few hundred warships and aircraft, and fewer than 50,000 men of the escort forces, were the fulcrum on which the free world's cause was so precariously balanced. . . . Had it failed, the results would have been catastrophic. The clear measure of the devotion of these men shall always be that they did not fail.

Of the Canadian Navy and its significant contribution to winning the war – mostly in crowded little Corvettes that reputedly would

---

* When the war began, Canada had only six destroyers and five mine-sweepers, and about 3,000 officers and men. By war's end there were 400 Canadian ships – mostly built in Canada – and 90,000 Canadians were at sea.

† Due to the Americans having to transfer so much of their strength to the Pacific after the awesome naval losses at Pearl Harbor. However, weeks before Pearl Harbor brought the U.S.A. into the war, American naval ships were helping unofficially to escort convoys across the first leg of the Atlantic crossing to Britain, and they were doing so openly from mid-November, with the passing by Congress of an amendment to their neutrality act allowing American warships to escort vessels into the war zone and American merchant ships to be armed.

"roll in wet grass," sailing in plunging seas where survival was unlikely if one was immersed in it beyond five minutes in winter, and where ships could become top-heavy with ice and capsize – Captain Waters would write:

> Most of the crews of its small ships had never seen the sea until they reported aboard. Their mistakes were many, but they proved to be one of the most important factors in keeping the Atlantic sea lanes open. . . . In their [naval] expansion the emphasis was at first on numbers, rather than quality, and their mistakes as they learned were sometimes painful, but any sailors who cruised those waters in the year of crisis should gratefully salute the RCN ensign whenever they see it.

Naval historian Captain S. W. Roskill adds,

> . . . because convoy battles have no names, the victory of May 1943 is scarcely remembered. Yet it was in its own way as decisive as the Battle of Britain, for never again was the German navy able seriously to threaten our lifeline.*

And Canadian Rear-Admiral L. W. Murray, commander-in-chief of the Northwest Atlantic, recognized the outsized bravery and steadfastness of the merchant marine sailors, without whom there would have been no ships moving in convoys across the ocean:

> I remember speaking to the captains and trying to reassure them that all would be well. But they knew, and they knew I knew that the probabilities were that 25 per cent of them would not

---

* Page 238 of *Bloody Winter*, quoting S. W. Roskill, *The White Ensign – The British Navy at War* 1939-45, U.S.A. Naval Institute, 1949.

reach the United Kingdom in their own ship, and that half that number would not reach there at all. For months this loosely disciplined service stood up to casualties like that and never faltered. No ship missed a convoy from Halifax because of malingering.*

---

* Page 253, *The Canadians at War*, Montreal: Readers Digest Association Canada Ltd., 1969.

33

EMPRESS OF JAPAN –

SCOTLAND

✳

NOT WISHING TO GIVE ENCOURAGEMENT TO THE ENEMY, LITTLE of what is happening in the Gulf of St. Lawrence and out in the Atlantic in the desperate and wide-ranging battle for the sea-lanes is revealed through official channels or through news reports at the peak of the crisis.

Still, enough is known about the frequency of Atlantic sinkings that all who are crowded into this troop train on Sunday morning, June 14, 1942, now approaching "an Eastern Canadian port," must cope with a growing sense of anxiety mixed with excitement as the first damp, seaweedy smell of the sea and the chill of its misty air filters in around the rain-spattered windows of the rushing, *clickety-clacking* railway cars, winding along the shoreline of a broad and foggy arm of the sea dotted with dozens of anchored ships.

"Bedford Basin," your knowledgeable companions declare, is where all Atlantic convoys assemble after loading at the docks of Halifax.

The cool air is a dramatic change from the weather inland. The train had been beastly hot yesterday as you passed through Maine, and you'd resented the fact that before leaving Petawawa in the dark two nights ago, they'd had all of you on the overseas draft change from cotton summer shorts and shirts to woollen battledress. Cooled only by air blowing in through windows raised here and there by daring souls willing to endure periodically spumes of coal-smoke and ash drifting back over the train, the cars were muggy and the mood of the troops became sour.

Mid-afternoon a riotous brawl threatened in the car containing Section 5. Jammed together with every inch of space taken up with sweating bodies and kit bags, and distempered by the heat and too many drags on illicit crocks of "alcool" bought during a lengthy stop at Megantic, Quebec, the gunners were getting ready for a free-for-all, and not just with fists you would discover, when the car's NCO, a "temporary acting-sergeant," chosen just before the draft left Petawawa, came seeking the help of the "conducting officers."

You'd arrived in the car just in time to interrupt the swing of an arm descending with a piece of board wrenched from a seat or some part of the car and aimed at the scalp of a nearby gunner. You and the other officers had to remain in the car for some time talking to them and assuring them they'd soon be getting near the sea and cooler air – droning on in that vein until drowsiness took over with the more inebriated and they began snoring.

Now it's so chilly your battledress is insufficient, and you fish in your kit bag for the sleeveless sweater your sister knitted to wear under the blouse.

The train pulls right onto the dock, and the troops, helped into their gear (webbing and backpacks) by the train's porters, pile off, form up, and are marched across the tracks and right up the gangplank of a great three-funnelled ship. Before leaving Petawawa, there'd been a rumour that the draft would be sailing on the *Empress of Japan*, and without an escort because of her speed. Incredibly, though the name has been painted out on her prow (preparatory to it being renamed the *Empress of Scotland*) the liner's interior – still luxuriously resplendent and provisioned as though for the civilian trade at Capetown before sailing to Halifax – everywhere displays the name she'd been using until a week or ten days ago on the Pacific. It is indeed the *Empress of Japan*!

It seems she just arrived from Capetown, South Africa, to where, four months ago, she brought refugees from Singapore. The British crew are very proud of the fact that this was the last Allied civilian ship out of that harbour before that great bastion of the Empire fell to the Japanese. The ship was so overloaded that men hanging from the rigging were in danger of falling overboard as she zigged and zagged to escape Japanese bombs. The Chinese helmsman, who was awarded the George Medal for saving the ship and its thousands of passengers, pointed with obvious pride to a gap where a short chunk of wooden rail was missing from its steel bedding-rail on an upper deck. The railing, he said, had been sheared away by a fragment of one of the bombs that just missed the ship as he swung it away from a swooping Jap plane.

However, the second part of the Petawawa rumour proves wrong. When the *Empress* finally pulls out of Halifax at 8:15 A.M., June 16, she is accompanied by another, slower, troopship, the *Letitia*, and escorted by two destroyers and a small aircraft carrier, reputed to be a converted banana boat, carrying, you are told, three old Swordfish biplanes only. One of these planes, the first day out, takes off to circle round and about the horizon on all sides, supposedly looking for U-boats. On returning to the bobbing carrier, the pilot finds it impossible to land and turns back in the direction of Newfoundland. Another crashes into the superstructure of the carrier on trying to reland after doing its patrol. If there is a third plane, it remains hidden in the carrier for the rest of the voyage.

There are twelve officers in your cabin with bunks for only ten.* The luck of the draw places you and another on mattresses on the

---

* Sharing the cabin with the author were Lieutenants Max Kaplan, Don Deacon, Tommy Coppinger, W. D. "Stevie" Stevenson, J. F. McIsaac, A. L. Fair, "Dizzy" Dean, W. D. Booth, Don Chute, Russ Everett, and F. Ray Irwin – the last named destined to fire the last rounds in anger on the Western Front in World War II. The official ceasefire took place at 8:00 A.M. on May 5, 1945, with the surrender of all German forces on the Western Front, *except* Dunkirk. Irwin was a flying OP officer with B Flight 665 Air OP Squadron. On the evening of May 7, using 25-pounders

floor, but since the bunks have no springs, it's as comfortable where you are.

The ship has a six-inch gun and a 12-pounder anti-aircraft gun on the stern, and two more 12-pounders on the bow. Also, at regular intervals around the sun deck and bridge, are Lewis guns in turrets resembling giant washtubs, but with the staves made of rough-cast steel four inches thick. Airforce gunners will man the Lewis guns and the permanent ship's staff the heavier guns.

There are 4,500 on board, including many British sailors from torpedoed ships; British, Canadian, and New Zealand airmen; civilian firemen on their way to London (one of them Tony Mc-Carthy, an Ottawa Roughrider); fifty nursing sisters; four civilian women; some British refugee children returning home; and the 3rd (Canadian) Medium Regiment.

The gunners that came aboard with you are quartered down on E Deck, five decks from the sun and two decks below the water-line, most of them sleeping in hammocks slung between pipes overhead, but some on mattresses on the floor. Needless to say, they spend most of their waking hours elsewhere on the ship, the weather being extraordinarily sunny, and, if not as calm as it was on setting out – when the *Letitia* steaming close by could be seen reflected in the intervening water – the wind never rises to gale proportions.

While no one reveals what course the ship is taking, it obviously is far to the north. When, to settle a bet one night around midnight, the lights are doused and the blacked-out porthole is opened, it is found to be broad daylight outside.

Everyone is required to carry at all times a life preserver in the

---

manned by Czechoslovakians – who had held the stubborn city under a siege of containment for months – he shelled the big guns of Dunkirk. A second shoot was called off the next morning, May 8, because there was a rumour the German garrison was preparing to surrender. In the afternoon, as Irwin was about to take off to engage another target, he was told all firing was to cease – it was VE-Day.

form of two kapok-filled pillows strung on tapes. And now and then the grating *aroo-guh* . . . *aroo-guh* . . . *aroo-guh* of the ship's klaxon sends everyone to their designated action stations to practise the order "Prepare to abandon ship." Your group gathers at a rather inadequate-looking wooden raft, which, you are told, is not meant to support such a large group riding on it, but with everyone in the water holding on to a rope pinned at intervals around its perimeter. This news inspires some disturbing speculation as to the time you might survive immersed in that cold-looking water down there seething past the ship.

Early one morning, during what appears to be another routine "Prepare to abandon ship" drill, there is some panic among those trying to get up from those lower decks below the water-line. Badly frightened by a series of ugly, horrifying *whams* against the hull of the ship, they scramble and jam the companionways until they learn they are merely the sound of pressure waves induced by depth charges flung from the stern of a destroyer some distance away, supposedly at a U-boat picked up on their sonar equipment.

The two troopships immediately change direction, and the other destroyer goes swiftly off towards the horizon in front, leaving the other circling the spot where it had, or thought it had, picked up a signal. For half an hour all are required to remain at their rafts or lifeboats before being released to go on with their card games, their letter writing, diary writing, patting the beautiful big honey-coloured tabby of the lower decks, or just lolling about on a stern deck, out of the wind, watching the flat-top rising and falling against the line of the horizon like the mortarboard on a hyperactive choir director.

On the evening of June 21, 1942, they announce over the ship's PA system that Tobruk has fallen.

This is sad news indeed. Long-besieged Tobruk was more than a stubborn bastion inhibiting the German advance across Africa, it had become a symbol of unquenchable Allied determination to resist and win in the end.

A pall of silence, broken only by the throb of the ship's great engines, descends on the officers' lounge, where only a moment ago conversation and laughter almost drowned out the piano on which the swinging Royal Navy padre, with a great left hand, had been "striding" out "The Lambeth Walk." Now it, too, is still, as the Padre, in his navy-blue turtleneck sweater, rejoins his fellow officers from the cruiser HMS *Penelope* at the next table, where they sit silently staring down at their drinks.* These quiet men – on their way back for "a spot of leave" in Britain while their ship, badly mauled in a "set-to" with the Luftwaffe near Malta, undergoes repairs in Boston – know better than anybody in this room the strategic significance of the loss of Tobruk.† The Germans can now renew their drive for Egypt and the Suez.

And this is only the latest in a series of defeats at the hands of the Germans and Japanese that began in 1940 with the fall of France, scarcely leavened by the periodic humiliations heaped on the Italian troops of Mussolini, the third member of the enemy tripartite.

For the past two years there has been a steady stream of disheartening stories: if it isn't news of great naval ships being sunk and land battles being lost in Russia, North Africa, and Asia, it's of whole countries, one after another, falling to the Germans in Europe and to the Japanese in the Pacific, until now the Germans are six or seven hundred miles inside Russia on a front stretching from Leningrad to the Black Sea, and the Japanese occupy the whole Pacific rim down through the East Indies and east through Borneo and

---

* The Padre, revered by his *Penelope* mates for having played more than a passive role when the ship was attacked again and again at Malta – carrying ammunition to the ack-ack guns pumping away at the diving planes – was thought (by all who came to know the story) to be the "sky pilot" in the popular song "Praise the Lord and Pass the Ammunition." However, five months later, on November 3, 1942, the Associated Press awarded the honour for coining the phrase to Lieut. Howell Forgy of Huddenfield, New Jersey, although he denied manning or serving a gun.
† The repaired *Penelope* was sunk by a sub off Anzio, February 18, 1944.

New Guinea and the other islands of the vast archipelago off the northern coast of Australia.

Just to review Allied defeats during the past two months is unnerving:

Apr 09:   Bataan falls – 35,000 Americans and Filipinos are taken prisoner.

Apr 30:   All central Burma falls to the Japanese.

May 01:   Mandalay falls to the Japanese.

May 06:   Corregidor surrenders to the Japanese – 16,000 Americans and Filipinos are taken prisoner.

May 15:   Japan completes its conquest of Burma.

May 19:   The Germans occupy all of Crimea, taking 100,000 prisoners.

May 28:   The Germans knock out the Russian force trying to retake Kharkov.

May 29:   A German midget sub badly damages the British battleship *Ramillies* and sinks a tanker with torpedoes in Madagascar harbour.

Jun 06:   The British counter-attack in Libya collapses after the loss of two infantry brigades and four artillery regiments.

Jun 09:   All formal resistance to the Japanese in the Philippines ends. In all, 140,000 American and Filipino troops were killed, wounded, or taken prisoner while attempting to hold the islands.

Jun 13:   The British suffer disastrous defeat at the hands of Rommel, losing 230 of their 300 tanks to superior German tanks at El Adem, making it possible for the enemy to move into Tobruk.*

---

* For a review of the years when the world was being overrun by seemingly irresistible supermen, see Appendix G.

PART FOUR: AUGUST 1942– APRIL 1943

The Failure of Dieppe Spurs More Intensive Training for Battle

34

ROYALS SHOT DOWN IN HEAPS
ON BLUE BEACH

—————————————— ✳ ——————————————

NO ONE IN 4TH FIELD IS SORRY TO LEAVE THE TENTS OF GREEN Street on August 14 to move into requisitioned buildings along country lanes and villages about two and a half miles north of Bognor Regis, though batteries are widely dispersed. RHQ is in a noble country mansion called Westergate Wood House; 2nd and 14th Batteries are at Walberton; and 26th Battery is some two miles away, centred on Barnham Junction, with more than a mile separating its troops.

On the morning of August 19, the BBC announces a Canadian landing on the coast of France at Dieppe, and suddenly a lot of things that have been bothering the curious for some time become clear: why Capt. George Browne went off on May 18 to act as a FOO for the Royal Navy practising landing infantry on a hostile shore; why, in the month that followed, two subalterns – "Moose" Saunders and Tommy Archibald – and twenty Other Ranks joined him for a hush-hush exercise known as "Simmer"; and where they were headed when they left in such a rush yesterday to catch up with the Royal Regiment of Canada on their way to Portsmouth.*

———————

* The two subalterns and twenty Other Ranks of 4th Field were to take over German field guns and turn them on the enemy. A FOO from each of the other two field regiments in the division also landed with the other two brigades. Capt. W. J. McCutcheon, of 5th Field, landing at Pourville

All day there are air-raid alerts, and dozens of Spitfires and Hurricanes range back and forth overhead, taking off from nearby Tangmere fighter station and returning from Dieppe to refuel and rearm. Radio reports provide few details, but imply the raid is meeting with success. However, by evening it is clear the raid was a disaster when only a handful of men – the remnants of assault battalions – return to Newhaven and other ports. At 4th Field, all is in readiness for returning comrades – rum, separate rooms, and hot food – but no one comes.

When next day there is still no word of the 4th Field men, they are presumed "missing," and a committee is formed to take care of their disposable personal effects.

Weeks go by with no news as to their fate. While the Regiment takes pride in the fact it was represented at a battle that will surely live for all time in the history of their country, much anxiety is aroused for friends who went on the raid when stories, from the few infantry survivors who landed and actually managed to get back, begin to circulate regarding the slaughter on the beaches, particularly on Blue Beach, east of Dieppe at Puys. Then, on September 11, comes some heartening news: Captain Browne is alive. He escaped the Germans and is now a Vichy French prisoner at Fort de la Duchere, Lyons, France. Incredibly, he reveals this through a regular cable to the Adjutant!

---

with Queen's Own Cameron Highlanders of Canada, was killed. Capt. H. B. Carswell, of 6th Field, was wounded landing at Pourville with the South Saskatchewan Regiment, and though wounded a second time remained on the beach for eight hours, observing and correcting the fire from the destroyers. He was subsequently awarded the first MC earned by a Canadian gunner officer in the war. The 3rd Light Ack-Ack Regiment, without their Bofors, armed with Brens and other small arms, were broken up into five separate parties. Some were held a mile offshore. Those who suffered most landed on Blue Beach at Puys with the Royals. Lieut. F. B. Carpenter and eight men were killed, and Lieut. McFetridge and nine Other Ranks were taken prisoner.

A month after the raid, the Regiment learns through official channels that Sgt. John W. Dudley, Lance-Bombardier F. H. Lalonde, and Gunner Donald McLean, along with eight officers and 201 Other Ranks of the Royal Regiment, died on Blue Beach at Puys – a narrow stretch of sea-lapped gravel, which for Gunner Carl Killeen, who went ashore with Browne that morning, will forever be "littered with dead bodies."*

Just how widely representative of Canada's regions 4th Field has become, through reinforcements over the years since the batteries were first recruited, is brought home by addresses of next-of-kin. Though a mere twenty ORs went to Dieppe, every province, with the exception of British Columbia, was represented, as well as New York State and Nebraska.

In September the Regiment hears the disturbing news that Dieppe prisoners are having to go about each day in chains, because the Germans found on the body of a dead Canadian officer a written order that Germans taken during the raid were to be tied up awaiting evacuation.†

During the fall, evidence that Browne has again escaped arrives on Col. Stan Todd's desk at Westergate House in the form of a

---

* Those who will spend the rest of the war in prisoners-of-war camps (Oflag 7B and Stalag 8B, Breslau, Poland, and Stargarde near Stettin):

Capt. Thomas D. Archibald	Gnr. Fulton James Adams
Lieut. Tait M. Saunders	Gnr. Charles Stanley Gray
Sgt. Leonard Joseph D'Arcy	Gnr. Archie Mills
L/Sgt. Irving Heller	Gnr. Joseph Krawda
L/Sgt. James George Potter	Gnr. Horden Jay Phillips
Bdr. Deans Cummings Lansing	Gnr. William Egill Sveinson
Bdr. George Leslie Gow	Gnr. Martin David Conrad Eager
Bdr. Harry Hancock	Gnr. William Mortimer Scott
L/Bdr. Morris Allen Demeray	Gnr. David Brown McIntosh
Gnr. J. Carl Killeen	(missing: Capt. George Browne)

† Daily manacling, begun September 1, 1942, did not end until December 2, 1943. See Appendix H.

cheerful little tourist postcard from Spain addressed to "Dear Uncle Stanley." Then nothing more for months. In the meantime, Combined Operations receives from Lyons, France, a remarkably detailed personal account of the Dieppe raid as Browne witnessed it, along with a wide-ranging critique of this first seaborne landing on the Continent that must surely prove of inestimable value to those planning "The Second Front."

Written while Browne was still in custody in Vichy, the document made it to Combined Ops and Canadian Military Headquarters on Trafalgar Square with the help of the American Consul in Lyons.* Unquestionably these nine single-spaced foolscap pages provide the single most important eyewitness account of the raid on Blue Beach, providing not only food for thought on equipment, fire-power, and tactics required for a successful seaborne lodgement on the Continent, but vivid images of great courage by men and officers among the awful carnage that day:

> In spite of the steady approach to the beach under fire, the Royals in my assault landing craft appeared cool and steady. It was their first experience under fire and though I watched them closely, they gave no sign of alarm, although first light was broadening into dawn and the interior of the ALC [assault landing craft] was illuminated by the many flares from the beach and the flash of the Bostons' [bombers] bombs.
>
> The quiet, steady voice of Captain W. B. Thompson [soon to die], seated just behind me, held the troops up to a confident and offensive spirit, although shells were whizzing over the craft, and we could hear the steady whisper and crackle of small-arms fire over the top of the ALC.
>
> The Royals touched down at 0535 hours . . . my first message to HMS *Garth* [a destroyer]: DOUG TOUCHED DOWN 0535.

---

* Report 89, Appendix "A", *Report on the Operation at Dieppe*, Dept. of History, Department of National Defence Headquarters. Sequence of excerpts modified to conform to sequence of events.

At the instant of touchdown small-arms fire was striking the ALC, and there was a not unnatural, split-second hesitation by those in the bow in leaping out onto the beach. But only a split-second. The troops got out onto the beach as fast as any of the "Simmer" exercises, and got across the beach to the wall and under the cliff. A and B Companies, landing immediately in front of the Blue Beach seawall, met intense and unexpectedly heavy machine-gun fire from a number of posts on the wall, sustaining very heavy casualties as they left the landing craft.

By the time we touched down the smoke laid by the RAF had almost completely disappeared, traces remaining only in the tree-tops above the beach. The beach was thus plainly visible to the Germans whose fire positions were extraordinarily well-concealed from our view. The Royals were shot down in heaps on the beach without knowing where the fire was coming from.

Their not unnatural bewilderment in this respect may have contributed to the fact that in five minutes' time they were changed from an assaulting battalion on the offensive to something less than two companies on the defensive, hampered by fire they could not locate. The narrow confines of the beach did not permit moving away from the fire to engage it in another position. Notwithstanding this the troops followed their leaders smartly where they could. The survivors who attained the comparative safety of the wall itself, were pinned to its face by enfilade fire from well-concealed positions on the flanks. Some of the wall machine-gun posts were put out of action, but at further heavy costs.

And in this regard, it may be permitted to mention the conduct of Lieut. [W. G. R.] Wedd of the Royal Regiment. Leaving the landing craft at touchdown with his platoon, he reached the wall with little more than a section [perhaps 10 men of 30], and there found he was still being fired upon by one of the wall posts, a pillbox. There being no other way of attacking the weapon, he left his corner of relative shelter and sprinted the short distance directly towards the pillbox with a 36-grenade. With complete disregard for his own safety, and displaying great skill, he flung the grenade through the fire-slit of the pillbox, killing all its occupants and putting the gun out of action. His body, riddled with bullets, was later picked up in front of the pillbox.

C and D Companies were landed at the extreme right of the beach, and Edward Force [some Royals, detachments of Black Watch and 3rd Light Ack-Ack, and the "prize troop" 4th Field] were landed west of the seawall under the cliff. D Company and the CO's party were in a sort of re-entrant on the western side of this wall's end spur. Edward Force and the prize troop were a hundred yards or more farther west.*

Remnants of C and D Companies, led by the Colonel [Doug Catto] then attempted to cut a path through the wire at the western end of the seawall and scale the cliff to the western prominent house. There was considerable delay here because D Company's bangalores [long tubes of explosive to blow wire] had been lost overside from the landing craft shortly after leaving the mothership through being improperly secured; and the bangalore-men of C Company were shot down in the water as they sprang out of the landing craft.

The only way through the wire was with wire-cutters. A path was finally cut by the Colonel, Sgt. Coles, and two Other Ranks. Lieutenant Stewart, who attempted to cover this operation by standing in the wire, upright with a Bren – the only position from which he might see from where the fire was coming – was shot down instantly though not killed. Cutting through the wire took some time and wasn't accomplished until after 0610 hrs at which time I reported to HMS Garth: DOUG STILL ON BEACH CASUALTIES HEAVY . . .

The path having been made through the wire, the Colonel led his party up the cliff to the top, between bursts of machine-gun fire. The party cleared the two houses at the top, immediately above the west end of the seawall, resistance being met in the

---

* Term "prize troop" means gunners who capture and man enemy guns.

first house only. Those who arrived at the top were: the CO, Capt. Hauser, Lieutenants Ryerson and Taylor, Sgt. Coles, and 11 Other Ranks of the Royal Regiment. Besides these were Lieut. McVetteridge [M. C. McFetridge], RCA, and the men of the Light AA Detachment, and myself as the FOO. The above were the only men of the Royals who got beyond the beach.

In the meantime the fire from A and B Companies was dwindling away to nothing, their casualties being so heavy. The remainder of C and D Companies, pinned into the re-entrant at the junction of the seawall and the cliff by accurate steady bursts of MG fire, could see nothing to shoot at. The battalion's 3-inch mortars were never fired, and scarcely set up; two crews being shot down in quick succession until there were no more mortar personnel left. Water and chalk from the cliffs jammed the Thompson sub machine-guns and Stens. And the 2-inch mortars in some cases being wet, could, only with difficulty and at reduced range, fire smoke bombs. There were not enough of these. The battalion 18-set would not function as, I believe, the microphone and key assembly had fallen into the water when leaving the ALC.

All this time, the remainder of the effectives having got out of the machine-gun fire by sheltering in the niches in the cliff-face on the beach, were now heavily engaged by German 3-inch mortars and stick grenades lobbed down from the cliff above. We sustained further heavy casualties from this mortar fire which the Germans were able to place well within twenty yards of the bottom of the cliff. The stick grenades, although not as effective as our M-36, were still very effectively employed and there seemed to be a lot of them. The DF fire of the German artillery (which I was told later by a German soldier was from 75-mm infantry guns) was apparently extremely well surveyed, for the shells burst precisely at the water-line, at impeccably correct interval and timing. I saw two ALCs sunk by hits or splinters from this fire. From a gunner's point of view, it was admirable shooting.

Then Browne explains why his signaller was unable to follow him up the cliff and allow him to communicate with the ships to bring down fire on the hostile battery up there:

> I saw the Colonel going up through the wire. My telegrapher, at that moment, was in the middle of a message. I told him to follow me as soon as he finished, and sprinted up the cliff after the Colonel. As it later appeared, machine-gun fire from a new position on the hill behind the fortified house on the left end of, and above, the seawall closed the gap in the wire and prevented any more men reaching the top. The Colonel and his small party were cut off from the remainder of C and D Companies on the beach. It was now nearly 0700 hours British time. Sounds of firing on the left flank had now died completely away. From the centre and the right flank we could hear intermittent bursts of German automatic fire and the steady detonations of their mortar bombs. From this we inferred that A and B Companies had been knocked out, and the survivors of C and D were still pinned down in the angle of the cliff and being cut up by mortars. We discovered we could not get back to the beach, nor could we get back to the cliff edge because of LMG [light machine-gun] fire from the left flank, up on the hillside. Just at this moment Lieut. Ryerson saw a strong patrol coming along the road through the trees towards us from the direction of the fortified house on the left flank.
>
> The decision was made to move toward Salvation Beach, west along the cliff top by the walled road, under cover of trees as far as they went. We would try to contact the Essex. Accordingly we struck through the small wood immediately to the west and above the beach, towards Notre Dame de Bon Secours . . . following the line of the walled road under cover of the trees, turning gradually south until Bon Secours. Ahead of us to the west across the walled road and beyond an open field of about 100 yards were the billets and gun positions of the 88-mm battery of the air photos. On our right, along the cliff edge 200 or 300

yards to the north, were three LMGs at that moment firing at our aircraft.

Behind us was the patrol which Ryerson had estimated at two platoons. Also behind us, at the junction of the Berneva-Puys-Neuville-Dieppe roads, were six-wheeled and eight-wheeled armoured cars, of which we were later informed by Lieut. T. D. Archibald, 4 RCA, who was led past these after his capture. On our left, across Puys-Bon Secours road, were the four-gun 75-mm infantry gun battery and a detachment of 88-mm ack-ack guns.

It was then getting on for 1000 hours, and the infantry guns were firing on the beach. They had previously been engaging the destroyer with, I was told, considerable accuracy, for when *Garth* came close in to engage shore targets at direct fire, she was forced to withdraw by bursts of gunfire from this battery which fell too hazardly close to her. One shell, it was rumoured, appeared to strike her on the bow.

A scout of our party who went out on the road to recce, was shot. The Germans had light machine-guns sited at each road and track intersection in this vicinity, with fields of fire in all directions.

Shortly after ten o'clock (or it may have been nearer eleven) while in the wood, we heard the survivors of the beach being marched past under guard. By noon it was apparent from the sound of firing we could hear from both RED and WHITE beaches, as well as from BLUE where there was none, that there was little or no land fighting, and that the operation had resolved itself into an air battle.

As far as we could see and hear from the wood, the German gunners had an unlimited supply of 88-mm, 20-mm, and LMG ammunition for ack-ack use, because they fired persistently and determinedly at every RAF machine they could see, without cease, right up until 1600 hours. The 88-mm battery of six guns on the cliff, between Notre Dame de Bon Secours and Puys, served its guns magnificently. It was low-level bombed at least four times and machine-gunned oftener by our fighters after 1000 hours, and each time the guns were back in action within a matter of a few seconds firing upon the departing aircraft. Once after a low-level attack only two guns were instantly back in action, but at other times always at least four. Twice we made a recce to the cliff edge to see what might be taking place on the main beach at Dieppe, but we could see neither the beach, which was just out of sight around the bend of the cliffs, nor any sign of the ships.

The situation suggested we were trapped. After long consideration the decision was taken to surrender. We surrendered at 1620 hours.

The Germans had casualties on Blue Beach. Lieut. Archibald, 4 RCA, saw their Aid Post above the beach at Puys full of German wounded. They were, however, by no means as numerous as ours.[*]

Browne then provides several pages of "observations" on equipment, tactics, and naval and air support of future landings. Much of this, he says, was "the gist of discussions held among remaining officers of the Royals at Verneuil where we were held prisoner for a week after the attack."

When a number of attacks are put in along a 25-kilometre stretch of coast, should they not all be put in simultaneously? This would give each individual attack a better chance of surprise. Further, is surprise easier to obtain than preparatory, heavy air-bombardment, which in our case quite probably would have succeeded where surprise, or the hope of surprise, failed? . . . At Blue Beach,

---

[*] Of the 542 all ranks in the Royal Regiment assault force, 464 were casualties – 227 killed, 136 wounded, and 101 prisoners. Of 5,000 Canadians taking part, nearly 70 per cent were casualties, 900 dead, 2,000 prisoners of war – many of them wounded.

where at the time of the landing the RAF had complete fighter superiority, dive-bombers could have been used . . . only a dive-bomber could have done immediate heavy damage to the seawall and the fortified house . . . It cannot be said here that naval bombardment failed, for it was not given an opportunity. As FOO, I was constantly in touch with the supporting destroyer through the good work of my telegraphist Wilkinson [a naval signaller] who continued to pass information messages to the ship until he was captured on the beach. But while on the beach itself, I could not see any origin to the fire poured upon us. On the cliff-top I was cut off from my communications to the ship . . .

Browne doubted *Garth* could have engaged the battery that kept her from coming in to engage targets. Though she was within range, the trajectory of her high-velocity shells could not have reached the German battery beyond the high cliff. Only looping shells with low propellant bombardment charges could have done so, and Garth had no bombardment charges.

His recommendations continue:

Frequently our own smoke obscured the situation for us as much, or more, as it did the enemy. When we wanted a screen badly . . . there was not enough to do the job. . . . Bangalore torpedoes made up of standard interchangeable sections of shorter length which one man could easily handle . . . would permit wider distribution of these aids against wire. . . . This would have saved us 20 to 30 minutes getting through the wire. And more wire-cutters should be available. At least 10 minutes were spent waiting for wire-cutters to be passed up. One pair finally arrived . . . I saw one man shot trying to get his wire-cutters up to the Colonel.

While Browne's No. 66 radio set (the 18-set modified for naval use) – carried ashore with aerial-mast unextended, and thus completely enclosed in waterproofing – remained dry and functioned perfectly, he recommends even better waterproofing of radio sets being carried ashore.

The Battalion HQ 18-set went dead as soon as the signaller stumbled into the saltwater getting off the landing craft, though well-wrapped in gas capes as a set on listening watch [with aerial stuck up in the air] can be. I was with the CO from the moment we reached the beach and he had no information from Brigade about the situation on the other beaches. Rockets or coloured smoke would have been of the greatest assistance here as with intercompany communication.

Browne spent much of his first hours as a prisoner at a makeshift first-aid post in Hotel Dieu in Dieppe, "a deserted convent which at one time might have been a hospital," but which then was devoid of running water and sanitary facilities.

The Sisters, French nuns, and a few French civilian women worked very hard trying to look after our wounded. The doctors, who were German, were busy looking after the last German wounded and despatching them to Rouen. At length the doctors got around to our fellows and did as much as they could for them with dressings on hand. The doctor in charge was an Oberstarzt, an ex-serviceman, good-humoured in a brusque manner, who worked hard to patch up our wounded. He was assisted by a German captain and a lieutenant and a Red Cross doctor . . . who from his costume appeared to be doing all the operating.
   A great part of the work, I learned later, was done by three of our MOs [medical officers] . . .
   Most of our stretcher cases were mortar-bomb wounds, very unpleasant and painful. From all the British and one French civilian (railroad employee) who were still conscious on their stretchers, there was not a murmur. Those who had cigarettes and were able to smoke sucked at a cigarette stoically; the others lay silent and uncomplaining. Not so the Germans who were

vocal and querulous in their pain. This was remarked by many of us as well as by French civilians in the hospital.*

---

* On October 3, 1942, a striking plaque, prepared by a special committee of Telscombe Cliffs, East Sussex, was unveiled in Telscombe Hall, where many of the soldiers who went on the Dieppe Raid had often attended dances and become acquainted with many townspeople. In 1997 the plaque was still there, appealing to all who enter the hall to remember those boys:

> Is it nothing to you, all ye who pass by?

> A tribute to the memory of those gallant goodhearted Canadian boys who spent so many happy hours in this hall and who passed on fighting for us on the Dieppe Raid August 19, 1942, knowing what ought to be done and doing it at all costs. They were worthy of their country.

> They shall be greatly remembered for God proved them and found them worthy of himself.

35

LIFE AT BARNHAM JUNCTION

———————————————— ✳ ————————————————

IT IS AS REPLACEMENTS FOR THE THREE OFFICERS WHO DIDN'T return from Dieppe that you and four other lieutenants (Howard I. Dawson, W. D. Stevenson, L. W. Lewis, and J. M. Lawless) on September 4 are removed from the sheltered existence at #1 CARU (Canadian Artillery Reinforcement Unit), where you have been taking "refresher courses" since arriving from Canada, and sent south by train to 4th Field, now stationed around Barnham Junction, about five miles north of Bognor Regis and the Channel.*

Here, with some exceptions (the most notable being a big smiling Jack Cameron, 26th Battery subaltern, the first officer you encounter after getting off the train, who arranges for a truck to take all of you and your kit to regimental headquarters two miles away), your reception is in the tradition of regular British gunner regiments, who expose newly joined junior officers to studied coolness and polite aloofness so as to reduce their egos to acceptable levels of deference.

From the outset all officers above the rank of lieutenant (and occasionally even some lieutenants) make it clear that you are some-

———————

* Five subalterns to replace two captains and one subaltern makes sense only if it is understood that frequently reinforcement subalterns were posted as supernumeraries to regiments to gain experience and at the same time to give the regiments a chance to look them over as future prospects.

what less than worthy replacements for the noble chaps who landed on the French shore. And Lt.-Col. Stanley Todd unequivocally declares this to be the case when the four of you are marched in before his desk by his formidable adjutant, Captain Harrison: "Left-right! Left-right! . . . Halt! Right turn! Stand-at . . . ease!"

After looking you over, each in turn, the stern, thin-faced, dignified colonel seems positively sad as he stares down at his desk blotter and quietly and reflectively informs you that you are joining a fine regiment, recently declared the best field artillery regiment in Britain; that you cannot be expected to replace the highly trained officers lost at Dieppe, but you will be expected to try; and that it is to be hoped, as time goes by, you will become valuable assets to the Regiment. It is a short speech, and he ends it abruptly with the words: "That is all." All in all, a pretty cold reception.

His stern adjutant, clearly sharing his disdain, takes over: "At-ten-shun! Right turn! Quick-march! Left-right! Left-right!"

Out in the front hall of the country mansion, noticeably shabby from years of suffering hobnail-booted occupants, Harrison assigns you to batteries. Slindon and Walberton figure in the location of the others assigned to 2nd and 14th Batteries. Happily you draw the 26th Battery and return with the friendly Jack Cameron to their officers' mess in a substantial house about half a mile from the station along a road lined with holly hedges and other less-well-groomed vegetation.

Helping you to carry your kit into the house – his every word, glance, and gesture making you feel welcome – Cameron leads you in through the entrance hall and right through the living room (the mess ante-room) to a ground-floor bedroom just beyond the fireplace. Here he immediately starts clearing a space for your folding canvas cot along the outside wall, between his cot and another low-slung affair he says belongs to fellow subaltern Len Harvey. As he struggles to open up your cussed cross-legged cot, he explains that Harvey, though several years his junior, is his boss, being the GPO (gun position officer) of Freddie Troop, for which he, Cameron, is the "troop leader" (the odd title by which the Ack GPO is known).

You, he says, will be assigned to Eddie Troop as its troop leader and be under the command and supervision of the GPO Lieut. "Stu" Laurie.*

At dinner you meet them and the other officers, including the battery commander, Major Don Cooper. As time goes on you'll learn that each is very much his own man – with his own personality, only superficially modified by the conformity imposed by the military – but for the moment, they come across as a clannish gang, whose whole universe is the narrow world of battery and Regiment.

Most have been over here since 1940 (one since 1939), and you are prepared for questions about what it is like back home these days. But they aren't the slightest bit curious about anything that doesn't have a direct bearing on the state of the unit and their mastery of gunnery. Clearly included among the subjects in which they have no interest are newly attached subalterns. By the end of the evening, you realize you have been, if not "sent to Coventry" (ostracized), then the next thing to it. When you inquire discreetly of Cameron why they are doing this to you, he says you'll not be fully accepted until you've "paid your dues." Everybody has to. He had to.

---

* In the artillery, lines of authority among officers are established by the titles of the jobs to which they are assigned, and authority to supervise and command fellow officers of the same rank is the rule rather than the exception. For instance, the battery Command Post Officer (CPO) is senior to the Assistant CPO, and to the Gun Position Officers (GPOs), who in turn are senior to their troop leaders, as the assistant GPOs are known. All are subalterns, and some being supervised possess longer service than their supervisors. Assistant CPOs are senior to the GPOs when they are acting as CPOs. Similarly, the Battery Captain (second-in-command to the Battery Commander) is senior to the two troop commander captains only when he is acting as Battery Commander. And it doesn't end at the regimental level. The highest ranking artillery officer in the division is the Brigadier CRA, the same rank as his boss, the Brigadier CCRA of Corps, and the Brigadier BRA at Army Headquarters.

Though explained in kindly fashion, he obviously agrees with their assessment: you are an untried greenhorn whose opinion is not sought nor welcome when volunteered. You feel abandoned by your new friend, and you burn with resentment. But you are determined your discomfiture will not show. And until you are accepted as a full-fledged member of the mess (a couple of weeks later), you retire to your cot each night after dinner to write letters, read and put down diary notes on everything you find novel or interesting about life at Barnham Junction.

The Battery Office is set up in what in peacetime was the village's bank, still clearly identifiable as Lloyd's Bank – a fact that never fails to inspire witticisms during pay parades as gunners pass before the likeable sergeant in charge of the office, whose name happens to be George Lloyd, son of Colonel Lloyd, who brought 4th Field to England.

Most of battery headquarters personnel live in unfurnished rooms in a requisitioned portion of the Railway Hotel across the street, but Sgt. Bill Montaigne and other battery command post acks live in a railway house beside the tracks with a most convenient, if illegitimate, supply of soft engine-coal piled high in their back-yard. (For what purpose no one knows, since Southern Railway is electrified.)

Eddie Troop is billeted in a couple of corrugated-iron Nissen huts in a field on the eastern outskirts of the village, and Freddie Troop is a mile and a half northwest of the station in a cluster of buildings at a crossroads distinguished by a pub with the unique name Labour in Vain that could be claimed by Eastergate or Westergate.

All sleeping accommodation is cold and draughty, but at least the army differentiates between sleeping on concrete and sleeping on wood and provides those men living in concrete-floored Nissen huts with steel-webbed (albeit springless) cots, while those who sleep in buildings with wooden floors, such as the parquet of the Railway Hotel, are issued straw palliasses on which to bed down.

One scuttle of coke is allowed for each stove or fireplace in each billet per day, and fires cannot be lit before four o'clock each afternoon. Living conditions by civilian standards are really quite crummy, but to all ranks regularly subjected to training schemes simulating the most primitive conditions they may face in action (stopping just short of using lethal fire to prove their point), the billets seem reasonably comfortable.

To men returning from living out of doors for days on end in blustery fall and winter rains – somehow surviving without tents or sheltering cover apart from groundsheets, greatcoats, and gas capes – those springless steel cots in Nissen huts look almost luxurious. And even the lumpy straw palliasses on the floor of the Railway Hotel can seem positively cosy in their rustling dryness, when rain is lashing the windows and the wind is rattling the doors.

The ration of only one scuttle of coke per day applying here in the officers' mess as well, no attempt is made to warm the house beyond the sitting room, or "ante-room" as purists prefer to call the room in a mess where you gather when you're not in the dining room, messing around with your food. And since the daily struggle to coax a bashful, smoky fire among the damp, mulish coke poured in the grate over balls of newspaper and a pitiful handful of twigs can only begin after 4:00 P.M., only this one room is reasonably comfortable by the time you are going to bed. Even your downstairs bedroom off the living room remains unheated and is so clammy that pyjamas hung on the wall in the frigid dampness absorb so much moisture in one day, they're unusable that night. Yours hang drooping from a nail over your camp cot, where they were deposited in September on arising your first morning here, and there they'll remain till they dry out next spring, while you continue sleeping in your long johns.

Though you sit down to meals at a highly polished mahogany table, the dining room is like an icebox, for the only heat it ever receives, apart from body heat, is what drifts in with the fumes from the gas-cooker in the kitchen. And the meals, prepared from precisely the same rations as those issued the men, exhibit the same interesting qualities; perhaps more so, since there's no provision in the establishment of a battery for an officers' mess cook, and a batman has had to volunteer to act the part. The fact he has no formal training in the culinary arts doesn't prevent him from assuming the traditional arrogance of a chef at the Savoy as he turns dried-egg powder into a moist, yellow, crumbly imitation of scrambled eggs, admittedly not too dissimilar from those concocted of the same yellow powder at that famous London hostelry.

Sugar, of course, is strictly rationed, and since the porridge served every morning is, for most officers, the only food offered in any twenty-four-hour period that would compare favourably in quality with memorable, prewar food, tempers can flare in the cold, grey light of dawn, and snide remarks are passed when someone thinks they spot a fellow "officer and gentleman" spooning more than his ration of sugar into his milk-laden bowl.

Sometimes there are palatable slices of fried Spam, but more often it's "soya-links" – imitation sausages which, regardless of how they are cooked, remain a repelling red on the outside and eternally pink on the inside, arousing latent fears of dread trichinosis, although you are assured there is not one corpuscle of real meat in the soya mash.

Like the reconstructed eggs, they are no better and no worse than the "bangers" served with great *élan* from under flashing silver domes at the Savoy these days. But toast is something else. When produced it is simply bread singed a spotty black and white, since toasting by gas flame calls for more skill and patience than the batman possesses or is inclined to display.

In short, officers' messing could be said to be "adequate."

On the other hand, messing for the men, being carried out at the troop level because of the distance between troops, is better than usual, since food cooked in smaller quantities can be produced with more care by the cooks, and is more *likely* to be, when the producers live in close contact with their caustic-tongued consumers. And you can testify with authority that, while the meals, deposited in mess tins held out by men lining up at Eddie Troop kitchen, may not be served with much style, they are vastly superior to those served on a mahogany table in a house half a mile up the road.

Still, variety, a most desirable feature of any menu, cannot help but be a continuing weakness of army messing. For instance, though you are supposed to be having one egg a week (judging from the little sheet of ration coupons they issue for a nine-day leave), you've seen only one egg in the last three months, and it was of Irish extraction and beginning to show its age. This can incite scrounging forays for such by men bored with the sameness of rations, and one morning your troop commander, Captain Wilson, receives a visit from a pensioner, living over the fence from Eddie Troop's Nissen huts. It seems he regularly counts his flock of three dozen hens, and this morning he was able to count only thirty-five instead of thirty-six.

Now, the pleasant, elderly man "sympathizes with the boys." Having soldiered in the First War, he "knows what it's like to yearn for a bit of a change of diet." Still, the loss of a laying-hen is a serious matter, for he and his wife depend on the income from the sale of the eggs to see them through. All of this is duly passed on to the men of Eddie Troop in the inimitable style of Captain Wilson – tersely and clearly, with tremendous restraint, in the manner of a man suppressing Vesuvian rage that could erupt at any moment. The culprit may escape detection this time, but should he tempt providence a second time, God help him.

Next morning the old man is back again, but this time smiling, as he reports: "Captain Wilson, a miracle of reproduction has oc- curred overnight. When, as usual, I counted my flock this morning, not only had the number returned to a full three dozen, there were two additional hens over the count!"*

---

* Months later a similar result accrued when the Regiment was confined to barracks at Sennybridge until the gunner or gunners unkown came forward with a very large and hard-to-come-by bright-green tarpaulin purloined from a piece of farm equipment or haystack on the way up from Sussex. For two days the farmer had followed the trail of vehicles

Throughout the fall and winter of 1942-43, 4th Field will remain in the Barnham area in a semi-operational role. An hour after dark, one battery puts its guns into action in camouflaged pits cut into the verges of a lane on the outskirts of Yapton, a mile or so southeast of Barnham, pointing towards the Channel three miles distant, in support of 4th Brigade infantry battalions taking turns standing to in positions of semi-readiness along the seafront at Middleton and Littlehampton.

Each night FOOs from the two troops of the battery taking its turn in the "stand-to" position, spend the night with the infantry, while at the guns all but the guards sleep in a nearby requisitioned house devoid of all furniture. At first all ranks are required to sleep fully clothed, but as time goes on regulations are relaxed, at least to the extent that boots may be removed. Information about the enemy indicates he is not in a position to conduct a full-scale invasion, but might try a raid in force somewhere.

At dawn the guns are manned with full crews for stand-to, and then limbered up and returned to their respective gun parks.

Morale is only fair. However important Dieppe may one day appear as a dress rehearsal for the invasion of Europe – guaranteeing certain immortality to infantry battalions sacrificed on its beaches – the immediate consequence to 2nd Division as a fighting force has been devastating. Units of 4th Brigade – the Essex Scottish, the Royal Regiment of Canada, and the Royal Hamilton Light Infantry – have had to rebuild completely with new officers, NCOs, and men. Clearly, action for them, and thus the supporting artillery, is a long way off. And the war is not going well. The Germans are on the rampage in North Africa, threatening to cut off the Suez Canal. And bets are being made on what day Stalingrad, one of the last Russian bastions, will fall.

---

carrying the unit sign "42" superimposed on a little square of red and dark blue (red on top and blue on the bottom). Next morning the front stoop of the hut assigned as a regimental office was piled high with green tarpaulins.

Closer to home, the Luftwaffe is showing signs of stepping up the air attacks on Britain. While using only a few planes at a time – flying in "down on the deck" to escape radar detection – these raids can be very destructive. Back in the spring, at the outset of these "sneak raids" as they've become known, the Regiment had a grand-stand view of one of them at Eastbourne, just four hundred yards from the hill on which the CO was holding an orders group.* Six planes came roaring up the valley behind the town, flying so low the men of 4th Field were looking down on them as they passed over the town, seemingly on their way back across the Channel.

Suddenly, with a tremendous boom, the town's monster gas-ometer tank blew apart in a great ball of flame and black debris.†

Every cloudy day, one or two Junkers 88s fly in from the Channel at treetop level to bomb and strafe surrounding towns and villages. One day one appears over Barnham, banking so low over the subway under the railway, you can see the face of the pilot looking at you. Circling, he drops a bomb, causing an earthquaking roar as it hits the gasometer.

Seconds later there is another shuddering boom as the plane, wounded by flying debris or by a shell from the storm of ack-ack it has aroused, crashes out of sight, sending up a column of black smoke beyond the village. Miraculously there are no civilian or military casualties beyond the crew of the bomber, for the concus-sion of the explosions shatters panes of glass in the living-room windows of 26th Battery's officers' mess more than a mile away. While accomplishing little in a tactical sense, these raids have a depressing effect on morale, reminding everyone that the Luftwaffe

---

* A meeting of officers for purposes of briefing and issuing operation orders.
† A huge steel tank filled with illuminating gas, the gasometer floats upside down in a deep reservoir of oil, held erect by an open network of steel girders, its own weight forcing the gas within it to maintain constant pressure throughout a network of pipes to gas stoves in the kitchens of the area.

still has the capacity to inflict frightful damage, and that if Russia falls, the Germans will turn the attention of all their planes on Britain.

Another grey, wet, chilly winter lies ahead, with the end of the war further away than ever. And morale is not helped by the cloak of smugness now assumed by the Regiment from having been named "the best" at fire and movement on the Salisbury Plain last summer, so noticeable during your abbreviated meeting with the CO the day you arrived. Seemingly it has not occurred to anyone that attaining such grand status might adversely affect enthusiasm for training, that much of the incentive to improve (so noticeable from the days when the new 25-pounders and quads arrived) might disappear. In the euphoria induced by this "smashing show . . . this super accomplishment," no one wants to be reminded of that one ranging round that landed *behind* the hill chosen by the CO to watch proceedings, its wicked thunderclap a stern warning that even "the best" can improve.

The effects of the drop in enthusiasm for repetitious troop deployments in local cow pastures, and for "dry shoots" with firing pins clicking on empty breeches, won't really show up until the Regiment attends its next practice camp at Sennybridge in Wales late in the fall. In the meantime, other training is emphasized, and some really imaginative devices are used to cure what the senior officers perceive to be residual deficiencies in the skills of 4th Field.

36

BRACKETING BY PUFFS OF
CIGARETTE SMOKE

————————————— ✳ —————————————

ONE GLARING DEFICIENCY IN TRAINING IS REVEALED WHEN 4TH
Field visits the anti-tank range on the floor of the valley behind
Beachy Head. Of course the quality of anti-tank shooting is entirely
dependent on the acquired skill of gun crews – in particular gun-
layers, who sight the gun and fire at the right instant, and the
sergeants, who must make quick estimates of ranges and deflections
as the shoot progresses.

When a gun position is attacked by tanks, the GPO becomes quite
superfluous, since once he indicates the quadrant from which the
tanks are approaching and gives the opening range, he must turn
over all gun control to his gun sergeants.

"Tank alert – southeast 1,000! Cheerio, chaps – see you Tuesday!"
is how Len Harvey (clearly borrowing a leaf from Dusty Miller's
Petawawa notebook) perceives his role as GPO.

In contrast, each Number One puts his gun on a specific tank by
throwing the trail around so the muzzle points roughly in its direction and gives his gun-layer the range in yards and the "deflection"
in degrees to "lead" the moving target with the graduated hairlines
in his telescopic sight.

Of course ranges and deflections constantly change as the tank
changes direction. It is not easy to hit a target that speeds up and
slows down and appears and disappears behind ridges – up and
down over folds in the landscape. This you learned on the layer's

seat of a 25-pounder during officers' training, and this the gunners of 4th Field find out when they try potting burlap-draped wooden frames, the size and shape of tanks, towed swiftly across the range some five hundred yards from the muzzles of their guns. Many of the burlap tanks make it across without being holed even once by a gun banging off its allotment of five rounds of solid-shot – the course of which can easily be followed because of the dazzling white tracer pellet in the base of each missile streaking at the target and ricocheting up and over the headland – some of them passing through the gloomy silhouette of the deserted and pathetic-looking restaurant building on the crest of the cliff before Beachy Head.

Since getting off just five rounds now and then could never produce expert open-sight gun-layers, some unsung genius has produced a device that allows a layer to lay his gun on a little cardboard-cutout tank (its miniature size suggesting distance) and have the accuracy of his lay proven by a bullet from a sawed-off .22-calibre rifle, which has been welded into the fuse hole in the base of an empty 25-pounder cartridge case, inserted in the breech of the gun and fired when the gun-layer pulls the 25-pounder's firing lever the normal way.

At first only static targets are used, but then a clothesline is strung across the wall of the miniature range, so the target can be towed across with some consistency. Now the gun-layer, with his eye glued to his telescopic sight and his hands constantly whirling his gear wheels, must learn to accommodate the sudden pitch and swing of the gun as his sergeant "throws the trail" to keep the muzzle pointing in the general direction of the target and so prevent him from "running out of traverse" as he fine-tunes the lay with his traversing gears. In a short time the speed and accuracy achieved by the gunners is astonishing, and interest in anti-tank firing techniques rises accordingly.

Another miniature range provides equally beneficial training for junior officers in the matter of conducting observed shoots at the OP – a serious deficiency in the training of subalterns due again to the rationing of ammunition. Naturally, first call on shells allotted for training in ranging techniques goes to the captains who will be moving with the infantry as forward observation officers. And though subalterns are expected to take over when their troop commanders become casualties, they rarely get a chance to range guns by observed fire. Thus the "miniature smoke range" erected in an empty room in Barnham by the Battery Command Post staff led by the CPO Lieut. Luke Lawson and his Ack CPO, Lieut. William Reynolds "Sink" Sinclair, following the directions of Major Don Cooper, proves of incalculable value in training you to range the guns and engage a variety of targets in appropriate fashion.*

Whether it is calling down a deluge of shells with a minimum of ranging on enemy infantry attacking over that hill; or bringing a single gun to "close-bracket" accuracy for a destructive shoot on that machine-gun post; or engaging with bold switches a "quick target" of tanks and armoured half-tracks roaring across the landscape, where speed must take priority over accuracy; or laying down a smokescreen to help the infantry disengage from a situation – regardless of what will be required of you one day as a FOO – you'll have confronted it and taken care of it here in this little room with its ingenious set-up.

It consists of a remarkably realistic landscape created on painted burlap sacking, planted with tiny trees and houses, representing an actual section of a real map. This rolling landscape of hills, roads, and villages is formed over chicken-wire pinned in waves on a wooden frame, some seven feet above, and precisely positioned over, grid lines painted on the floor. The painted grid corresponds with the grid lines of the map provided the "FOO" sitting on a raised bench overlooking this "landscape."

When the FOO calls for a round on a chalk pit on the side of a hill – providing what he considers to be the map reference from his map – he hears a voice say "shot one" at such and such range, and

---

* Various targets require different scales of fire and number of guns involved.

a few seconds later a tiny puff of smoke appears at the chalk pit, if his map reference is accurate, or somewhere else if it isn't.

Down on the floor underneath the burlap vista, two fellow officers acting as GPOs perform the function of the guns. Receiving the map reference, they mark it with chalk in the appropriate grid square on the floor. Then, positioning the base of the smoke machine over that point and raising a long, glass tube to the burlap sacking, they send up a puff of smoke. Future corrections by the FOO, which are never map references, must be converted into such on an artillery board, reversing normal procedure at a troop command post.

This can be a little slow, and when the ammonia-induced-smoke device fails, the "GPOs" down under have to smoke cigarettes like mad to produce the required "shots" through the burlap, with a corresponding deterioration in the quality of the air in the room. But the overall effect is so uncannily realistic that every hour of instruction on this range under Major Cooper or Troop Commander Don Wilson is worth many trips to an OP on the ranges – trips you can never hope to make. And clearly Harvey and Cameron, taking their turns under the guidance of their troop commander, Capt. Dave Blyth, feel the same way.

What this experience does for your confidence level alone makes this training device worthwhile – confidence being half the battle when carrying out a shoot with an IG from Larkhill or Sennybridge looking over your shoulder. And when one day you have to engage real enemy targets in action, such confidence surely will be priceless.

37

"LEANING INTO THE BARRAGE"

——————————— ✳ ———————————

EVERY NOW AND THEN, WHILE STILL ON THE NEVER-ENDING round of "schemes," which usually involve only dry-firing, the Regiment travels east some fifty miles along the Sussex coast to Alfriston range, a couple of miles north of Seaford. Here they deploy and fire off a few desultory rounds of H.E. at a selection of chalk pits or stoney skeletons of buildings such as Black Cat Farm, lying in scattered, broken sorrow among the humpbacked, gorse-covered chalk hills known as the South Downs.

Reached by way of a barely negotiable, deeply rutted, chalky goat track, rising steeply out of the quaint little village of Alfriston with its ancient inns (including the famed Star, at whose fireplace King Alfred reputedly dozed off and allowed the cakes to burn), the ranges are very small compared to the vast acreages of Senny-bridge. Though greatly expanded by the requisitioning of surrounding farms since the Regiment first fired here in November 1941 (into a target area of only five hundred yards square), it is still known as a "postage-stamp range." Nevertheless, the Alfriston range offers many more training opportunities to Canadian gunners than does Sennybridge.

Certainly, it is at Alfriston that most junior officers have gained their first regimental experience in control of troops firing live ammunition as troop leaders, gun position officers, command post officers, and troop commanders. Unquestionably, the word

Alfriston will forever arouse special (if mixed) emotions among officers and men.

While there are no barracks or usable buildings on the range, and all ranks must bed down on the exposed slopes of the treeless South Downs, the weather (unlike Sennybridge) can be entirely pleasant, occasionally providing sunny days and starlit nights. Even when gun positions and observation posts on the open crests of the hills are lashed by rain and wind howling in from the Channel five miles away, there is consolation in the fact that you are here only for a one-night stand.

And if, as sometimes happens, you are among the lucky ones who get the chance after dark to visit the warming hearths of the charming pubs of Alfriston, the discomforts of the night disappear completely for a while and are greatly leavened for the rest of the night by much good spirit flowing through your veins.

Alfriston provides many days to remember, but none more memorable than the day of September 25, 1942, when all ranks of the Regiment learn by personal experience what it is like to run forward behind a barrage, placing your trust in the accuracy of others plotting the "lifts" on artillery boards, and laying the guns.

A composite battery of officers and gunners, selected from all six troops of 4th Field, fires the barrage into a suitable valley of the South Downs before the curious eyes of Lt.-Gen. Harry Crerar (former gunner), commander of 1st Canadian Corps, Maj.-Gen. J. Hamilton Roberts, another former gunner, now in command of 2nd Division, and the present CRA Brigadier, P. C. Tees.

Officers, gunners, signallers, acks, drivers, motor mechanics, clerks, cooks, storemen, and batmen – every man not required to man the eight guns involved in the shoot – will run up a grassy, gentle slope with Lieutenant-Colonel Todd, "leaning into the barrage," as those keen battle-school instructors (who have never participated in the breathtaking experience themselves) like to put it.

While common sense tells you those crashing orange-and-black flashes – causing the ground to shudder beneath your running feet

– are a safe distance ahead, it seems as though you are running right at them as you feel their hot breath and are enveloped in a continuous reverberating roar. After the briefest pause between lifts – lying prone on your stomach in the grass, with much heavy breathing and the sour taste of the drifting acrid fumes in your dry mouth – the muffled *crump*ing begins behind and the vicious sizzling and crackling overhead as the earth before you again flashes and spouts with furious overlapping thunderbolts.

Officially, the interval between this charging mob and the barrage is supposed to be three hundred yards, but it is probably less than two hundred. It *seems* less than a hundred. Just keeping abreast of the Colonel, who seems determined to lead the pack all the way, you are running over shell-pitted ground so close behind the crashing, threshing storm, you are leaping over gashes in the earth still steaming and smoking from the explosions that gouged them.

Is the CO, in his zeal, leading all of you to outrun the forward progress of the barrage; will you arrive at the next lift just as the shells start to fall on it? Fearful, but in a strange way exhilarated, you churn up the last hundred yards of the slope, arriving breathless and leg-weary on the "objective." Unscathed, but totally subdued by the awesome experience, you find yourself wondering how the infantry can be expected to engage the enemy in combat with any vigour after such a run, even with the enemy stunned and bewildered from having suffered the full force of that horrific maelstrom and not inclined to rise up with enthusism to repel a foe rushing at them as the shelling ends.

For days afterward, those shattering concussions, with their hot, sour breath seemingly just a few yards in front of your feet, churning up the slope with hundreds of others, remain remarkably vivid.

And the gunners who manned the guns, and the NCOs who supervised the gun-laying – all of them men of long experience in firing live ammunition – tell you how they prayed they wouldn't make an error and drop one short on their buddies.

The officers and their command post acks, responsible for working out the predicted fire plan and applying "corrections of the moment," to compensate for the effects of wind, temperatures, and air pressures on the shells looping over the Downs, confessed that, after checking and rechecking their work, they "sweated blood" waiting for a report from up front on the results of their work – so agonizingly slow in coming, at least one GPO came to believe there'd been a disaster.

Of all the valuable lessons learned during years of training, this has to be not only the most dramatic, but also the most meaningful. All who ran behind the bursting shells knew their lives were in the hands of others applying tiny switches to dial-sights and range cones, and levelling their bubbles on sight-clinometers on the guns hidden in the hills a mile or two behind them. Every yard they ran forward, they ran in dread of a shell falling short, tearing them to pieces – the same feeling all men of the Essex Scottish, the Royal Regiment of Canada, and the Royal Hamilton Light Infantry will feel each time the Regiment supports them in the attack with a barrage, or drops neutralizing fire close-in to their positions to subdue an enemy counter-attack.*

The profound meaning of all these impressions has been imprinted permanently on the mind of every member of 4th Field. And you are proud you were there when you are told the reason so many generals came to watch was simply that this was the first time all ranks of an artillery regiment had ever been obliged to run behind a barrage fired by their own guns. Clearly, Colonel Todd is an innovator, especially when you add this unique training experience to the fact he is seeing that infantry officers of 4th Brigade get some instruction in ranging the guns on targets, just in case it one day comes in handy.

---

* Though seemingly a rehearsal for firing barrages over the heads of the infantry, this doesn't occur until the spring of 1944, only weeks before being involved in the real thing. At Alfriston, during night exercises, 4th Field fires barrages involving each battalion in turn: the Essex on March 27, the Royals on the 28th, and the Rileys (RHLI) on the 29th.

38

MAP-READING

———————————— ✳ ————————————

FACTORED INTO THE TRAINING OF OFFICERS OVER HERE IS AN unusual dimension provided by the devious, labyrinthian British roads, which the simple road systems of North America could never provide – thoroughly and conclusively preventing complacency or smugness afflicting any officer for long. Regardless of how qualified or experienced he may be, or how elevated his rank, he knows – and he knows that all the Other Ranks know – he's not immune to errors in map-reading.

There are, of course, no roadsigns in Britain, all of them having been removed in 1940 to confuse invaders. Thus all officers have had to learn the idiosyncrasies of British maps and roads – often in the most embarrassing circumstances while leading a convoy of vehicles astray – since expert knowledge of map-reading is not enough to ensure the most assiduous officer from taking a wrong turn, especially in the more densely populated southern counties of this blessed isle.

For instance, all officers have to learn the hard way that when a map clearly shows a Y in the main road through a small town, they must not count on it being obvious which of the openings they are approaching is the correct route to follow. In fact, the road they want – clearly shown on the map as the main road – more likely than not forms no part of any visible Y, but takes off at right angles, or worse still curls right back in the direction from which they've been coming, appearing to disappear between two buildings and looking for all the world like an alley leading to nowhere. While the wrong road, one that will lead them into a hopeless mess of misleading map-reading, clearly forms the only distinct Y as you approach that road junction.

And still worse may lie ahead for the poor leader of the convoy, for errors are not readily discovered in a country where there are more than enough hamlets, road junctions, and roundabouts to satisfy any map-reader for some considerable time that he's on the right road, regardless of which road he chooses.

When finally it dawns on him he's not on the right road, and, in a cold sweat, turns the convoy around to go back, even more complications may develop. Not knowing exactly where he now is on the map of Great Britain, or precisely where the error was made, further errors are almost inevitable – particularly on a drizzly, foggy night in the blackout.

While officers have continued to improve their map-reading skills over the years, the struggle for mastery of the English road system is unceasing. And it's clear that as long as the Regiment is in Britain, these deceptive roads will never relinquish their capacity to reduce even the most self-assured officer of unquestionable ability to a quivering mass of embarrassment, struggling to hide his chagrin as he supervises the turning around of his convoy, each gun and each limber having to be manhandled separately because of the constricted space of the barnyard into which he led them. That he's one of the most alert, well-trained, earnest officers in the Canadian Army – who may one day be a famous jurist of a superior court, a cabinet minister, or a leading industrialist owning much of the real estate of an entire city – cannot save him at this moment from appearing a perfect nincompoop in his own eyes and the eyes of all those involved in physically manhandling the guns and trailers around in the mud, or worse, of the barnyard.

Your worst experience so far is driving back and forth on a main public road skirting Sennybridge ranges at least five or six times (fortunately without convoy), looking for a road leading in to a map reference on the ranges you'd been given to recce for the guns, before concluding that a farmhouse lane – passing through a closed gate into a barnyard and two more gates beyond – is the correct road!

Stories of predicaments arising out of errors in map-reading are legion, but even as you laugh at the latest tale, you know it could well have happened to you. Like the story of Capt. Tommy Richardson, the Regimental Quartermaster, who, one rainy, black night in the fall of '42, on the way back from a scheme, led his little convoy right out onto the runway of a bomber airdrome that has the peculiar distinction of having hangars on one side of a highway and runways on the other.

In the fog, thinking he'd arrived at a crossroads, he had his driver turn onto a taxiing strip used to move bombers across the road from one side of the station to the other. And for the next half hour, he went round and round the airfield, cursing the inadequacy of British maps and establishing a legend of bewilderment for RAF types responsible for landing planes on that field, while the other drivers in his little convoy, taking "independent action," contrived to escape the encircling military police.

Whether or not the runway lights actually were turned on to allow Tommy to find his way out to the highway, as is claimed by his driver, it must remain one of the great map-reading-débâcle stories of all time.

Because of the natural desire of the senior officers to end up after a long day of convoy driving with the same number of vehicles following them as when they started out, the most-junior officers (subalterns below the seniority of CPOs) are required to take turns on motorbikes riding herd on the convoy, not only ensuring convoy discipline, but supplementing the efforts of the despatch riders doing point duty at every road intersection that might be confusing to drivers, who, for one reason or another, have let the vehicle in front of them get out of sight.

It is said that drivers have been known to drop in for a quick one at out-of-the-way pubs while seeking directions. To save them all this trouble and expense, subalterns spend hours on motorbikes, rushing up past the seven-mile-long line of trucks and guns of the Regiment snaking along narrow, winding roads with little room to spare on either side. Frequently, you brush ivy-covered stone walls and the flat sides of quads with the sleeve of your trenchcoat, and hold your breath as you roar through blind intersections at seventy miles an hour – all for the purpose of getting to the head of the convoy to point the direction to passing vehicles so that, when the last one passes, you can get on your motorbike and start all over again making it up to the head of the convoy.

Fortunately, you were exposed to a wonderful MC (motorcycle) course at #1 CARU that familiarized you with the Norton motorcycle, standard issue to all line units. Besides having to follow your instructor, a former dirt-track racer, on a lot of "road running," you were also taught "cross-country riding" in the vicinity of Hindhead: nursing your machine through shallow, stony streams without stalling halfway across; "walking" the rugged smoking machine through gorse, deep sand, and up a high staircase of haphazard rock ledges forming the dry bed of a cataract; and riding in a standing-up position, down and up the incredibly steep sides of the "Devil's Punchbowl."

Still, convoy work – which keeps an entire ward at Number 14 General Hospital, East Grinstead, well-stocked with officers recovering from broken limbs and concussions suffered in motorcycle accidents – can be learned one way only: by doing it.

And so it is with so many things required of a subaltern joining a field regiment already well-advanced in its training, particularly one that has just been named "the best." While better-trained technically than probably any of the officers who joined the day war broke out, you arrived knowing nothing of the day-to-day responsibilities of officers in a functioning regiment. Fortunately, sergeant-majors and senior acks are tremendously helpful. And you realize there is considerable truth to the claim that NCOs have to train all new reinforcement officers.

39

SENNYBRIDGE

———————————— ✳ ————————————

TO ANYONE UNACQUAINTED WITH THE PRINCIPAL ARTILLERY training camp in Britain, located among the hills of central Wales, the charming name Sennybridge will probably invoke a pleasant image of a village basking in the sunlight, distinguished by a notable stone bridge spanning a mountain stream.

But to Canadian gunners visiting Sennybridge for training periods, invariably in late fall and winter (the British seemingly having exclusive use of the ranges in the summer), the very word "Sennybridge" will forever raise images of bitter, cold, wet weather unique to the Welsh hills: fog one minute, rain the next (sometimes mixed with hail), followed closely by heavy snow flurries, which, in their turn, can cease abruptly, allowing shafts of startlingly bright sunshine to break through roiling black clouds with dramatic suddenness, briefly turning the sweeping folds of hills and valleys into a tourist-poster scene of pastoral beauty, even to splashing a spot of brilliant light on some snowy-white sheep grazing on the slope across the valley.

The warm, drying rays usually last only long enough to entice you into loosening your heavy clothing and removing a couple of layers before a bone-chilling fog starts rolling in. Then the cycle begins again, the icy rain lashing the silent guns and the gunners huddled around them with their backs to the wind, vainly trying to stay dry in a sodden, dripping world – all bundled up in knitted

Balaclavas stuffed under steel helmets and water-shedding gas capes of camouflaged oilskin enshrouding bulky greatcoats and leather jerkins that make them look like so many multicoloured cocoons.

There are days when firing is held up for hours by dense fog, which some maintain is not ground fog at all but low-lying clouds, which plague these hills, reasoning that real fog can be dissipated by wind, while Sennybridge fogs are actually nourished by gale-force winds blowing in over the western mountains from the Irish Sea.

And for the officers, in addition to the misery of the weather, there is the almost nauseating tension, afflicting most severely the junior officers, aroused by the fear of making a mistake in front of a Sennybridge IG while being watched by their colonel, and frequently by Brigadier Tees, CRA of 2nd Division.

Every time a training session at Sennybridge comes around, all ranks groan inwardly as they remember past "practice camps," waking up in the dark each morning to the raucous sound of a poker banging on an empty coal-scuttle in draughty, cold, unprepossessing barracks, donning layers of sweaters, greatcoats, and leather jerkins to face another bone-chilling, drizzling, grey morning and another day of dawn-to-dusk exposure to every possible variation of atrocious weather on pitiless, treeless, mountain slopes.

Sennybridge: a world of haversack lunches, issued unwrapped at breakfast – one *cheese* sandwich (a chunk of cheese amidst splinters of margarine between two remarkably thick chunks of bread), and one *jam* sandwich (qualifying for the name by virtue of a small reddish stain in the centre of one of the other two slices of bread).

Sennybridge: a world of vehicles having to be winched out of the clinging mud of sodden fields, of guns having to be manhandled through the muck, and of freezing fingers – aching and raw – struggling to secure unbelievably heavy, slithering, steel tire-chains around mud-encrusted wheels of trucks stalled halfway up an icy mountain track in the predawn hours of a windy winter morn.

Sennybridge: a world of rush-rush-rush to wait-wait-wait, where the constant requirement to get the guns into position, hours before shooting is actually scheduled to begin, is regularly mocked by endless waiting at the guns, sometimes for fog to dissipate, but mostly because only one gun is being used for tediously slow, methodical ranging to obtain "short brackets" by hesitating junior officers called upon to make their decisions under the close and forbidding scrutiny of those gods of the ranges, the IGs.

Products of gunnery staff courses at the School of Artillery – set up at Larkhill in 1920 to establish principles, standards, and rules of artillery, and qualify selected officers and NCOs as instructors so they could carry enlightenment to all artillery units – IGs will never be anyone's favourite people, though unquestionably they are necessary for the development of competent regiments, and to ensure uniformity in procedures essential when large formations are linked together.*

And clear evidence of their worth can be found in the pride and confidence the acks have developed in their knowledge and skills since being exposed to the many hours of intensive training last summer under the visiting IG from Larkhill, Major Borton – a pride and confidence that unquestionably have helped form and stabilize the very character of the Regiment. Months after he'd left, you could still hear arguments between acks being settled by reference to the teachings of Major Borton.

But IGs also have the power to ruin careers with their criticism, and since their scrutiny is inescapable when the Regiment is in training at Sennybridge, they evoke widespread tension among all the officers. Ostensibly the Regiment is here to practise firing guns and sharpen officers' ability to range on targets, but all know that the real purpose is to be examined and criticized by IGs. A single, casually uttered sentence, providing an insecure CO with a reason

---

* In December 1942, the Canadian School of Artillery was set up at Bordon, Hants, by Lt.-Col. Eric Harris (former CO of 26th Battery) using Canadians qualified on the War Gunnery Courses at Larkhill. It moved to Seaford in 1943.

for writing an "adverse report" on an officer, can lead to that officer's removal and more often than not "a bowler hat."*

It's unlikely the subject of Sennybridge will ever be raised among officers of the Regiment without someone recalling the story of an officer who was given a "bowler hat" simply because a Brigadier CRA saw him smoking – not an inoffensive cigarette or manly straight pipe, but a curved pipe that rested on his chin. Somehow his choice of pipe attracted attention to perceived deficiencies in his make-up that might have a bearing on his effectiveness as an artillery officer, and right after the Regiment returned to its home base in Sussex, he'd been "adversed" out as unsuitable officer material.†

---

* To officers on leave in London, bowler hats on civil servants in White-hall came to be seen as symbols of "Civvy Street."
† Unlike most officers who received adverse reports, he not only retained his commission, but ended the war as a Lt.-Colonel.

40

PAYING YOUR DUES

---- ✳ ----

THERE'S A FEELING OF TENSION WHEREVER YOU ARE IN Sennybridge Camp, but it's almost unbearable for a junior officer in an OP (observation post). Even on the way up, riding in the back of a truck with other subalterns summoned to take their turn at ranging the guns on a target, you can feel the anxiety rising and see unmistakable signs in eyes and body language that it's now a case of every man for himself.

The OP is a low-slung concrete structure some fifteen or twenty feet long and about eight or ten feet wide. There is a chest-high open port running along the side overlooking the target zone, with a wooden shelf just below the sill on the inside providing a place for signallers to rest telephones and message pads, and officers their map boards.

The corrugated-iron roof, while offering no protection against a wayward "short round" fired from behind, at least keeps out the rain, hail, and snow – the shelter's only concession to comfort, for in addition to the long wide-open port, there is a doorless entrance at the rear, only partially closed off by a blast-wall guarding against splinters from wayward shells. Combined, the front and back openings provide ready access to the frigid winds sweeping eternally across these exposed mountain slopes, now and then howling and whistling through this wretched hovel in gusts so ferocious they threaten to shake the fluttering slabs of corrugated iron from their moorings on the roof poles.

An uncomfortable silence lies over the assembled group, broken only by the sounds of the wind and the heavy, nervous breathing of the junior officers waiting for "the guillotine to drop," particularly evident in the most recent junior officer to be called to take his turn at ranging on a target selected by the IG.

This IG is distinguished by the sheepskin jacket in which he is bundled, and his grossly long hair, cascading from beneath his stained and beaten-up red-banded forage cap. Of all the physical features, mannerisms, and other mysterious factors at work to create the aura of invincibility and flawless judgement that surrounds this man and causes even colonels and brigadiers to ascribe to him qualities of wisdom the ancients reserved for their gods, the most impressive is his long hair curling down over his collars, outrageously affronting all regulations regarding conduct becoming an officer and a gentleman. That he can get away with hair so long, in full view of such power as surrounds him each evening in the mess, buying him drinks and hanging on his every word, is proof beyond all shadow of doubt that he truly is an exalted being.

Naturally, he's suitably equipped with a terribly British "it's-all-a-great-towering-bore-don't-you-think" accent, which, in other circumstances, such as in the "gentlemen only" bar of the Shireland pub in Birmingham, would be scorned as pure la-di-da, but here serves only to reinforce the image of a war-weary survivor of bitter battles starting around Dunkirk and stretching across the sand dunes and deserts of North Africa.

As you wait your turn, you study your map and try to relate its wiggling contour lines to the surface of the earth lying out there. You know only the map reference of the OP. The whole landscape is devoid of houses and roads and other normal distinguishing features, and as you search the lay of the land down the grassy slope that falls away quickly out in front into a hidden valley and up the treeless slope opposite into overlapping folds of hills and ridges, you realize that only the contour lines (the wandering lines on the map that establish consistent heights at twenty-five-foot intervals above sea level, providing a certain picture of the topography) offer any hope of identifying the map reference of a target out there.

Suddenly your name is called, and you move over and place yourself in front of the wooden shelf beside the IG. For a moment he keeps you waiting, saying nothing, looking out over the misty valley, as the wind howls mournfully through cracks under the eaves of the creaking roof. When finally he deigns to speak, what comes forth is a drawl so very affected, so studiously casual, it sounds almost supercilious:

"You see that prominent white *grovel* pit on the *fawood* slope directly out in front?" stretching his arm out full length in front of his face, and sighting over his knuckles. "Well, now, three degrees – aw . . . four o'clock – you'll see a brown *scaw* – a spot of dead *gawse* I should think. Right. Well, five degrees – six o'clock – you'll see another slash of white, which we take to be another trench. Now, it seems the infantry are being held up by a machine-gun firing from that trench. You will engage and destroy it."

Turning to the signaller, with his notepad and telephone, you order, "Eddie Troop – right section target – H.E. 109 – Charge III."

As you listen to him repeat your orders into the phone, you study your map. In the awful silence, you shiver and hear yourself puffing as you blow on your fingers to warm them so you can hold onto your Chinagraph pencil and mark your map. You must pin down the location of that damned white scar, but the map is just a blur of contours.

You peer out again through your field-glasses at the faraway slope to examine the position of that white scar. Oh hell – you've lost it! You have to go back to that prominent chalk pit to orient yourself all over again. What was it he said, "three degrees – 4:30 o'clock"? Yes, yes, there's that patch of brown gorse. Now, six o'clock, five degrees – or was it six degrees, five o'clock? Oh gawd, you're lost – it's a bowler hat for sure!

Out of the corner of your eye you can see the CO, the 2 IC, and your battery commander shifting their feet impatiently, and you struggle to suppress the panic that will blind you.

Finally you see it: a white scar at six o'clock. In your field-glasses it looms so much bigger you hadn't recognized it. And there is a ridge right behind it – where the map shows a contour line. But is that the ridge, or is the ridge that scribble of contours shown on the map this side of it to the right?

What is it that Don Wilson is always preaching? "Be bold!" That's it. But no . . . that applies only to corrections when you've lost a round in dead ground. If you lose your ranging round in one of those valleys out there, you'll be bold. But now time is passing; you must get on with it. As confidently as you can, you mark a tiny **X** with your Chinagraph pencil on the talc covering your map where you think the chalk scar is located. Then, affecting a voice you hope sounds appropriately decisive, you give the signaller the switch from zero line to the line you've measured with your protractor, drawn from your pivot gun to target. Then you provide the "angle of sight" calculated to compensate for the remarkable difference be-tween the height of the gun and the height of the target above sea level. You follow this with the range in yards and the order "Right ranging – fire!"*

Oh, please, let it be right! It's got to be right . . . there's no other ridge between you and the target . . . except perhaps that fold in the ground over there. Surely not! If only the damn thing lands where you can see it. You recall the horrific tales of officers losing all their ranging rounds and having their shoot stopped by an IG after they had thrown a dozen rounds back and forth across those same hills without once seeing a wisp of smoke rising from those distant, muffled *crumps*.

So as to be ready for the shell's arrival out there, you calculate how many seconds it will take to cover the distance from gun to

---

* "Right ranging" means that the right-hand gun of the troop, or of the section being used, will conduct the ranging.

target, when the gun position reports it's on its way driven by Charge III.*

But when the signaller reports "shot one," you lose track of what you are supposed to be counting and are caught preoccupied with the crackling whisper overhead, as a flash of orange and black gushes up from the slope, about 250 yards beyond and to the left of the white scar. Mentally marking the spot where the round landed as its echoing roar reaches you and its smoke drifts away, you order another round at a range 400 yards less, so as to establish a line on the ground from gun to target.

Another faint *crump* from the rear, another sinister whispering overhead, another flashing explosion over there, and you have your line. Or have you? The smoke dissipates so quickly. And you are no longer entirely certain where your first round landed. Oh hell, it doesn't matter. At least you know the line is left of the chalk pit about two hundred yards, and you've got to move it over to the right.

"Be bold!" you almost imagine you hear Wilson admonishing you. The guns are about three thousand yards from the target. You recall the little rule-of-thumb table of the number of degrees and minutes subtended by a hundred yards at various ranges from two thousand yards up to six thousand: "three, two, one-and-a-half, one-ten, one." Since gun to target is about three thousand yards, and the next round must be switched two hundred yards to the right, you give the order to the signaller: "More four degrees – Repeat."

The round whistles up and lands exactly where you think it should. You add four hundred yards to the range to get a "bracket." Then you split it by dropping the range for the next round by two

* Charge I (646 feet per second or 215 yards): 4.65 seconds per 1,000 yards.
Charge II (987 fps or 329 yards): 3.00 seconds per 1,000 yards.
Charge III (1,463 fps or 488 yards): 2.05 seconds per 1,000 yards.
Super Charge (1,742 fps or 581 yards): 1.70 seconds per 1,000 yards.

hundred yards. It lands just down the slope in front of the scar. You order "Repeat," and again the orange-and-black puff goes up in front of the scar. You raise the range by a hundred, and, hallelujah, it lands just beyond the scar! You split the hundred yards and go into fire for effect: five rounds' gunfire with the one gun. They all fall short. You split the bracket again by adding twenty-five yards, and one of the rounds seems to clip the top edge of the scar.

Immediately the IG drawls, "Stop. Very well . . . you could have confirmed the top range of your bracket with another round before going into fire for effect, but all in all a very good shoot. Next."

You glance at Major Cooper as you step back out of the way. He doesn't smile, but the way he nods his head tells you he's pleased. Those many hours spent at the miniature smoke range he initiated at Barnham for the junior officers have just paid off, and he knows it.

You retire to a corner of the bunker. It's all over. You didn't blow it – no bowler hat this time.

The sense of relief is incredible. You unbutton your coat, for you are sweating as though from great exertion. Then, as the tension leaves you, you start shuddering with the cold – and are suddenly aware you're encased in clammy, sodden woollen underwear. But you don't care; you can't resist smiling. In fact, you feel like laughing boisterously, but since that's absolutely taboo in the circumstances, you enjoy the heavy shuddering that racks you now and then as a substitute expression, a form of release for the triumphant joy and relief you are feeling.

41

PLACES OF WARMTH AND
SONG AND LAUGHTER

※

EACH EVENING AFTER SUPPER, RECREATIONAL VEHICLES (JUST the regular tarpaulin-hooded 30-hundredweight trucks) take loads of gunners into Brecon, some ten miles away to the east, or Llandovery, about the same distance to the west. Along with other junior subalterns, you take your turn at being in charge of a couple of trucks.

Technically you are responsible for seeing that if you start off with sixty men in two trucks, you bring sixty back to camp. But since you normally leave Sennybridge in the dark, not knowing just who you have in the back of the trucks, and drop them off in the dense blackout of a narrow street of a town whose layout is a complete mystery to you – where they proceed to scatter hither and yon to pubs of their own choice – you are completely dependent on them finding their own way back to the trucks in the impenetrable gloom after the pubs close at ten.

Somehow they never fail to show up. And friends won't let a truck pull out until they've checked to make sure all their pals are aboard, resulting in a roll call of names raucously acknowledged before the truck engine is revved up.

While no one who has been with the outfit for any length of time would think there is anything remarkable in this, to you it is striking testimony of a deeply rooted soldierly discipline maturing in the men of 4th Field. They may be loaded with suds – so loaded they won't go more than a couple of miles before they'll be stomping the steel floor of the truck to get it to stop so they can lean over the tailgate without risk of falling ass-over-teakettle onto the road – but they make sure they're on board that truck with their friends when it pulls out in the dark on its way back to the Regiment, adding their voices to the roaring chorus singing to pass the time: "I've got sixpence – jolly, jolly sixpence – I've got sixpence to last me all my life . . ." or "Nellie put your belly close to mine" or "Roll me o-ver in the clo-ver – roll me over, lay me down and do it again . . ."

There being a perfectly good canteen in Sennybridge Camp, you've sometimes wondered why so many choose to pay the penalty of these long, cold trips, standing up in the back of a windy truck under the flapping tarpaulin, just for a few beers in a pub. But, of course, no NAAFI canteen has ever offered the cheerful warmth of a British pub filled with song, chatter, and laughter.

You are just as susceptible. Though the officers' mess is quite comfortable, and might even be judged splendid in comparison to most village pubs, you still are quick to respond when fellow subaltern Len Harvey suggests you both "get the hell out of this stuffy hole and run over to the Bear in Llandovery." The Bear is your favourite watering-hole in all of Wales for several reasons, not the least of which is a charming mutt of a dog that loves to have a lick of your Scotch in a saucer. As time goes on, he can become quite boisterous, even to knocking over the glasses of the unwary as he skids exuberantly across the bar in his usual grand finale before falling asleep and snoring noisily beside the fire – by which time you and Len are ready to go up to the proprietor's own living quarters for dinner.*

---

* Visiting the Bear in 1988, the author asked the current proprietor if he remembered the little mutt with a taste for Scotch. He didn't, but an older customer recalled that for the last years of his life, the little dog had suffered

At her own dining-room table, the publican's wife provides each of you with two fried eggs, two thick slices of ham, a bowl of French-fried potatoes, real butter for your bread – topped off by homemade apple pie, real cream, and tea. And this glorious parade of rare goodies, which could not be had at any price at the Savoy or the Ritz in London, is served up by a smiling, motherly lady for three shillings, just so long as you don't inquire why these luxuries have not been swept up into the general rationing dragnet afflicting this island. Stuffed, you doze off in indescribable bliss beside the coal fire glowing in the grate and sleep until your driver comes to collect you at closing time.

One Sunday you take a truckload of gunners over the mountains to Merthyr Tydfil, more than twenty miles away. It being the Sabbath and this being Wales, where it is illegal to purvey alcoholic beverages on Sunday, the pubs are technically closed – at least their front doors are locked and the shades drawn. Gunners, accustomed to pubs in England being open at certain hours seven days a week, are dismayed, until they hear, coming from within an inn on the main street, the muffled, cheerful chatter of a pub crowd enjoying themselves. Assuming the pub has just closed, they inquire from the bobby along the street what time the pubs will open again. He informs them that pubs are not allowed to open at all on Sunday. However, if they wish to have a pint, they could just go down that alley there and rap on the back door.

The thirsty 4th Field types do as the bobby suggests, and no one seeks out the truck to go back to camp until the pubs truly close up shop at ten and turn their customers out into the foggy, pitch-black night.

You can see nothing as you wait at the rear of the truck in the phenomenal quiet that pervades a blackout even in a city. Here, there isn't even a chuckling diesel bus motor idling at a nearby bus stop to break the stillness. And apart from a faint tinkle of female

---

a form of arthritis and the landlord's daughter transported him about town in a perambulator.

laughter now and then, and distant "cheerio"s as friends part, there is only the rustle of dozens of shuffling feet making their way home along nearby narrow streets.

Then one voice – a distinctly Welsh high-pitched tenor – begins to sing: "*We'll meet again, don't know where, don't know when – but I know we'll meet again some sunny day . . .*"

Instantly, on all sides, voices take up the song in full-throated harmony, in a manner reminiscent of a well-drilled mass choir at a song festival. The sound grows and swells up and down the streets until at last it seems the whole town is reverberating with song.

It is an experience so splendid, that if you live to be a hundred, you will not likely forget this earnest, beautiful rendition of a lovely song by random choristers bursting forth spontaneously in the night. Could this occur anywhere else in the world but here in Wales? Tears well up in your eyes as you recall the stories told you this very afternoon by an older resident – stories of days of poverty before the war when these people of Merthyr Tydfil suffered the worse hardship from unemployment in all of Britain.

There must be more than one way to measure wealth.

42

SNAFUS UNLIMITED

—————————————— ✳ ——————————————

NORMALLY, WHEN THE GUNS ARE LIMBERED UP FOR THE LAST
time at Sennybridge, and the regimental convoy sits waiting for the
signal to pull out on the two-day two-hundred-mile drive back to
home base, it's a pleasant moment for all: the Regiment is getting
away from the critical scrutiny of the IGs and returning to a much
friendlier atmosphere and benign climate down in Sussex. Officers,
especially, tend to relish feelings of relief that once again they have
escaped earning a "bowler hat."

This time, however, there's no pleasant feeling of accomplishment. Everything that could go wrong, did go wrong, starting the
night before the camp got underway, on October 20, at Sennybridge railway station when the guns and ammunition limbers were
being taken off the flatcars of the train on which they'd travelled up
from Barnham Junction, the first and last time 4th Field guns ever
moved by rail.

It was sometime after midnight when word came that the train
had arrived with the guns, and you were sent with a convoy of
quads and gun crews to take charge of the unloading. The railway
siding was up at the top of a steep incline from the road, and the
guns and limbers had to be manhandled down to quads parked at
the foot of the incline. Either the brake on one of the limbers failed,
or was not applied properly by a crew member. Whatever the
reason, one of the first limbers off the train, fully loaded with half a

ton of ammunition (thirty-two shells and thirty-two cartridge cases), turned into an unmanageable runaway, bowling down the hill in the foggy darkness, narrowly missing you and a group of gunners alerted at the last second by a warning shout.

Gathering speed, it knocked over Gunner Bill Stevens, who'd been trying to manage the brake, and ran over his legs just before it reached the first quad at the foot of the hill. There Sgt. Howard S. Cameron, who was guiding the limber's tongue as best he could – gallantly trying to steer it past the quad – fell, and one of the limber's wheels rolled up onto his midriff just as the tongue, scraping along the pavement, jammed under the side of the quad with an ugly metal-scrunching jolt.

And there he lay, pinned to the wet pavement, until you and the gunners, who had rushed to his aid, could remove the ammunition from the limber and lift the still-considerable weight of the empty limber enough that he could be dragged free. Though he was still conscious, and remarkably calm as you covered him with a great-coat, common sense suggested his chances of surviving the effects of that crushing weight were slight, and you despaired he'd still be alive when the ambulance arrived. But he was, and still astonishingly calm and cheerful as he was taken away – first to a civilian hospital at Brecon and then to a British Military Hospital at Whitechurch, where he was diagnosed as having a ruptured diaphragm and with some organs repositioned somewhat, but functioning.*

Throughout the whole time in Wales, the weather, always foul in these hills in the winter, was especially uncooperative, with powerful winds, rain, hail, and snow. And whenever it calmed

---

* "Howie" S. Cameron not only recovered but went on to become first an IG at the new Canadian School of Artillery, Seaford, and then in 1944 a commissioned officer serving with 19th Field Regiment. After the war he became an orthopaedic surgeon. Residual effects of his accident at Sennybridge, according to Dr. Cameron, were taken care of in 1947, when his "diaphragmatic hernia was repaired" and his spleen, which had migrated into his chest, was removed.

down a little, a thick blanket of fog rolled in, closing down the shoot, including one battery fire-and-movement manoeuvre at a crucial moment. Then, on the final day – the last chance the Regiment had to redeem its reputation – a dense fog prevented all observed shooting from dawn until dusk.

As might be expected, following the normal pattern of things, all the frustration of the senior officers of the Regiment, which had been building for days, immediately focused on the shortcomings of the subalterns, when they heard at a final post-mortem, attended by all the officers, the critical remarks of the long-haired supercilious senior IG, and the comments of the CRA of 2nd Division, summed up by Brig. G. A. "Nick" McCarter, CCRA of the Corps: "I'm sorry, gentlemen, but this regiment is not ready to fight."

Lieutenant-Colonel Todd, clearly devastated by the verdict, made it clear that to hear the Regiment so described, only a few weeks after being judged number one at Larkhill, was "unbearable." And the regimental war diary, with remarkable restraint, will record, "It was an unexpected statement to hear after our previously excellent record of being the best field regiment in the RCA."

Immediately it was obvious to all above the rank of subaltern, that all the problems encountered by the Regiment resulted directly from "the subalterns not taking over." How could it be anything else? After all, the majors and captains were already wearing on their epaulettes badges of rank that had come to them in recognition of their competence.

That 90 per cent of the snafus at this camp were directly traceable to the atrocious weather is ignored completely by all those whose opinions count for anything. A god of gunnery has spoken, and it would never do to question the basis of his severe judgement. In fact, it would be worth an officer's career even to suspect that the poor, shaggy-haired sod might simply be suffering from a very human case of Sennybridge ranges frustration, inflamed by a heavy head-cold brought on by standing around all day in a draughty concrete OP bunker waiting for the fog to lift, passing the time wondering how much longer he can possibly endure these endless days on these wretched ranges, watching nerve-racked officers muddle through shoots on white scars containing imaginary machine-guns.

However, among those who would consider such thoughts treasonable, the judgement of the IG is accepted; the shortcomings of 4th Field, imagined or otherwise, will be dealt with, and this spells unpleasantness for the subalterns for the foreseeable future – at least until the unit regains its confidence and reputation at another practice camp.

When the regimental convoy is about to set off for Sussex, and the silent limbered-up guns and vehicles sit waiting – some on the road leading off the ranges, but most just helter-skelter along a grassy slope bordering the road – you can feel the gloom hanging over it.

Suddenly, resounding across the valley and surrounding hills, in the bell-tone notes of a perfectly pitched trumpet swinging in march-tempo, is a familiar tune from an old Dick Powell film: "Shipmates stand to-geth-er, *don't give up the ship*. Fair or stormy wea-ther, we won't give up, we won't give up the ship! . . ."

At first it seems a strange choice for a trumpeter of an artillery outfit. But as you listen, you find it comforting in a warm, human way. It's loud and defiant, if not downright disorderly in the military sense. It's a kicking-over-the-traces, a sassy "you-may-kiss-my-ass-Sennybridge" serenade.

Whether Gunner Bob Wilson, of Don Troop, 14th Battery – standing with his head and shoulders and trumpet protruding through the hatch of a quad – knows it or not (and you suspect he does), his horn is telling everyone, "Don't take too seriously all the BS those frigging Limeys have been dishing out. Hang on to your sense of humour. They haven't got to me – so don't let them get to you!"

You can feel that swinging trumpet puncturing all the puffed-up dignity and stripping away the sense of tragic destiny that's been hanging over the Regiment since last night. You find yourself smiling as you whistle along with him, and by the time the signal to "Wind up engines and move off" is passed down from troop to troop by the subalterns assigned to motorbikes to ride herd on the convoy, you know that every soul in the outfit, from the Colonel down to the lowliest gunner, feels better because of that corny rallying horn, blown so beautifully by a truly great trumpeter.

And though the memory of one snafu after another out on these ranges will linger, creating the impression of a wasted practice camp, this is far from the truth. In fact this may well have been the most enlightening Sennybridge camp ever, for it was here, during a period of classroom instruction, that officers were introduced to an entirely new and revolutionary system of fire control that will allow incredible concentrations of shells to be brought down on an area no larger than a football field, just two or three minutes after a FOO calls for fire on a target. The pendulum, which, back in 1940, had swung away from large groupings of guns (because of the slow, methodical management of large numbers) to fast-moving, small groups (as few as a four-gun troop moving in a jock column with a company of infantry), has swung back to a central position that combines the best features of large concentrations of fire-power with speed of application.

43

MIKE, UNCLE, AND
VICTOR TARGETS

———————————— ❋ ————————————

TREMENDOUS CHANGES, MADE POSSIBLE BY IMPROVED EQUIP-
ment and procedures, have taken place in gunnery within the living
memory of many here in Britain, and this was underlined in startling
fashion in a pub in Birmingham, during a recent nine-day leave, at
a chance meeting with a retired artillery sergeant-major of the Boer
War era.

Each evening for several in a row, on arrival at the Shireland pub
across Portland Road with your host Bob Cotton (master machinist
by day and chief air-raid warden of Edgbaston District by night),
Bob's friends in the "Gentlemen Only" bar had expressed regrets
that you had again just missed meeting The Gunner, who'd been
in for his nightly pint and gone: "What a pity. You and he would
have so much in common."

So when this much-postponed meeting finally took place, an
unusual expectant silence descended on the room as you were
introduced.

Deferring to the venerable Gunner, you waited for him to begin.

"I expect things have changed somewhat since my time," said
he. "I understand you now engage most of your targets by indirect
fire."

Fortunately, those who frequent the "Gentlemen Only" at the
Shireland abhor a vacuum and are always ready to fill a gap in the
conversation, for you were struck dumb, it never having occurred

to you that you would be meeting a gunner who had never seen guns engage targets in any way other than by "direct fire" over "open sights."

According to Petawawa's walking encyclopedia of gunnery, Sgt.-Major Dusty Miller, procedures for firing guns indirectly – from concealment behind woods or hills, following directions from forward observers far ahead and out of sight of the guns – evolved from lessons learned in the South African War, fifteen years before the outbreak of World War I. High-powered rifles and high-explosive shells, accurately delivered by rifled guns (the spiral grooves imparting spinning to the shells stabilizing them in flight) made deployment of field guns up at the front in full view of the enemy a suicidal procedure. The last time field guns were purposely deployed in the ancient way to supplement the fire of rifle companies – firing over open sights at the advancing enemy, clearly visible to the gun-layers – was when the British made a stand during the retreat from Mons at Le Cateau on August 27, 1914, with predictably disastrous results.

Only anti-tank guns, which by their very nature must be placed at strategic points along the front, are now required to fire over open sights, and they, to survive, depend on camouflage and concealment. How could you ever explain to this old gunner that over at Sennybridge in Wales, just before coming up here on leave, you'd been introduced to a new procedure in gun control that will allow a forward observer of lowly rank to engage moving targets (such as attacking infantry) with torrents of shells from twenty-four guns of a regiment, seventy-two guns of the Division, or 216 guns of the Corps field regiments, within three or four minutes of him broadcasting a map reference and a scale of fire.

It's hard enough for you, fresh from that Sennybridge course of instruction on the matter, to accommodate such an innovative concept of flexible, movable, irresistible fire-power being placed in the hands of junior officers. Until now all courses in gunnery to which you have been exposed have been conducted in such a manner as to leave the impression that the rules governing the deployment and control of the guns, if not actually etched in stone and unchangeable as the laws of nature, were, at the very least, expert conceptions proven in the crucible of war – the distilled experience of generations of highly qualified professionals and not subject to amendment or modification by anyone. And reinforcing this view have been the stern, inflexible positions taken by the IGs.

Thus it has come as something of a shock to realize that gunnery is still evolving, that because of the development of better radio communications since 1940 – both by way of better sets and better signal procedures – new methods of target-plotting and fire control have been invented, allowing forward observation officers to bring to bear on a target tremendous concentrations of guns within three or four minutes (concentrations which previously would have taken an hour or more to arrange) and which can be moved about the landscape in even less time, following a moving target such as tanks and men coming at you or a distant enemy transport column moving across the front. All a FOO has to do to get all guns of his regiment on a target is to prefix the map reference of his target with the words "Mike target – Mike target – Mike target," the repetition being merely to ensure all the signallers (manning the sets at regimental headquarters, the three battery command posts, and the six troop command posts) are alerted.*

As all gun crews are ordered to "take post" (man the guns), each troop command post is plotting the target on its *own* artillery board and reading off the line and range unique to its four guns.†

If fire is urgent, the FOO feels secure in the accuracy of the map reference of his target, he may go right into fire for effect with all

---

* "Mike" is merely the communications code word for the letter M. At the outset, before the old British phonetic alphabet was modified to clarify radio communications with the Americans, the word was "Monkey."
† The line and range to target from the "pivot gun" (the right-hand gun of the troop) are used as the line and range for the other three guns of the troop as well.

guns of the regiment, letting the normal "zone of dispersion" of the shells take care of any inaccuracy caused by wind and weather. But if the FOO is not sure of his map reference and needs to "range" onto the target, he merely adds, "Right-ranging – fire." The pivot gun of the first troop reporting ready is given the job of ranging for all of the troops.

Each subsequent correction to the fall of shot of that one ranging gun is plotted independently on each of the six troop artillery boards, and the guns of each troop are switched as necessary following each correction. Thus, all troops are ready when "fire for effect" is ordered at a scale of fire by the FOO.

This is possible because the FOO uses the "cardinal-point" method when ordering corrections, giving the distance and direction from the point where the last shell landed to the actual target, such as "Northwest 200." The genius of this method lies in the fact that cardinal-point corrections are applicable regardless of where the forward observation officer or his guns are located in relation to the target. (See Appendix I.)

If a FOO needs to call down all seventy-two guns of the three field regiments in the division, he simply uses the prefix "Uncle target," repeated three times, before the map reference of the target. Immediate response to his broadcast is possible only because each regimental headquarters maintains two radio transmitters, one netted to the sets of the regiment and one to divisional headquarters, allowing RHQ to receive the call from a FOO on one set and transmit the appeal to divisional headquarters on the other, alerting the other two regiments with sets netted to divisional headquarters.

And since the procedure is the same at every gun position throughout the division, the speed of response is almost as fast. But instead of 240 rounds (at Scale 10), it will be 720 rounds descending on an area about the size of a football field in a matter of a few seconds. And if the prefix "Victor target" is used, and the same scale of ten rounds' gunfire is ordered, all 216 field guns of the nine field regiments of the Corps will pour down 2,160 rounds on that target area. A "William target," involving every gun in the army not engaged on another target, is almost inconceivable.*

And this new capacity to concentrate such colossal fire-power and shift it about on moving targets within minutes (something four-star generals and field marshals of other nations can only dream of having) is not just available to senior officers at brigade, division, corps, or army headquarters, but is at the disposal of the troop commanders, who on occasion may be only lieutenants acting in the place of captains.

This is remarkably different from the way the American gunners control observed fire. Showing much less trust in the judgement of their forward observers, their system provides for officers of more senior rank, located in a fire-control centre back at the guns, making all decisions related to the importance of the target, the number of guns that will engage it, and the number of rounds that will be fired on it. The reasoning behind this is that senior officers back at the guns are more likely to have cooler judgement than junior officers immersed in the heat of battle, who might tie up the guns on the less important targets. This is precisely the way senior British officers in the Boer War thought when the guns changed over from direct fire to indirect fire, and control moved away from senior officers at rear headquarters to forward observers of lowly rank.†

---

* The first and only William target involving Canadian guns mentioned by the official history (Col. G. W. L. Nicholson's *The Gunners of Canada, Vol. II, 1919–1967*, Toronto, McClelland & Stewart, 1967, page 204) was delivered on the Italian town of Aquino at 1:00 P.M. on May 23, 1944. In little more time than it takes to read this page, nineteen field regiments, nine medium regiments, and two heavy regiments unloaded seventy-four tons of explosive on the "already battered town."

† Brig. Shelford Bidwell, on page 143 of his learned treatise on artillery – *Gunners at War* by Arrow Books Ltd., London, 1972 – commenting on this reluctance to place such fire-power at the discretion of junior officers, states: "The admirable United States Artillery has never trusted its forward observers and treats them merely as technical fire controllers and sources

Now, placing the awesome fire-power of Uncle or Victor targets at the discretion of anyone below the rank of brigadier has again aroused fears among the British brass. At the outset, it was planned to have the Brigadier CRA, or his representative, go forward into an OP in the zone most likely to be critical, armed with his own command radio network to call down all the guns of the division or corps onto targets of his choosing. Fortunately, this was abandoned as being impractical, as well as a gross misuse of the divisional commander's artillery adviser.

Troop and battery commanders are well equipped to make quickly all necessary decisions on the use of the guns on "targets of opportunity." Being always at or near the cutting edge of the battle, and constantly referring to the map, they usually are the best-informed officers on the current situation on any battlefield. And when they combine their knowledge and judgement with the knowledge and judgement of the company commander or battalion commander to whom they are attached, they are in a better position than anyone in a rear command post to assess the situation and apply the weight of shelling where it is likely to do the most good – particularly at the height of the battle, when infantry communications tend to break down and brigade headquarters and divisional headquarters can be, for long periods, completely out of touch with what is going on up front.

Now the hottest subject for bull sessions in the mess is the implications of being able to bring down fire of irresistible force on a counter-attacking enemy. And from the depth and breadth of the questions raised it is clear that some, at least, recognize that the course and outcome of future battles involving British and British

---

of intelligence: they report, but may not order. The decisions concerning the importance of the target, the numbers of guns to engage and the scale of fire are taken as the result of cool deliberation and a study of situation maps in a fire direction centre far in the rear. It is an orderly and logical process, but in British eyes it is not nearly fast enough. We decided to trust men at the front."

Commonwealth forces will be influenced as much by decisions made by artillery officers at the regimental, battery, and troop commander levels, as by the generals.*

And you find yourself speculating quite seriously that had the unbearable intensity of Mike, Uncle, Victor, and William targets been available to the BEF in 1940, the German drive might well have been stopped cold in Belgium.

In the 1941 book *Return Via Dunkirk* (the same book used to sell "the reluctant gunners" on the artillery), the point is underlined that a forward observation officer was expected to do most of the technical work in the OP when firing on observed targets, sending back detailed fire orders that could be applied directly to the four guns of the troop he was ranging. "Gunbuster," the author, describing how he occupied his first OP in action in May 1940, some sixteen miles west of Brussels, might have been describing the occupation of an OP in 1918: "With the help of a Number 7 Director, rangefinder, artillery board and my O.P. Ack, I settled down to the business of doing a silent registration of the zone under observation: taking the switches, ranges and angles of sight of possible targets, as well as drawing a panorama of the zone and filling it with the necessary data, identifying positions such as churches, woods, farmhouses and hamlets."

---

* Lt.-Gen. Sir Brian Horrocks (veteran of World War I, Dunkirk, North Africa, and Northwest Europe in command of British XXX Corps from Normandy to the end of the war) would unequivocally declare the superiority of the British and Commonwealth artillery in being able to concentrate in three or four minutes storms of shells on targets. This ability he attributes to fast and accurate survey: "The core of the Royal Artillery (and all the Commonwealth artillery using the same weapons and gunnery procedures) was the fantastic accuracy of their survey units. . . . Neither the Germans, nor the Russians, not even the French who were always supposed to be the masters of artillery systems, could approach the accuracy or weight of concentrated fire-power which I had at my disposal within minutes." (Sir Brian Horrocks, *Corps Commander*, Toronto: Griffin House.)

Thus encumbered by equipment, handicapped by unreliable radio communication, and unable to concentrate quickly on any
target all the guns of his regiment, let alone the guns of a division
or corps, it is a miracle the guns did as well as they did in covering
the withdrawal and preventing a disordered rout, as they constantly
faced a fluid front and fast–moving mobile German columns threatening to outflank them, forcing the BEF back to Dunkirk.

44

WALTZING MATILDA AND YANKEE

DOODLE DANDY

———————————— ✳ ————————————

THERE IS AN ATMOSPHERE OF UNUSUAL OPTIMISM ABROAD IN London when you and fellow subaltern Len Harvey arrive on leave the last week of November 1942 – a result of a surprising order from on high that "a maximum number of personnel be granted leave immediately," reinforcing an already strong rumour that the Canadians are about to be sent into action as a result of the great British Commonwealth victory in Africa.

General Montgomery announced on November 5 that British forces had won "a complete and absolute victory" in Egypt and that the German Afrika Korps was "in full retreat." However, it took a few days for people here in Britain to become fully conscious of the extent of the victory at some obscure place called El Alamein, said to be about a hundred miles from Cairo. But when Churchill underlines its importance in a speech on November 10, the whole world takes notice.

Though Eighth Army, during General Wavell's era in North Africa, had effectively destroyed the Italian army, taking masses of prisoners, it somehow didn't rate in the public's mind as a victory significant to the outcome of the war, for it was not against the chief enemy, Germany. This is the first real drubbing administered to the Germans by British and Commonwealth forces in this war, and the word "Alamein" quickly comes to suggest a turning point in Allied fortunes. Prime Minister Churchill, as usual, says it with precision:

"It is not the end. It is not even the beginning of the end. But it is the end of the beginning."

General Rommel's main forces in North Africa, which in June took Tobruk and thirty-two thousand British Commonwealth prisoners, had relentlessly pursued a discouraged British Eighth Army, and by August were poised for one last drive that would carry them the last hundred miles to Cairo and the domination of the Suez Canal. From this menacing position, Rommel's troops have been defeated and routed by a hodge podge of New Zealand, Australian, South African, Indian, and British divisions, welded together into a formidable fighting force with a new pride in itself by Monty, who himself is projecting a new image of cocky confidence in theatre newsreels and newspaper photos. In his black beret with two hat-badges, his turtleneck sweater and baggy pants, he seems to be saying, "Yes, I'm good – so good I can wear whatever I want, and nobody can say anything."

Weeks may pass into months before the Germans are completely driven from Africa, and a string of vicious engagements ranging across two thousand miles of coastal regions may still lie ahead, but this smashing victory at Alamein, and the picture of beaten and tattered German forces in full retreat, brings joy to hearts and smiles to faces all over Britain. For the first time since France fell in June 1940, leading into a two-year stretch of the most disheartening disasters, the tide seems to have turned.

While victory was expensive (particularly for the Australian, New Zealand, and 51st Highland Divisions), with 13,500 wounded or missing, the Germans suffered much more. By the time Rommel was forced to retreat, thirty thousand of his men were prisoners (ten thousand Germans and twenty thousand Italians), and he'd lost a thousand guns and all but fifty of his five hundred tanks.

The twelve-day battle began on the night of October 23 with a massive barrage of nine hundred guns – the majority of them 25-pounders. Again, in the dark early hours of November 2, momentum was restored by another thundering barrage from the guns of two army corps. And it will be through blurred images of guns

firing and men pressing forward, lit only by the muzzle flashes of
these crucial 25-pounder bombardments – featured by every newsreel cameraman and every photographer – that the world will remember this historic battle.

You buy every issue of every London paper and study fuzzy
pictures of Eighth Army soldiers in baggy shorts, their helmets tilted
in a cocky way, bouncing over rough desert terrain with their rifles
held at the "high port," or running crouched over, their long bayonets determinedly pointing at the enemy as they go forward, their
way lit by the sheet lightning of the guns belching away on the
barrage that broke things open. You almost imagine you can hear
the skirl of the piper who marched with the 51st Highland Division
into the attack. And wherever you go, someone is whistling "Waltzing Matilda," unconsciously honouring the Australians.

Adding to the buoyant mood are reports of continuing success
of the British and American combined forces now menacing the
Afrika Korps from the northwest, guaranteeing that Rommel will
be driven completely from Africa. Four days after El Alamein,
107,000 American and British troops, fresh from North American
and British shores, landed from five hundred ships at Casablanca in
Morocco on the Atlantic coast and at Oran and Algiers on the
Mediterranean coast and became involved in continental man-
oeuvring and skirmishing with the remnants of Rommel's forces.

Optimism clearly dominates the thinking of the ex-newspaper
types in battledress, masquerading as soldiers under the title "public
relations officers," when you visit their wonderfully cluttered office
with the familiar atmosphere of a newspaper "city room" – filled
with the sound of clacking typewriters and desks strewn with paper
– at CMQ (Canadian Military Headquarters) in Canada House, a
noble edifice on Trafalgar Square meant to house the Canadian
High Commissioner and his staff.

And over on Fleet Street, at the Canadian Press Office, there is
even an earnest reference to "after the war," something you rarely
hear over here and, until now, always with a sardonic grin on the
face of the speaker.

Out in the street the only person who isn't smiling is a bobby presenting his customary official poker-face as he stands next to the shell of a building on which can be discerned the remains of a sign "Geographi . . . We Map the World." But when a grinning delivery boy on a bicycle, whistling George M. Cohan's "I'm a Yankee Doodle Dandy," winks at the bobby as he passes, the bobby breaks into a broad grin and winks back. And the thought strikes you that those winks and grins mean plenty of grief for men who would challenge a people who could erect a sign declaring, "We Map the World."

By the time you are on your way back to the Regiment, a song, from a new Bing Crosby film, inducing painful nostalgia, is going round and round in your head: "I'm dreaming of a white Christmas – just like the ones I used to know . . ."

Back at the Regiment it is clear that going into action is not imminent, but hush-hush training is. Lieutenant-Colonel Todd, Majors Cooper and Cowan, Captain Graham-Brown, and Lieutenants Harvey, Grange, and Murdoch, along with 121 Other Ranks – taking six guns, limbers, and quads, two carriers, and a motorcycle with them – board a train at Chichester for the north for training in "combined operations," always involving assaults from the sea.

On December 17 there is a news report that "The United Nations" – a nebulous body conceived in Washington last January, with signatures by twenty-six sovereign nations, vowing to employ "their full resources, military or economic, against those members of the Tripartite Pact of Germany, Italy, and Japan and its adherents" – make a promise to the world that "crimes against the Jews will be avenged." This same day, British Foreign Secretary Anthony Eden tells the House of Commons that Germany is "now carrying into effect Hitler's oft-repeated intention to exterminate the Jewish people in Europe." Jews are being sent to Eastern Europe "to be worked to death in labour camps" or "deliberately slaughtered in mass executions." This is the first public statement by any official that a campaign of genocide has begun against European Jewry, and is duly reported by the daily papers and the BBC. But in the crush of events crucial to the prosecution of the war, no one dwells on the subject.*

---

* Eden obtained his facts from Jan Karski, a special courier of the Polish underground, who secured his safe passage to Britain by bribing corrupt German officials with money provided by the Jewish Underground. Karski also carried his message to the United States. Though his credentials gained him audiences with President Roosevelt and foremost publishers of American newspapers and magazines, he returned to Poland discouraged by the low level of response he'd aroused. In October 1981, then a professor at Georgetown University, testifying at the International Liberators' Conference arranged by the United States Holocaust Memorial Council, Washington, Karski told the author (attending as the liberator of Westerbork Camp, the collection centre for Dutch Jews) he was so disillusioned by the weak response by the Christian world to the Jews' plea for help that he had become a Jew.

45

HAPPINESS IS A CHILD ON A
GUNNER'S LAP

———————— ✳ ————————

YOUR CHILD WAS TO BE BORN ON OR AROUND DECEMBER 13, but here it is the 20th and no word whatsoever. By now you are beginning to get really worried; something surely has to be wrong.

Your erratic, preoccupied conduct must be getting on the nerves of the other officers in the mess, for Don Wilson takes you aside and tells you "the best way to stop feeling sorry for yourself is to get stuck into organizing a Christmas party for the local kids." He says you can make a start with the great box of magnificent toys and dolls – the like of which have not been seen in England since before the war – that just arrived from de Havilland Aircraft in Canada, employer of the wife of the troop's signal NCO, Bombardier "Red" Johnston.

Bless the wisdom of Don Wilson! With only four days to Christmas Eve (the last possible day for a children's party) and so much to be done, thoughts of Canada recede from your mind.

You are astonished at the enthusiasm and cooperation of all ranks in Eddie Troop, starting with Gunner H. W. Walton, the troop cook. In a most cavalier fashion he impounds next week's sugar ration for the troop so he can make up dozens of sugar-coated doughnuts and still have enough for a round of well-sweetened cocoa for the kids. And when Sgt.-Major G. F. Dennis asks the men on morning parade if they'll forego a rare issue of a bag of peanuts, as well as their weekly ration of hard, poorly sweetened, but very precious bars of chocolate, they all vote to toss them into the pot for a treasure hunt in the village hall, where the party is to be held.

Curt Embleton, the YMCA Auxiliary Service bloke, supplies a proper Santa Claus suit for Walton to wear when he arrives in RE, the troop's tracked Bren gun carrier, to hand out the gifts. Also, Embleton promises to be present with his sound projector to show a swatch of Mickey Mouse cartoon films to the kids, which should be a real treat since none of them will ever have seen a movie, it being against the law for children to attend movie houses "for the duration" because of the possibility of a bomb landing on a theatre full of children.

Finally, for what promises to be a really great party, every last detail is laid on – everything except the *kids*. With no village paper to spread the word, you decide the only way to deliver invitations is to get on a motorbike and chase up and down roads looking for women accompanied by small children.

Not surprisingly this business of roaring up behind women pushing prams with toddlers in tow, and yelling an invitation at them over the noise of the burbling motor, while they comfort the tiny tots hiding in their skirts, produces no more than a dozen committed guests. But then one of the accosted women suggests you approach the teacher of the "baby class" at the school. Eureka! The pleasant teacher, though she will have to move forward the time of their class party, "for which the kids have worked so hard with so little resources," will cooperate, for she knows how generous the Canadian parties for kids can be. All she asks is that each child be picked up at the school by a gunner prepared to take responsibility for the child getting to the party and home safely afterwards.

In all, thirty kids and several mothers show up, and the party is a great success, even though you, as master of ceremonies, make one blunder after another. At first the kids seem totally lacking in vivacity, and during the treasure hunt, their gunner foster-parents have to find all the treasures hidden for them about the room.

Finally one mother whispers, "Do you intend to feed the children? At children's parties in England, the children expect to eat first and play games afterwards."

Then, when the cocoa is served, well-sweetened with the gunners' sacrificial sugar rations, the kids take one look at the rich brown stuff and ask plaintively, "May we have some tea, please!"

However, they adore Mickey Mouse and Popeye, and are quickly taught by the gunners, on whose laps they are sitting, to scream and shout in good old Saturday-matinée fashion each time the lights are turned out for the next reel of film. And the whole business seems especially worthwhile when you see some of the older gunners – fathers who haven't seen their children for more than two years – hugging a child to their chests and staring wistfully into space as the lights come on.

But you have one last *faux pas* to deliver. Vaulting up on the stage, you tell the kids you have just received a signal from the North Pole that Santa Claus is about to arrive right outside the door! In the total silence that follows, one of the mothers, near the apron of the stage, leans forward and whispers, "You mean Father Christmas, I think." This the kids recognize, and a loud whoop of approval goes up.

Outside, Walton, resplendent in his fiery red suit and white whiskers waving in the breeze, puts on a great show as his carrier roars round and round the deserted cattle market, showering the cheering kids with candy kisses (from your mother's parcel) each time he passes. His natural girth gives him real credibility, which is further enhanced when at last he gets out of the carrier carrying his great sack and leads the kids back into the hall to start distributing his awesome gifts. The kids can hardly believe the glory of the trucks, the fire engines, and the dolls, some as large as the children receiving them.

Just as the party ends, despatch rider Cy Reader brings you a cable. It's from Canada. You open it with shaking hands. But it is merely a report (several days old) that the baby is reluctant to enter this world.

To allow armoured corps drivers to drive and maintain tracked vehicles, the Canadian government bought 250 obsolete two-man tanks from the United States in the summer of 1940. They were of a 1917 French design with a beaver-tail stuck out behind to prevent them toppling backwards when climbing out of a ditch. (National Archives of Canada, PA-197870)

One wonders what Colonel (later Maj.-Gen.) Frank Worthington, responsible for all tank-training in Canada, is thinking as he climbs out of the odd lightly armoured vehicle in October 1940. (National Archives of Canada, PA-197871)

Second Division leaving Halifax for Britain, August 1940 – 4th Field on the *Empress of Australia*, built to carry the Kaiser on a world tour and seized by Britain for reparations in 1918. (National Archives of Canada, PA-197864)

Second Division leaving for Dieppe, August 18, 1942, for a dawn attack the next day. (National Archives of Canada, PA-197863)

The
Brockville
Officers'
Training
Centre, in
the early
spring of
1941.
(National
Archives of
Canada,
PA-197875)

The first 25-pounder fired in Canada, in April 1942, one of four guns of A Troop, E Training Battery, A1 Training Centre, Petawawa. The shells were especially fitted with test fuses, and the fire was observed by VIPs from Ottawa. The troop, partially trained on 18-pounders and 4.5-inch howitzers, had only four nights and one day of training on 25-pounders, but pulled off the shoot like veterans. (Author's collection)

The tough part of the motorcycle course for officers at #1 Canadian Artillery Reinforcement Unit, Bordon, Hampshire, began on the steep slopes of the Devil's Punchbowl, near Hindhead. (National Archives of Canada, PA-197858)

If he stalls, water will get sucked into the motor and he may have to "walk it" back to camp. (National Archives of Canada, PA-197859)

A guncrew of 14th Field Regiment, 3rd Division, awaiting the order to
fire at a dawn shoot on Sennybridge Ranges, December 1942.
(National Archives of Canada, PA-190940)

A 5.5-inch medium gun-howitzer, capable of firing an 82-pound shell
18,200 yards (almost eleven miles) or a 100-pound shell 16,000 yards.
(National Archives of Canada, PA-197860)

The Churchill I tank was a 38.5-ton monster (compared to the 29.69-ton American Sherman), but was armed with a pea-shooter 2-pounder gun. (National Archives of Canada, PA-197829)

A much-loved padre, Rev. Ray McCleary, who left 4th Field after three years to become the chief padre of 3rd Division, which assaulted the Normandy shore on June 6, 1944. After the war, he became famous, through the support of the *Toronto Star*, for his efforts to reclaim delinquent youth in the vicinity of his Woodgreen United Church by establishing a "boystown" drop-in centre and making regular appearances at Juvenile Court on behalf of his young "pals." (Donald J. Grant, DND, National Archives of Canada, PA-143929)

A Spitfire, marked with the white-and-black stripes used for easy identification on all Allied aircraft flying in close support of ground troops in Normandy, taking off for a sortie over the bridgehead. (Canadian Forces Photo Unit, RE-20421-1)

The North Nova Scotia Highlanders and the Highland Light Infantry landing on D-Day at Bernières-sur-Mer, Normandy. (National Archives of Canada, PA-137843)

Christmas Eve you have to take the regimental hockey team to Brighton for a game. When you arrive back at Barnham station late that evening and are picked up for the drive to the stand-to position at Yapton, where 26th Battery is on duty for the night, the gut-clutching worry, that Wilson calls "feeling sorry for yourself," threatens to take over when your driver starts whistling that new hit song, "*I'm dreaming of a white Christmas, just like the ones I used to know . . .*"

The night is frigid, and the crystal-clear sky, drenched in stars, is criss-crossed with the silent shifting shafts of searchlights. Memories of past Christmas Eves are inextricably mixed up with wondering what is going on in Canada. Was the child stillborn, and they are not telling you until after Christmas – or is it something even worse? You fight to suppress the memory of a funeral for a relative, a joyful, pretty young woman who died of "complications" having her first child. You're glad when you get to the stand-to billet and the gang of officers playing poker, though you decline to get into the game. In your present mood, it doesn't seem quite right for Christmas Eve.

At dawn, when the guns are taken out of action and all ranks assemble in front of the battery office in Barnham preparatory to taking off in trucks for an early-morning service laid on for the Regiment in Chichester Cathedral, a barrel of beer is produced by Major Don Cooper and consumed from tin cups out in the frosty street. Taken on empty stomachs, all get good mileage out of a couple of draughts each. So when the men of 4th Field raise their voices in the first hymn, "Come All Ye Faithful," they almost drown out the ethereal boys' choir and the deep, full-throated organ swelling through the great church.

Padre McCleary conducts the service, and his Christmas message evokes striking images that will remain long after the service ends: of him, on a recent night, stumbling along in the pitch black of the blackout, tapping his way with his blackthorn cane, when "suddenly and silently the heavens burst forth into a perfect whiteness of light" as the searchlights were turned on seeking enemy planes droning overhead. And in the brightness he pictured "the ancient shepherds sitting chatting on the hillside when suddenly the heavens declared the Glory of God . . . as the Eastern Star shone forth and proclaimed to all mankind, the Light of the World had come."

On returning from Chichester, you are kept so occupied collecting British searchlight and ack-ack gunners from Tangmere and Ford airfields to take them for dinner at regimental headquarters, you miss dinner in the village hall. By the time you find and deliver the last man and get back to Barnham, there isn't a drop of gravy left; in fact, they are washing the pans, which is not surprising when you consider the ration is one 16-pound bird for every sixty-four men – four ounces per man, including bones!

Feeling even sorrier for yourself than last night, you return to the deserted mess, fry up a can of bully beef into a hashlike consistency, and consume it with a slice of bread and "marg."

On Boxing Day you attend a meeting in Petworth regarding 2nd Division hockey playoff arrangements. When the meeting breaks up at noon, and you and your driver drop in for a quick one at The Swan pub, you are surprised to find the place empty.

When you ask the publican where are all his customers, he sadly tells you, "Oh, it is a very sad time for the village. No one feels like celebrating. You see, just before Christmas a German plane dropped a bomb on the school, killing most of the children."

Thirty-eight years after this terrible tragedy, the memory will still be vivid for F. C. L. Wyght, who was visiting old buddies of his former regiment, then stationed in the village of Petworth, when they were throwing a Christmas party for the kids:

They'd invited all the youngsters – about 60 or 70 aged between six and eleven – to a party. The QM [quartermaster], who could whip the hind teeth out of a skunk without promoting a whiff, from somewhere produced a turkey that was converted into a mountain of sandwiches. The village bakery produced more than enough cookies and cakes. A tree was found and decorated.

The entertainment was a most catholic offering. Eddie Watkins, probably the finest pianist in 1st Cdn Div, led the kids in a sing-along and two girls played very creditable Spanish guitars.

Another of the girls, a flawless classical beauty with long golden blonde braids, put on a one-girl show of gymnastics to rival June Pressier who reigned in those days. Somehow Eddie picked up the cadence and gave her a background rhythm. Almost 40 years later I still remember that performance. It was a great party and all went home happy.

The following quotation belongs to the early days of '43: "The Village of Petworth in West Sussex became almost as childless as Hamelin after the Pied Piper had taken his revenge. A scared German pilot, to gain speed, dumped his bombs during lesson time on the local school."

Our company was on the scene within minutes and out of the ruins took 47 forever still small bodies.

I never asked about the blonde gymnast. I never will. In my mind she had to go on – to survive and become the beautiful woman she was promising to be, to marry and have dozens of beautiful children and so close the gap that particular horror created in the lives of so many.*

Three days later on December 29, back at the mess at Barnham, just as you're sitting down to lunch, despatch rider Cy Reader delivers the long-awaited cable:
EIGHT POUND DAUGHTER BORN CHRISTMAS DAY FEEL WONDERFUL HOW ABOUT YOU DARLING ALL MY LOVE.

---

* F. C. L. Wyght, "The Darkest Year," *Legion*, December 1981, 21. Wyght doesn't give the name of regiment.

46

NO ONE WISHES ANYBODY A
HAPPY NEW YEAR

※

OFFICERS AND MEN OF 26TH BATTERY, HAVING BEEN HELD IN isolation on Christmas Eve at the stand-to position, were unafflicted by the resentment aroused in the men of the other two batteries, who had been ordered to attend an ENSA concert party in an Arundel theatre when most of them would have preferred to join in parties with friends in their favourite pub. That some had been invited to spend this special eve in private homes counted for nothing when they tried to get themselves excused.

The whole business of providing an evening of bright musical-hall-type entertainment was an error in judgement on the part of the Padre, the one man most sincerely concerned with the welfare of the men of 4th Field. That most of the men had made other arrangements was discovered too late; the theatre was booked and the concert party was on its way down from London. An audience had to be there.

So all the officers and 125 men from each of the two batteries not on stand-to (2nd and 14th) were ordered to attend. As it happened, the pubs were just opening up when the disgruntled men were being paraded to trucks for the drive to Arundel. And though the required number of bodies were present in the theatre, their spirits were elsewhere. To top things off, the performers were not very good, and their performance was not helped by the openly hostile audience, who provided evidence of their rancour at every opportunity.

As usual, the blame has been attached to the junior officers, who (according to the unit diary) showed a lack of leadership. By noon Christmas Day, after spending some time in the nearby pubs, the worst of the resentment had disappeared, but still the 2nd Battery Christmas dinner was uncharacteristically quiet, enlivened only now and then by the odd rude remark and razzberry directed at anyone daring to speak, including the Battery Commander Major Steuart-Jones, just when the CO was paying a visit.

All week this sour attitude maintains in 2nd and 14th Batteries, and when the Regiment is ordered to conduct a shoot at Alfriston ranges on New Year's Eve – clearly as punishment for its sins – resentment spreads to personnel of 26th Battery, who until now have maintained an amused aloofness. There's a nasty edge to the usual beefing as the guns are deployed and the men are bedding down among the ice-coated gorse in a driving December rain that lashes gorse and groundsheets all night. War Diary comments about the morning shoot are hardly surprising: "Response from the guns is slow, gun drill bad, communications hopeless."

One gun is laid twenty degrees off line and drops a round right out of the ranges entirely, and the regimental War Diary, showing unusual perspicacity and frankness, will state, "The attitude of the men during the exercise was one of resentment for having to work on New Year's Eve. Again lack of leadership on the part of junior officers was extremely noticeable." However, when the Regiment returns from Alfriston, all ranks manage to see the old year out in the true spirit of over-indulgence. And as aching heads are counted next morning, and attempts made to reconstruct the night, you are grateful you chose to stay home in the mess.

Battery Captain Tommy Richardson is totally unable to account for the fact he was found sleeping on the ground in front of the mess by someone coming home after midnight. And several officers, well-oiled from a lengthy spell at the Railway Hotel bar, cost the

Major a packet when finally they turned up at a fund-raising auction for the Women's Auxiliary Voluntary Service, which supplies the van in which Mrs. Stacey brings tea each morning to the troops, Mrs. Stacey being the lady across the road with whom the Major's wife and little girl room and board. Not realizing they were bidding against each other, the hazy crew, mindful of the fact their battery commander had earlier strongly urged them to be generous in their bids, forced the Major to go on raising his bid for the dozen eggs he was determined to acquire, until he paid the awesome price of forty-six shillings, about $11.50 Canadian.*

Most everyone looks back on the evening with varying degrees of regret, but after a bit of "the hair of the dog that bit you," all are ready to face the Colonel's "at home" at noon at Westergate House.

As it happens, the party gets off on the right foot when Adjutant John Harrison proposes a toast to Colonel Todd who was listed for an OBE in the New Year's Honour List. Then roommate Len Harvey, who knows you are carrying a big box of cigars sent over by your wife in anticipation of the birth of your daughter, but that you are too shy to pass them out, enlivens things by conducting you around the room from group to group calling out, "Meet 4th Field's newest legitimate poppa!" And while you hand out the cigars, he chants an illogical ditty he composed while in his cups last night: "*Today is the day we give babies away with a half a pint of beer.*"

Still, everybody seems exceedingly happy for you and is pleased to get a big Whiteowl cigar. And by late afternoon, all are having such a good time they are reluctant to see the party end.

And Major Cooper decides it shall not. Overtaken by an absurd wave of goodwill, unquestionably aroused by generous dollops of the sour, cascara-like rum punch, he invites the officers of 14th Battery to drop in at 26th Battery mess for "a stirrup cup on their way home." And he details you and "Sink" Sinclair to rush ahead to concoct a punch.

---

* In 1990 money, almost 115 dollars, or ten dollars an egg.

This you do, with concentrated lemon juice, sugar, and two bottles of gin in a giant aluminum washbasin. While surprisingly palatable, it is so strong even the most temperate souls are conducting themselves in the strangest fashion by the time they are taking off about 6:00 P.M. And as soon as the Major leaves to go home to his wife and little girl, who live across the street, the house quickly grows still, as one after another of the remaining officers grope their way to bed.

Once in your bedroll, you are conscious only long enough to remark how strange it was that no one actually wished anyone else a happy new year today, and flake out pondering the implications of Jack Cameron's muffled retort, "Surely it would have been even stranger if they had!"

So, when at 7:30 P.M. the Major unexpectedly returns to the mess, all are dead to the world. Shaking everybody awake, he orders all to get dressed, washed, and combed, and follow him in fifteen minutes over the street for a party at the Bolchitrudes, a get-together (he'd forgotten to mention earlier) especially arranged for the officers of 26th Battery and some Land Army girls working on nearby farms far from their homes and families in the Midlands and other parts of Britain.

While recognizing the thoughtfulness of the Bolchitrudes, you can hardly stay awake long enough to get your pants on, let alone take part in a social affair. And you are not alone; some are so stupefied that even the Major's loudest, severest tone makes no impression on them. But on you, he will not give up. You cannot escape by turning your face to the wall. The party must have a piano player, and he knows that now and then you have passed as such, having seen you clunking out hymns at church parades and, occasionally, at Saturday-night dances in Barnham village hall, substituting for the one-and-only Gunner Ralph "Coop" Cooper, a truly great jazz-piano man with the regimental orchestra.

Concentrating his efforts in the ground-floor bedroom you share with fellow subalterns Cameron and Harvey, his attack is so impressive and sustained that by the time you have capitulated and are standing upright and he has poured down your throat the dregs of that breathtaking punch, scooped from the bottom of the wash-basin, you find your room-mates are up and about too, knotting their ties, and brushing their hair.

Somehow, you get through the party, aided by gallons of strong tea and delicious bits of this and that from a beautifully arranged table of sandwiches and sweets, some of which, being recognizably of Canadian origin, were clearly contributed by the Coopers. And while the Major, by the time "Auld Lang Syne" is being sung, is snoring in a chair in the corner, you are quite enjoying yourself – as is Cameron, who also has stuck it out in noble fashion to the end.

Harvey, saying he was bored stiff, left early, supposedly to return to bed, but when you and Cameron get back across the road to your bedroom, his cot is empty. Not until dawn does he finally come staggering in, covered with mud and cursing the depth of the slit trenches (for use in case of an air raid) outside the back door. It seems he fell in one on his way home and was unable to climb out until he sobered up.

Fortunately it is Saturday, with only a half-day of duties for all – all except for "Sink" Sinclair, who is the designated duty officer and must spend the whole day in the battery office.

47

MORE DAYS TO REMEMBER

AT ALFRISTON

———————————— ✳ ————————————

MOVEMENT OF OFFICERS IN AND OUT OF THE REGIMENT, WHICH in one year will see more than a complete changeover of senior officers, including two changes in command, begins in mid-January, when Lieutenant-Colonel Todd becomes Brigadier CRA (Commander Royal Artillery) of 3rd Division, and is replaced by Lt.-Col. William Fleury, a former 26th Battery commander, who more recently was 2 IC of 6th Field.

Changes in leadership cannot help but raise anxieties and affect morale, particularly the loss of a commanding officer who has won the respect of all ranks for the high level of training achieved during his regime. No amount of weather-induced snafus at Sennybridge could ever erase the pride they share with him in having been declared "the best" at Larkhill last summer.

And not only the Regiment will miss this first-class gunnery officer. In addition to helping 4th Field attain a new level of maturity, he laid the foundations for an extraordinarily effective partnership with the infantry battalions of 4th Brigade in action – a partnership based on knowledge and trust realized through lectures he'd provided infantry officers on the various ways artillery can be used most effectively. He'd even gone so far as to bring infantry company commanders to observation posts at Alfriston to illustrate the speed, accuracy, and fire-power of the guns, and to give them an elementary course on how to range guns so that if ever they find themselves without an arty representative and needing fire, they'll be able to call for it and the appropriate number of shells on target.

In addition to the disturbing effects of officer changes, rumours greatly influence morale in 1943 – which rises steeply with each whisper that action is imminent, and falls precipitously when the rumours prove false. Such rumours start early in the year, possibly the result of optimism inspired, first, by Montgomery's smashing victory at El Alamein and the subsequent success of the British-American operation that ousted the Germans from North Africa, and, second, by the success of the Russians in entrapping 270,000 Germans at Stalingrad, killing 147,000 and capturing 91,000, including twenty-four generals and a field marshal.

Whatever the reason, rumours will continue to come and go as the Regiment takes part in strenuous training for battle, involving no fewer than sixteen schemes, varying from one-day stands to two weeks, some of them combining wide-ranging manoeuvres with shoots on firing ranges.

In between all these schemes, the Regiment frequently visits Alfriston for more first-ever experiences.

One of these is firing the guns following the directions of a "flying OP officer," an artillery captain trained to fly a little Auster aircraft "right down on the deck," back and forth behind the guns, rising up just in time to observe the arrival of each ranging round on his distant target, then dropping down to a grass-cutting, hedge-hopping level behind the guns so as to present a more elusive target for enemy fighter planes or ack-ack guns while figuring out his corrections in range and line for the next round and radioing these corrections down to the guns.*

Life for the flying OP can be complicated, as he must maintain his orientation and read distant map references while piloting a

---

* The first Air OP Squadron, RAF, formed October 1942, went into action in Tunisia, November 1942. Training of officers for Canadian OP squadrons began shortly after. Mark III Austers, fitted with flaps, self-sealing petrol tanks, armour on pilot's seats, etc., were in service by 1943.

plane in strange configurations, up and down, back and forth, over the gun position, so low to the ground he must tilt up one wheel of his fixed undercarriage to pass over a cow resting in a meadow, and having to remember – after hearing "shot one" in his headphones – to count the seconds it will take his ranging round to reach the target so that, just before it is due to arrive, he can whip his plane up high enough to see it land and make the necessary corrections before going into "fire for effect."

As far as the guns are concerned, an Air OP shoot is conducted in the same way as any "observed shoot." However, for the first time ever, you see a propeller-driven aircraft rise vertically and fly backwards.

On your arrival with an advance party to lay out your Eddie Troop position, you are amazed to find an Auster sitting in a tiny bit of open space surrounded by shaggy clumps of gorse, its pilot leaning against it, smoking. How on earth did he land on the top of this hill, with no more than fifty feet of flat, unobstructed landing space?

He explains his plane will fly at thirty-five miles an hour, and since it faced into a gale-force wind blowing steadily from the Channel, he simply throttled back the engine until he lowered his plane like a leaf to the ground. He says the wind is so strong today, he could actually fly his Auster backwards. When you appear sceptical, he promises to give you a demonstration when he takes off.

After the guns arrive and are put on line ready for the shoot, he requests the help of some gunners to grab hold of the tail and the tip of each wing to prevent the plane from rolling forward until he has the motor roaring at full throttle. When he gives the signal to let go, the little plane leaps forward about thirty feet and up into the air about thirty feet, from where it rises up and up, roughly over the same spot, higher and higher, until it is up about the height of a church steeple. Then as he eases off on his throttle very gently, almost imperceptibly the Auster moves backwards across the gun position. When he's backed it a quarter of a mile or so, he flips up one wing to catch the gale, and, with engine roaring, he swings away at great speed.

But not all Alfriston "firsts" have been in the field of gunnery.

One sunny Saturday afternoon, 4th Field officers join what appears to be a gathering of all officers of all Canadian and Home Guard units in Southeastern Command, assembled around the slopes of a natural amphitheatre on Alfriston ranges overlooking an open, grassy valley for a demonstration of German infantry tactics.

Several loudspeakers have been set up across the valley directed at the hillside and its dense cover of humanity, and, there being no wind, the instructor's explanations of what you are to look for as events unfold, come through very clearly.

The Germans, it seems, are in the habit of purposely pulling back under heavy attack, and then, before the elated, victorious Allied troops have a chance to consolidate their new position, they ferociously counter-attack, driving the Allied troops back where they came from.

The whole business is illustrated by squads of troops, half of them dressed in bluish grey German uniforms belted in at the waist, wearing jack-boots and German helmets, and firing German machine-guns as they run bent-over across the valley. It is a most impressive way of getting across the message, which could prove extremely valuable to you someday soon.

However, it doesn't end there. The instructor involves the entire vast crowd in a mass language-learning exercise, of astonishing effectiveness. You, who unquestionably have the lowest possible aptitude for foreign languages, find yourself learning the German words of command painlessly. The instructor down in the valley, by way of his microphone, invites the crowd to "drill" the squad in German uniforms, by repeating after him the German commands in roaring unison: "*Achtung – Stillgestanden!*" (Atten-tion!); "*Achtung – Marsch!*" (Quick march!); "*Achtung – Halt!*" (Halt!), and so on.

Armed with your new knowledge, and advised that, on return to your unit, you should teach all ranks in your troop these words of command so that they might more readily control prisoners of war, you proceed to do just that. As there is no troop commander at the time to say yea or nay – Don Wilson being on leave – for several days on morning muster parade and during the regular, half-hour route march along an overgrown lane and its strangely isolated little pub, The Cherry Bush, only German commands are used by you and Troop Sergeant-Major Dennis.

Surprisingly, all members of the troop take to them readily, and Major Cooper is so impressed that when he accompanies the new CO, Lieutenant-Colonel Fleury, on an informal inspection of billets and vehicle lines, he has you put on a demonstration drill out in the field using only German commands.

Then comes that remarkable day at Alfriston when from the heavens there drifts down on 26th Battery an abundant supply of material for the manufacture of waterproof, windproof outer-skins for bedrolls, something the planners and the famous backroom boys never thought to provide the troops. Suddenly, there, lying among the gorse on the gun position, is this considerably deflated barrage balloon – not one of those baby balloons that small boats tow about the harbours, but a full-sized London giant.

Reasoning that in its present debilitated state it could never find its way back to London or wherever it had been tethered, men of initiative and imagination begin slicing the waterproof skin into chunks just big enough to enclose a bedroll of army blankets. But before it is entirely sliced up, the battery command post gang, directed by the CPO Stu Laurie, garners enough of the material to allow for the manufacture of weatherproof troop and battery command post shelters.*

After much trial and error, and the application of limitless ingenuity and hard work by the battery equipment-repair man, a

---

* Two glaring deficiencies in army issue equipment were the lack of waterproof covers for a man's roll of woollen blankets, and weatherproof shelters for command posts where highly technical work on vulnerable sheets of paper on artillery boards had to take place in the rain under the stingy hood of the button-down canvas cover.

splendid command post for Eddie Troop evolves in the form of a fabric-enclosed attachment of easily assembled pipes, anchored to the rear of, and extending out from, GA, the troop command post truck. But Laurie's first try at producing a practical battery command post is a disaster. While it, too, is supported by a pipe frame, it is a four-sided, freestanding structure retaining much of the form and character of its free-spirited, high-flying ballooning ancestor. Woefully short of ballast, it fails to survive even one night on the South Downs when erected on 26th Battery's next visit to Alfriston.

At first the wonderful protection provided by the flapping cloth, holding out the roaring, drenching gale, arouses new levels of satisfaction and pleasure in Laurie's staff, including his Ack CPO, Lieut. "Sink" Sinclair, as he and the acks go about setting up the artillery boards and arranging in systematic order a sophisticated set of talc-covered proformas, along the lines of Sands Graphs (some created by the CPO himself and all designed to make life easier and more efficient) – unquestionably the most formidable array of such devices ever seen in a command post anywhere. But it's a grim night, perhaps the grimmest the Regiment will ever spend at Alfriston, and you will have special cause to note this and remember, for you are manager of the regimental hockey team scheduled to play their final game for the championship of 2nd Division in Brighton tomorrow morning (January 7), and your request that the players be allowed to remain back in billets to get a good night's rest was disallowed by the CO himself.

A bitterly cold wind, driving inland fog and rain from the Channel, lashes the gorse-covered gun positions and the gunners, who are trying to get some sleep in sodden blankets among the gnarled roots and dripping, prickly bushes. Morale is very, very low throughout the Regiment, mutinously low, for every man huddled in his bedroll or under a gas cape, trying not to shift position and force shuddering skin to warm up still another icy spot in his sodden long johns, knows that the 4th Field Regiment needs tomorrow's training shoot about as much as the chef at the Ritz of London needs another cooking course.

But fortunately there are men who can see humour in even the most miserable situations and by an apt remark turn on smiles and laughter. Every outfit has a few of these rare people – its true leaders, regardless of their rank – who continually threaten to drive it asunder while actually cementing it together with the strange glue known as "morale" by the officers and "soldiering" by the men.

Suddenly, a bullhorn voice, with the peculiar snarl of authority associated with regimental sergeant-majors, penetrates over the wind and the rain: "All right! Everybody up for kit inspection!"

For a split second there's no reaction. Then, with the recognition that it is only one of their own, rolling in from an unauthorized visit to the Star Inn down in Alfriston, a torrent of abuse is let loose, couched in the most colourful of four-letter words, telling Sgt. "Doc" Lavigne in the most explicit fashion where to go and precisely what to do when he gets there.

But for a long time after, the windy darkness is filled with lively shouts back and forth and gales of laughter. And somehow the whole damned, insane business seems to make sense, and everybody goes to sleep feeling much better if no more comfortable.

When Troop Sergeant-Major Dennis wakes you gingerly just before dawn, he cautions you to move judiciously, for accumulated in a sagging canvas basin between your legs is a pool of icy water at least four or five inches deep. He brings you two bits of news: first, during the night the gale blew 26th Battery Command Post and its contents into oblivion across the Downs; and second, your plan to withdraw the hockey team from the playoffs in protest against the inconsiderate treatment by the CO has been discovered, and Capt. Don Wilson has declared, "Come hell or high water, 4th Field will participate in the playoffs today, and you are to get your ass down to the kitchen in a cowstable at the foot of the hill, prepared to embark for Brighton with your team forthwith."

Frustrated and burning, you are sloshing through the ankle-high mud of the gloomy stable, lit only by the hissing flames of the oversized blowtorches the cooks use to prepare food in the field, when you come across a man who is in an even fouler mood than you.

It seems "Sink" Sinclair has been up all night, urged on by his CPO to ever more assiduous efforts to try to recover all those precious proformas, scattered far and wide by the same wind that blew away the command post tent. "Stumbling around in the flaming dark," growls Sink, "in the flaming rain, searching through the flaming gorse for bits of flaming paper and flaming proformas, with flaming lamps-electric that couldn't shed enough flaming light to find your flaming socks if they were on your flaming feet!"

Suddenly you find you are laughing. And while this does nothing to improve Sink's outlook on life, it certainly does yours. So when you stick your head in under the canvas hood over the back of the 30-hundredweight truck to make sure everybody is aboard before taking off for Brighton, you are able to present a more encouraging countenance to your droopy-eyed hockey players. Surprisingly, you receive only a couple of pointed scowls for having failed to get them the night off back in billets, most noticeably from Sgt. "Scotty" Cameron, the coach, and Sgt. Stan Crossett, the ex-NHL defenceman who played with Ivan "Ching" Johnson on the New York Americans. Sgt. Keith McConnell actually smiles a pleasant goodmorning, and that pair of irrepressibles, Bombardier Ron Hooper and Sgt. "Lefty" Phillips, seem as "full of pee and vinegar" as usual.

However, your high-scoring "kid line" – Gunners George Hillier, Jim Corbett, and E. C. Walker – always up and raring to go, do not present an inspiring picture this morning. Huddled together in the chilly gloom of the truck, heads pulled down in the collars of their greatcoats, they obviously intend to sleep all the way to Brighton.

On arrival at the Brighton Ice Arena all tumble stiff-limbed out of the truck with just enough time to pick up equipment from a storage room, making sure they get a stick of correct length and blade, and skates that fit and aren't both for the same foot. Watching them make their way to the dressing room, loaded with shin-pads, gloves, pants, sweaters, and socks, you are thankful the poker-faced

Sergeant Cameron is in charge of the bench and not you. They try hard, but they lose by the lopsided score of 10-4 to 6th Field, a good team, but one 4th Field might have beaten had they rested in billets last night.

Still, all end up having a good day in Brighton – mainly because they are inside, out of the wretched wind and rain that sweep in off the white-capped Channel all day long – happy in the knowledge that the CO and his 2 IC, to whom they attach more than a little blame for the CO's callous decision not to allow them to remain behind in billets last night, are still out on Alfriston ranges getting drenched and chilled to the bone while they are warm and dry. Afternoon tea in the upstairs restaurant in the arena, ensconced at a window providing an unobstructed view of the ice surface and the last game of the day, takes on an aura of outrageous luxury when you visualize those intense senior officers in sodden trench coats standing in the wet gorse, braced against the gale sweeping across their exposed hillside OP.

Then there's the friendly warmth of Sherry's bar, former British heavyweight champion Tommy Farr's bar, and still later the Dome dancehall, when Gunner Oliver Ament, your driver – on the pretext of wanting to make sure he gets the truck conveniently parked at the Royal Pavilion (where everybody has been told to gather at 10:30 for the trip home) – suggests you might like to spend the last hour or so there. And never having been in the spacious hall, which once served as a luxurious stable for its incredible neighbour – the oriental-style palace with swirling domes and minarets, built for the Prince Regent, who became George IV – you readily agree.

When Ament goes off in search of a dance partner, and you settle down with a drink to watch the vibrant mob of swinging couples crowding the floor, you are struck by the fact all the men are in uniform, but all the gals are in dresses, whether or not they're in the services.

48

A NEW TROOP COMMANDER
EVERY SECOND WEEK

---------------------------------- ✳ ----------------------------------

WHEN DON WILSON LEAVES TO COMMAND A BATTERY IN 12TH
Field, for a long time you are acting troop commander, which is
unusual, for clear seniority lists are maintained at Corps and the
officer next in line for promotion can be readily established. However, the mystery of why and for whom the position is being held
open is resolved on the night of January 30, 1943, when two 4th
Field officers enter the brightly lit American Bar in the basement of
the Park Lane Hotel in London, and find a well-groomed and
polished George Browne sitting there with a gin-and-lime in his
hand, smiling from ear to ear. Of how he came to be there he can
say little, beyond the fact that the French Underground helped him
down into Unoccupied France, for a time disguised as a nun.

After days of interrogation by Intelligence, he is allowed to rejoin
the Regiment. Of course, his return provides an excuse for a classic
4th Field bash at the Royal Oaks pub, drawing representation from
all parts of the Regiment, but especially 2nd Battery. Everyone
wants to get close to one who so recently was over there with the
Germans, and competition is heavy among those setting up drinks
for George "Huntley" (his code name at Dieppe), with predictable
results.

Long before the publican's "Time, gentlemen, please!" resounds
over the hubbub, the guest of honour has assumed a reclining
position on the floor. And when Sgt. Ed Howker of RHQ deems

it fitting to say, "Excuse me, sir," as he steps over the good captain on his way to the bar, he draws forth the gracious response, "No apology required, sergeant. As you see, I am a bit unsteady on my feet tonight."

Seconds later, he delivers another classic line when Lieut. Samuel Grange asks him, "Could I get you a fresh drink, George?"

"Oh, I suppose so. I might as well be drunk as the way I am."

When next day he becomes your troop commander, you look forward to getting the lowdown on how he managed to survive in Occupied Europe. But he's disinclined to discuss details. After escaping German custody, the French Underground helped him get to Unoccupied France, but he was interned by the Vichy French. Again he escaped, only to fall into the hands of the Italians after the occupation of Vichy France by Axis forces on November 11, 1942. While being taken by bus to Grenoble on December 7, he escaped again and this time made it to the Pyrenees via Toulouse.

After an exhausting trek over the snow-covered mountains in the depth of winter, he reached Andorra in the company of two Spanish smugglers. From there he was repatriated by way of Gibraltar, arriving in England on January 26, 1943.

His style of command is so like that of his old pal Don Wilson, you are looking forward to working with him. But he never really gets a chance to settle in before he, too, is promoted and leaves for 1st Division wearing on his shoulders the crowns of a major, and on his chest the ribbon of a DSO (Distinguished Service Order) awarded "for gallant and distinguished services in the field." It being a decoration seldom given to anyone below the rank of major, all assume it is recognition of his three escapes from enemy custody, and the priceless information he brought back for those who must one day plan the real invasion of Hitler's continent.*

---

* Browne would serve in Italy in 1943–44 with 1st RCHA and in the late winter of 1945 become CO of 14th Field of 3rd Division for the battle for the Rhineland.

Your next troop commander, Capt. Dave Ely, arrives wearing pilot's wings on his battledress blouse, having just qualified as a Flying OP Officer. It's clear he won't be around long; he's expecting a posting to a new Air OP Squadron presently being formed. Actually, he remains only long enough to introduce you to an old mariners' method of foretelling the weather, taught at the RAF flying school. It seems the weather people, not being privy to meteorological conditions in Occupied Europe, have taken to reading the weather from changes in cloud formations, the way deep-sea fishermen have traditionally foretold the coming weather.

When your latest troop commander, Capt. Bill Graham, arrives one Saturday evening recently, he gains a most peculiar impression of the level of good order and discipline extant in 4th Field. Resting before the fire in 26th Battery officers' mess, deserted except for Stu Laurie engrossed in a book, Graham is astonished to see someone (you) stagger into the house in a wrinkled sweatshirt, mud-caked pants and sneakers, and pass on into the ground-floor bedroom beyond the fireplace without eliciting a glance from Laurie concentrating on his book.

And before he can assemble the nerve to inquire what possible reason there might be for an officer arriving home at eight o'clock in the evening in such a state, two gunners come in the front door carrying another subaltern feet-first, dressed in the same informal style, and perhaps even muddier. At the door of the ante-room, they pause to inquire of Laurie, "Where shall we put him, sir?"

"In there," says Stu, nodding towards the door of the bedroom. And when the bearers have deposited the inert Harvey on his cot and departed, Laurie, as though recognizing the new captain deserves an explanation, says, "Len's home," and returns to his book.

Graham waits several days before raising the subject with you – waits until he is convinced by observation that 4th Field is not a complete loony bin, but rather a highly disciplined unit, adhering to the same rules of dress and conduct, and showing the same respect for accepted social divisions between officers and men, as any regiment in Britain.

While you find his description of Stu Laurie's phlegmatic response to a bizarre situation hilarious, it doesn't make it easy to
provide an explanation for your inexcusable conduct that night –
of which you have never before been guilty, and never again shall
be. To arouse even a modicum of understanding, you have to go
through the whole story with its origins in a snap midnight inspection of gun positions three weeks ago at Alfriston ranges by the
2 IC.

You and all the other gun position subalterns had been awakened
in turn that night by Major Steuart-Jones and informed that your
gun guards were either asleep or less than alert, since he had not
been "challenged" when he approached your position. At dawn,
an appalled Colonel Fleury attributes this "incredible apathy on the
part of gunners and NCOs" to "a lack of leadership by the subalterns," which translated means you failed to warn them that they
should be on the lookout for the enemy disguised as a Canadian
major striding boldly into their gun positions, singlehandedly trying
to take over twenty-four guns. The result is an unprecedented
decree by the CO that for one month all subalterns in 4th Field
would be confined to barracks except when carrying out assigned
duties.

Befogged by sleep and totally bewildered by the fact that there
had been no inkling of an imminent invasion either from the BBC
or military channels, you and the other fuzzy-headed subalterns,
suddenly aroused from your bedrolls, had felt defenceless. Smitten
by a terrible sense of dereliction of duty, all of you had accepted
your sentence without question. But as time went by, reason began
to reassert itself.

That a Sussex villager or Welsh sheep farmer would vandalize
your gun position is unthinkable. You are living among people
whose sense of responsibility as citizens – exceptionally high in
normal times – has been raised to levels unequalled in history by
the demands of the times and a spirit of service and sacrifice on
behalf of the common weal. So just what in hell are the gunners
guarding the guns against? After several nights of reflection and

lively discussion, you and your fellow confinees conclude (as the gunners had long since concluded) that guards on the guns on the lonely Downs of Sussex or on the bleak hills of Sennybridge are about as necessary as "tits on a bull," as friend Harvey puts it.

Even Jack Cameron, normally capable of laughing off what he likes to refer to as the "weird and wonderful demands of the high-priced help," was incensed by the implied insult of the chastisement, which he considered far too severe for the "crime." After all, battery officers' messes are never locked, and frequently are left totally unattended for hours on end, with the officers' personal kit in unlocked trunks in the bedrooms, and the usual stack of beer and liquor in unlocked cupboards.

And with each passing week, the confined-to-barracks sentence rankled more. Confined to the mess from dusk to dawn each week-day and all day Sunday was hardly a chore, for it was where most officers would normally be found anyway, but that the subalterns should be singled out for such indignity and insult, ignoring all other levels of command, struck all as unfair. And watching the grinning captains walking out for a bit of socializing with the natives in the evening became more and more irritating. So the stage was set for a rebellious incident when an opportunity presented itself.

It came on the Saturday you and Len Harvey were detailed by the Battery Commander to take part in a divisional cross-country run around Goodwood Park and racetrack.

Since the weekend confinement to the mess was more irksome than during the rest of the week, you didn't protest. But by the time the event was over and you – having lost the coin toss to Len for the seat beside the driver in the cab of the truck – were bumping back to the Battery, huddled down on the cold, steel floor in the back of the 30-hundredweight with a bunch of equally disgruntled gunners, who had wanted even less than you to don sneakers, old trousers and sweatshirts, and plough through muddy fields of Good-wood Park, you were in a mutinous mood.

So when the truck, letting off the last of Freddie Troop gunners, stopped directly in front of the Labour in Vain as it opened for the evening, Len had only to nod at the pub door, and you, shuddering with cold and drenched in self-pity, were with him heading for the bar for a warmer-upper, oblivious to the fact that neither of you was dressed for walking out. However, the publican, noting your attire, invited Len (whom he appeared to know well) and you to use a private room behind the bar. Very sensible, for it soon would be dark, and you could walk home in the blackout unseen.

If only you had returned directly to the mess, you'd have learned you were free to go abroad that evening. Special dispensation had been secured by Major Cooper from the Colonel to release his subalterns and their billfolds to attend another fundraising dance in the village hall on behalf of the WAVS (Women's Auxiliary Voluntary Service) and Mrs. Stacey's "tea van." But in your ignorance you proceeded to have a "warmer-upper" of Scotch with a chaser of mild and bitter. The combination went down so well, you had to have another. If possible, that went down even more smoothly than the first. Quite incredibly, the third round seemed to be an improvement on the other two. Things became a little fuzzy from then on.

Just when you decided it was time to go home, while you both could still manage the long walk in the blackout, Len discovered the existence of Mrs. Stacey's fundraising WAVS dance nearby and insisted you both attend, for "it would be a dereliction of duty not to make a contribution towards that dear old gal's great work on behalf of the troops." Afraid he might get into real trouble if he went over there alone, you followed along, wondering how on earth you were going to stop him from going in. Just outside the village hall, nature intervened. As he leaned over a low stone wall beside the roadway to throw up the excess of liquids he'd taken on an empty stomach, he passed out draped over the wall. Stopping a couple of his gunners on their way to the dance, you asked them to get the duty truck and deliver Mr. Harvey home to the mess. Then you walked home, which was no small feat in the inky blackout. You hoped Captain Graham would understand your disinclination to fraternize on your way to bed through the ante-room.

Far from assuming a superior posture, Graham seems tremendously relieved. And you and he get into a wide-ranging discussion of the astonishing level of tolerance Other Ranks can extend to "boozing officers" – even to out-and-out alcoholics, of which there are at least a couple in every outfit. There never seems to be any fall-off in the respect and deference shown officers because of their alcoholic escapades, many of which have been highly visible over the years.

And this is not because Other Ranks automatically extend tolerance to other deficiencies of character in their officers. On the contrary, they can be extremely critical. One officer, whose stock-in-trade is dirty jokes, within days after arrival at the Battery became an object of contempt for many in his troop. On making discreet inquiries, you were told it wasn't that they were put off by the subject matter of the jokes, but rather that their officer would indulge in telling them. They simply expected a man whom they were obliged to salute, and whose orders they had to carry out without question, to be a cut above the average, with an advanced sense of decency and morality.

49

"SPARTAN"

❋

IN MARCH THE REGIMENT IS INFORMED THAT 1ST CANADIAN
Corps is "to be brought up to full strength of equipment," and about
the same time it is whispered that 1st Division is about to participate
in something really hush-hush.

Then, just before the start of Exercise "Spartan," scheduled to
begin March 1 and run for two weeks – the largest and most realistic
war manoeuvre ever held in Britain – suspicions that the Regiment
is actually going into action are aroused by a two-day rehearsal for
"leaving for a battle zone outside Britain." Conducted under the
name Exercise "Elm," everything designated for storage, including
officers' trunks, is tagged and collected in a central place, and all
military pamphlets and documents are packed in boxes marked
"Destroy by fire."

When these procedures are repeated on the eve of "Spartan,"
with even more stringent security precautions, including censorship
of mail at the unit level, many are convinced "Spartan" really spells
action. Even when it turns out to be just another scheme, the sense
of actually going into action persists, to the benefit of all taking part.

As the name "Spartan" implies, men are expected to survive with
minimal food and rest. Each man is allowed only one blanket, and
conditions are so arranged through constant movement that it is
difficult for anyone to get any sleep or hot food. Your endurance
is continually being tested under pressure, as constantly you are

confronted with emergencies devised by the umpires or derived from some master script somewhere. Obstacles to fast moves are placed in your way: signs reading "Bridge blown – unusable," or "Crossroads mined." And they compound your problems by declaring essential vehicles and key personnel "casualties" at the most awkward moments.

In this massive confrontation of two armies – First Canadian Army breaking out of a bridgehead, and a British army (heavily supported by swarms of fighter aircraft) attempting to contain the break-out – there is such a high degree of realism in the struggles to outmanoeuvre the "enemy" that, long after, men engaged in the real thing in Sicily and Italy, writing to comrades in England, will say, "It's just like 'Spartan,' but with real shells and bullets."

Of course the only casualties in "Spartan" are from accidents – mainly motorcycle accidents as despatch riders (Don Rs) and officers race over heavily congested roads. But the shock and horror of gruesome death is present one morning when a tank crew is discovered squashed dead by their own tank settling on them during the night. It seems they decided to sleep under it, and when its tracks started to sink, it settled so gradually that by the time the sleeping men knew what was happening it was too late to escape. Then, the last night of the scheme, there is the shocking business of a damaged RAF Wellington bomber trying to make it home from a raid.

Posted overnight as a liaison officer (a glorified Don R) at 2nd Division Headquarters, you are dozing off, sitting on the ground beside your motorbike, leaning against the side of the caravan of Maj.-Gen. "Ham" Roberts, when you hear the irregular throb of the approaching bomber, seemingly headed for a landing field nearby, skimming so low in the blackness overhead you can hear the air rushing by its wings. It barely passes over when it crashes with a terrible flashing roar that shudders the earth, blowing body parts and pieces of airplane, the largest being the engines and wheels, over a wide area.

When the General comes out to ask what happened, he remains for some time, watching the flames flicker and glow in the field just over the road, pursuing the conversation with you in a very concerned and fatherly way. When he learns you are from 4th Field, he tells you he, too, was a gunner before being made divisional commander. Then, to your embarrassment, he asks for your assessment of the exercise so far.

Of course, you haven't a clue. Living the blinkered life of a GPO – fully occupied with getting the guns from one position to another and responding to unending demands for fire (albeit "dry fire," with firing pins clicking on empty gun breeches) on barrages and "targets of opportunity" sent back by the FOOs moving with the infantry – you've had no time to consider what the infantry and tanks may have been accomplishing. Also, you are very nervous talking to this famous man who led the Dieppe Raid. You tell him, however, that as far as you can tell, things have been going quite well. With this he readily agrees – so readily and so heartily, you sense he is badly in need of reassurance, even when it comes from a lowly gunner subaltern.

But your assessment proves correct, when shortly after dawn, "Spartan" is called off, a day early, with 2nd Division infantry near Oxford, having "fought" their way north about a hundred miles from the Channel at Brighton, clearly accomplishing what they'd been ordered to do: "break out of a bridgehead."

Somehow the umpires make sense out of all the goings and comings of units lost, units rerouted, and units bogged down in endless traffic jams, and decide that "Spartan" (at least from the invaders' point of view) was a success, though the brass are said to be disappointed in the very good weather that persisted throughout the whole two weeks. The chief purpose of "Spartan" being to expose men to exhausting conditions, the planners had counted on the normally foul March weather of England to deny sleep when they and the umpires ran out of other nasty ideas. But while it was very cold at night and each morning the ground was covered by a white frost, it was the driest two weeks in memory for this time of year.

Clearly, breaking out of a bridgehead is the role for which 2nd Division is being prepared and for which it will be put to use when the inevitable invasion of the continent takes place. As in "Spartan," this is the stated purpose of Exercise "Welch" late in April, involving another thirteen days and some 150 miles of "fire and movement" for 2nd Division.

50

CHICKEN AU DIABLE

———————————— ✳ ————————————

UNLIKE "SPARTAN," "WELCH" IS NOT ALL "DRY FIRING." THE scheme kicks off with a shoot with live ammo on West Downs in Sussex, and ends at Sennybridge with another shoot on Easter Monday after an unforgettable bivouacking on the ranges – unforgettable because of the violent form of diarrhoea that sweeps through the Regiment with dramatic suddenness.

The bowels of the Regiment are so distraught, the shoot, scheduled for first light, has to be delayed until almost noon. And when finally the Regiment is able to limber up for its move to Builth Wells for a week-long training camp at the north end of the ranges, it is late afternoon, and the coarse, winter-withered grasses on the adjacent slopes nearby are undulating in a cold wind that has been freshening noticeably since the pale sun began to wane and sink among the western peaks.

It's a familiar sight: the guns hooked to their limbers and the limbers to the quads resting helter-skelter about the slope, ready to move off in convoy down the steep track to the main highway, bound for Builth Wells about thirty miles by way of Brecon. Some of the quads sit at such precarious angles, you marvel at the nerve of the sergeants, standing with head and shoulders out of open hatches in the roofs of their humpbacked vehicles, waiting for the signal to move off. Although remarkably stable vehicles, equipped with bull-low gearing and four-wheel drive for climbing and descending very steep grades, they can still roll over. (One did roll over on these very slopes on a previous occasion.) And before they roll, they can roll their gun.

Before climbing into GE,* you go from vehicle to vehicle, checking on the state of the gunners' inner workings driven haywire by bacterial action in the food last night. You have to know if their bowels have regained a degree of stability not requiring frequent stops in addition to the normal convoy halts of ten minutes every hour.

The problem began when the Regiment was late in arriving yesterday to put the guns in position and settle down for the night – much later than expected by the cooks on the advance party who had prepared a special Easter treat. Huge cauldrons of steaming-hot canned chicken in a creamy sauce were allowed to cool down, and had to be reheated when the Regiment arrived. It had grown dark by the time a long lineup of ravenous gunners formed and the cooks began slopping generous dollops of the creamy chicken into clinking mess tins. In the dark, no one had read the warning on the cans: that the contents, once heated, must *not* be reheated. The reheating did no harm to the flavour, and all ranks gobbled up every speck of their grub, remarking how unusually good it tasted.

But during the night, disasters began to happen as men were wakened suddenly for guard duty. Sound asleep in your bedroll in the tentlike command post attached to the rear of your GE, you were totally unaware of the mounting crisis until the first grey light of dawn was creeping over the frost-covered gun position. Awakened by the buzzing of the field telephone on the ground beside your head, you raised the clammy handset to your ear and were greeted with one of the strangest wake-up calls any man ever received: "Whatta we going to do about it – make plugs for their rear ends?"

---

* "G" standing for gun position officer and "E" for Easy Troop, which used to be Eddie Troop under the old phonetic alphabet.

The voice was easily recognizable as that of the Ack CPO William Reynolds "Sink" Sinclair, but his words made no sense whatever. And since Sink has been known to hit the sauce a trifle too heavily now and then, you offered him the friendly advice, "Go back to sleep and sober up, you silly bugger."

Chortling merrily, he persisted: "Look, I'm just passing on a message from RHQ. The shoot won't be starting on schedule. It's been postponed indefinitely – at least until we can keep gun crews on the guns."

"Sink," you asked in mounting bewilderment, "what the hell are you talking about?"

"You mean it hasn't hit you yet?"

"What hasn't hit me?"

"Raise the side of that tent of yours and look out."

In the misty dawn light, in all directions, men were squatting with their pants down. Just then, Sergeant-Major Dennis, followed closely by two gunners carrying shovels, came striding briskly in the direction of a gunner pulling up his pants. Spotting your up-turned face from under the drapery of the tent wall, he paused a moment to explain:

"We're the covering squad for those who don't make it to the hedge. I take it, sir, it hasn't hit you yet. Well, it will, and it can be pretty . . . uh . . . drastic! My advice is to move very slowly. It's when you move that it hits you."

And it was while you were pulling on your boots, preparing to go outside to assess the situation, that the vicious cramps struck. You barely made it to the hedgerow.

The shoot finally got underway just before noon, and as soon as the shoot ended, the order came to limber up and prepare to move.

Now, waiting to move off, you need to know if there are any residual effects of the plague, starting with Sergeant-Major Dennis in the cab of TL (troop leader's vehicle), having given up his motorbike to your recently acquired troop leader, Lieut. Sid Darling, who has been delegated to ride herd on the convoy. You are more than a little surprised to find Dennis alone in the cab, seated behind the steering wheel, while overhead on the roof, sitting hunched over, with his feet dangling down in front of the windshield, is Gunner M. J. Wilkinson, the regular driver, wearing a most woebegone expression. And for this he can hardly be blamed, for the wind has taken on a cold edge, and, once the light goes, it is bound to grow even colder.

Why on earth is he up on the roof?

Wilkinson remains grimly silent, but the Sergeant–Major answers your question with one of his own: "Can't you smell him, sir? There's no way I'm going to ride in the cab with that!"

There being a certain identifiable redolence in the vicinity, and suspecting the subject is most painful for the poor man perched on the cab roof (a man for whom you had developed a high regard when you were troop leader and he was your driver), you drop the subject and return to your vehicle, where you get the whole story from your driver.

It seems Wilkinson is in the habit of sleeping in the back of his truck in preference to the ground. However, unlike other trucks, with high steel boxes hooded over by tarpaulins held up to standing-room height by tubular frames, TL has just a shallow, wooden-sided equipment box to carry behind its cab, with a tarpaulin stretched over the top and lashed down tight with a rope attached to clips around the outside. Having had trouble the previous night with the tarp blowing off the shallow box, leaving him exposed to the rain, Wilkinson, after settling down for the night, had a friend spread the tarpaulin over the box and lash it down snugly. The friend, of course, was to return at dawn to undo the knots and release him.

However, during the night, Wilkinson had required immediate release from his canvas prison for the same reason everyone else was heading for the hedgerow. But when he called, no one came, and the more he struggled to break out, the worse it was for him and his immediate surroundings. When at dawn his friend finally showed up, Wilkinson was in such a rage, he was afraid to let him out. Not until "Wilkie" swore a solemn oath he wouldn't kill him, did his friend release him.

Now, having no change of clothing, the poor man is doomed to be aired on the roof of the cab all the way to Builth Wells.

PART FIVE: APRIL 1943– JANUARY 1944

Morale Becomes the Big Problem

51

MEN LIKE OFFICERS WHO TRY
TO UNDERSTAND

THE BUILTH WELLS TRAINING CAMP IS BROUGHT OFF VERY smoothly in contrast to the endless snafus that occurred at Senny-bridge last fall, and by the time the Regiment is pulling out to return to Sussex, the IGs declare the Regiment has put on "a very good show."

But on the last day of the camp, while your troop is providing the guns for a bunch of quick-firing targets called for by the captains in an OP somewhere, a tragedy begins to enfold that will depress Eddie Troop for a very long time. Sid Darling, troop leader and assistant GPO – a splendid young man, handsome as a movie star and possessing the most charitable of natures, who, in just a few weeks, has won the respect and affection of every man in the troop – collapses on the gun position with an excruciating stomach ache just as the guns are deploying for fast action. Rushed to the hospital in Builth Wells, he is found to be suffering from a burst appendix.

And this is not the worst of it. When he enlisted, he'd kept secret the fact that he was a haemophiliac – "a bleeder" – who, were he to suffer any deep cut, such as an incision to remove an appendix, would bleed to death unless the serum derived from rattlesnake poison could be located – a substance seemingly unavailable at this time in Britain.

And for three weeks after the Regiment returns to Sussex, all in Eddie Troop agonize over reports on "Mr. Darling's" deteriorating

condition regularly reported by Padre McCleary, who is in touch
with the hospital in Wales through his church links. As the town
becomes aware that an exceedingly robust young Canadian officer
is slowly bleeding to death in their hospital, at least one of the
churches holds a special mid-week service to pray for his recovery.

The day the Padre comes back from visiting the hospital and tells
you it is only a matter of hours, that "the poor boy's so weak, his
jaw is being held up with a bandage," you assemble the troop to
inform them and invite all who may believe in Divine intervention
to engage in silent prayer. You are a little uneasy as you offer the
suggestion, but for several minutes all stand silent and unmoving,
most with their eyes closed. It is not something you will soon forget
– a hundred men praying for the life of a young officer whom they
have known only a few brief weeks, but loving the sympathetic,
understanding nature that caused him to listen with concern to all
their beefs.

Sid dies the next day and is buried in Brookwood Military
Cemetery.

For days a pall hangs over your troop, and it is not really dispelled
until the Regiment takes over the anti-raid positions near Worthing
of 3rd Division, which is being sent to Scotland to practise disem-
barking from landing assault craft on a stormy beach. Now morale
rises dramatically. Not only are all batteries well-billeted – 2nd in a
large tennis club, and 14th and 26th in requisitioned houses in
Bramber and on the outskirts of Worthing – but everyone is talking
about an order from on high that the unit is to be fully mobilized
by May 1, 1943.

Of course rumours that the Allied invasion of the Continent is
imminent reach a new peak as quarter stores get bags of new equipment, including Sten guns, though these light automatic weapons,
meant to replace the sleek tommy-guns taken from the unit to arm
1st Division for whatever they are about to get into, are a disappointment. Not only do they look like something assembled by the
plumber down the street, they don't work worth a damn. When
Capt. Bill Graham and you try them out in a nearby gravel pit, you

are unable to get off more than two or three rounds at a time before they jam.

Still, the feeling that 2nd Division will soon follow 1st Division into action somewhere keeps morale at a high level, and when 4th Field goes to Lydd Camp in the latter part of May, it breaks all records set by other regiments in "manhandling guns" over a gruelling obstacle course that includes a section of that wide, slithering waste of gravel for which Lydd is famous – a desert of shiny round pebbles of indeterminate depth through which it is difficult to walk, let alone manhandle 3,640 pounds of 25-pounder gun. A 14th Battery gun crew does best of all, cutting five minutes and forty seconds from the previous best time. And all ranks enthusiastically approach courses in tank and aircraft recognition, and an introduction to German booby traps and mines.

But when the gunners learn they are not going into action, but are going to assemble under canvas in the wooded parkland of Arundel Castle for the summer, morale plummets. They feel they've been had. During the seemingly endless round of schemes and training camps in every kind of weather (often digging trenches and gun pits simulating action), they've done their best and put their hearts into it. They have not beefed at being kept away from their reasonably comfortable billets and denied the pleasure of meeting with pals in favourite "locals" for a pint or two at night, and they have put up with endless, boring days of silly make-believe war that may be valuable for staff officers, but clearly is of little value to overtrained gunners.

In fact, they have done everything required of them to get ready for action, represented to them as being just around the corner. That this turns out to be nonsense they find intolerable. Not knowing just whom to blame, they direct their frustration at the Colonel and his 2 IC.

Though unintentioned, you become one of its first victims when your own troop decides to express, in the classic manner of gunners, their displeasure at being pushed and driven hither and yon for weeks on end to no real purpose. Their opportunity comes when the Regiment moves over to the Alfriston ranges and your troop is chosen to provide the guns for some "observed shooting" by the subalterns.

As the methodical business of delivering ranging rounds at various ranges and switches – requested ever so slowly and deliberately by each subaltern up in the OP obtaining his "close bracket" on some chalk pit or gorse bush – goes on throughout the day, you are irritated, but not unduly disturbed, by the number of times you find guns pointing somewhat less than parallel to the rest when "fire for effect" is called for. Though time and again you have to call to Sergeant-Major Dennis, who is acting as troop leader, to check the line of a gun, you never suspect intentional errors in gun-laying, but rather put it down to a combination of fatigue and boredom.

So when you are summoned by your Battery Commander to take your turn up at the OP, and are told to leave Sergeant-Major Dennis in charge, you merely warn him to remain alert to possible errors in laying.

When you arrive at the OP hill, the 2 IC is conducting a lecture with the other officers, and Colonel Fleury takes you some distance away to conduct your shoot. This turns out to be a wild one – so wild that by the time he calls a halt to it, he could hardly have failed to recognize that something extraordinary is at work back at the guns to distribute shells about the landscape in direct and visible opposition not only to your most explicit corrections, but to all logic.

For some inexplicable reason, however, it suits his purpose to blame you. And not only that, he gathers about him all officers of the Regiment, who had been absorbed in the 2 IC's lecture, and introduces the subject by saying, "I have just witnessed what has to be the worst shoot in the long history of artillery."

He carries on in this vein for some time, but you aren't listening; you are planning what you are going to say to those "crazy bastards" at the guns. And when you get to face Sergeant-Major Dennis, you can hardly believe your eyes. He is grinning from ear to ear, totally oblivious to the fact that that screwed-up shoot was *your* shoot, by *your* guns, and had incited the Colonel to crap all over you in front of all the officers of the Regiment.

Later, when the guns are out of action and the Regiment has moved down to bivouac for the night in the broad, green valley facing Beachy Head tank-range, where all gun crews are to engage in a tank-shooting contest tomorrow, Dennis seeks you out with a message from the sergeants. They are all terribly sorry, and will make it up to you tomorrow by winning the barrel of beer the Colonel has put up for the troop scoring the highest number of hits. While relishing their chagrin and grateful for their belated sympathy, you still burn. And, of course, you write off as childish bravado their promise to restore your status in the Regiment by winning the tank shoot for you. But then you never before have had the chance to witness what gunners are really capable of accomplishing when they truly set their minds to it.

Next morning, when it is Eddie Troop's turn on the guns, all that time spent at the miniature anti-tank range, snapping tiny .22-calibre bullets at targets, pays off. With astonishing frequency, the glaring white tracers, sizzling in the base of the solid-shot, streak through the burlap tanks rocking up and down, appearing and disappearing in the trench that wiggles across the front some six or seven hundred yards away.

Each of the twenty-four gun crews fires five rounds, and when it is over, Eddie Troop, with more than 80 per cent hits, is an easy winner – far above the 55 per cent average considered remarkably good for the Regiment as a whole.

Major Cooper, fully aware of all the hours you've spent with your gun crews on the miniature range, instructs you to position yourself in front of your troop lined up by the Sergeant-Major to receive the prize.

But the Colonel views matters differently. Ignoring you, he calls the four gun sergeants forward to be congratulated. So much for all those endless, nauseating sermons that "the subalterns are failing to take over," that "the subalterns must start providing more leadership."

52

"BUT NO DAMNED FLOWERS"

---- ✳ ----

THOUGH POINTEDLY IGNORED WHEN THE KUDOS IS BEING handed out for your troop's great display, you seem to have drawn the attention of the 2 IC, for immediately after you're told to report to Major Steuart-Jones in a nearby house, where he and the other senior officers were billeted last night. There, to your dismay, you learn you are now "Regimental Mess Secretary," as he passes on the simple but forbidding terms of reference: "This being the first chance in months for the officers to mess together, and perhaps the last regimental mess before going into action, Colonel Fleury wants it to be a memorable one, the finest mess in the history of 4th Field."

Shocked, you hasten to tell the 2 IC that if he searched through the entire army, he could not locate a more unsuitable candidate for mess secretary, that you are singularly ill-equipped, having had no appropriate experience whatsoever in Civvy Street. While you don't actually go down on bended knee, begging to be released, you feel you should, for you sense disaster lurking down the road.

But he won't listen. You were highly recommended for the job by your Battery Commander. You *can* do the job. You *will* do the job.

And so you cease to be GPO of Eddie Troop and become full-time mess secretary, responsible for the maintenance of three marquee tents of varying sizes: one, representing the ante-room, sheltering a bar; a larger one providing a dining room; and a small one, the kitchen.

Your first task, after seeing the tents are erected close to each other, is to establish a duty roster of batmen to service most of the needs of these centres of activity – the exceptions being the positions of cook and barman, each of whom must be chosen for his experience and (at least in the case of the barman) his integrity.

The tents are reasonably new, but tents are tents and ground is ground, and while the combination may produce a charming setting for a garden party in the afternoon, overnight they lose all appeal as functional quarters for anything involving human beings.

There's almost a forbidding quality to the gloomy tent harbouring the bar, furnished at the outset with wooden folding-chairs. The mess tent is a bit better. The tables are just issue folding-tables, butted together to form a U-shape, the closed end providing a head table for the senior officers, but when draped with white tablecloths they look great. Obviously a hangover from a previous age, the white cloths give the place quite a civilized appearance, though the batmen are not at all thrilled with the prospect of the frequent laundering and pressing they'll require.

Whatever else is required of a mess secretary, you will have to pick up as you go. On canvassing fellow subalterns as to what they think would make for "the finest mess in the history of 4th Field," a consensus suggests, first, a well-stocked bar with plenty of Scotch (which all recognize will not be easy these days), second, as many eggs as you can scrounge, and third, bags of strawberries and other fruits and vegetables in season. But no damned flowers!

The strength of opposition to their mess dues being "squandered" on flowers is explained by Stu Laurie when he advises you not to follow the example of the last mess secretary, "Moose" Saunders (captured at Dieppe), who had made it a habit of arriving back at the mess from a buying trip well-oiled and singing happily, but with the back of his truck filled with flowers and little else.

Regimental Orderly Officer Bob Douglas, who you are told has good connections with booze suppliers in London (from Civvy

Street connections with Gilbey's Gin), advises you to collect mess dues from each officer in advance and head for a warehouse operated by the NAAFI (Navy, Army, Airforce Institute) where, in addition to condiments and other things not supplied through regular rations, you may buy the monthly ration of liquor (a bottle and a half per officer) and eggs (if available, at the rate of one egg per officer per week).

To your astonishment, the NAAFI produces cases of Scotch, rye, rum, and gin, and *crates* of eggs. They tell you their records show no one from 4th Field Officers' Mess has come to claim their rations of these precious items for months, and so large credits have built up. Obviously, battery messing officers have been drawing rations in the name of their batteries, not in the name of the Regiment. But of course you don't mention this to the NAAFI counterman helping your driver load up the truck.

Nor do you reveal anything to reduce your reputation as a genius among your fellow officers of 4th Field when they find the bar flooded with Scotch, and each morning – for days on end – two eggs gracing their breakfast plates – fried, scrambled, or boiled according to taste.

That you have succeeded in producing the best mess in the history of 4th Field is conceded without argument by everyone below the rank of the Commanding Officer and his 2 IC. Patiently you wait for them to add their commendation. Finally, one evening, just after you get back late from a buying expedition and have settled down to your supper in the mess tent, now deserted except for the senior officers up at the head-table dawdling over their coffee, Major Steuart-Jones beckons you. At last, you think, a moment of triumph, a bit of recognition before the Colonel and other senior officers! But when you get to him, he points at his coffee cup and tells you to taste it and tell him if you think it is something that should be served in an officers' mess.

Stunned, you accede to his request. It's cold, but otherwise it tastes as usual, the way most coffee tastes over here: passable, but with faint, mouldy overtones possibly induced by the eternal damp, particularly when stored in a tent. You mumble to this effect.

At this, Major Steuart-Jones – affecting an accent so tee-reebly, tee-reebly British it would do justice to the most pukka of pukka officers of the most pukka regiment on "the northwest frontier" putting his servant in his place – says, "If you cawn't get the cooks to pre-pah a decent cup of cawfee, then you must do it. Go out to the kitchen and brew us a fresh pot."

As you pass down the tent, past the remnants of your dinner, you are in despair. Only a very brave man or a total fool would invade a cook's domain and openly insult him by taking over his stove. And you are neither that brave nor that stupid. Diplomatically, you try to explain your mission to the cook, and why you must remain to carry in the pot, but the looks you get and the stream of comments made to an unseen third party while the coffee brews, suggest you have inflicted a wound that will not heal for a long time. And the fact he is black does not help your relationship with him at this point.

Delivery of the steaming pot is an anti-climax. Only the 2 IC and a couple of other majors are still there. Unwilling to interrupt the conversation, the 2 IC points at the cups and makes a pouring gesture. When you have tipped out the old dregs in the cups on the ground and filled them up, he sends you away with an imperious wave of his hand.

Your next hassle with your high-ranking critics takes place in the Colonel's office with the door closed. He is very put out. It seems that at the mess buffet on Saturday afternoon for officers and their guests, before the party moved on to the great hall of Arundel Castle for a dance hosted by the Duke and Duchess of Norfolk, one of the lady guests had been embarrassed by having to report there was no toilet paper in the latrine set aside for the use of the ladies.

Obviously the latrine, a primitive four-holer like all the others in camp, had been looted of its precious paper by a gunner with a provident bent – one wishing to ensure a supply of the stuff for the next scheme and so obviate the need to use letters from home in the normal manner of all troops, who invariably leave the landscape dotted with crumpled-up little blue airmails.

As the Colonel proceeds to accuse you of something worse than dereliction of duty, implying you should have guarded against such a possibility, something inside you snaps. Standing up, you tell him that from the start you warned you were totally unsuitable for the job, had begged Major Steuart-Jones to get someone else, but he wouldn't listen . . .

The Colonel starts yelling, "Sit down! Sit down and be quiet!"

Determined to speak your piece, you charge on: You have tried to do your best – which, in the judgement of others, is damned good – but you obviously can't satisfy him or the 2 IC, so why, in God's name, not get someone else?

By the time you are finishing, you too are shouting.

When at last you sit down, the CO is livid, but for a long time he says nothing as he writes furiously on a notepad. At last, tearing out two pages filled with notes, he pushes them across the desk to you. Then, in an astonishingly calm voice, he explains that one is a list of things he wants done "without fail" by 1700 hours today, and the other a list of things he wants checked out every day. Among these is "the toilet paper in all latrines." And he's added a new one: "There will be fresh flower arrangements on the headtable every day."

On the long list of things you are to complete "before 1700 hours" is "Pick up chesterfield and upholstered chairs from the recently abandoned battery messes near Barnham," and it's late in the day when you finally get around to it. By now you are very tired, and on the return journey you are catching forty winks as your driver lets his 30-hundredweight truck roll freely down one side of the steep valley of Whiteways Crossroads so as to roll up the other side as far as he can before gearing down. Just as he's getting into low gear for the long climb up the hill, a military policeman on a motorbike pulls alongside, wakes you up, and hands you a speeding ticket. The speed limit, designed to save wear on tires, is fifteen miles an hour, and it seems your vehicle, now crawling up the steep hill, was doing in excess of fifty on the way down into the valley.

Having ridden so long in vehicles careening at breakneck speed trying to keep up with regimental convoys threatening to pull out of sight, you are not overly impressed by the ticket. And so, when, a couple of weeks later, as you are eating your late and solitary dinner in the mess tent, you are collected by the Colonel to go with him to divisional headquarters, you are mystified. All the way there, and while you wait with him in an outer room, you are given no clue as to the nature of your visit. So it is with incredulous ears you hear yourself ordered to remove your wedge cap and *march* in before the ruddy-faced Brigadier Tees, waiting behind his desk. Exhibiting all the signs of a man whose appetite for good food and fine brandy have been sated, he looks at you almost benevolently as he says:

"You are charged with being responsible for a vehicle exceeding the speed limit. Now, if that was all there was to it, I would tell you, 'Don't be a young fool – go home and don't do it again!' But Colonel Fleury tells me you will only carry out written orders. Now, this is a very serious charge indeed, and I took the trouble to look up your service record. It is a very good record. Why the sudden change? I want to hear your side of the story."

Totally embarrassed, crushed by the indignity of it all, feeling utterly betrayed by the outrageous accusation, you think, What is the use? And you hear yourself saying, "Sir, if you can't believe a senior officer under your command, why would you believe me?"

For a moment the florid-faced Brigadier puffs up so much, it looks as if he may explode. You can almost see steam coming out his ears. But then the truth of what you unwittingly implied sinks in. For a long time he says nothing. Then turning to the Colonel, he says:

"Colonel Fleury, I think we have to use some common sense here. I think, on the strength of his record, this officer deserves another chance. I want another report in a month's time."

Then turning to you he growls, "In the meantime, you are grounded."

Bewildered, you ask, "Sir, I know what grounding means in the airforce, but I don't understand what it means in the army?"

"You are forbidden to ride in the front of any vehicle, for any purpose whatsoever, for a month."

Riding back to camp in the car with the CO is a most uncomfortable business – he in the front chatting amiably with his driver, and you in the back alone, fighting a sense of hopelessness, and struggling not to give in to a gnawing feeling that you must have some major personality defect or character deficiency to arouse such hatred in that soft-spoken man up front showing such polite consideration for his driver's views on the current success of 1st Division in Sicily, who thinks that Sicily will be the springboard for the invasion of the Italian mainland.

As you listen to them discussing the latest news from down there, you find yourself imagining what 1st, 2nd, and 3rd Field Regiments are going through. At this very moment, while 2nd Division is playing at war here in England, they could be throwing shells at the enemy or sheltering in holes from enemy shelling. And with these thoughts you suddenly are able to put tonight's Alice-in-Wonderland affair in proper perspective.*

---

* At 2:45 A.M., July 10, elements of twelve American, British, and Canadian divisions from Montgomery's British 8th Army and Patton's 7th U.S.A. Army landed on the southeast corner of Sicily. The landings caught the ten Italian and three German divisions in Sicily by complete surprise. In the first twenty-four hours 160,000 Allied troops, along with 600 tanks and 1,000 pieces of artillery, landed in Sicily against little resistance. Two days later against stiffening resistance, requiring American 1st Division near Bagusa to drive off a German attack with 100 tanks, six airfields were reported captured, and Syracuse captured by the British. On July 16 Canadian troops captured Caltagirone, while U.S. forces took Barrafranca and Porto Empèdocle, bringing about a quarter of the island under Allied control. Palermo, the chief city, fell to Patton's army on July 22.

53

LIVING WITH THE SPECTRE
OF A BOWLER HAT

⁂

HAVING TO LIVE FOR A MONTH WITH THE POSSIBILITY OF AN adverse report that could send you packing back to the holding unit and possibly all the way back to Canada, labelled "unsuitable officer material," is a nerve-racking experience you never expected could happen to you.

At the outset it seems you're engaged in an uneven struggle. As you proceed to serve your sentence, while fulfilling your duties as mess secretary, you expect to become the laughing-stock of every gunner and NCO in the Regiment as daily you ride out of camp in the back of a truck on foraging expeditions to greenhouses and market gardens, and later return, still riding in the back, under the canvas hood among the vegetables. Surely you will come to be seen as a regimental joke, someone not worthy of commanding troops.

But it doesn't work that way. It is not you who becomes the object of scorn when it becomes known that the Colonel was instrumental in getting you relegated to riding in the back of vehicles when he paraded you before the Brigadier on "a lousy speeding charge." To the drivers especially, who know the speeds they must attain when catching up in convoy, "somebody has to be nuts."

And the troops don't take kindly to seeing one of their officers treated with contempt by senior officers. They see it as an obvious insult to their intelligence and judgement when an officer to whom they are expected to show deference and salute, and whose orders they must carry out without question, is held up to ridicule. And the men of Eddie Troop eagerly support you when one day you are ordered to return to them for an hour or so to try to carry out a "perfect troop deployment," which the Major IG from Larkhill, currently visiting the Regiment, has been seeking, but never getting, from each troop in turn; always some little details have been neglected by the GPOs or the Other Ranks.

When Major Cooper seeks you out at lunch and tells you to collect your steel helmet, skeleton webbing, compass, and map board, and report to your Eddie Troop, which he says is drawn up and waiting for you, he adds that the Colonel expects you to ride as usual in the rear of GE under its canvas hood. And that is how you arrive on the position, in full view of all the officers of the Regiment assembled with the Larkhill IG on a nearby hillside, hanging out of the back of the truck and peering around the side of its canvas hood, with your map board flapping and you shouting directions to your driver, alone in the cab up front, on which way to turn and when to stop.

If, after watching this weird entrance, the IG expects a snafu from this crazy-man's troop, he is disappointed. Before taking off in GE, you just had had time to let the Sergeant-Major know *they* were out to get you today, that they were looking for a perfect deployment, and that "No one *walks* on the position today." And they don't.

The way the Numbers One leap down out of their quads to direct them to the flags you planted, and the way their crews pile out of those quads and get their guns up and locked on their platforms, and trailers unhooked and in place, you'd think you were watching a military tattoo. Gun-layers leap onto their seats almost before the trails hit the ground, fixing their dial-sights in place ready to accept the bearings you call to them from the director. While well aware that Eddie Troop, like every troop in the Regiment, is capable of doing a perfect troop deployment with their eyes closed, you can hardly believe the speed of their response. And evidently every piddling detail is taken care of, for when you are waved forward to the hill where the officers and the IG are assembled, the 2 IC says he has no criticism, and the Major from Larkhill says he has none, either.

Next day, they have you do a crash-action deployment – again riding in the back of a truck, peering around the tarp to maintain your orientation. And to add to your difficulties, this time, they don't allow you to use your own troop, but deliver you to Freddie Troop, limbered up and waiting. Again you have only a moment to appeal to the gunners' and NCOs' sense of fair play, informing their Sergeant-Major Richardson that they (the CO and the 2 IC) are contriving to get you a bowler hat, so please, let no one walk today. But it works the same magic it did with Eddie Troop; the deployment is flawless and the fastest you've ever been involved in. The Larkhill IG finds nothing to criticize.

Afterwards, when you are thanking Troop Sergeant-Major Richardson and the NCOs, you are astonished to learn your stock has been rising throughout the Regiment ever since reports of your stormy confrontation with the Colonel over the missing latrine paper (overheard by the orderly room clerks at RHQ) began circulating.

Though this information is comforting, you are aware there's the better part of a month to go, and it's only a matter of time before you make some stupid mistake or fail to do something, even if you are able to escape the ambushes they must surely be plotting, more determined, now, than ever to get you.

The feeling of being trapped in a situation from which there is no escape induces a strain that is almost intolerable. But then fate takes a hand. Overnight you become seriously ill.

54

GARNONS

———————————— ✳ ————————————

WHAT YOU THINK IS A HANGOVER TURNS OUT TO BE A ROARING fever, so high the MO packs you off to the casualty clearing station, where they diagnose your problem as sinusitis, and send you on to 14th General Hospital. Here, a specialist (who'll be returning to Montreal to teach at McGill's medical school after he finishes with you) feeds you massive doses of sulfa and snares a couple of oversized polyps from your nose and antrums.

This leads to a fortnight at a convalescent home for Canadian officers established up in Hereford in a castlelike country mansion called Garnons, rented by the Massey Foundation from the owner, who, you are told, owns everything, including villages, as far as the eye can see in all directions from the considerable hill on which the great stone pile rests.

The living conditions at Garnons, where most of the regular staff of the owner appear to have been kept on, are so luxurious you marvel the place is not overrun with convalescing officers. But after a few days you will come to understand how its reputation could have preceded it, turning off its prospective clientele. Even after a few hours, the place begins to give you the creeps. There is a gentle-but-insistent pressure on you to take advantage of the tennis courts and riding stables, and when you try to take advantage of its library, overly solicitous hostesses sweetly involve you in activities obviously intended as occupational therapy, such as tooling leather.

However medically beneficial tooling leather may be, it doesn't seem to be the proper activity when friends are engaged in deadly struggles to push through the valleys and over the hills of Sicily, and hundreds of airmen (the RAF by night and the American Airforce by day) brave torrents of flak to attack German industrial cities.*

With each passing day, you feel more and more like a shameful malingerer, particularly at lunch and dinner as a servant hovers about, ensuring your wine or cider glass is always topped up. And each night when you open the door to your room and find the bedside lamp glowing and your bed awaiting, with its silken spread and rustling rich sheets turned down just so, your sense of being a contemptible counterfeit is very disturbing.

To break the smothering spell of this dream-world of affluence, the current crop of convalescents – a pretty good cross-section of Canadian mavericks, detesting stuffiness and pretence to the point of being inverted snobs, organize junkets down across the fields to a crossroads pub in the valley.

Down there, in what must be one of the most unprepossessing pubs in all of Britain, you and your jolly mates, pestered by hordes of flies, partake of warm, flat brown ale while resting on uncompromising wooden benches with sternly upright backs, in preference to leaning back in one of the deeply upholstered chairs, with their flowery effeminate slipcovers, in the lounge of the great house and ringing for a servant to bring you a glass of cool cider or pint of cold ale.

---

* On the night of July 24–25, Hamburg, with three thousand factories, most of them on war production, is hit by 2,396 tons of bombs dropped by 740 RAF planes. The next night Essen was hit by 2,032 tons of bombs, reputedly shutting down the Krupp works. The following night, July 26–27, Hamburg was again bombed by 739 RAF planes dropping 2,417 tons of bombs, including large numbers of incendiaries that started fire-storms, which developed winds up to 150 mph and temperatures of close to 1,000 degrees Centigrade.

Even guys with broken legs encased in casts, barely able to get about on crutches on level ground, insist on joining in these pilgrimages, blithely ignoring the problem of the return journey until they and their more healthy companions – on whom they must depend to pull and push and otherwise support their tottering ascent back up the hill – are well into their cups. Thus they guarantee still another epic struggle to regain the summit and the great grey eminence, where the world of super-decorum soon puts an end to all the happy, if fuzzy and raucous, bantering, as each is invited politely but firmly to go to his room and get dressed for dinner.

On Saturday, July 31, the Honourable Vincent Massey, Canada's High Commissioner in London, comes up from the city in time to preside at dinner. You draw one of the places near the end of the table at which the great man is placed. This proximity proves embarrassing as time goes on and he chooses to regale his young dinner partners with what he considers to be a humorous anecdote involving a meeting he had with Benito Mussolini in the early 1930s. Triggering this recall is the sensational news coming out of Italy since last Sunday, July 25, when the Italian people, including some of their most prestigious generals, revolted and arrested Mussolini.

The whole point of Massey's anecdote, obviously told for what he perceives to be its humorous content, is his acute, knees-knocking discomfort on being ushered, with studied, intimidating pomp into the presence of the Italian dictator. Everybody else at the table clearly thinks it's hilarious. Remembering that in the fall of 1938 Massey had led a move by British Commonwealth ministers (meeting in Australia) to declare support for Chamberlain's appeasement moves, you bite your tongue, but you can't hide the fact you think his confession disgusting.

It seems he had been sent to Rome to represent Canada's official position with Mussolini on a matter of great consequence, but was reduced to a quivering mass of nerves by the treatment meted out by the arrogant little bastard. It began with a seemingly endless walk through echoing marble halls and a succession of doors opening and

closing with resounding bangs behind him as his name was announced in stentorian tones at each doorway by an armed guard
splendidly garbed to impress visitors. Finally the last door opened
and he found himself in a huge room, empty but for Mussolini,
who was sitting on a raised dais underneath a giant gilded eagle at
the far end of the room.

No word or gesture of welcome was extended to the timid little
man from Canada as he made his way with quivering legs across
the vast expanse of marble floor, the room echoing with each
footfall, to stand like a schoolboy in front of the dictator, for there
was no chair in sight. Nor was there any response from the dictator
when he presented his credentials.

Not until it was clear the meek Canadian was thoroughly dis-
comforted and totally embarrassed by his predicament did the imperious bully remove his fists from his hips and clap his hands to
summon a flunkey to bring in a chair on which his visitor could
collapse.

Why anyone would think this story humorous is beyond you.
That any Canadian envoy would accept such shabby treatment, and
later glory in his own embarrassment, is beyond your comprehen-
sion. That the envoy in question had all the advantages of growing
up in a family of great wealth and influence makes it even less
understandable.

When you think what he and others like him could have done
to control that puffed-up Italian jackal when he first defied the
League of Nations and showed Hitler it could be done with im-
punity, you have difficulty suppressing the urge to shout at him,
"For God's sake, man, are you still blind to what you appeasers did
to us?"

Fully aware, however, of what that could do for your career, you
remain silent. But what you are thinking clearly shows, for when
he turns to you and his eyes catch yours, his countenance falls and
he frowns in bewilderment. It's at this instant you decide you have
had enough of Garnons. Next day you get them to take you in to

Hereford, where you can get a train to Bordon and #1 CARU, the only route you have to get posted back to the Regiment, having been struck off strength when you went to hospital.*

---

* When on leave or taking a course, soldiers remain on the strength of their regiment, but when they go for medical treatment beyond the casualty clearing station level, they are "struck off strength" and when discharged from hospital are posted to an appropriate reinforcement depot.

55

BACK TO 4TH FIELD

———————————— ✳ ————————————

AT BORDON THE THOUGHT OCCURS YOU WOULDN'T HAVE TO go back to 4th Field and Fleury-Jones's persecution if you could get yourself posted to one of the 1st Division field regiments getting ready to invade mainland Italy with the British Eighth Army.

To your pleasant surprise, on presenting your story to the Colonel Commandant as you walk back to the mess together after having served as a sort of aide-de-camp to him during church parade and a drumhead service on the main parade square of the depot, he promises you a place on the next draft to the Mediterranean. He tells you he himself is the victim of comparable silliness – a purge of "mature" officers from regiments.

Highly knowledgeable on how to conduct oneself in territory under observation by the enemy, he says he was summarily removed from command of his regiment when a young umpire on a scheme, after disdainfully watching him crawling up to the crest of a hill to an observation post, turned in a report that this old man was still fighting the last war and was out of touch with the realities of a fast-moving modern battle. The Colonel understandably gets real pleasure in finishing his story by telling you, "That presumptuous fellow was one of the first casualties in Sicily . . . lost a leg . . . presumably preferring to run up, rather than crawl up, an exposed slope."

While you await the next draft to the Mediterranean, the kindly Colonel appoints you "Heath Fire and Paratroop Picket Officer," which entitles you to a truck and driver, ostensibly to help you track down heath fires and any paratroopers that may be wandering about, but also providing you with a pleasurable degree of freedom of movement. For a while, life is quite pleasant, until one night your room-mate – who is technically in your charge until his trial for bouncing a cheque – returns from playing bridge with the Colonel, wakes you up and tells you that you are going back to Canada on a draft of "officers with regimental experience" required to train new officers in Canada.

While you long to go home, this is not the way. You don't sleep a wink, and are waiting for the Colonel Commandant when he arrives at his office next morning. He understands your feelings completely, but his hands are tied – unless, of course, your Regiment requests your return. You ask him to call 4th Field, and he gets Adjutant Capt. Brit Smith, who says, of course, they want you back, they have been wondering where you'd got to.

Thus you return to 4th Field, but not as GPO of Eddie Troop, 26th Battery, Major Don Cooper having decided (you surmise) he doesn't need a subaltern who so easily ruffles the feathers of Colonel Fleury and the 2 IC. In contrast, Major C. M. "Bud" Drury, now in command of 2nd Battery, welcomes you with unusual warmth, as though he knows the story from within and is ready to challenge anyone who tries to revive the situation you were in before going to hospital.

Drury, unfortunately, soon leaves on a staff course, and the new battery commander, Major Gordon Wren, doesn't have much time for subalterns with tarnished reputations.

For a while you share the responsibility for Battery Command Post with the CPO, Lieut. Bill Murdoch, the only serving officer in 4th Field who rose from the ranks after enlisting as a militia-qualified sergeant on September 2, 1939.* Murdoch served as a fellow NCO

---

* Others were sent for officers' training, but served with regiments other than 4th Field.

with Sgt. "Scotty" H. Cameron, his CPO Ack, and there naturally exists between them the bonding of the 1939 "originals" of the Regiment in which no late-arriving subaltern can hope to share. Further, Cameron (in peacetime the town clerk of Bowmanville) carries a poorly disguised resentment that he, too, hasn't been commissioned, which shows each time you have to check his work for accuracy – a duty you cannot shirk.

While acks, by continuous practice of their specialties, are better qualified than most officers in their skills as surveyors, they can make errors, and the officer in charge is held responsible. Acks, always conscious of the terrible consequences of errors, understand this, and, with one notable exception, are only too happy to have their work checked. The exception is Scotty Cameron, universally recognized among his peers as a superior ack – one who never makes a mistake.

Naturally, he commands the respect of all officers working with him, but to Scotty this is not enough, he must periodically have the satisfaction of embarrassing an officer. So any officer having the temerity to question the accuracy of his work must be prepared to suffer "the treatment." First, there's the nose in the air and the staring off at a distant horizon. Then, in his dour, poker-faced fashion – without uttering a word but with a slight sigh of resignation that says it all – he picks up his slide-rule. A couple of deft movements and it's set and read, examined and laid to rest on the artillery board. Assuming again that air of studied patience that only a man who has been forced to engage in a waste of time to humour an officer might display, he resumes his nose-in-the-air, staring-at-the-horizon posture, as he sniffs, "There's no error."

This, of course, obliges the officer to recheck his figures under his contemptuous gaze, knowing he'll find, as usual, his ack is right. While this does not encourage a happy working relationship between officer and ack – a relationship that is normally warm, friendly, and mutually respectful in most command posts – having an ack that never makes a mistake is most comforting to a new assistant command post officer when he is in charge and a barrage is called for with really not enough time to prepare it before H-hour.*

---

* Cameron was eventually posted as an IG to the Canadian School of Artillery, first established at Bordon by former 4th Field Lt.-Col. Eric Harris, and moved in 1943 to Seaford College on the coast.

56

MUDDY MORALE OF

MONKS COMMON

✳

CONFORMITY BEING OF FUNDAMENTAL IMPORTANCE TO THE functioning of the armed forces, officers at all levels of command do their best to adhere to general standards of conduct, not only those set out in rules and regulations, but also those governed by fads, fashions, and practices believed to be currently in vogue throughout the British army.

Nevertheless, the personality and character of each officer always show through in the way he conducts his responsibilities and in where he places emphasis in matters of good order and discipline, sometimes with disturbing consequences when he is the commanding officer of a Regiment and has a wide range of prerogatives not available to officers of lesser rank. One CO may be totally preoccupied with attaining high standards of training, while his successor shows himself to be incapable of overlooking the pickiest of details in dress and conduct.

Both may be severe taskmasters, but the one who leans towards what old soldiers aptly refer to as "chicken shit," will at best irritate, and at worst arouse morale-destroying anxiety among all ranks as officers and NCOs, down through every level of command, make sure they "cover their asses."

Whether an officer is stiff-necked with little sense of humour or has a terrific sense of humour and a highly developed tolerance for the weaknesses of human nature – whether he is a slave-driver or a natural leader, approaching each job with contagious enthusiasm – are matters of tremendous consequence to the men under him. Men can accommodate all types, from *laissez-faire* blokes to ramrod martinets, but when they must adapt to a different regime every few weeks, imposed by a new CO, a new battery commander, or a new troop commander, the experience can be traumatic.

Soldiers don't like change. Change arouses suspicion. Even when the change might raise the quality of existence, it can stimulate demoralizing anxiety. Once men are used to a routine (even a miserable, boring routine), they prefer to stay with it. This you learned last winter, when, as acting troop commander, you decided to do something about the excessive time devoted to maintenance of equipment, currently being used simply to fill in time, there being a limit to the number of hours a troop can devote to troop deployments, anti-tank drill, signal exercises, and the like. Every morning after muster parade and a short, but brisk, route march for a couple of miles, signallers were routinely dispersed to see to their equipment in one of the huts, drivers to their vehicles parked under camouflage nets around the perimeter of the hedge-enclosed field, and gun crews to the open gunsheds in the cattle market in the village behind the Railway Hotel.

Just what signallers do in the way of maintenance is a mystery, but they seemed happy enough mucking through mounds of cables and sorting through equipment, while gossiping and brewing up a cuppa now and then.

Vehicles do require some maintenance, of course, and drivers devote much time to keeping their quads and trucks spotlessly clean inside and out. Clearly, however, they have to find ways of putting in time, and many of them go in for painting the insides of their quads and truck cabs in bright colours – Paris green, pale blue, or light grey, with knobs and handles in bright red – in contrast to the drab exterior of camouflage splotches of dark green, olive-green, black, and khaki.

And while endless hours on gun maintenance seem to present no real problem for the gunners, just watching them go through the same stupefying routine each morning and afternoon was enough to drive you batty. First, they removed the canvas muzzle- and breech-covers and pulled the gun through with an oily swab. Then, carrying on desultory repartee and exchanging the latest rumours, they took the breech mechanism apart, laying it out on the breech-cover on the ground, and began to rub endlessly each glistening little part with an oily swab of cotton waste. When mid-morning tea-break arrived, they reassembled everything, restored the breech- and muzzle-covers, and headed for a tearoom up the street, or to the WVS tea-van when it was their turn to have it. After tea they came back, took off the muzzle- and breech-covers, re-moved the breech mechanism, and carried on until noon. At noon, they restored everything and went to lunch. On their return to the gunsheds after lunch, they removed the breech-cover, took apart the breech mechanism, and again took up the task of rubbing each oily little part and gossiping until tea-time, when they packed up everything and went for tea.

So, one particularly cold and wet morning, you'd decided to change matters. At the noon muster parade, you announced that henceforth all maintenance would be completed in the morning, leaving each afternoon for either sports, on a volunteer basis, or "internal maintenance," a euphemism for staying out of sight in their sleeping-quarters in the Nissen huts, washing clothes, writing letters, reading, or sleeping.

But were they grateful? Were you looked upon as a hero? Hardly.

Within a week Sergeant-Major Dennis was begging you to re-store the old routine. Morale had sunk to such a level that discipline was becoming a serious problem. Incredibly, once they were again condemned to spending their afternoons in draughty, cold, open gunsheds among the freezing puddles of the animal market, the Sergeant-Major reported morale restored.

No, soldiers don't like change. And there have been endless changes in command at all levels of the Regiment this year, starting back in January, when Colonel Fleury became the new CO. Soon after, his 2 IC, Major Frank Ernest Goulding, left for 8th Army Field and was replaced by Major E. Steuart-Jones, leaving a vacancy in 2nd Battery that was filled by a new arrival, Major C. M. "Bud" Drury.

Then Major McGregor Young, 14th Battery Commander, left to become 2 IC of 14th Field, 3rd Division, and was replaced by Major G. A. Cowan. But soon Cowan left to conduct a party of German prisoners-of-war to Canada, and was replaced by Major Gordon Savage from 1st Field Regiment.

Then Major Steuart-Jones left to take command of 2nd Field in Italy, and was replaced as 2 IC by Major Don Cooper, who was replaced as 26th Battery commander by Major Cowan on his return from Canada. And when Major Drury left for a staff course, Major Gordon Wren came to take over 2nd Battery.

And there have been at least as many promotions of captains, in and out of the Regiment, including Capt. John Harrison, who had been adjutant of 4th Field since 1940 and was something of an institution, if also something of a martinet, earning the title of "Colonel Harrison" among the subalterns. Still, morale rises briefly in the latter part of August and early September while the Regiment takes part in a most realistic scheme held in the Southhampton area. Known as "Harlequin," the exercise is designed to test the port administration's handling of large bodies of troops embarking in assault craft. But to those taking part, it appears to be not just an exercise, but the real McCoy.

Unit censorship is in effect for six days, the whole area is cut off from England and put under a heavy security blackout, and the Regiment is divided into several parties and allotted to various types of craft. Daily, thirty officers and 150 Other Ranks practise loading and off-loading vehicles. On September 6 – the same day the camp is inspected by Gen. Bernard Paget, commander-in-chief of the home forces, and by Lieutenant-General McNaughton, commander of Canadian forces in Britain – all ranks are issued "48 hours' landing rations" and "emergency rations." So when next morning, as the Regiment moves down to the embarkation "hards" (concrete ramps), Spitfires engage a swarm of enemy fighters in a sputtering, whining dogfight directly overhead, all doubts disappear; this is, indeed, for real!

But then suddenly the scheme is called off, and the Regiment returns to mildewing kits in mouldering tents on the damp ground beneath the trees at Arundel Castle.

From this point on, morale deteriorates, for it is now clear the unit is not going into action in the foreseeable future. And at this most unpropitious time, the spirit level of 4th Field is seriously unbalanced when its beloved Padre, Ray McCleary, leaves to become chief padre of 3rd Division.*

So when the Regiment moves into draughty, corrugated-iron Nissen huts, sitting like bleak islands in a sea of glistening mud, at Monks Common near Horsham, facing another grey, wet English winter – their fourth Christmas away from Canada – morale drops to an all-time low.

The deterioration, however, has been so gradual it seems not to have registered with the leadership of the Regiment, many of whom are new to their command. But to you, who have been away, it is shocking to see how low morale has sunk in a few weeks, even among the junior officers.

When you mention this to fellow subaltern Ted Dack, who'd been a course-mate at Brockville and Petawawa and is now troop leader to GPO Jack Cameron in Freddie Troop, his comment is, "This outfit is just about ready to blow." And knowing the distaste that had grown up between you and Colonel Fleury before you left for hospital, he adds, "Just keep your nose clean – sit back and watch it happen." And this is about all you can do, for you are no longer GPO of Eddie Troop, where you could have provided some leadership, but are Ack CPO of 2nd Battery, with very little responsibility for anything of consequence when the guns aren't in action.

---

* Replaced by Honorary Captain L. B. Begg.

As though to guarantee a further drop in morale, one after another, all three battery commanders and the second-in-command of the Regiment are replaced.*

Then, incredibly, not only are some subalterns unaccountably shuffled between batteries on some whim of the senior officers, but groups of six or more subalterns are sent off for a week at a time to a gunnery course run by Division in Holmbush House, a requisitioned house on a road north of Worthing. Thus, when every officer who has been around long enough to be trusted by their troops is most needed to defuse problems at an early stage, a high percentage are not there. In fact, they themselves are being demoralized by having to take instruction on how to lay out a gun position, orient a director, plot an artillery board, and the like – elementary stuff, which they could carry out with their eyes shut if need be, having done all of it under pressure during schemes in every imaginable condition of terrain and weather.

Meanwhile, back at Monks Common, the CO feels it necessary to call the NCOs together and lecture them on the discipline of the unit!

By now the mud is beginning to play a role, becoming so bad from continuous rain that all the vehicles have to be parked along the road outside the camp until a stable vehicle-park and access road can be built by the Regiment's own efforts. For weeks the gunners are required to move awesome quantities of rubble from bombsites in nearby towns, transporting it in regimental trucks, which are, of course, not dumptrucks and must be emptied as they are filled, a

---

* Major "Bud" Drury left for attachment to 5th Armoured Division Headquarters to gain staff experience before going on a staff course, and is replaced in 2nd Battery by newcomer Major Gordon Wren. Major Cooper leaves to take an IG course, and is replaced as 2 IC by Major Gordon Savage from 14th Battery. Major R. W. Corinstine arrives to take over 14th Battery. Major Cowan leaves 26th Battery for Italy and is replaced by another newcomer, Major William F. Carr.

shovelful at a time. There seems no end to it, and jokingly the thing becomes known as "Richardson's Bypass" after quartermaster Capt. Tommy Richardson, who is in charge.

But while it may appear a matter of humour over dinner in the officers' mess (an event for which officers are now obliged to "dress" in their serge each night), it isn't funny to those who line up for their grub, slopped into mess tins in the dining hall, after being out in the lashing rain all day on the end of shovels butting into awkward lumps of rubble.

And then, on top of everything else, lurking in the shadows of everyone's consciousness at this time of year is the irrepressible longing for home and its unspeakable cousin, homesickness – something never openly discussed by soldiers. Whether they think it would be evidence of a character weakness, an unmanly emotion unbecoming of a warrior, or because everything surrounding the subject is so painful that even to broach it would open the floodgates of memories and suppressed emotions with embarrassing if not dangerous consequences – whatever the reason – you never hear an officer or Other Rank confess to being homesick.

Whether every man here suffers from periodic bouts of this malady that baffles description, or suffers with the same intensity, is impossible to say. The few who have their wives or fiancées over here may be reasonably free of the affliction, and even some of those with comfortable arrangements with mistresses may be immune. But for the majority it surely is a cross to be borne, though the army does not officially recognize it as a distinct hazard to morale.

How others manage to control it after years of separation, you do not know, but you suspect that most see to it that their attentions are concentrated on duties and diversions as far removed from memories of home and loved ones as possible. This is the only way you can manage it – backed up by your long-standing determination not to dwell on home and family but to forget every precious memory from that far-off life of other times that could be a source of torture and frustration, most particularly memories of those last wonderful days and nights of your brief married life, made all the more precious at the time by being rationed and by the feeling that time was running out.

At first it was very hard, but with the passage of time the periods between bouts of this malady have grown further and further apart. And so it must be for others. But the threat is always there, and the pain of homesickness can surge through you at any time, day or night, with excruciating intensity, triggered by a particularly warm, loving letter, a startlingly realistic photo, or a parcel containing a pair of socks so soft and so woolly you can't resist pressing them to your face, knowing that every inch of that lovely yarn has been fondled by her beloved hands.

So, during the last days of November, as Christmas letters are being composed for loved ones at home (special letters, recalling the sweet memories of glorious Christmases past), and the first Christmas parcels begin to arrive from Canada, morale in the Regiment sinks further still. So low does it sink that the Catholic padre from Division, after one of his weekly visits to the Regiment, feels obliged to report to Brig. R. H. Keefler, now the CRA of 2nd Division, that he thinks there could be a mutiny at 4th Field unless something is done.

Shortly after, on a grey and bleak afternoon, a staff car flying the CRA's pennant turns in through the gate of Monks Common, and, sailing right past the Regimental Office, pulls up outside the mess hall that doubles as the NAAFI canteen. There, the Brigadier leaps out, stomps inside, and after establishing himself at a table, despatches a soldier running to locate the RSM (regimental sergeant-major) and tell him to call an immediate muster parade here of the entire Regiment – all personnel except commissioned officers. He wants no officers present when he questions the men as to what is wrong with 4th Field.

When all are assembled, he explains he has come to find out what they think is wrong with the Regiment and how *they think* things might be improved. He gives them five minutes to appoint spokesmen – three from each troop. All the rest will then clear out.

Later, a couple of NCOs, who were among those chosen as spokesmen, tell you a consensus was forthcoming "loud and clear": the Colonel was held to blame for all problems, imagined or otherwise.

There surely will be a new commanding officer soon. Significantly, the Brigadier departed the way he came, without going near RHQ. Quite obviously he was looking for evidence to confirm what he already had learned from other sources. Could one of those have been the senior IG from the Larkhill School of Artillery, who must still be laughing at the peculiar colonel of 4th Field who had one of his subalterns lead his troop in a crash action while hanging precariously out the back of a truck, holding on with one hand while clutching his map board with the other – peering around the truck-roof tarp, trying to see where he was going and to read the map at the same time?

Nor would such a story – making for a good chuckle over the port in the messes of the high and mighty – have done much good for the career of Brigadier Tees (now on his way home to Canada) when it became known that he was the one who decreed that a subaltern in one of his units should, for a month, view the world backwards from underneath the tarpaulin hoods of trucks.

There are some officers, particularly the newly arrived majors, who believe that Brigadier Keefler's dramatic, unannounced arrival at Monks Common, and his afternoon of interviews with the Other Ranks, was really unnecessary, that things would have worked themselves out if left alone. And there are others, equipped by long experience in the Regiment,* who contend the wrong man is taking the rap, that Major Steuart-Jones, who recently left to take

---

* While there are several subalterns with two or more years' service with the Regiment, only two officers remain of the original 1939 roster: Capt. John Drewry and Capt. Tommy Richardson. (Another "original," Lieut. Bill Murdoch, still serving with the unit, was a sergeant on enlistment.)

command of 2nd Field in Italy, contributed most to the lowering of morale in 4th Field.*

---

* That this may have been so is borne out by the fact that, as lieutenant-colonel, Steuart-Jones continued his demoralizing ways in Italy until summarily removed from command of 2nd Field the day his gunners succeeded in "sending a message" to his CRA by turning in a ridiculously bad anti-tank training shoot. Padre Eldon Davis, of 3rd Field, who periodically covered off 2nd Field when their padre was away, in his book on the Italian campaign, *An Awesome Silence*, described this in detail in a chapter entitled "The Judgement of the Gunners." Of events leading to this, he wrote:

> As that cold and extremely wet winter progressed, and the guns could no longer be dug in below grade (simply because the pits would fill up with water and collapse) forty thousand sandbags were issued to each regiment . . . to be used to erect low, circular walls around the guns. However, the new CO commandeered ten thousand of them to build a shell-proof shelter – providing living quarters in one end and regimental headquarters in the other end. He further ensured his safety by roofing it with steel rails covered with more sandbags. His next act was even more repellant to the battle-seasoned troops. While on an inspection of a battery, that had been driven out of drowned slit trenches and were using an old farmhouse (the only whole house in the area) as sleeping quarters, he ordered them out into the open. He claimed it would be sheer favouritism if they were allowed to continue to use it. As soon as it was vacant, he set up an officers' mess in it. The morale of the Regiment plummeted. While there wasn't any ranting, quiet anger burned with intensity. This often took the form of stories of World War I tyrants being found with a bullet in the back of their heads. While I believed these threats to be mostly talk, a way of letting off steam, I counselled moderation, and hoped and prayed they'd take my advice.

(Page 98, Eldon Davis, *An Awesome Silence*, Carp, Ont.: Creative Bound, 1991.)

57

THE REGIMENT'S FOURTH
CHRISTMAS AWAY FROM HOME

———————————— ✳ ————————————

WHILE NO CHANGES OF ANY CONSEQUENCE IN THE LOT OF THE men of 4th Field are immediately discernible, the shock of the CRA's dramatic intervention has an immediate uplifting effect on morale, and by Christmas the unit is in surprisingly good spirits.

Of course there is the normal annual party for the children of the locality, this time featuring Father Christmas arriving in the turret of a Ram tank recently acquired by the Regiment for training forward observation officers and their crews in the use of a tank as an OP vehicle. The towering tank, turned a startling white for the occasion by the application of gallons of whitewash, is escorted by a team of Don Rs on their motorcycles, making as though they are towing it along with red and green streamers attached to its flanks.

And on Christmas Day 1943 the cooks outdo themselves, and the officers, fulfilling their traditional role as waiters, are able to serve the men what the diary calls "one of the finest dinners ever organized by any regiment."

Then, for a couple of hours in the afternoon, those gunners who choose to repair to a nearby cow pasture as spectators are provided with some unforgettable entertainment by what is billed as a sporting event, but which in the event smacks more of the traditions of the Roman Coliseum. Officers meet the NCOs in a slipping, sliding mêlée on the gunky playing-field in a half-soccer, half-rugby game using two balls – one round and one egg-shaped – which could have been confusing to the players (it certainly was to the spectators), except that seldom does a foot or a hand make contact with a ball of any shape. And when, after the game, the mud-encrusted glad- iators (particularly those with the greatest number of bruises and abrasions), gathering at the nearby Dunhorse pub for a post-mor- tem, are asked why more attention wasn't paid to the general pro- gress of the balls up and down the field, they reply in astonishment, "Balls? What balls?"

There are, as always, many away over Christmas, some by choice and some on special assignment. Those who have wives or fiancées over here arrange to have leave at this season and are the envy of all. But for those on course or on assignment, dependent on the hospitality of strangers over Christmas, the outlook can be bleak.

So when men on course at Rhyl in North Wales learn that the people of the town intend to throw a party for the strangers in their midst on Christmas Day, they are both surprised and much excited by the prospect. Included among the Canadians is Sgt. Keith McConnell, the motor transport sergeant of 2nd Battery, who, on completing a course in loading and off-loading waterproofed ve- hicles from assault landing craft, had been asked to stay on a few weeks as an instructor.

Rhyl, a seaside resort town in peacetime, with miles of broad beaches, is an obvious choice for such training, but, ironically, the training takes place on the beach of a nearby lake – fresh water being less corrosive to metal than saltwater, and the winter winds not so severe inland. On the coast gale winds can be so strong that sand lifts from the beach and sifts in around the windows of the third-storey seafront billets of McConnell and his mates.

Training carries on right up to Christmas Eve. McConnell, knowing from experience how cold it can be in wet clothes in the biting wind, rides cross-legged on the roof of the cab of the truck as it rolls down the ramp off the landing craft and the water swirls in through the cab as high as the steering wheel. And there he remains when the inexperienced driver stalls his vehicle (as most of them do), making it necessary to have the vehicle winched ashore. An NCO with a big heart, who'd normally never ask a man to do anything he wouldn't do himself, McConnell had quickly learned to deny his principles in the vicinity of that icy lake. But he winces each time he orders another poor trainee out of his stalled vehicle, down into the freezing water to wade ashore, catch hold of the hook of an exceedingly heavy winching cable of a land-based truck, and, struggling and stumbling, tug and drag the awkward snake from its winding spool, back out through the frigid water up to his armpits, to go down under the water at the front of his swamped truck and find the towing ring onto which to hook the cable.

The prospect of the men spending Christmas away from all their friends as well as families had bothered McConnell very much as the day drew near. So when the people of Rhyl stepped in, inviting trainees as well as their instructors to a Christmas party at the town hall, he could hardly believe their good fortune. Canadians always throw parties for the English kids in their areas at Christmas, but never expect to be on the receiving end because of severe civilian rationing, which is more stringent with each passing year.* And so they're overwhelmed by the generosity of the people of Rhyl when they enter the great town hall Christmas afternoon and confront tables of food under a giant streamer strung across the room reading, "Merry Christmas and A Happy New Year."

Naturally, the supply of truly rich seasonal goodies is sparse; even the best will in the world cannot overcome wartime rationing in Britain. But there is plenty of draught beer, good fellowship, joyous singing, jokes, and laughter. And above all there is an abundance of pretty female partners for the dance floor – gals bubbling with happiness at being home on leave from grimy factories, smelly cowbarns, and drab service barracks.

---

* Twenty-two ounces of meat and two and a third ounces of butter per person per week, and two and a half eggs per *month* in 1943.

58

REDESDALE — THE LAST
TRAINING CAMP

———————————— ✳ ————————————

THE YEAR 1944 BEGINS QUIETLY, WITH NO INDICATION THAT plans for operations of tremendous magnitude involving 2nd Division and the Regiment are about to be put in motion. There are troop deployments on cold, clear nights in the surrounding fields, road building in the camp at Monks Common, and the usual training in small arms, anti-gas, signals, and gun drill, none of it carried out with any enthusiasm.

Because camp maintenance requires so many "fatigues," one full battery must always be totally on "duties," while a second battery supplies "details" for all tasks with which they are unable to cope.

After dinner, officers assemble in the ante-room to listen to a lecture, when there is one, and to drink too much when there isn't. Whiskey is unusually plentiful, frequently arriving by the case from London, courtesy of ex-4th Field subaltern Bobby Douglas and his prewar connections with Gilbey's Distilleries.

Then, on January 17, the long-awaited signal arrives: the warning that little time remains to get ready for action, that only forty days remain for units to bring themselves up to scratch in every way. After that the Regiment will become part of a large plan that will disregard the training requirements of individual units.

Although many can't help being sceptical (after all the previous false alarms), most believe that these instructions are authentic, and morale gradually rises to a high level. Training takes on real meaning, concentrating on matters of some consequence in action: mine-laying, arming and throwing grenades, and firing the new one-man anti-tank weapon, the PIAT (Projector Infantry Anti Tank). The 32-pound PIAT launcher – employing both a heavy spring (which must be cocked with some force, using both hands and feet) and a light propellant charge – is able to hurl a two-and-a-half-pound tail-finned bomb with a "hollow charge" capable of burning instantaneously a tiny hole through the turret of a tank and sending a lethal shower of molten steel ricocheting around inside. It can be fired from the shoulder, but there is a heavy kick. Firing duds in practice with notable inaccuracy at anything beyond twenty-five yards, it is clear the PIAT gunner, to be certain of hitting a tank, will have to close in well below the hundred yards suggested as its lethal range against tanks.*

Officers are issued extra bullets for their pistols and encouraged to practise firing them, something most officers have never done. At first you find it difficult to hit a tree as thick as a man only a few feet away, even when you take plenty of time to aim the thing, let alone wheel around and snap off a shot as you are warned you most likely will have to in action.

Then some unusual night training for subalterns and other ranks is laid on. Troops take turns learning how to establish infantry defensive positions and conduct infantry patrols – both "listening" and "fighting" patrols under the direction and guidance of infantry officers. Dressed in dungarees, head and neck encased in a Balaclava, face blackened in real commando style, creeping stealthily across a black landscape of farm hedgerows and the backyards of village cottages, attempting to capture before you are captured, can be exciting as well as instructive.

---

* Hollow charge or shaped charge, on impact with the target, bursts forward in a thin jet so incredibly hot that in a split-second it sears its way through armour several inches thick, the molten metal ricocheting around within the tank.

And now and then there are pleasant interludes, as when you are "captured" by a civilian – a member of the Home Guard investigating strange noises coming from his garden – and you and your patrol are given the choice of a glass of light ale or a shot of whiskey before pressing on with your mission.

On February 3, a few new 60-hundredweight trucks arrive, and you learn that all the trucks and quads, first received in 1941, will be replaced before you go into action. Fourth Field will take them on a last convoy way up to the border of Scotland to an artillery camp at Redesdale in Northumberland, fittingly the longest trek they've ever made – a round trip of about 750 miles. That every vehicle makes it there and back under its own power says something for the high level of maintenance by drivers and motor mechanics, for they are deemed to be worn out, with the lighter vehicles showing thirty thousand miles on their speedometers, much of which was recorded while churning over the worst country England and Wales have to offer, bumping over gorse-covered hills and grinding through mud up to their axles.

The convoy leaves before dawn on February 9, and is passing through the heart of London as the city awakes. Broken into blocks of twenty vehicles each at the southern outskirts, each block is escorted through the main streets by the Metropolitan Police on motorcycles, sometimes at forty-five miles an hour. In just an hour and a half, the whole Regiment is passing out into the northern outskirts. The whole business is brought off with incredible smoothness, causing no sensation among the blasé Londoners, who seemingly see nothing odd in a stream of trucks and quads roaring around Hyde Park Corner past the artillery monument and across Piccadilly with 25-pounders bouncing behind them.

Three overnight stops are needed on the trip north: first, a bivouac area near Stevenage, then in tents pegged down on Doncaster racetrack, and the last night in huts at Catterick camp. The weather is extremely cold, especially in the north, and officers and ORs on motorbikes, or riding in open Jeeps and carriers, are almost frozen by the time the convoy stops each night.

The weather remains bitterly cold throughout, and snow flurries frequently swirl across the barren moor ranges that straddle the border between England and Scotland, where a tall, stark gibbet still stands silhouetted against the sky at a point where the snaking road runs over the crest of a hill – a prominent spot where in times past, the body of a sheep thief, hanged for his crimes, could be left dangling as a warning to others.

You are warned to stick to marked tracks on the ranges, for bogs can swallow a pony, a sheep, or a man on a motorbike. The range map, showing gun areas in England and target areas in Scotland, carries names of landmarks of almost storybook quality: Ogre Hill, Hearts Foe, Witch Hill, Witch Crag, and two brooks named Black Burn. The officers' mess, a gloomy house down a craggy slope where the winds swirl and howl beside the road leading out of camp, begs the label "Withering Heights," but it already carries the unique name Burhopecrag Hall.

. Every night, except the last, all ranks sleep under cover, and while the wooden barracks are spartan, the men are grateful to be warm and dry, though some sleeping huts are crowded due to a fire that occurs the first night – an event that will dominate the consciousness of 4th Field throughout the rest of the time in camp, arousing smiles and guffaws each time someone chooses to recount his personal experience that night. Even the final monster shoot – involving the seventy-two guns of 2nd Division, a regiment of medium guns, and a regiment of 7.2-inch heavies – will not displace it as the outstanding memory gunners will carry away from Redesdale.

In addition to a 2nd Battery sleeping hut, a hut housing regimental quarter-stores is gutted. While this might be viewed as a disaster by the uninformed, Quartermaster Capt. Tommy Richardson and his staff see it as a most fortuitous event, since it allows them to write off a great list of "unaccountable shortages" accumulated over several months and about to be discovered by a quartermaster general's inspection, scheduled the day after the Regiment returns to Monks Common. In fact, Richardson looks upon the fire as "an act of God" and refuses to take seriously a rumour that his quartermaster sergeant, "Doc" Lavigne, conspired to have his pal "Bull" Hunter and friends start the blaze "accidentally on purpose." Though Gunner "Buck" Saunders and others could have told Richardson how astonished they were to find that as fast as they threw equipment to safety out one window, it was thrown back in through another.

While the "Act of God" theory will always be suspect – especially for those who know that the fire started from overproof rum being spilled on and about a red-hot stove – the way things combined to allow it to burn on and on undisturbed by any firefighting efforts could suggest there may have been supernatural interference at that. First, when the camp fire-engine rolled up, attached its hose to a nearby hydrant and pointed its high-pressure nozzle at the fire, nothing came forth but a little burp of air. On investigation it was found the hydrant had fallen over, never having been attached to any water pipe. By then the fire-engine was bogged down and couldn't move to another hydrant. Then the big, heavy LAD recovery vehicle brought on site to pull down the walls of the burning building so as to save the next one to it, settled up to its axles in mud beside the fire-engine. Then a procession of quads, brought on site to winch it out, became equally well stuck.

When Saunders and his fellow drivers were ordered by someone to get the fire extinguishers from their trucks, they had to come up with excuses fast, that it wasn't working or had been lost, for each and every extinguisher was filled with petrol to keep them heavy with something that wouldn't freeze, to prevent discovery that the extinguisher fluid, excellent for dry-cleaning uniforms, had long since been used by said drivers. Where innocents obliged the officer's order, the blaze was greatly enlivened.

By the time the fire was brought under control by water tossed on it by a bucket brigade, everyone was in such hearty spirits that even those who had to sort out wet equipment in the dark and sleep in a windowless shack, in beds made up over the water-covered floor, did so with jokes and laughter. The greatest merriment was reserved for the story that "Bull" Hunter was looking forward to receiving a medal for rescuing one of the cooks who'd been left sleeping in the burning hut.

The good spirits shown at the fire continue during the whole training camp, through intensely cold weather and atrocious mud up on the ranges. Except for one poor show during regimental fire and movement, the Regiment is highly commended by the resident gunnery experts. This is very satisfying to all ranks, who firmly believe this will be the last training camp before going into action.

The trip back to Sussex is uneventful except for one brief moment during a scheduled stop when a passing fighter plane suddenly turns up its nose and climbs almost vertically at incredible speed until it is only a speck overhead, producing a *scrootching* sound as it goes, unlike the industrious hum of a Spit. Later you'll learn that this remarkable plane is a jet-propelled Gloster Meteor, about to be placed in service.*

On March 11, "Bud" Drury returns as Lieutenant-Colonel Drury, replacing Lieutenant-Colonel Fleury, who, shortly after returning from Redesdale, quietly departed for a job at #1 CARU, the holding unit at Bordon.†

---

* The only Allied jet aircraft to fly operationally in World War II, the British Gloster Meteor went into service in the RAF in July 1944. Its main role was to intercept V-1 flying bombs, thirteen of which they destroyed. In 1945 it achieved the record speed of 606 miles an hour.

† Lt.-Col. William Fleury, who could have remained in the safe depot job, voluntarily reverted to a major, and as a battery commander in 12th Field arrived in France in advance of 4th Field.

PART SIX: JANUARY 1944–
JULY 1944

Approaching the Final Showdown on the Continent

59

THE YANKS ARE COMING

---- ✳ ----

BY EARLY 1944, ALL RUMOURS THAT 2ND, 3RD, AND 4TH Divisions might be joining 1st and 5th Divisions in Italy cease, as it becomes steadily clearer, by the nature of the training and the heavy build-up of troops in Britain, that you are being reserved for the invasion of Hitler's "West Wall," which cannot be put off much longer.

The build-up is becoming increasingly evident as more and more Americans appear on trains and on the streets of popular leave centres in all parts of the island. Members of the Regiment coming back from leaves in Scotland, particularly Edinburgh, report an astonishing number of Yanks in the pubs and shops.

And on regimental moves, as on the way to Sennybridge in late September for the culminating shoot of the massed Corps Artillery in Exercise "Victor-Blast" (that began with digging-in and firing first at Alfriston and then at Larkhill), you frequently meet and pass convoys of spanking new American trucks with cigar-chewing GIs behind the steering wheels, managing to maintain universally recognizable blasé expressions, though it is obvious their driving skills are being tested to the limit as they wheel their big vehicles along the narrow, winding roads. Not only are they unaccustomed to driving "on the wrong side of the road," but they are also handicapped by having to drive with steering wheels on the left side of the cab of their American trucks, not on the right as in your trucks designed for driving on the left-hand side of British roads.

On leave in London, you get the distinct impression that the Yanks aren't just coming – they're here. Like everybody else on leave in the great metropolis, they head for the West End, but they are somehow more visible, for they tend to congregate in great numbers on Trafalgar Square, Leicester Square, and Piccadilly – particularly around Piccadilly Circus. There they lounge by the hour, chewing gum and "holding up the buildings," seemingly perfectly happy and content just watching the girls go by as though they are still back home on Main Street U.S.A.

After dark, they practically take over the dance floor in the converted Covent Garden Opera House, not numerically, for they are still outnumbered by British and Commonwealth troops, but because they require lots of space for their fantastic displays of acrobatic "jiving." And while they are worth watching, you can feel the resentment and bile rising among the British servicemen spectators. Already envious of the relatively well-heeled Canucks, they find this totally intolerable.* They brought their girls here to have them snuggle up and dance with them, not to have them watch the Yanks with obvious fascination and growing admiration.

Surely it was in this corner of the West End in answer to the query "What have you got against us Yanks?" the immortal words were first heard: "You're overpaid, you're oversexed, and you're over here."†

---

* British soldiers received one pound and one shilling a week – about $4.70 in Canadian funds (based on a $4.47 pound), compared to $10.50 a week for Canadians (based on the new pay rate of $1.50 a day as of December 15, 1942) and $14.42 a week for the Americans. By then, Canadian allowances for dependants of servicemen were more generous than for any other Allied country: $72.60 a month for wife and one child, compared to the American allowance of $62.00 and the British of $33.22. (Figures from page one, *Ottawa Journal*, December 16, 1942.)

† The Australians claim it was in Australia this was first expressed.

American uniforms and accents add to the hubbub and crush of your overcrowded, favourite watering-holes and restaurants, and their "outrageous tipping" is being blamed for inflating prices of all items not covered by government price controls, including the services of the "Piccadilly Commandos."

Even many Americans, who were here before the big influx of their fellow countrymen, have been heard to complain about the heartless greed of London's ladies of the night. In the bar in the basement of the Park Lane Hotel along Piccadilly, you overhear a couple of soldiers attached to an American transport company stationed near the hotel complaining that the price had more than doubled overnight from two pounds to five.

This, of course, is only of academic interest to Canadian veterans of the English scene, who, having assembled their leave money with the greatest difficulty (more likely than not through many long hours on their knees at back-breaking games of chance), would rather be found dead than part with their hard-earned bob on such adventures. In this, they feel superior to their American cousins, pitying their naivety – that they would think it necessary to pay for it when this blessed isle is swarming with thousands of able-bodied girls, living away from home and the inhibiting eyes of family and neighbours: land army girls, factory girls, members of all three services, many of them as aggressive and determined as any soldier on leave to live it up for a few hours, or a few days, with a jolly, willing companion before returning to their dreary factories, their chilly barracks, or smelly barns.

And like their unmarried sisters, many lonely married women, who for years have not seen husbands on service in the Mediterranean or the Far East, succumb to a yearning for male companionship and invite substitute mates to share their hearths and beds when on leave – mending their socks, bleaching their greying handkerchiefs, and more often than not sending them back to their units with more "brass" in their pockets than when they started their leave.

Mercifully, the number of wayward wives will never be known, but that it could be very high in some localities was illustrated in startling fashion one day last September at Arundel.

On the way back from London on a late afternoon train to the regimental encampment at Arundel Castle, Padre McCleary found himself in a compartment with half a dozen heavily tanned soldiers in tropical shorts and puttees. In answer to his obvious question, they told him they'd just been flown back from the Mediterranean, with so little notice they'd had no chance to warn their families. At least two of them were married. How surprised their wives would be! The Padre told the story at dinner in the officers' mess tent. Immediately, it was carried by the mess stewards to the kitchen, from whence it spread like wildfire. Within half an hour, the whole Regiment knew that two long-absent husbands had returned to two wives in Arundel. But no one could answer the question "Which two?"

And so that evening no one seemed to leave camp. It was as though Arundel had been declared "out of bounds." Tent lines, normally deserted and silent from about 6:00 P.M. until at least 10:00 P.M., that night seethed with life – softball games, horseshoe-pitching, clothes washing, guitar playing, and sing-songs. The whole camp looked for all the world as though the Regiment had been "confined to barracks."

By the next evening, through devious reconnaissance methods and a mysterious, but reliable, communications system (never duplicated in official military intelligence circles), the homes of the returning veterans were pinpointed and the information discreetly distributed, so that after dinner, the 4th Field tent lines took on their normal, abandoned appearance, at least until the pubs closed.

Yes, in this one matter, the Canadians and Brits enjoy feeling superior to the Yanks, to the point of contempt. But deep down, the Canadians and the Brits are most grateful that their American cousins are at last arriving in significant numbers to thicken up the invasion forces, for everyone knows it will be a grim, if not impossible, task to land and sustain a lodgement on the Continent long enough for it to be built into a force strong enough to carry forward the final lethal strike at the heart of Germany. The Dieppe disaster, only a year and a half ago, proved that.

One indication that closer cooperation between the armies may be expected soon is the revision of the phonetic alphabet signallers use in place of regular letters of the alphabet to spell out key words and avoid errors in spelling such things as place-names. Now "Ack," for the letter A, has become "Able," and "Beer," for B, has become "Baker," and so on.

Officially, the new phonetic alphabet has been in use since late in 1942 or early 1943, when they mongrelized the old British – Canadian phonetic alphabet in a union with an American concoction. But while it is generally used in wireless procedure when passing coded messages and spelling out words that might be confusing, it has never been adopted universally in the common labels and expressions in day-to-day conversation among artillery types. And it is most unlikely that it ever will. Who could ever bring himself to use "Dog Roger" in place of "Don R" – so splendidly appropriate for a gallant, intrepid despatch rider.

An observation post remains an "O Pip" or just plain "OP" and seldom, if ever, will it be referred to as an "Oboe Peter." And while a thoroughly capable artillery surveyor, serving as a GPO Ack (gun position officer's assistant), might not object to being called an "Able," he's still called an "Ack."

Radio is still referred to as "R Talk" for RT, meaning radio telephony, a label which, by all common sense, should never have survived with British forces up to this generation of signallers. However, you wouldn't want to bet on its early demise, for it is living proof of the durability of military labels. This one has survived for decades, in spite of the fact the British public has never, since radio came into common use, referred to it as such. Radio is "the wireless."

You must admit, however, some labels are distinct improvements. For instance, "Baker Troop" does suggest a greater dignity of purpose than "Beer Troop," however accurately the latter might on occasion describe B Troop. And certainly "Mike target! Mike target! Mike target!" – the signal calling for concentration of all twenty-four guns of the Regiment on a target under the newly devised gun-control system – has more of a martial ring to it than the phonetic label with which it began life: "Monkey target! Monkey target! Monkey target!"

At any rate, it has been made clear that, from now on, you must at least take the new terms into use in passing radio messages, since codes will be sent in the new alphabet. And the emphasis given to the order would suggest that cooperation with the Yanks in battle conditions is not too far away.

60

A CONTINUOUS DRONE
OVERHEAD

———————————— ✳ ————————————

ALMOST EVERY NIGHT, NOW, IT SEEMS TIDAL WAVES OF RAF Lancasters and Halifax bombers drone overhead in an ominous chorus on their way to raids on Germany, with Hamburg, Bremen, or Berlin frequently the targets mentioned in the morning by the BBC.* And even as you listen to the news being intoned by a blasé announcer – "For the second night in a row our bombers have attacked industrial targets in the Ruhr basin . . ." – high overhead, long white streaks of vapour trails are determinedly forming behind a flock of silvery American Fortresses and Liberators, flying so high they are barely visible in the brilliant blue sky, on their way out towards a variety of targets on the Continent.†

———————

* By 1944 the RAF was an international force. In addition to large numbers from more than a dozen countries serving in anonymity with the RAF (as were hundreds of Canadians), a significant number of squadrons identifiable with the country of origin of those manning their ground and air crews were flying with the RAF, as shown by the following breakdown as of D-Day: British, 330; Canadian, 42; South African, 27; French, 27; Australian, 18; Polish, 13; Indian, 9; New Zealand, 6; Czechoslovakian, 4; Norwegian, 4; Greek, 3; Dutch, 3; Belgian, 2; and Yugoslav, 1. Statistics from Robert Goralski, *World War II Almanac*, 1944–45, London: Hamish Hamilton, 1981, page 322.
† By mid-1943 more than one thousand U.S.A. bombers were flying out of England.

Revisiting Barnham Junction, you are struck by the day-long stream of Bostons, Mitchells, and the new twin-fuselaged Lightnings, flying out to patrol the Channel from Ford airdrome three miles east of Barnham. And from Tangemere, three miles northwest of Barnham, Spits, Typhoons, and Mustangs come and go endlessly, conducting sweeps over northwest France, where they are shooting up trains and railway yards, their choice targets being hard-to-replace locomotive boilers if one can judge by the endless newsreel shots of exploding locomotives.

Now and then you identify a Canadian-made plywood Mosquito flying out of Tangemere, and with pride – for you are told that these sleek, twin-engined, two-man planes have established themselves as the fastest assault planes now in service in the world, capable of outflying all enemy fighters while delivering a thousand-pound bomb-load as far as away as Berlin. And your nationalism is tickled by the report that American Flying Fortresses have had to add so much armament to defend themselves against enemy fighters, which have been knocking them down at an awful rate during their daylight raids, they've had to reduce their bomb-load to less than can be carried by a couple of Mosquitoes capable of outrunning the German fighters.*

By now much of the romance that surrounded the fly-boys during the early years of the war has faded, and their image as dashing heroes in overstuffed jackets, sheepskin-lined boots, and bulbous helmets, has been replaced by an image of Commandos with Balaclava-shrouded heads, blackened faces, and razor-sharp knives, stealthily slitting the throats of unwary guards patrolling cliffside paths along Hitler's West Wall across the Channel.

Until recently, your latent envy of men wearing wings on their breasts could still be aroused by the sight and sound of a low-flying

---

* By 1945 Mosquitoes could carry up to four thousand pounds of bombs. A B-17 Flying Fortress could carry a bomb-load of only 6,000 pounds.

Spit squashing the roadside trees almost flat with its slipstream, as it pretended to "beat up" the regimental convoy on Exercise "Spartan," or by a newsreel shot from the cockpit of a fighter strafing a train, its smoky tracer trails streaking down at a locomotive until its boiler burst. But then two separate and radically different experiences with surviving airmen put an end to all your regrets that your deficient eyesight had prevented you from becoming a pilot.

The first was with a fighter pilot back in the officers' ward of Number 14 General Hospital, just after he awoke from a remarkably dense slumber induced by a whack on the head while "pranging" his ailing fighter on the beach near Beachy Head after having nursed it back from a train-busting sortie in France. For more than five days he had snored peacefully in a bed opposite yours, checked periodically by pulse-taking nurses, but otherwise left to his own devices, unencumbered by intravenous tubes, oxygen tent, or other hospital paraphernalia.

When he awoke, he had no idea where he was. His last memory was the bumping of his Mustang as it skidded on its belly on an open stretch of sand near Beachy Head. He was without bruises or visible scratches, and climbed out of his bed unassisted. Donning an issue dressing-gown hanging beside his bed, he wandered around the ward, orienting himself by way of questions as to the place, the day of the week, the date, and other essentials. In a ward dominated by motorbike casualties and even less remarkable cases of jaundice, pneumonia, sinusitis, and the like, he was a fascinating figure, and you took the first opportunity, while he was having a cup of Bovril after being examined by a doctor, to ask him about his dicey low-level sorties over enemy-occupied territory.

With becoming casualness, he said that until this incident, the worst thing that had ever happened came about when he pulled his fighter out of a steep dive after strafing a locomotive in Normandy, on a morning he'd taken a stiff dose of laxative. Somehow his description (mostly implied) of riding his plane home that memorable morning stripped away much of the glamour which, over the years, you had attributed to the occupation of fighter pilot.

Then, more recently, on leave in London, all your residual regrets at not having been accepted for air crew disappeared forever just off Piccadilly Circus, in a basement bar known as "Crackers" decorated with propellers and other mementoes from the Battle of Britain, a favourite haunt of airforce types, particularly pilots from Biggin Hill airdrome.

You'd dropped in early in the evening on the off-chance you might run into someone you knew, and was surprised to find this very popular watering-hole, normally crowded and noisy with chatter at this time of day, totally deserted except for two in airforce-blue standing at the bar. And just as you received your drink, you heard one of them say, "Cheerio, old man, see you around."

Recognizing there were now just two of you, standing a few feet apart leaning on the bar, and thinking that perhaps he might turn out to be an interesting partner at dinner, you turned to him, intending to stretch out your hand and volunteer your name. Instead, you fell back gasping in shock, for he, who from the back had looked so fit and normal – standing so upright, square-shouldered, and gallant in his well-tailored flying officer's uniform – face-on looked like a monster. Obviously a victim of flame, his face was still being rebuilt by the surgeons. In place of a human nose, a long, looping, tubular affair had been grafted, the free end of which was pasted onto his cheek with adhesive tape. Scar tissue around his mouth distorted his smile into a baring of his teeth in what seemed to be a vicious snarl.

The voice issuing from within was probably normal in every way, but your brain was no longer functioning.

Later, again and again, you would curse your immaturity – your lack of imagination that prevented you from instantly projecting yourself into that poor man's shoes – recognizing that within that horrible visage resided a man like yourself, who had not been changed in any way by the searing flames, who'd retained all his faculties intact, and had all the needs as yourself for companionship. But you were totally unprepared for such an encounter, and you cravenly bolted your drink and excused yourself, just as his previous companion – and God knows how many others before him – had done this evening.*

---

* Only among the people of East Grinstead, Sussex, where burn victims lived, during their long period of skin-grafting and convalescence, at Queen Victoria Hospital, were they met without embarrassment and embraced as much as possible into the life of the town.

61

UNADULTERATED B.S.
BUT MONTY IMPRESSIVE

※

ALL FORMAL INSPECTIONS ARE TEDIOUS, AND THE EARLY months of 1944 are marked by a succession of them, starting with the Colonel and leading on to inspections by the CRA, the Corps Commander, General Montgomery (now the designated commander-in-chief of all Allied ground forces for the invasion of the Continent) and finally a cursory, but significant, one by His Majesty King George VI.

Having been put through the normal stiff-necked, rigid formalities of the first three inspections, and knowing (at least by reputation) Monty's demanding nature, it is taken for granted his inspection will call for the ultimate in drill and discipline. And so it is no surprise when the officers and men of 4th Field, along with the three battalions of 4th Infantry Brigade, are lined up on marks surveyed in artillery directors on the vast grassy sward that constitutes the playing fields of Christ Church School.

You are told you can smoke, but because the great man abhors the smell and the sight of tobacco, all cigarette butts must be placed in your pocket, extinguished as best you can on the backs of cigarette packages held in the hand. You must not, for any reason, shift the position of your feet, which, though not actually individually surveyed in position, have been dressed and re-dressed successively by keen-eyed troop sergeant–majors, battery sergeant–majors, and regimental sergeant–majors, until the lines of each troop, each battery, and each regiment are as straight as the chalk lines that *were* surveyed in with artillery directors.

Suddenly a far-off, high-pitched, dominant voice calls, "Par-a-a-de! Ah-ten-n-n-n . . . shun!"

Some 3,500 left boots thump as one on the thick turf, and for a few seconds there exists that eerie silence you'll always associate with standing rigid, among thousands of other rigid men, awaiting inspection, a vast silence broken only by the mewing of a mourning dove and the faint desultory barking of a distant dog worried by the recent shouted commands.

Then, incredibly: "Par-a-a-de! Stand-at . . . ease! Stand . . . easy."

Mystified, you look across the field, where a small knot of officers – obviously the senior officers of the division – are clustering around and shaking hands with one wearing a black beret and the slightly humpbacked look you have come to associate with Montgomery from his pictures.

How strange to be stood-easy to witness this! It could only have been on Monty's suggestion, his way of letting everyone know he is aware how tedious it is to stand at attention waiting for an inspection to start.

Already he is making an impression.

For some time you watch the élite chatting amiably together. Then one of them, detaching himself and facing into the square, calls, "Par-a-a-de!"

Ah, here we go, back to normal, you think, as you slap your left hand on your right wrist behind your back and wait to spring to attention on the next command. But it does not come. Instead comes a complicated set of instructions unlike anything ever heard on a parade ground before:

"On the order, 'Move now,' the two front ranks will about-turn and close to within five paces of the facing rear ranks, leaving a corridor just wide enough for the Inspecting Officer to pass along. Officers will position themselves in front of their troops within the corridor. All ranks will stand-easy and position themselves so each can see the Inspecting Officer and he can see each of them as he moves down the corridor between the ranks. There will be no saluting. "Par-a-a-de! Move . . . now!"

The about-turn of the front ranks is reasonably normal in its execution, but the move forward towards the facing rear ranks is a kind of shuffling shambles. Still, a narrow corridor is formed, and while all ranks are crowded together shoulder to shoulder – reminiscent of the civilian crowds of 1939 lining the streets to catch a glimpse of King George and Queen Elizabeth during the royal tour – a respectful silence, unusual in its quality and duration, is maintained as you wait.

And in a minute or two you see the famous figure coming from the left, walking very slowly, his hands behind his back, his head swinging first to the right and then to the left, ensuring he looks into the eyes of every man. He passes only two feet from your nose. And, for the split-second his eyes are locked on yours, you find yourself having to fight the urge to come to attention and salute this most famous of all Allied commanders – the hero of El Alamein, the leader of the legendary Desert Rats, the ingenious field commander who defeated Field Marshal Rommel in North Africa and is now welding together another massive American, British, and Canadian force to cross the Channel and lock horns again with his wily old enemy in whom Hitler has entrusted the defence of his "West Wall."

While still marvelling at the man's dramatically informal way of meeting new troops under his command – a style that couldn't be more suitable to the Canadian soldier's way of thinking – you hear off to the right, "Around me, gath-uh!"

Looking that way you see Monty standing up in a stationary Jeep that's been brought there for the purpose, waving his arm around in a circle over his head. Immediately, a stampede starts towards him from all directions. And when a dense crowd has formed around him, and all is quiet, he proceeds (in his clipped, abbreviated manner, speaking in short simple sentences) to assure the multitude – particularly those serving with battalions reconstituted since Dieppe – that this time it will be quite different. Of course he doesn't mention Dieppe, but his meaning is clear as he explains the methods he used so successfully in North Africa: "We simply looked around for a sea against which we could drive them, where they would be forced to surrender or die. Very simple – very easy – nothing to it at all."

He speaks of the superiority of the Allied "air armadas dominating the skies over the Continent, weakening the enemy's capacity to wage war," and extols the "superior equipment and superior training" being given the assault forces. Finally, he emphasizes the importance of "writing off" as many of the enemy as possible at every meeting, not allowing them to escape to fight again at shorter lines of defence:

"Once ashore, we shall look around for a sea or other formidable water barrier against which we can drive him, and there force him to surrender or die. Very simple – very easy – nothing to it at all."

It is unlikely that in this crush of men about his Jeep, hanging on to his every word, alert to every nuance, there is a man who isn't aware he is listening to so much unadulterated B.S., and gunners will later go out of their way to so declare in your presence. But the overall effect is tremendously positive. Everyone cannot help but draw comfort from the cocky confidence of the man who is to lead them in the final, decisive battles across the Channel – especially those wearing the shoulder badges of the infantry battalions wiped out in 1942 in the last attempt to gain a foothold in France.

A few days later, on March 9, you find Monty's sauntering, informal, eyeball-to-eyeball inspection has spoiled you for all normal, formal inspections when King George VI inspects 2nd Division, lined up shoulder to shoulder, three-deep, along both sides of a country road. Your eyes, rigidly fixed at "eyes-front," get only a fleeting glimpse of the royal visage as he strides by, without looking right or left, seemingly carrying out a formality, fulfilling the tradition that all troops going into action be inspected by His Majesty.

Of course Monty is one of a kind – the first Allied commander to achieve heroic stature in this war, who, recognizing the inspirational value of a leader who manages to capture the popular imagination as a field commander who always wins, works hard at nurturing this image.

Would any other general, past or present, about to assume the heavy responsibilities of GOC of vast invasion forces, have taken time to visit war factories to salute the men and women working around the clock in shifts turning out weapons and shells for those forces?*

After the inspections by Montgomery and the King, it was thought that the Regiment was finished with inspections. But no, the Commander of 2nd Division must have a go at it, and for him it is back to the formal parade-ground manner of doing business, best expressed by the old acorn "Hurry up and wait!" invented to cover the army's habit of getting the troops packed up, polished up, lined up, and otherwise ready and waiting for something to happen, long before the event is actually scheduled.

Stemming from an ever-present fear that something awful must happen if an inspecting officer is kept waiting, it means that at each level of command a safe cushion of time is added, advancing the timetable. Since there are a great many levels of seniority on the way up from troop commander to divisional commander, it is only logical there will be a great deal of "hurrying up and waiting" leading up to a divisional inspection. However, the accumulated waiting-period cushions imposed on 4th Field for the inspection by Divisional Commander Major-General Foulkes on May 31, 1944, is so utterly ridiculous as to border on outright cruelty.

The order to be at a "dispersal point," which turns out to be the gate of the parade ground, at 0940 hours, means getting up at dawn

---

* Monty's casual manner of dress (baggy pants, beret with two hat badges, and flight jacket in cold weather) struck the King as being too informal and he instructed Alan Brooke, Chief of the Imperial General Staff, to "draw Monty's attention to dress regulations." At the same time, Churchill, not relishing Monty's high profile getting any higher by his visits to factories and his speeches to factory workers, told Alan Brooke to renew the directive against generals making public addresses.

so as to be blancoed, polished, inspected, and mounted in vehicles at least two hours before. Then, on arrival at the parade ground, the Regiment is formed up on parade to await the arrival of 5th and 6th Field, 3rd Light Ack-Ack, and 2nd Anti-Tank Regiments at 10:25 (a cushion of forty-five minutes) to take part in a rehearsal at 11:00 (a further cushion of thirty-five minutes) in preparation for the actual inspection by the Div Commander at 2:30 – a really good cushion of three and a half hours!

This means the officers and men of 4th Field are left standing in their "dressed" lines on the inspection field from 9:40 A.M. to 2:30 P.M. – just ten minutes short of five hours – waiting for the actual inspection when they are obliged to stand rigidly at attention for another twenty minutes.

This extraordinary example of military megalomania, occurring only a month after you were inspected by the commander-in-chief of all Allied ground forces preparing to invade the Continent, underlines the extraordinary informality of Monty's leisurely stroll among his troops standing easy as spectators, inspecting *him* even more keenly than he inspected them.

In early April, Exercise "Step," a seven-day affair conducted in the Alfriston area, is remarkable only because for the first time ever the code of dress for personnel on gun positions is relaxed to a level of informality considered suitable to gunners in action. (There's a rumour that Monty, the informal dresser, had a hand in this.) Now, all the last-minute details of a unit about to go into action are completed. Parades are held to check each soldier's paybook to see that his medical shots are up to date, and to check his "dog-tags," the two identical reddish fibre identity-discs hanging on a string around his neck, one of which, in case of death, will be left on the body and the other cut off for recording purposes. Kit bags are painted with unit colours, serial number (42), and the owner's rank, name, and number.

Then, on April 16, an advance party leaves camp with only its leader, Major Gordon Savage, knowing where they are going. Not

until well on their way are they told their destination is a concentration area just north of Dover, among hundreds of Canadian,
British, American, Polish, and Free French units awaiting the start
of the cross-Channel invasion.*

---

* During this rather hectic period, Regimental Sgt.-Major A. C. Hanks,
who had been RSM since May 1940, left for a job with the Auxiliary
Services and was replaced by Sgt.-Major A. J. Addie of 14th Battery, who
in turn was replaced as 14th Battery Sgt.-Major by E. H. "Ed" Blodgett.

62

WALDERSHARE PARK

———————————— ✳ ————————————

THE CONCENTRATION AREA FOR THE REGIMENT, AND SEEMINGLY
most of 2nd Division, turns out to be a rolling stretch of Kentish
countryside centred on a beautiful grove of mature deciduous trees
and carrying the name Waldershare Park, some two and a half miles
as the crow flies from Dover and the sea.

Here you will remain until D-Day, whenever that shall be, cut
off for security reasons from the rest of the country by a line drawn
across the counties bordering the Channel. No phone calls are
allowed out of the restricted zone, and no one can cross the line in
either direction without special permission. And now every letter
must be read and censored at the unit level, a tedious daily task for
one subaltern per troop.

All along the road from Dover there are unit signs one after
another, and at crossroads a confusing clutter of regimental signs,
and signs pointing to Division and Corps headquarters. And when
on pass to Dover, Folkestone, Ramsgate, Margate, or Deal – all
within the restricted zone – you see shoulder flashes of endless
variety. Everything you observe suggests you are occupying valuable space, that each and every acre in the south of England is
accounted for.

Along tree-lined lanes, mounded under hoods of corrugated iron,
are piles of bombs, cases of ammunition, land mines, coils of barbed
wire, and engineering stores of all kinds. In some places tanks and

vehicles (seemingly for future replacement needs) are parked nose-to-tail, rank upon rank, to the horizon.

Until now a "corps" was just a word, a vague way of speaking of a collection of three or four divisions, but seeing the vast numbers of men and vehicles and guns in a single corps, jammed into a relatively small area, you get some concept of the dimensions of the colossal operation about to be set in motion.*

So vast are the invasion forces, their concentration areas stretch all the way from Weymouth in the west to Margate in the east – some two hundred miles across country, and double that by coastal roads. A single regiment like 4th Field, which until recently loomed large in your world, now seems rather insignificant.

Refresher training in gun drill and troop deployment is attempted, but there is little enthusiasm. The feeling is general among both officers and men that if you don't know your job now, you never will.

Quarter-stores becomes the hub around which all activity revolves. Each day brings new lists of equipment to be turned in, replaced, or issued. Such things as "shell dressings," with their ominous implications, are issued, and anti-gas equipment is checked for deficiencies.

Old vehicles are still being replaced by new ones. Great cans of waterproofing "gunk" (a plasticine-like substance made of grease, lime, and asbestos) pour into quarter-stores, and each day a

---

* While just six divisions (three American, two British, and one Canadian) are earmarked for the initial assault on the Continent, a total of 39 divisions are concentrated along the coastal regions from Cornwall to Kent – 20 American, 14 British, 3 Canadian, one French, and one Polish, plus hundreds of thousands of special forces, corps troops, lines of communication and supply, and headquarters units. Indication of the numbers involved can be gained from the fact that by July 25 more than 1,450,000 will have crossed to the Continent: 812,000 Americans and 640,000 British and Canadians, plus a Polish Division and a French Division.

few gunners and NCOs attend courses on how to waterproof vehicles to allow them to be driven ashore through water flowing over their engines.

The "paper war" in the orderly-room tent increases.

All ranks live in tents – the officers in crowded marquees and Other Ranks in too few bell tents. Some of the tents are old and leak when it rains, but there is little beefing, for all know that soon living conditions are bound to be a lot worse. And there are a goodly number of beautiful sunny days.

The Regiment shares its grove with 5th and 6th Field Regiments, and recreational facilities are pooled. Each night there is a movie shown by Curt Embleton of the YMCA Auxiliary Service in the marquee tent, which also houses the wet canteen run by friendly NAAFI girls well able to hold their own with the fastest-talking gunners.

Every evening, until it grows dark and Embleton can get the movie underway, cries of "Baby wants new shoes . . . ten bob says he won't make his point . . . Two quid says he will . . . Blow on 'em buddy . . . Comin' out with a natch . . ." and many other less-intelligible incantations, leading up to roars of delight intermingled with moans of despair, emanate from the canteen tent, where, allegedly, quite scandalous sums are being won and lost in games of chance.

Officially frowned on by the powers that be, crap games are tolerated whenever extended periods of boredom could generate more serious problems than those associated with men having "nuppence to spend, and nuppence to lend." And in the Victory Loan Campaign, 4th Field subscriptions are the highest in the Division, forty-five thousand dollars, an astounding total in view of the fact a gunner is paid only $1.50 a day. Clearly, some of the boys have been winning a good share of those monster pots built up by the high-rollers from at least two regiments.

Battery commanders and their signallers go off on a hush-hush scheme, and a few days later troop commanders and their crews do the same. On their return they'll say only that they were "practising crossing a tidal estuary." This, of course, arouses speculation as to where such training might be useful – from Holland to the Riviera.

A corporal of the 19th Light Aid Detachment of REME (Royal Electrical and Mechanical Engineers), attached to the 4th Field to look after vehicle repairs beyond the resources of the regimental motor mechanics, is brought in under Military Police escort charged with "assaulting and offering violence to a superior officer." It is a most unusual case, made all the more unusual by the fact the "superior officer" is reported to have been a WAAF (Women's Auxiliary Airforce) warrant officer.

The Regiment draws its first White* Armoured Scout Car, resembling a 1920s touring car with a canvas roof, but with a hardened steel body varying in thickness from 6-mm to 12-mm. Steel shutters fold up in place of windows, and another shutter folds down over the windshield, leaving only narrow slits for the driver and officer in the forward bucket seats. Intended for use as a troop or battery command post vehicle, the eighteen-foot, five-ton car, powered by a 110 HP Hercules engine, is capable of fifty-five miles an hour, and will accommodate five men and their equipment. Originally designed as an American cavalry scout car, it is equipped with four-wheel drive.

Subalterns Gordon Lennox and Bill Murdoch, along with three ORs, leave for a parachutist-jumping course, and this arouses all sorts of speculation as to the possible role 4th Field may be expected to play in support of a big parachute drop that will surely take place on D-Day or shortly after.

Afternoons are given over to sports, and now and then the calm air of Waldershare Park is shattered by the bullhorn voice of one Lieut. Kenneth Hatheway Turnbull (ex-police chief of a Northern Ontario town) roaring "Heave!" as he exhorts to greater effort the

----

* The name of its manufacturer, not its colour.

regimental tug-of-war team that won the divisional track meet and is now in training for a corps meet.

For the officers the most entertaining daily event is the volleyball game organized after supper each evening by Colonel Drury and brought to an all-time height of intensity by Major Gordon Wren. No one who has ever played a game with or against Wren could ever again look upon volleyball as anything but the most competitive of sports. Babe Ruth at the height of his glory never played with more flamboyant verve than the ruddy-faced, chubby Commander of 2nd Field Battery.

For a while the days pass pleasantly, with no one working very hard, until waterproofing of vehicles becomes a priority. Groups of vehicles are taken to a central place where, under supervision of Ordnance, the first stage is carried out. This mainly involves the welding onto the engine of each vehicle a vertical intake manifold, reaching up as high as the roof of the cab, so that when the vehicle is being driven off a beached landing-craft into three or four feet of water, a sudden swelling surge of surf will not be sucked into the engine causing it to conk out.

Back in the regimental vehicle park, all but the few vehicles required for moving rations and recreational personnel are placed under strict orders to not be moved for any reason, and are cleaned as they have never been cleaned before. Every inch of every engine, down to the smallest detail, is scrubbed to its original factory lustre, for waterproofing "gunk" will not stay affixed to anything soiled by oil or dust.

At the corps sports meet, staged at Maidstone, Lieut. Bill Knapp, recently attached to 4th Field, wins the half-mile race and the profound gratitude of all of the 4th Field officers who had backed him with heavy bets. Remarkably, the slight, pink-cheeked lad is in such good shape he hardly worked up a sweat in pulling off his triumph. However, members of the regimental tug-of-war team are drenched in perspiration after losing out on the final pull of the day.

Lieut. Jack Owen and Capt. George Nixon leave for a course that will qualify them as "Flying OP" officers, the envy of at least half the subalterns in the Regiment who had applied to take the course.

63

THIS BLESSED PLOT

ON MAY 24, THERE IS A COMMEMORATIVE SERVICE FOR 2ND
Division in Canterbury Cathedral, and you are among the eighty-
five members of the Regiment privileged to attend. The realization
that D-Day is now imminent imparts special meaning to the occasion, and some memories will surely remain indelible, beginning
with the opening surge of "*O Canada! Our home and native land*"
reverberating among the soaring beams and roof trusses of this
ancient cathedral from two thousand Canadian throats, so filled
with pride of home they drown out all but the most piercing descant
of the choir's boy tenors and the deepest thunder of the great organ.
In the subdued, echoing quiet afterwards, you listen to the measured
voice of the "Red" Dean* and stare at the stained-glass windows of
the chancel, new when the Magna Carta was signed at Runneymeade – "The Lord shall preserve your going out and your coming
in . . . nor shall we forget that it was you Canadians who led the
attack on Dieppe and struck the prelude note of the now imminent
Second Front . . . and I would dare add, when Nazi-fascism is torn
out of their hearts, as torn out it must be in the end, then with the
great German people we may together build a world more akin to

---

* So labelled by the British press because of his socialist views, and the
warmth of his enthusiasm for the perceived accomplishments of the Soviet
Union.

that for which we pray when we say, 'Thy Kingdom come, Thy will be done on earth as it is in heaven.'"

When the service is over, and you are filing out into the sunlit grounds, it suddenly occurs to you that you have fallen in love with this island, that it has become "your Britain," and that you will feel bereft when the day arrives for you to leave it.

Your friend Lieut. Al Fair, a natural-born Anglophile with whom you'd shared training, had predicted on the way over to England on the *Empress of Japan* that it would happen, claiming everyone sooner or later fell in love with Britain if they stayed long enough. But being a sixth-generation Canadian on your Scottish side and ninth-generation Canadian on your Norman side, and, like most Canadians unable to maintain a neutral position, let alone have warm feelings towards a society perceived to be structured on classes, you'd thought this most unlikely.

Though raised pro-British and honouring the Crown, you had not been impressed by many of the Englishmen you'd met in Canada, who, though they'd emigrated to gain a better life, never tired of telling all and sundry how much better things were in the "old country."

Still, you took pride in your British origins as you relished the superior quality of things *Made in Britain* – starting with the world's fastest automobile (Sir Malcolm Campbell's), the fastest motor boat (John Cobb's), the fastest plane (the forerunner of the Spitfire, known as the Supermarine, which won the Ryder Cup race for that title in 1931, giving the RAF its third win and the cup in perpetuity), the fastest train (the *Flying Scotsman*), the largest ocean liners (*Queen Mary* and *Queen Elizabeth*), the peerless Rolls-Royce engines and hand-crafted cars, and an endless list of consumer goods, from Scotch whisky to tartans, from fine bone-china to Sheffield steel knives, from lavender soap to style-setting suits from London's Savile Row – not to mention hats and shoes and shirts and "plus-fours," the pants worn throughout the world after being seen in pictures on the person of the Prince of Wales, *the* style-setter of style-setters throughout the 1920s and 1930s.

Fair claimed you could always tell how long a guy had been over here by the way he talked about the Brits. The newcomers inevitably sneered at such things as the railway locomotives – so unimpressive in their subdued puffing and their shrill, effeminate whistles – ignoring their incredibly smooth and rapid acceleration from stations provided by superb multi-expansion engines, with no banging and clanking between the cars held apart by spring-loaded bumpers.

You, of course, had been guilty of dozens of misconceptions shared by North Americans about English life. Their customs and ways of doing things had seemed so strange, and on first encountering them even startling, such as the night you slid your bare feet down under the bedclothes in the Park Lane Hotel Annex in London and encountered with horror what you thought was some kind of animal, in fact a warm "pig" (a crockery affair full of hot water) inserted in the bed an hour or two before to reduce the clamminess of the moisture-laden sheets and comforter, the inevitable product of unheated bedrooms in winter in wartime Britain.

Your love affair with "this blessed plot" probably began with your earliest exploration by bicycle of the beautiful countryside around Bordon Camp in Hampshire, when you were astonished to find that those thatched cottages and low-beamed coaching inns in the films weren't just cooked up for the movies; there actually *were* thatched-roof cottages with families living in them, and ancient timbered coaching-inns, right out of a Charles Dickens story, still renting rooms and serving steak-and-kidney pie with beakers of ale for lunch. And while few Brits have ever reminded you of Ronald Coleman, David Niven, Leslie Howard, Robert Donat, or Laurence Olivier, few would fit the image of that other Hollywood creation – the bumbling, befuddled blimpish stereotype intended as comic relief.

Still, you'd gone on thinking you would never get beyond being vastly impressed by the "old country's" cathedrals, her cultivated, gardenlike landscape of hedged-in fields, and her legendary institutions of learning, governing, and preserving her wondrous heritage. But somewhere along the way you began to think of this country as *your* country – your Britain.

Your Britain is the Britain of damp nights when the air smells sourly of coal gas from thousands of chimney pots, especially during a pea-souper fog in the blackout, occasionally so dense you can make your way along the echoing canyons of deserted downtown city streets only by feeling your way with an outstretched hand, wiping the smooth plate-glass of store windows and along the rough brick or stone façades of banks and other noble establishments, as you did one night recently in Birmingham on your way to New-street station. On that occasion, led on by the sound of hissing steam of a resting locomotive, after the buses had ceased running and no other living soul but you shuffled along the pavements, at each intersection you stumbled over the big water-main left above ground next the curb, where it would be easier to repair after a bombing.

Your Britain is the Britain of endless queues of disciplined, patient, orderly, uncomplaining people – queues for everything, from getting on a bus to buying sweets or cigarettes or newspapers, not to mention block-long queues for desirable things in short supply, which often attract shoppers who haven't a clue what the queues are for but, knowing there must be something worth waiting for to attract such a lineup, feel compelled to join them.

It is the Britain of ration coupons for nearly everything, where whole families have to pool their accumulated clothing coupons to outfit a girl member who is getting married on short notice.*

It is the Britain of incredibly clean streets, where every gum-wrapper and empty cigarette package is placed in a paper-recovery

---

* This was required when the author's wife's cousin, Beryl Marsh, of Birmingham, decided (shortly after her father's death on duty as an air-raid warden) to marry her fiancé, airman Gordon Hipkiss, the weekend he was posted to the RAF in Burma – a not untypical spur-of-the-moment decision by couples facing separation "for the duration" and perhaps forever.

bin, and every piece of aluminum foil is added to someone's growing ball that will one day become part of the skin of a Spitfire or a
Lancaster bomber "to give them back some of their own."

It is the Britain of a people with universal respect for laws they
consider sensible (even jailing for a month the great Ivor Novello,
composer and star of the musical *The Dancing Years*, which has been
running since 1938, when he is found guilty of using illicit gasoline*)
but who will laugh their heads off when the government one day
says they can stop carrying their anti-gas respirators everywhere
they go, having long since removed it from its little khaki carrying-
case and replaced it with their lunch or whatever else they want to
carry.

It is the Britain of glowing coal fires in friendly corner pubs
smelling of whisky, gin, bitter lemon, and endless foaming pints of
mild and bitter drawn up from barrels in the cool cellar by publicans
pulling on tall, colourfully painted, clublike levers with the odd
name "beer engines" – pubs of history and of legend, pubs with
character, and pubs with no character whatsoever, but all of them
exuding warmth and hospitality wherever you choose to push
through their blackout curtains into the bright light and hubbub of
laughter and overlapping conversations, frequently made impossible
by a clanking piano, never quite in tune, but pounded with vigour
by a volunteer trying, and sometimes succeeding, to get people
singing *"I've got sixpence, jolly-jolly sixpence . . ."* or *"Lilly of
Laguna . . ."* or *"You can't trust the specials like the old time coppers,
when you can't find your way home."*

It is the Britain of unheated, dark interiors of blacked-out night
trains, eternally jammed with service men and women – every
inch of their compartments and corridors packed with humanity,

---

* Novello first gained fame for his World War I song "Keep the Home
Fires Burning," which was still being sung in the pubs in the 1940s as his
"Waltz of My Heart" from *The Dancing Years* was being played over and
over on the BBC and at dances.

but always the thoughtful voice calling, "Room for one in here," when an outside compartment door opens and clunks shut with that distinctive heavy latching sound of a British passenger train.

It is the Britain of abiding respect for privacy in every situation where people must crowd together, most evident in train compartments, where people will travel with elbows touching for two hundred miles or more and never exchange one word, but also jealously guarded as a precious commodity at home in areas of densest population. Here, people who have lived side by side for up to fifty years still keep in the best repair the solid board fences separating their narrow backyards and the brick-and-stone walls (combined with stubby wrought-iron railings and gates) enclosing postage-stamp front yards of blocks and blocks of row-houses distinguished one from another only by the colour of the front door and the painted wooden frames enclosing identical front windows, each pane criss-crossed with masking tape to inhibit flying shards of glass in case of a bomb landing nearby. And though the lady of the house may stand and talk for half an hour with a highly treasured neighbour on a morning when there is a legitimate reason for communicating, most mornings they respect the fence and the other's privacy as they putter in their gardens or sit in the sun to write letters or read with no fear of interruption over that sacred line of wood.

It is the Britain of the middle class – a class so wide-ranging and all-encompassing as to seem not to be a class at all but to embrace all Britons but those occupying the great country mansions, dotted here and there about rural England – God-fearing, respectable, stable, loyal, dependable, hard-working, courageous people, many of them filling demanding jobs by day and then firewatching on rooftops when the air-raid siren sounds the alert at night.

It is the Britain of total commitment to the prosecution of the war, even to the extent of conscripting all single able-bodied females for the factory, the farm, or one of the three services – something no other Western nation (Allied or enemy) has done.* This level of commitment is illustrated over and over by chance meetings with people from all walks of life who are contributing significantly to essential production.

On many occasions recently in the presence of older men like friend Bob Cotton (machinist by day and air-raid warden by night), and young women like Joy Marsh (the head nurse of the emergency ward of the main Birmingham hospital during the worst of the Blitz), you have begun to feel like a phoney, having done nothing but carry out guard duty on the south coast when not on training schemes.

Soon, you hope, that will be rectified.

From May 28 to June 6, the command post staffs of all three batteries are away on a secret operation, "Fortitude South," involving round-the-clock wireless transmissions between each other and with division and corps headquarters, using unfamiliar call letters and spouting (what seems to them) nonsensical garbage totally unrelated to reality.

All who take part in the scheme are reluctant to discuss it. They say it is a scheme to test communications up and beyond the corps level, but clearly it is some sort of feint to confuse the Germans as to the intentions of the Allies. There is no end to the number of transmitters involved, and the airwaves are simply jammed with messages as 4th Field command post officers and signallers follow word-for-word the prescribed script of timed messages – initiating some messages and responding on cue to others – hour after hour, around the clock, for ten days.

Months after the fact, you will learn that this scheme was part of a huge pattern of deceptions called Bodyguard – six major ones and thirty-six subordinate ones. "Fortitude South" was meant to

---

* Of sixteen million British women aged fourteen to fifty-nine, seven million were in the Services or working in industry by mid-1944.

convince Hitler that he should leave his Fifteenth Army intact at Calais, that American General George Patton was in command of not just one army but a group of armies called First U.S. Army Group in the southeast of England, readying to spring across the Channel to gain the principal invasion bridgehead in the Pas-de-Calais, an area of broad beaches suitable for landings and much closer to England than Normandy. Operation "Fortitude North" was to convince him to leave his twenty-seven divisions in Scandinavia to fend off an Allied invasion over there by a fictitious British Fourth Army, created in the mists of Scotland by twenty-four officers and two hundred and thirty-four Other Ranks, most of them radio operators exchanging on-air messages from rooms under Edinburgh Castle – messages appropriate for the maintenance and movement of vast numbers of men and materials, carefully crafted for the ears of enemy monitors and agents in Britain.*

---

* In addition to these radio exchanges, large numbers of inflated rubber tanks appeared overnight in the open fields of Kent. Six divisions only are to carry out the initial assault to gain a firm foothold in Normandy. These divisions will be: 29th U.S. Division of 5th Corps; 4th U.S. Division of 7th Corps; 1st U.S. Division of 1st Corps; 3rd British Division of British 1st Corps; 50th British Division of 30th Corps; and 3rd Canadian Division of 2nd Canadian Corps. The Canadian 3rd Division is composed of the following: 7th Brigade, with the Royal Winnipeg Rifles, Regina Rifles, and Canadian Scottish Regiment; 8th Brigade, with the Queen's Own Rifles of Canada, le Régiment de la Chaudière, and the North Shore Regiment; and 9th Brigade, with the Highland Light Infantry of Canada, the Stormont, Dundas and Glengarry Highlanders, and the Nova Scotia Highlanders. The division will be supported by the 2nd Canadian Armoured Brigade made up of: 6th Armoured Regiment (1st Hussars); 10th Armoured Regiment (Fort Garry Horse); and the 27th Armoured Regiment (Sherbrooke Fusiliers). Battalions in the first wave ashore will be the Royal Winnipeg Rifles – with C Company of the Canadian Scottish Regiment attached – the Regina Rifles, and the North Shore Regiment. The Canadian 2nd Corps consists of the following divisions: 2nd Infantry Division; 3rd Infantry Division; 4th Armoured Division; and Polish Armoured Division.

64

D-DAY

---　✳　---

ON JUNE 6 — A BRIGHT, SUNNY, UNFORGETTABLE MORNING —
the eight o'clock BBC news quotes a German report that Allied
parachutists landed in Normandy during the night and that seaborne
landings have begun at several points along the coast of France.

As the news spreads throughout the camp, all ranks seek out
vehicles carrying 38-sets (walkie-talkies) that can be tuned to the
broadcast band of the BBC, which this morning is almost entirely
given over to bulletins and commentaries related to this great event.

Speaking to the people of Western Europe, General Dwight
Eisenhower, Commander-in-Chief of the Allied Invasion Forces,
in his terse distinctive style – burping his words as though they've
been bottled up for a long time – addressing "the people of France,
Belgium, and Holland" tells them, "In the early hours this morning
British, American, and Canadian troops began landing on the north-
west coast of France," and warns them to evacuate the coastal areas.
Immediately afterwards, General de Gaulle of the Free French
Forces in Britain repeats the warning in French.

Subsequent BBC broadcasts tell of the great cathedrals and the
little country churches of Britain filling with people to pray for the
success of the invasion, and when "God Save the King" is played,
it stirs you as it has not done since that awful hour almost five years
ago, when it became clear that war had finally come, and you –
clutching your beloved's hand – stared at your little Viking radio

and listened to this same recording by the Grenadier Guards Band wavering across the Atlantic that sunny September Sunday.

Throughout the morning, bulletins, derived from BBC broadcasts, are posted in battery areas. And a map of France is pinned up on the bulletin board outside the regimental headquarters tent and marked with little red circles on the coast of Normandy, representing bridgeheads secured by each of the British, Canadian, and American assaulting divisions.

As you examine the map, you find yourself thinking of Lieutenants Jack Mitchell, Cliff Chadderton, and Bill "Cozy" Aiken of the Royal Winnipeg Rifles, who, if things went according to plan, were in the first wave to hit the Norman shore this morning. You wonder if they made it safely.

You wonder especially what happened to Cozy Aiken, a tall, good-looking, personable guy who, a few weeks ago, shared with you and his old Winnipeg buddy, Gordon Lennox, his concern about the role his platoon was to play on D-Day in taking a "great god-damned pillbox."

Over a lunch of steak-and-kidney pie, and an afternoon of endless gin-and-lemons in a little upstairs bottle-club tucked away in a narrow back alley off Piccadilly in London, he talked of little else. Again and again – with increasing frequency as the afternoon wore on and an alcoholic haze set in – he'd asked you, "My friend, give me your honest opinion. I am to lead the first platoon of the first company of the first battalion ashore – now, what do you think my chances are of making it to that god-damned pillbox?"*

---

* Years after, you would learn from Chadderton that that huge pillbox or casemate was located at the west side of the mouth of the Seulles river at Courseulles. Aiken's corporal, Bull Klos, who had his Sten gun blown from his hands by a mortar bomb, strangled the first German to confront him, but was himself killed a few minutes later by a mortar bomb. Aiken, leading his 3rd Section, then climbed a ladder and got into the pillbox and silenced it. In the process he was shot through the chest and was evacuated to England. The wound, fortunately, was not too serious, and

Intrigued by reports from drivers returning from Dover of civilians lining the cliffs to watch convoys of freighters – their decks black with troops – steaming west through the strait, hugging the English coast as shells from the German guns near Calais burst in the sea around them, you and fellow subaltern Doug MacFarlane concoct an excuse for a quick visit to the coast to see for yourself.

When you get to Dover, there is a "shell-warning" in effect, and it is with some difficulty you escape the solicitous attention of an ARP warden who wants only to guide you to an underground shelter. When finally you and MacFarlane find a position along the steeply sloping face of the cliff west of the town, secure in the belief that the Germans are after the ships today and will leave Dover alone, you discover a freighter has been hit and is lying motionless just offshore, streaming black smoke low across the sea, partially obscuring other freighters sailing by with agonizing slowness.

Suddenly you hear a fearful wail that quickly grows into an ugly, intimidating howl just before a great black waterspout leaps towering from the sea between the burning ship and the shore, and a monstrous roar rolls up the valley and reverberates over the land, echoing and re-echoing down the coast.

Training your field-glasses on the misty thin line on the horizon that is the French shore, said to be twenty-one miles distant, you try to catch the muzzle-flash of the German gun. After a long wait, you are rewarded: a bright pin-prick of light. Counting "hippopotamus one, hippopotamus two, hippopotamus three . . ." you

---

he recovered to return to the regiment as adjutant. A second great casemate on the east side of the river mouth was taken that morning by the Regina Rifles with the help of tanks of the 1st Hussars firing point blank at close range.

make it to about hippo forty-five when you hear the ominous wail of the incoming giant shell.*

Immediately there is another great black waterspout (this time beyond the burning ship), and again the horrendous reverberating roar.

You could stay watching there for the day, but you and Doug have regimental responsibilities back at Waldershare Park, and you leave without knowing if that disabled freighter survives, and if any other ship in the convoy is hit.

As the days go by, and the thrill of D-Day passes, the sense of being left out of it begins to take hold as no word comes for 2nd Division to proceed to ships for France – something expected from June 12th onwards, because of a rumour that has persisted all spring that 2nd Division would be sent in on D-plus-seven (seven days after D-Day) to lead a "break-out from the bridgehead."

Officers and men settle down to an uninspiring routine: checking the waterproofing, checking tire pressures, touching up the paint here, covering with grease there, reading about France, talking of France, practising French words and phrases provided by a little booklet issued to each man for that purpose, studying the London dailies and the intelligence map on the easel outside RHQ, playing cards, playing volleyball, writing letters, and forever theorizing and speculating as to when you'll be "going over there."

---

* 1,323 pounds if it is from one of the 40-cm (15.75-inch) Adolf guns at Blanc Nez, and slightly less if from one of 38-cm (15-inch) guns positioned at Cap Gris Nez.

65

ARE YOU REALLY THERE?

———————————————— ✳ ————————————————

ONE MORNING, WHEN YOU GO DOWN TO THE WAGON LINES to supervise the removal of the waterproofing gunk from some parts of the engines long enough for the sweating to dry out, you are accosted by a very excited Wally Driemel, a Baker Troop signaller, inquiring if you heard your song "Are You Really There?" on the BBC last night. Driemel is vastly disappointed when you tell him you gave up listening for it a long time ago.

Driemel developed a fondness for the melody from hearing it played at Saturday-night dances by the regimental orchestra,* and by its swinging piano player, Signaller Ralph "Coop" Cooper, doing impromptu solo performances on pub pianos.

———————

* The 4th Field Orchestra, in demand for many dances by other units in 2nd Divison, was small but loaded with talent. When the principal violinist somehow managed to wangle a medical discharge in early 1944, he immediately joined Geraldo's famous orchestra at the Savoy. And "Coop" Cooper, who collected a crowd wherever he sat down to play, ended up doing precisely that nightly for years after the war, at the Hotel Metropole in Toronto. And whenever the composer of "Are You Really There?" was in Toronto and felt the need to have his ego restored, he'd visit Coop's bar. Spotting him coming through the door, Coop never failed to pull his mike boom over and say, as he began to play it, "Here comes the composer of this great war song." And they loved Coop so much they never failed to give it a big hand.

The song had come to you one night in a hotel room in London
– words and music fully developed – from some strange well of
homesickness, nostalgia, and longing. None of the books you'd
read about the miseries endured by soldiers in the last Great War
prepared you for the cruel torture a soldier endures from too vivid
a recall of memories of his beautiful young wife. In your earliest
days over here at the reinforcement depot at Bordon, in the middle
of a sleepless night on duty as orderly officer, you decided you must
consciously and systematically go about the business of forgetting
her, at least to the extent of suppressing all thoughts of her except
when reading her letters and writing to her. This was during that
dispiriting time immediately following the Dieppe Raid, when the
dismal conclusion became inescapable, as the full extent of the
disaster began to seep into everyone's consciousness, that if we
didn't have the strength to pull off a sneak raid, a full-scale invasion
could not even be contemplated in the foreseeable future.

Sitting on the side of your camp cot in the orderly room, smoking
one cigarette after another, waiting for the dawn, you'd finally faced
the obvious fact that your separation was bound to stretch into
years, and might well be permanent. And that if you ever were to
sleep again, all your most precious, tender memories of her as a
living, breathing person must be made to fade away to manageable
dimness: the sound of her voice, her laugh, the way she walked,
the softness of her skin, the fullness of her lips – all you shared with
her in joy and passion, and which in your loneliness you most
desperately want to relive – had to be banished from your mind.

Since that night you have acted as though your relationship has
always been on paper only: photographs, envelopes smelling of
perfume, letters with lipstick-imprints of her lips beside words like
"yours forever," reducing her to the status of a fantasy, vague and
wonderful, and, in the manner of all authentic fantasies, impossible
to attain. And though you regularly receive parcels and letters –
little blue airmail letters, always smelling of her perfume with every
corner exquisitely filled in with loving thoughts in the most micro-
scopic handwriting imaginable – your memories of life with her

(once so vivid they caused physical longing bordering on pain) have, through long suppression, faded to the point where they resemble dreams more than reality.

In the daily routine with the Regiment, preoccupied with duties and problems, and never entirely alone day or night, you are now able to keep thoughts of home easily at bay. However, homesickness can strike with full force when you are on leave, particularly the first day, when it seems you should be heading home or for a haven somewhere. Though clean hotel rooms and restaurant meals are in themselves tremendously desirable luxuries, there is the longing to share them with her, which inevitably arouses old memories, some too good to be true, as though concocted in a dream. And it was during the first night of a nine-day leave, while in an alcoholic haze, that you wrote the song the BBC played last night.

Passing through London on your way to her relatives in Birmingham, you fell among friends at least as thirsty as you. And after visiting many too many pubs and "bottle clubs" (licensed to remain open when pubs close for their mid-afternoon hiatus), you'd decided it would be entirely unwise to take a train anywhere. In fact, in your overloaded state, if you didn't get a hotel room right away, you could fall asleep in an odd position anywhere. Being Saturday evening, however, a hotel room would be hard to come by. In desperation you took a taxi to the Park Lane, where at least you were known.

Waiting, clutching the end of the registration counter for support, you despaired as you listened to the polite but weary lady behind the desk repeating the litany:

"No reservation? Oh, I'm sorry – we've no rooms left."

When it was your turn, you could only say, "I need a room badly."

And she, bless her dear heart, replied, "You most certainly do." And filling in your registration card for you, she slid a key under one of your hands clutching the desk.

Going up in the elevator, you seemed to be an object of interest to the couple who got on with you – an airforce officer and a lady you took to be his wife – the kind of beautifully matched pair that always arouses in you a mixture of envy, jealousy, nostalgia, and longing homesickness. And whenever you spot such a pair on their way up to their bedroom in a hotel, you are sent into deep melancholia or back down to the bar to blot out all conscious thought.

As you prepared, with some care, to step out of the elevator at your floor, they proceeded to discuss you as though you weren't there.

She: "Don't you think you should help him?"

He: "No, he's all right."

She: "How do you know?"

He: "I can tell by the way he holds his head."

While disconcerting, you found his vote of confidence – heard just as the elevator doors closed behind you – encouraging. And you proved him correct. But barely, for the only thing you remember from that point on was awaking to the sound of rapping on your door by the waiter with your breakfast tray. How you made it to your room, undressed, and got into bed, you will never know.

So in the morning when you let in the waiter with your breakfast tray and were clearing off the desk so that he could put it down, and found you were removing a sheaf of used, hotel note-paper on which someone had crudely drawn the staff lines of a musical composition and scribbled in notes and words, you were more than a little curious. But then, to your astonishment, you discovered the handwriting was yours, unmistakably yours, and the lyric revealed sentiments that had been haunting you constantly for days on end, but which, until now, you'd never expressed in words.

> There's no such thing as the present:
> We live by the past in the future
> Memories arranged by our hearts,
> Bring dreams without effort or tutor.
> I have my memories too, but they are too good to be true:
>
> (Refrain:)

Are you really there? Or are you just illusion?
Do you breathe and smile – do you feel warm emotion?
Was there really music in the air? .
Did that bellhop really see confetti in our hair?
Were there drives by moonlight – did you wear blue chiffon?
Do you go for autumn? And did we dance till dawn?
There are many things to prove to me you care,
But, darling, I can't help repeating: Are You Really There?

The music had remained a mystery until you could get to a piano, for while you can compose and arrange by ear, without a piano, you have never mastered the art of sight-reading a voice line and translating it into sound. After eating, you had gone next door to the King George Officers' Club, where they had a big grand piano. There you'd had to wait for a Canadian airforce officer, newly arrived in England, to finish amusing himself playing current North American hits, including "A Paper Dolly," which he said was "very big at the moment back there."

While waiting, you had pondered the mystery of where those words, scrawled by your hand in an alcoholic stupor, had come from, speculating that possibly the idea expressed in the verse may have been inspired by something you'd found profoundly moving in James Hilton's *Good-bye, Mr. Chips* which you'd read not long before while up at Garnons convalescent home in Hereford. The aging Chips, alone beside the fire, is recalling far-off days when his beloved young wife was at his side.

What a host of little incidents, all deep-buried in the past – problems that had once been urgent, arguments that had once been keen, anecdotes that were funny only because one remembered the fun. Did any emotion really matter when the last trace of it vanished from human memory; and if that were so, what a crowd of emotions clung to him as their last home before annihilation! He must be kind to them, must treasure them in his mind before their long sleep.[*]

When at last you got to the piano and picked out the tune, you were impressed, so impressed you decided to offer it to the BBC Armed Forces Network musical show hosted weekly by a Canuck named Jerry Wilmot. Acquiring some proper music paper, you'd made a clean copy with simple piano arrangement, and took it out to the BBC tower, where you played it for Wilmot. He, too, was impressed, at least enough to accept it and promise to have it orchestrated and played by Robert Farnon's orchestra on his show – though just when, he couldn't say.

His advice had been to listen in each week. But after tuning in religiously for several weeks and being disappointed each time, you'd finally given up the vigil.

Driemel had not. And he is very sad you missed hearing "a great presentation of your song."[†]

So are you!

---

* From James Hilton's *Good-bye, Mr. Chips*, Toronto: McClelland & Stewart, 1934, p. 46.

[†] The presentation could well have been "great," for arranger and orchestrator Robert Farnon stayed on in London after the war and became world famous for his arrangements and orchestrations of popular music.

66

VERGELTUNGSWAFFE — I

--- ✳ ---

NOW EVERYTHING IS DEFINITE, YET NOTHING IS DEFINITE. YOU are going to France, but you don't know when. You are water-proofed for a wet landing, but you may make a dry landing. You have five-hour passes to spend money, but officers cannot cash cheques. There is lots to write home about, but security prevents you from writing about anything you see. You are full of expectancy; you are bored stiff. There is little time left to do anything worthwhile, but time hangs heavily on your hands and there doesn't seem to be anything worthwhile to do. You are surrounded on all sides by great masses of men, yet you feel stangely isolated.

Air letters from Canada take only six days, but it takes eight days for a letter to travel only eighty miles here in England, and men with British wives only a short train-ride away are shut off from them within a circle of twenty miles' radius that cannot be breached even by phone.*

On June 12, while standing-by, waiting for the CO to begin an inspection of vehicles and equipment, Lance-Bombardier J. H. Barton, a popular member of 2nd Battery, collapses and is rushed

---

* Lance-Bombardier Ken Munro earned a severe dressing-down by Major Carr and lost his promotion to full bombardier (already on orders) for making a promised call to his fiancée when he should have been on duty with the Major.

to the nearby field hospital, where he dies at 1:45 P.M., the victim (it is later established) of a cerebral haemorrhage.

Because of the stringent rules restricting movement in and out of the security zone, only the Padre, H/Captain L. D. Begg, accompanies the body for burial at Brookwood Military Cemetery, about twenty-five miles southwest of London. On his return, he holds a memorial service. Held outside under the trees, it might have been impressive, but it wasn't. It was merely a mouthing of some of the platitudes of the funeral service, and when the little circle of Barton's friends, hesitatingly, without accompaniment, are asked to sing all four verses of "Unto the hills do I lift up my longing eyes . . ." the result is an uninspiring drone. It all seems so pitifully inadequate as a farewell to a comrade, and after the service, Barton's closest buddies express their regrets that Padre McCleary wasn't still around to give the eulogy.

One man suggests, "Old Friar Tuck would have had everybody laughing and crying at the same time."

"Still," says another in a thoughtful way, "from now on, where we're going, burial services are likely to be even less formal."

This ends the discussion, and all disperse quietly, each man thinking his own thoughts.

On the night of June 13 there is an air raid. You wake to the sound of a stormy barrage. Ack-ack guns are cracking and booming all around – the earth-shaking thumping of the heavies mixed with the rhythmic pounding of the Bofors, like men shingling a roof. Lifting the side of the tent, you see myriads of tracers streaking almost horizontal to the ground, trying to hit a strange plane with a burbling motor scudding overhead at low altitude, caught in the beams of searchlights, its tail seemingly on fire and spouting flames. Though it takes no evasive action, the ack-ack guns fail to hit it, and it continues on a steady course inland until it is lost from view. The firing dies down, but the *blattering* sound of the strange plane can be heard fading in the distance for some time.

Several times throughout the night, the stormy ack-ack barrage is put up, and in the morning on the way to breakfast, pieces of

ack–ack shells are picked up outside the tent. Discussion over breakfast consists mainly of derogatory remarks about the inability of the
ack–ack gunners to knock down an already partially disabled plane
flying in a straight line "with its tail on fire." Only Lieutenant
Turnbull suggests they are "pilotless aircraft," a suggestion that draws
much scornful laughter from his peers, who, in their brief contact
with the voluble Turnbull since he joined the Regiment only a few
weeks ago, have come to take his stories with a grain of salt, such
as the recent golden-plover shoot he claims to have enjoyed with
old friends of his family on some great country estate in Ireland.

But the eight o'clock BBC newscast proves him entirely correct
when it reports the first attack in history by robot jet planes on
London, "flying bombs of tremendous destructive power."

From this day on, at all hours of day and night "buzz bombs," as
they come to be known – because of the distinctive sound of their
"ram–jet" motor – scud in over Kent at low altitude, sometimes
pursued by fighter planes that always seem to be too far behind to
shoot them down.*

And now you learn that weather is playing a role in preventing
the Division from going to France. From June 19 to 23, a Channel
gale rages along the Normandy coast, so strong it wrecks the artificial
harbours (code named Mulberry) and sets back all landing and
shipping schedules.

There is, according to the BBC, vicious fighting in the area north
of Caen. Afraid of rust sweating in the sealed–up gun barrels, the

---

* Until the ack–ack guns were provided with the proximity fuse – an
ingenious device jointly developed by the Americans and Canadians,
based on a British idea that placed a tiny radar transmitter and receiver in
the nose of each ack–ack shell that would automatically explode the shell
when it was passing lethally close to a buzz bomb – Hitler's "revenge
weapons" had a fairly easy time making their way to London. In the first
twenty-four days of this new Blitz, 2,754 flying bombs struck the London
area, killing 2,752 persons and wounding thousands more, according to
Prime Minister Churchill. (See Appendix J.)

gunners have to remove the waterproofing and pull the barrels through with oil.

Cherbourg Peninsula is cut by the Americans. The guns are again waterproofed for passage through saltwater.

Cherbourg is said to be under siege. The one operating headlight on each vehicle (albeit painted over and blacked-out save for a hole the size of a nailhead emitting only a faint beam) is moved over to the right fender, for they drive on the right side of the road in France.

The fall of Cherbourg is imminent. Officers are again allowed to cash cheques, and the number of men allowed out on five-hour passes increases.

Cherbourg falls. It is a very windy day today in camp.

Then one afternoon comes the warning order for the Regiment to move to a "marshalling sub-area" from whence it will move onto boats for France. It is brought back from 2nd Division Headquarters by Capt. Malcolm "Tim" Welch, the adjutant. At 1:40 A.M. July 2, the Regiment will set out for London and the East India docks where vehicles, guns, and men will be taken aboard ships for Normandy.

At last, after all those years of training – of shoots at Sennybridge and Alfriston, of deploying in every kind of filthy weather on every kind of gorse-covered down, bare mountain, foggy moor, and soggy cow pasture, of playing at war on exercises and schemes run by "umpires" with mimeographed scripts – you are going into action.

Over the years, for days without number, everyone over here, regardless of rank, has had to confront and manage frustration, boredom, and periodic lowerings of the spirit to levels that could only be described by the expression "totally browned off." This will never be appreciated by anyone who has not for years been denied all the freedoms civilians take for granted, including the freedom to come and go as you like and to pick and choose where you live, where you sleep, what you wear and what you eat, and (equally important) when and where, and with whom, you eat it.

Now, however, everyone draws strength and courage from the very harshness of the life they have been living. There is a real sense of belonging to a brotherhood forged and tempered by years of hard training and discipline – fully prepared and ready to confront whatever the future has in store. And you feel, surging through the Regiment, that stimulating sense of purpose that motivated all to enlist in the first place, and which, since 1940, has underpinned and sustained morale at a remarkably high level.

APPENDIX A

THE PLUNKETTS' MARCHING SONG

"WE'RE ON OUR WAY"

We're on our way! We're on our way!
We're on our way to Berchtesgaden!
And every day, in every way
We're one day closer Berchtesgaden.
When we get there, you can be sure,
There'll be a high-dee, ho-dee, hey!
For with Chamberlain's umbrella,
We will spank the little fella,
Singing: Hey! Hey! We're on our way!

As recalled in 1997 by 1939 2nd Battery "originals" ex-Brigadier Ted Beament and ex-Gunners Carl Killeen and Hervé Dupuis, all of whom also remembered the tune and sang it without hesitation though they had not had occasion to sing it since their route-marching fifty-seven years before.

While the melody obviously made for a good marching song, the lyric was from the same shallow well of inane bravado from whence sprang the early British war songs "We're Going to Hang Out Our Washing on the Siegfried Line" and "Run Rabbit Run," the latter commemorating the demise of a rabbit on a lonely heath, reputedly the only casualty from one of the first bombs dropped on Britain.

Not until the German *Blitzkrieg* overran Western Europe with brutal efficiency, and Hitler was pictured standing on a promontory in the Pas-de-Calais staring across the Channel at England, did the lyrics of popular songs start to reflect concerns of consequence, which, when married to well-developed melodies, projected profound tenderness, yearning, poignancy, hope, and the nobility of the human spirit.

APPENDIX B

HOW "HAM" ROBERTS GOT HIS GUNS BACK TO ENGLAND

(an excerpt from *The Gunners of Canada*)

Early on the 17th [June, 1940], Headquarters Brest Garrison, to ensure that the evacuation of all personnel would not be jeopardized by attempts to save equipment, issued orders for all transport to be destroyed. Even the guns of the 1st Field Regiment [RCHA] were endangered. A report in the regimental diary shows how close they came to being lost.

> At 1100 hours Lt.-Col. [J. H. "Ham"] Roberts went to Garrison H.Q. and fought for nearly two hours to save the guns. Colonel Mackie, the garrison commander (an ex-cadet of the Royal Military College of Canada), was very helpful, but eventually had to order the guns and tractors to be destroyed. This was countermanded by wire. But shortly after, the order to destroy came again. Lt.-Col. Roberts pointed out that his guns were on the dock and guaranteed to load them within an hour. So a zero hour of 1600 hours was given and as much as possible to be loaded in that time.

> Loading began at once "before any more minds could be changed." It was then 2:15, and by the four o'clock deadline there had been put on board the steamer *Bellerophon*, not only the Field Regiment's 24 guns, but also 12 Bofors [ack-ack] guns, seven predictors, three Bren carriers and several heavy technical trucks belonging to other units. Then came the grim task of destroying the Regiment's gun tractors [quads], while French civilians stood by waiting to salvage what they could of the remains. Drivers drained the oil from their vehicles and then ran the motors until they seized. After that they went to work with picks and crowbars on the engines, batteries, R.T. [radio telephony] sets and other equipment. It added little to the gunners' peace of mind to note that when the *Bellerophon* pulled out into the harbour, though she was well-packed with troops, there appeared to be still room enough to have taken all the equipment that had been on the docks.

(From pages 70-71, G. W. L. Nicholson, *The Gunners of Canada: The History of the Royal Regiment of Canadian Artillery, Vol. II, 1919-1967*, Toronto: Mc-Clelland & Stewart, 1967.)

APPENDIX C

". . . D'YOU TELL ME AS YOU DIDN'T KNOW THEY WAS THERE?"

The following is told by Ian V. Hogg on page 120 of his book *The Guns: 1939-45*, published by Ballantyne Books, New York, 1970. At the time of publication the author was one of only sixteen holders of the distinguished rank of Master Gunner 1st Class in the British Army:

In the summer of 1940, when things looked their worst, an acquaintance of mine, then an officer of long service who had, in the dim past, been trained on railroad guns, was despatched with a companion to reconnoitre likely sites on the coast of England to which the few available railroad guns could be sent. Having studied the map, they came to the conclusion that a little valley near a main railway line would be suitable providing a short spur of track could be laid into it, and they set out to study the ground. Walking through a wood they were surprised to find a rusty single track leading right towards their selected valley, though not shown on the map. Pleased with their good fortune, they followed the tracks into the valley where the rails disappeared into two weatherbeaten sheds. Peering through the cobwebbed windows, they discerned dimly what seemed to be some form of machinery. Feeling that here was a good place to park a pair of guns, they broke the lock on one door and entered the gloom. Before them was a gleaming 9.2-inch railroad gun. The other shed proved to hold another one. At this juncture, they were disturbed by a posse of police and troops alerted by a suspicious shepherd – people were very touchy at that time and place – and with them came an elderly pensioner who turned out to be the caretaker of the two guns. Yes, they were fully serviceable; yes, they'd been there since 1918 and he was paid every week through the local Post Office to keep them clean and greased, and so he had, and bless me, sir, d'you tell me as you didn't know they was there?

APPENDIX D

THE 25-POUNDER: A SUPER WEAPON

All artillery weapons are a compromise between the need to produce the biggest possible impression on the target (the heaviest possible shell, but slow to deliver) and the need to produce quickly a torrent of shells (smaller, less destructive, but deliverable for lengthy periods), keeping in mind that the bigger the weapon, the less mobile it must be – which, in the case of field guns closely supporting the infantry, is an overriding consideration. The speed with which field guns can be moved forward behind an advancing front and brought into action at a new gunsite may well decide the outcome of a battle.

Also to be considered in designing the perfect weapon is the loading weight of its projectile, which should be no more than twenty-five or thirty pounds if gunners, hand-loading the weapon, are to sustain a high, uninterrupted rate of fire for long periods – the kind of shelling considered most effective in keeping enemy heads down when our infantry is attacking, neutralizing enemy gun or mortar batteries, and destroying enemy counter-attacks.

Finally, there is the choice between a gun and a howitzer. The powerful propellant charge of a *gun* will produce a high muzzle velocity and thus longer ranges with a high degree of accuracy, but will not be able to reach targets sheltering behind steep hills or in deep valleys because of the relatively flat trajectory of its shells; and the lighter propellant charge of the *howitzer* produces shorter ranges and slightly less accuracy, but loops its shells on high trajectories over hills and into deep valleys unreachable by the gun.

All these compromises were recognized and reflected in the design of a field piece the like of which the world had never seen before: the British 25-pounder of 1938.

First, it is both a gun (low trajectory) *and* a howitzer (high trajectory). This is possible through the introduction of a cunningly designed range-cone, allowing the gun to be laid at widely varying elevations to get the shell to target, depending on whether a low, medium, or high charge is used to propel the shell. Varying the charge is possible, because the cartridge case is separate from the shell. This allows the gun crew, on orders, to remove one bag or two bags of the three (red, white, and blue) bags of cordite to reduce the propellant charge and increase the looping effect of the shell: removing the blue bag to get Charge II, and removing both blue and white bags to produce Charge I, a charge so low that on dull days the shells can be glimpsed fleetingly as a vague shadow.

Loading shells is facilitated by the vertical breech-block, which, when dropped open, provides a loading shelf for ramming the shell. And when the cartridge case is inserted behind the shell, protruding lugs are pushed aside, releasing the breech-block onto springs that make easier the closing of the heavy block for firing. Experienced gun crews can get off ten and twelve rounds a minute, though the "intense" rate of fire for 25-pounders is officially listed as only five rounds a minute.*

Deploying a 25-pounder ready to fire is easier than for any field piece in the world, for there is no need to level off a gun platform. It carries under its trail its own level platform, resembling a large steel-spoked wheel, hubbed at the centre and connected to the sides of the box trail by two arms that lock in position when it is dropped from its carrying position and the gun's wheels are hauled onto it by the towing quad. The claws on the bottom of the platform, pressed into the ground (even on a roadway) by the gun's 4,032 pounds, obviates the need for the trail's spade to dig in, which allows one man to swing the gun in a complete circle of 360 degrees traverse, something no other field gun in the world can do, and which, in fluid warfare, can be extremely useful.

Coming out of action for a fast move is equally simple: when the gun trail is hooked to the ammunition limber, which is hooked to the quad, and the arms holding the platform to the trail are unlocked, the quad simply rolls backward a few feet, pushing the gun's wheels off the platform so it can be raised and secured under the trail in seconds.

The weight of shell was raised 50 per cent from the World War I 18-pounder, and its range increased from 9,500 yards to a maximum range for its high explosive shell of 13,400 yards, and 11,000 for its smoke shell. In 1943, the weapon was fitted with a "muzzle brake" to reduce the wear and tear on the recoil system, particularly when "super charge" was used with a muzzle velocity of 2,000 feet per second expelling armour-piercing solid-shot against tanks.†

---

* Sgt. G. "Lefty" Phillips's crew on No. 4 gun, Able Troop, 2nd Battery just south of Caen in August 1944, timed with a stopwatch by Lieut. Bob Grout, got off seventeen rounds in one minute.

† The brake is simply an extension of the gun's barrel, containing large transverse holes in its thick sides to catch some of the expelling gases in their forward rush out of the muzzle and inhibit the barrel's thrust towards the rear.

APPENDIX E

ARTILLERY BOARD

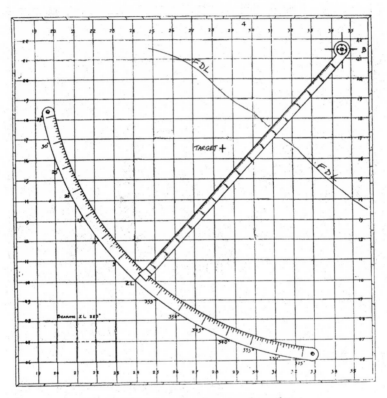

The artillery board set up and ready

When the pivot gun is plotted in the appropriate grid square, and the zero line is drawn from it along the designated bearing, a brass pivot is pinned over the pivot-gun dot and a steel "arm" (to measure the range in yards to targets) is placed on this pivot. Now a steel "arc" (engraved with degrees and minutes) is centred over the zero line and thumbtacked down at the extremity of its companion "arm," allowing switches from zero line, as well as ranges between gun and target, to be read off quickly when targets are plotted in appropriate grid squares on the board to an initial accuracy of 100 yards where only six-figure map references are possible, but to 25 yards when eight-figure coordinates are supplied for the target.

APPENDIX F

LOSSES AT SEA

Of the 785 German submarines sunk by the Allies in the North Atlantic, 246 were sunk by ships and 245 by shore-based aircraft.

From September 1939 to May 8, 1945, the Allies lost 5,137 ships in the North Atlantic.

MERCHANT SHIPPING LOSSES IN ALL THEATRES

	Ships	Tons
United Kingdom	4,786	21,194,000
Japan	2,346	8,618,109
Germany	1,595	7,088,779
United States	578	3,524,983
Norway	427	1,728,531
Holland	286	1,195,204

(Canada merchant ship loss was only 68, totalling 330,254 tons.)

NAVAL LOSSES IN ALL THEATRES

The largest number of naval vessels lost by the Allies, 676, were American, but of these, 396 were landing ships, landing craft, and miscellaneous "district" craft. Counting only significant fighting ships, the British Navy suffered considerably more than the Americans:

	Battleships (& Battle Cruisers)	Cruisers (Hvy & light)	Carriers	Destroyers & Destroyer Escorts	Subs
U.K.	6	27	7	164*	74
U.S.	2	10	11	82	52

---

* Including twenty-two corvettes.

Among the Axis powers, Japan's navy suffered most:

	Battleships (& Battle Cruisers)	Cruisers (Hvy & light)	Carriers	Destroyers & Destroyer Escorts	Subs
Japan	11	36	20	133	129
Germany	9	7		101	785
Italy	2	14		55	107

(The statistics above are from pages 448 to 455, Robert Goralski, *World War II Almanac*, London, Hamish Hamilton Ltd., 1981.)

APPENDIX G

A GRIM CAVALCADE OF DEFEATS

Only by perusing the following litany of defeats and losses in material and personnel (including British civilian casualties) suffered by the Allies from September 1940 until June 21, 1942, can the reader fully grasp how close the world came to sinking into what Churchill foresaw as a "new Dark Age, made more sinister, and perhaps more protracted, by the lights of perverted science." Even those who lived through these anxious years tend to dwell on those rare occasions of shining success – such as the RAF in the Battle of Britain in the summer of 1940, the Royal Navy's sinking of the German battleship *Bismarck* (May 27, 1941), and the American navy's triumph over the Japanese fleet at Midway Island the first week of June 1942 – and forget how often utter despair threatened, and how the free world hung on every brave word and confident growl from Churchill, and the ringing optimism of Roosevelt's every utterance.

1940	Sept 23:	Attempt by Free French, with British support, to occupy Dakar in French West Africa fails and British battleship *Resolution* severely damaged.
	Sept 30:	British civilian casualties for Sept: 17,600, 6,954 dead.
	Oct 31:	British civilian casualties for Oct: 15,000, 6,334 dead.
	Nov 14:	Coventry bombed by 450 planes dropping high explosive (503 tons) and incendiaries (30,000); killing 554 and wounding 865, and destroying 60,000 buildings, including 75 per cent of the residential areas.
	Nov 19:	Birmingham heavily bombed.
	Nov 28:	Liverpool heavily bombed.
	Nov 30:	British civilian casualties in Nov: 10,800, 4,588 dead.
	Dec 11:	British lose 624 capturing 38,000 Italians at Sidi Barrani.
	Dec 31:	British civilian casualties in Dec: 9,000, 3,793 dead.
1941	Jan 03:	Australian 6 Div takes Bardia, capturing 30,000 Italians.
	Jan 09:	British cruiser and destroyer sunk, and the aircraft carrier *Illustrious* put out of action west of Malta.
	Jan 11:	British cruiser *Southhampton* sunk off Malta.
	Jan 22:	Brits and Aussies take Tobruk capturing 25,000 Italians.
	Feb 28:	January to February, British civilian casualties: 5,300, 2,289 dead.
	Mar 23:	In one week, 59,141 tons of shipping lost in North Atlantic.

Mar 31:   British civilian casualties in March: 9,800, 4,259 killed. Since Blitz began, 28,859 killed, 40,166 wounded.

Apr 06:   Yugoslav defences collapse to 2nd Panzer Division. Six British generals lost in sandstorm in Libya and captured.

Apr 07:   British lose Benghazi to Germans.

Apr 09:   2nd Panzer Division takes Salonika, Greece.

Apr 10:   9th Australian Division pulls back into Tobruk.

Apr 20:   Greece capitulates to the Axis forces.

Apr 24:   British and Commonwealth forces evacuate 40,000 men from Greece, leaving behind 22,500 dead, wounded, or captured, along with 8,000 vehicles and 207 aircraft shot down by the Germans.

May 10:   Heaviest raid on London kills 1,436 and wounds 1,792. The House of Commons, Westminster Abbey, and the British Museum hit.

May 20-30: Allies lose Crete − 15,000 evacuated, but left behind are 45,000 dead, wounded, or captured. The British lose 46 planes, along with an aircraft carrier, three cruisers, and six destroyers − all sunk.

May 24:   German battleship *Bismarck* sinks pride of British navy, battle cruiser *Hood*, between Iceland and Greenland. Of a crew of 1,419, only three survive.

May 27:   Battleship *Prince of Wales* badly damaged and withdraws, but battleships *Rodney* and *King George V* track the *Bismarck* and sink her 500 miles west of Brest.

May 30:   British civilian casualties April to May: 23,600 of which 11,438 are killed.

Jun 22:   Germany attacks Russia and advances 200 miles in six days.

Jul 09:   Russians lose 2,500 tanks and 1,500 artillery pieces as 290,000 of their troops surrender at Vitebsk.

Jul 10:   German Panzer units within 10 miles of Kiev.

Jul 16:   Smolensk falls to Germans.

Jul 22:   In one month Germans take 720,000 square miles of Soviet territory.

Aug 30:   Leningrad's last rail link severed.

Sep 19:   Kiev falls − Russians lose 350,000 men, 3,718 guns, and 884 armoured vehicles.

Sep 22:   Leningrad cut off.

Oct 06:   Russian Ninth and Tenth Armies surrender, including 100,000 men and the entire general staff of Ninth Army.

Oct 12:   Women and children being evacuated from Moscow.

Oct 16: Another nine Russian armies – 80 divisions – destroyed by Germans, who take 663,000 prisoners at Bryansk and Vyazma.

Nov 08: Hitler claims to have inflicted eight to ten million casualties on Russians. Russians report losses up to October 16 as 350,000 killed, 1,020,000 wounded, and 378,000 taken prisoner.

Nov 12: HMS *Ark Royal* torpedoed and sunk off Gibraltar. Allied shipping losses for month 750,000 tons.

Nov 19: Australian cruiser *Sydney* sunk by German surface raider off west coast of Australia.

Nov 22: British offensive stopped by Rommel in North Africa.

Nov 23: German surface raider *Atlantic* is sunk after claiming to have sunk 22 merchant ships in 20 months of operation. South African 5th Brigade virtually annihilated by Rommel in North Africa. Germans take Rostov in Russia.

Nov 24: British battleship *Barnham* sunk by sub in Mediterranean.

Nov 27: German Panzers within 19 miles of Moscow.

Nov 30: British civilian air raid casualties October to November: 866, 351 killed. Leningrad is cut off and facing starvation (11,000 starved to death in November).

Dec 02: Japanese planes put the U.S. Pacific Fleet anchored at Pearl Harbor out of action, sinking four battleships.

Dec 08: Japanese planes hit Philippines. (Half the bombers of the U.S. Far Eastern Force are destroyed.) Japanese land on Malaya and Thailand. Singapore and Hong Kong bombed.

Dec 09: Japanese occupy Bangkok, Thailand.

Dec 10: British battleship *Prince of Wales* and battle cruiser *Repulse* are sunk off Malaya by torpedoes dropped from planes. U.S. garrison on island of Guam surrenders to Japanese.

Dec 15: British driven back in Malaya, Burma, and Hong Kong. British cruiser *Galatia* sunk off Egyptian coast by sub.

Dec 16: Japanese invade British Borneo.

Dec 19: British battleships *Queen Elizabeth* and *Valiant* seriously disabled in Alexandria harbour. British cruiser *Valiant* hits mines off Malta and sinks with one survivor.

Dec 21: Massive Japanese landings in Philippines.

Dec 23: Wake Island falls to the Japanese, leaving United States with no base between Hawaii and Philippines.

Dec 25: British Hong Kong garrison, including 1,000 Canadians, surrender to Japanese. Losses defending the colony are 11,848, including civilian casualties. Japanese suffer 675 killed and 2,079 wounded.

	Dec 30:	British drive halted in Libya by superior German tanks.
1942	Jan 06:	British offensive in Libya halted, though British claim Rommel's Panzer Group Africa suffered 38,000 casualties, and view their offensive as a victory.
	Jan 16:	Burma invaded by Japanese.
	Jan 17:	U-boat sinks ship off U.S. coast.
	Jan 19:	British Borneo surrenders to Japanese.
	Jan 23:	Japanese invade Solomon Islands.
	Jan 25:	In Libya, 1st British Armoured Div. routed by Germans. British lose 96 tanks, 38 guns, 190 trucks, and 12 aircraft.
	Feb 05:	*Empress of Asia* sunk near Singapore.
	Feb 10:	82,423-ton liner *Normandie* burns in New York harbor.
	Feb 13:	Three British transports for Malta sunk off Alexandria.
	Feb 15:	Singapore – believed impregnable – falls to Japanese, and 64,000 British, Indian, and Australian surrender after 9,000 of their comrades die in combat. Total casualties of Allies in 70-day Malayan campaign: 67,340 Indians, 38,496 British, 18,490 Australians, and 14,382 volunteers from the resident populations. Of the 139,000, 130,000 are prisoners. Japanese casualties: 9,824.
	Feb 23:	Oil field at Santa Barbara, California, shelled by Japanese sub. Stalin claims war has turned against Germany.
	Feb 26:	U.S. aircraft-carrier *Langley* sunk by Japanese off Java.
	Feb 27:	In the three-day battle of the Java Sea, Allied navies – British, U.S., and Dutch – suffer worst defeat of the war. Using torpedoes with effective range of up to 25 miles (five times the U.S. and British models) on February 27, the Japanese sink the Dutch cruisers *De Ruyter* and *Java*, the Dutch destroyer *Kortenauer* and the British destroyer *Electra*. On the 28th the Japanese cruisers sink the American cruiser *Houston* and the Australian cruiser *Perth*. And on March 1, the Japanese sink the British cruiser *Exeter* (of River Plate fame) and the destroyers *Pope* and *Encounter*.
	Feb 28:	Japanese land on the north coast of Java.
	Mar 06:	Batavia falls to the Japanese.
	Mar 08:	Rangoon, capital of Burma, falls to the Japanese.
	Mar 10:	All Allied forces in Dutch East Indies surrender.
	Mar 19:	Japanese complete occupation of Sumatra and Timor.
	Mar 23:	Andaman Island in Bay of Bengal occupied by Japanese.
	Mar 31:	Allies lose 273 merchant ships (834,164 tons), 95 of them in the North Atlantic during March.
	Apr 05:	British cruisers *Dorsetshire* and *Cornwall* sunk by Japanese.
	Apr 08:	In four days, Japanese sink 28 supply ships (144,400 tons).

Apr 09:   Bataan falls – 35,000 Americans and Filipinos prisoners.

Apr 10:   British aircraft carrier *Hermes*, a destroyer, a corvette, and two tankers are sunk by Japanese planes off Ceylon.

Apr 30:   All central Burma falls to the Japanese.

May 01:   Mandalay falls to the Japanese.

May 02:   British cruiser *Edinburgh* is sunk coming back from Russia.

May 03:   Japanese invasion fleet threatening Australia intercepted in Coral Sea. United States lose more ships but Japanese invasion is off.

May 06:   Corregidor surrenders to Japanese – 16,000 Americans and Filipinos taken prisoner.

May 11:   German U-boat torpedoes transport ship in St. Lawrence River. German planes sink three British destroyers in Mediterranean.

May 14:   Waters off Newfoundland mined by German subs.

May 15:   Japan completes conquest of Burma. Germans eliminate all Russian forces from Crimea except in Sebastopol.

May 19:   Germans occupy all of Crimea, taking 100,000 prisoners.

May 28:   Germans knock out Russian force trying to retake Kharkov.

May 29:   German midget sub badly damages British battleship *Ramillies* and sinks tanker in Madagascar harbour.

May 30:   First 1,000-bomber raid on Cologne: 1,455 tons of bombs, two-thirds incendiaries, causing 12,000 fires, 1,700 conflagrations – 486 people killed, 59,000 made homeless.

Jun 04:   First U.S. success in Pacific: Japanese turned back at Midway Island, losing four aircraft carriers and a heavy cruiser.

Jun 06:   British counterattack in Libya collapses after loss of two infantry brigades and four artillery regiments.

Jun 09:   All formal resistance to Japanese in Philippines ends. In all, 140,000 U.S. and Filipino troops killed, wounded, or taken prisoner while attempting to hold the islands.

Jun 13:   British suffer disastrous defeat at the hands of Rommel, losing 230 of their 300 tanks to superior German tanks at El Adem, making it possible for the Germans to move into Tobruk.

Jun 21:   33,000 British and Commonwealth soldiers surrender in Tobruk.

APPENDIX H

DIEPPE REPRISALS

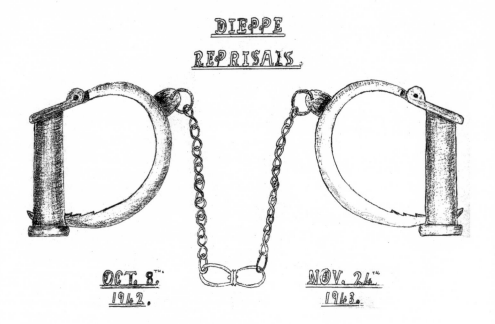

Pictured above are the manacles the Canadian Dieppe prisoners were obliged to wear each day from October 8, 1942 to November 24, 1943, though within days a way had been found to unlock the steel cuffs and remove them when the guards were not in view. The chain between the steel cuffs was about fifteen inches long. The drawing was done by commando prisoner A. J. Wallis.

APPENDIX I

THE GENIUS OF CARDINAL-POINT RANGING

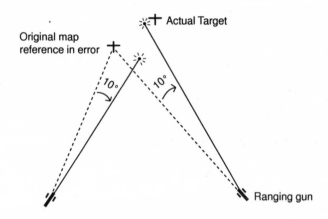

This diagram is meant to show that an order from a FOO switching the muzzle of the ranging gun "right" (or "more") 10 degrees at 4,000 yards moves the impact zone of its shells northeast (close to the target), but the same order applied to a gun sitting 4,000 yards west (left) of the ranging gun would deposit its shells 750 yards south of the target. Thus the FOO needs to order cardinal-point corrections, which, in this instance, would be "Northeast 1,000," the estimated distance and direction of the target from the first ranging round. Each troop command post would plot the new dot on its artillery board and read off (with its arm and arc) the switch and range peculiar to its position in relation to the target, which, in the case of the non-ranging gun in the diagram, would be "more six degrees – 4,000 [yards]."

Actual plotting of successive ranging rounds is accomplished using a little square of clear, stiff plastic (equalling a grid square) in which lines of holes have been punched (scaled a hundred yards apart) radiating from the centre to all the cardinal points of the compass. The centre hole is placed over the dot of the last plotted round, and if the correction is "Northwest 1,000," the ack counts along the northwest line of holes to the tenth hole and plots a dot through it with his pencil, to which he then swings his arc and reads off his new range and switch for *his* four guns. By continuously re-plotting the ranging rounds on their artillery boards, each troop in the regiment, division, or corps can follow the movement of that one ranging gun and be ready to go into "fire for effect" immediately it is called for.

APPENDIX J

THE DESTRUCTIVE POWER OF THE V-IS AND THE BRITISH–CANADIAN–AMERICAN PROXIMITY FUSE

Before the Canadians clear the Channel ports and overrun the launching sites for the V-1s in the fall of 1944, those 25-foot-long pilotless craft carrying one-ton warheads will kill 5,479 people in Britain, injure 15,934, and destroy or seriously damage 1,104,000 homes,* 149 schools, 11 churches, and 95 hospitals. In total, 8,000 of these *Vergeltungswaffeln*, as the Germans know them, were fired on Britain. Of those, 2,300 reached London. (As reported by Robert Goralski on page 324 of his *World War II Almanac* published by Hamish Hamilton, London, 1981.)

The buzz-bomb menace, which, for several weeks at the beginning, seriously reduced production of goods and services vital to the prosecution of the war (according to the diary notes of the Chief of the Imperial General Staff General Alan Brooke) was brought under control by the timely arrival on the ack-ack gunnery scene of the proximity fuse – a Canadian–American invention based on a British idea. Shells from the 3.7-inch ack-ack guns, which would have sailed past a few feet from a buzz bomb, were caused to burst and send lethal fragments into the buzz bombs' vitals when a tiny radio-transmitter signal bounced back from the pilotless monster.

The Americans developed the tiny radio transmitter and receiver. Canada supplied the design for a dependable power supply, which had to have long storage life but produce instant power to the little radio transmitter as the shell left the gun. Regular tiny batteries, with their limited shelf life, were useless, but scientists at the National Research Council in Ottawa, working with industrial scientists in Toronto, produced the answer: a battery that would remain dormant until activated by acid from a tiny vial broken within the fuse by the shocking *wham* of the propellant charge sending the shell on its way.

---

* Representing one quarter of all British homes destroyed or seriously damaged by enemy action during the war.

APPENDIX K

OFFICERS OF 4TH FIELD REGIMENT RCA

July 7, 1944	May 8, 1945
A/Lt.-Col. G. M. "Bud" Drury	Lt.-Col. McGregor Young
Major G. C. Savage (2 IC)	Major Don. Wilson (2 IC)
" J. O. Wren (BC 2nd Bty)	A/Maj. J. M. Cooper (BC 2nd Bty)
" J. W. Dodds (BC 14th Bty)	Major J. L. Drewry (BC 14th Bty)
" W. P. Carr (BC 26th Bty)	A/Maj. J. F. Brown (BC 26th Bty)
Capt. G. M. Welch (Adjutant)	Capt. S. G. M. Grange (Adjutant)
" R. C. Jim Morrison	A/Capt. A. N. Allan
" E. Stu Laurie	Capt. G. G. Blackburn
" Gordon M. Hunter	A/Capt. R. E. R. Borland
" Jack L. Drewry	Capt. F. J. Davis
" A. Brit Smith	A/Capt. D. D. Edwards
" Jack E. Thompson	A/Capt. R. J. Haig
" W. L. Stuart-MacLeod	Capt. W. L. Hutcheon
" Reg. F. Parker	" E. Stu Laurie
" Sammy G. M. Grange	A/Capt. G. T. Lucas
" T. G. Richardson, (RQM)	Capt. W. D. Stevenson
" B. T. Dunham (MO)	" D. L. MacDonald (QM)
" D. A. Shain (dental officer)	" P. C. Voloshin (MO)
" J. D. MacDonald (paymaster)	" D. A. Shain (dental officer)
H/Capt. L. D. Begg (padre)	" J. D. MacDonald (paymaster)
Lieut. A. E. Adams	H/Capt. A. M. Laverty (padre)
" A. S. Barber	Lieut. B. C. Ackerman
" G. G. Blackburn	" A. S. Barber
" J. A. Cameron	" D. G. Buckley
" J. L. P. G. Corbeil	" J. E. Butler
" T. E. Dack	" J. S. B. Cadieux
" H. T. Dawson	" A. C. Cagney
" W. L. Dunning	" J. L. P. G. Corbeil
" J. Gerby★	" R. S. Cork
" R. C. Grout★	" W. Craig
" W. L. Hutcheon	" R. E. Davis★
" W. W. Knapp	" W. L. George
" G. E. Lennox	" R. C. Grout
" C. T. Lucas	" O. D. Hancock
" J. D. Macfarlane	" W. E. Hanley★
" R. A. McCarey	" L. B. Hunter★
" W. E. Murdoch	" R. A. McCarey
" D. M. Patrick	" D. MacDonald
" J. E. Richardson★	" E. J. Macrew★

★ Supernumeraries not posted to batteries.

Lieut. W. D. Stevenson
   "   K. H. Turnbull
   "   L. A. Verdeil
   "   C. E. Williams

Lieut. J. E. McLean
   "   W. G. B. Miller★
   "   W. E. Murdoch
   "   J. L. Nesbitt
   "   D. M. Patrick
   "   A. W. Reid
   "   J. E. Richardson
   "   R. F. H. Russell★
   "   L. W. Spurr
   "   F. H. Toman
   "   F. G. Thompson
   "   E. C. Williams★

Of the forty-three officers on strength on arrival in Normandy, July 7, 1944, only twelve were still with the Regiment at war's end ten months later.

INDEX

A-1 Training Wing, Petawawa, 155
abandon-ship drill, 90, 91, 199
ablution stands, 60
Achilles (N.Z. cruiser), 49
acks (*see* gunnery)
Adams, Gnr. Fulton James, 207*n*.
Addie, Sgt.-Maj. A. J., 374*n*.
"Adler" (*see* operations)
Admiral Graf Spee, 49
Africa, 267
Africa Corps, 269
AFS (Auxiliary Fire Service), 117
Ailsa Craig, 92
Air OP, 285
air raids (German), 106, 400
Aitken, Lieut. Wm. "Cozy," 390
Ajax, HMS, 49
Alamein (*see* El Alamein)
Aldershot, 94, 95, 99, 105, 106,
    110–14, 116, 117, 129
Alfred (the Great), 232
Alfriston, 134, 232, 233, 279, 283,
    286, 287, 288, 289, 291, 295, 314,
    357, 402
Algiers, 269
Allies, 387
Ament, Gnr. Oliver, 291
American Airforce, 327
American Bar (Park Lane), 292
American Consul, Lyons, 208
American forward observers, 263
ammunition reserves, 158*n*.
Andora, 293
Andrews Sisters, 62
angle of sight (*see* gunnery)

Anglesey Island, 99
Antwerp, 53
Anzio, 200
Arc de Triomphe, 67
Archibald, Lieut. Tommy, 205, 207*n*.,
    213, 214
"Are You Really There?", 396–7
Armed Forces Network, BBC, 398
armies: 8th British, 267, 268, 269,
    322*n*., 331; 4th British (fictitious),
    387; German 15th (Calais), 387;
    Italian, 267; 7th American, 322
Armistice Day, 39, 67
Armoured Regiments: 6th Armoured
    Regiment, 388*n*.; 10th Armoured
    Regiment, 388*n*.; 27th Armoured
    Regiment, 388*n*.
Arondora Star, 71
ARP (air-raid precautions), 99
artillery batteries (other than 4th
    Field): 51st, 17; 57th and 59th
    Heavy (Newfoundland), 98;
    Superheavy X and Y RA, 97, 98,
    30th Light Ack Ack, 163
artillery boards (*see* gunnery)
artillery regiments (other than 4th
    Field): 1st Field RCHA, 4, 59, 82,
    92, 96, 97, 174, 175, 293*n*., 322,
    338; 1st Field Brigade RCA, 17;
    2nd Field, 322, 344; 3rd Field, 322,
    344; 5th Field, 138, 205, 373*n*.,
    377; 6th Field, 121, 141*n*., 206*n*.,
    283, 291, 373, 377; 8th Army
    Field, 337; 11th Army Field, 131*n*.;
    12th Field, 292; 14th Field, 293*n*.,

338; 19th Field, 255; 3rd Medium, 198; 3rd Light Ack Ack, 109n., 206n., 373; 6th Light Ack Ack, 163, 210; 2nd Anti-Tank, 373

Arundel, 278; Castle, 313, 319, 339, 360

Ashdown Forest, 130

assault landing craft (ALC), 346

Associated Press, 69, 200n.

Athenia, 23

Athlone, Earl of, 74

Atlantic, Battle of, 190, 191, 415

Atlantic convoys, 195

Auster, 284

Australia, 201, 268, 269, 328, 358

Australian (RAF) squadrons, 363

Axis forces, 293

Bagusa, 322n.

Baldwin, Stanley, 22

Banbury, 94

Bangalores, 215

barges (German), 125

Barnham Junction, 205, 218, 221, 225, 226, 249, 275, 276, 277, 281, 320, 364

Barrafranca, 322n.

barrage (*see* gunnery)

barrage balloon, 6, 93

Barrie, 77

Barriefield, 51, 58

Barton, Lance Bdr. J. H., 399

Basher, Lt.-Col. Headley, 35n.

Bataan, 201

batteries (*see* artillery)

Battle of the Atlantic (*see* Atlantic)

Battle of Britain, 99, 118n., 193, 417

battle drill, 123, 124

"battle-school," 124

Bay of Biscay, 191

BBC, 205, 363, 393, 398

Beachy Head, 228, 229, 315, 365

Beament, Major C. E. "Ted," 17, 30n., 40n., 45, 47n., 55, 82, 109n., 131n.

Bear (Llandovery), 251

Beaver Club, 115

Bedford, 132

Bedford Basin, 195

Beedie, Betty, 13

BEF, 50, 53, 57, 67, 76, 265, 266

Begg, H/Capt. Padre L. B., 339n., 400

Belgian (RAF) squadrons, 363n.

Belgium, 28, 53, 109, 389

Bellerophon, 407

Berlin, 8, 17, 50, 99, 363

Big Ben, 118

Biggin Hill, 366

Billings, Gnr., 45

Birmingham, 91, 259, 384, 386

Bismark, 417

Black Cat Farm, 232

Black Sea, 17

Black Watch (Royal Highland Regiment of Canada), 210

blackout, 93, 384

Blanc Nez, 392

Blenheim bomber, 24n.

Blitz, 113, 120

Blitzkrieg, 26, 169

Blodgett, Sgt.-Maj. E. H. "Ed," 374n.

Blue Beach, 205-17

Blum, Leon, 22

Blythe, Capt. Dave, 231

Bodyguard (misinformation campaign), 387

Boer War, 155, 259, 263

Bognor Regis, 205, 218

Booth, Lieut. W. D., 197n.

Borden (*see* Camp Borden)

Bordon, Hants, (#1 CARU) 52, 330, 331, 353, 383, 394

Borton, Major H. S., 141, 242

Boston, Mass, 200
Boston (plane), 208, 364
Botwood, 6
Bournemouth, 110
Bowmanville, 333
Bracken, Gnr. George, 114
Bramber, 312
Brecon, 250, 255, 303
Bremen, 363
Bren Gun Carriers, 106
Breslau, 207n.
Brest, 96, 174, 407
Brickwall House, 129, 130
brigade (RCA), 1st Field, 17
brigades (Canadian): armoured, (2nd) 388n.; infantry, (4th) 35n., 126, 225, 283, 368, (6th) 123, (7th) 388n., (8th) 388n., (9th) 388n.
Brighton, 118, 275, 289, 301
Brighton Ice Arena, 290
British child refugees, 70-72
British Columbia, 145, 207
British Commonwealth, 5, 50, 68, 268, 267, 328
British Empire, 19, 52, 68
British Expeditionary Force (see BEF)
British School of Artillery, 155
British War Office, 42, 96, 123, 146
Brittany, 96
Brockville Officers' Training Centre, 145, 146n., 147, 150, 154, 165, 339
Brooke, General Sir Alan, 372n., 427
Brookwood Military Cemetery, 312, 400
Browne, Lieut. (Capt.) (Major) George, 45, 205, 206, 207, 207n., 208, 292, 293n.
Browne, Major G. S., 161, 169
Brümsbutel, 24
Buckingham Palace, 99
build-up for invasion, 357
Builth Wells, 303, 307, 311
bumpf, 155

Burhopecrag Hall, 351
Burma, 201, 384n.
Burwash, 135
buzzbomb (see V-1)

Cadet Corps (schools), 21
Caen, 123n., 401, 412n.
Cairo, 268
Calais, 55, 91
Caltagirone, 322n.
Cameron, Sgt. H. "Scottie," 290, 291, 333, 334n.
Cameron, Sgt. Howard, 255, 255n.
Cameron, Lieut. Jack, 218, 219, 220, 231, 281, 282, 339
Cameron Highlanders of Canada, 24
Camber, 126
Camp Borden, 76, 78, 133
Campbell, Jack, 20, 189
Campbell, Sir Malcolm, 7, 382
Canada Corner, 139n.
Canada House, 269
"Canada" shoulder badges, 81
Canadian Armoured Fighting Vehicle Training Centre, A-8, Borden, 80n.
Canadian Artillery Reinforcement Unit, #1 (see CARU, #1)
Canadian Artillery Training Centre, 171
Canadian High Commissioner, 269
Canadian Military Headquarters, London, 208
Canadian Press, 269
Canadian School of Artillery (Seaford) 242n., 334
Canadian Scottish Regiment, 388n.
Canadian squadrons, 363
Canadian Training School ("battle-school"), 124
Canadian War Measures Act, 11
Canadian Women's Army Corps (see CWACs)
Canterbury, 97

Canterbury Cathedral, 381
Cap Gris Nez, 392n.
Capetown, 196
cardinal-point ranging, 425 (see also
    gunnery)
Carlisle, Gnr. C. W., 106
Carpenter, Lieut. F. B., 206n.
Carpenter, Major F. N., 100
Carpenter family, 100n.
Carr, Major. Wm. P., 340n.
Carr-Harris, Lieut. Peter, 64
carrier (Bren Gun or Universal), 133
Carroll, Daphne, 71-2
Carswell, Capt. H. B., 206n.
CARU, #1, 52, 55, 218, 239, 330, 353
CARU Commandant, 331
Casablanca, 269
casualty stats: Brit civilian, 113n.;
    Dieppe, 214; El Alamein, 268;
    Libya (Brit), 201; Pearl Harbor,
    135n.; Russian-Finland war, 51n.;
    Stalingrad, 284; Tobruk, 268; V-1
    bombs destroyed, 427; Warsaw, 11
Catterick, 350
Catto, Lt.-Col. Douglas, 208, 210, 212
Cave, The, 138n.
CBC, 44n.
Cenotaph, 117
censorship of letters, unit level, 375
Central Canada Exhibition, 33
Chadderton, Lieut. Hugh Clifford,
    390
Chalk River, 61
Chamberlain, Neville, 5, 7, 11, 17,
    19, 20, 22, 52
Channel, 56, 125, 126, 218, 401
Chaput, Mrs., 189
Château Frontenac, 87
chemical shoots, 138
Cherbourg, 402
Cherry Bush, 287
Chez Moi club, 366
Chicago, 18

Chichester, 270, (cathedral) 275, 276
chief of the imperial general staff, 121
child refugees, 70
Chinese, 20, 197
Chopin, 26
Christ Church School, 368
Christmas: 1939, 44, 50; 1940, 112;
    1941, 135-36; 1942, 272-77; 1943,
    345-347
Churchill, Rt. Hon. Winston, 21, 23,
    52, 53, 57, 67, 91, 121, 267, 372n.,
    401, 417
Churchill tanks, 29n., 76n., 401
Chute, Lieut. Don., 197n.
Citizen, 16, 38, 39, 71
Clapham Junction, 119
close bracket (see gunnery)
Clyde, 92, 95
CMHQ (Cdn Military Headquarters),
    269
Coats, Battery QM Sgt., 102
Cobb, John, 7, 382
Coburg, 37, 80
Cocked Hat Woods, 120
Cohan, George M., 270
Coles, Sgt. (Royal Regt.), 210
Coliseum, 24, 37, 48
Columbia Records, 44
Combined Operations, 208
commandos, 364
Commonwealth (see British
    Commonwealth)
compass march, night, 153
Compiègne, 66, 67
compulsory service, 168n.
Connery, Lance, 59, 60
conscription (see compulsory service)
Constanza Harbour, 17
contour lines (see gunnery)
Cooper, Major Don, 141n., 220, 230,
    231, 247, 249, 270, 275, 280, 281,
    282, 287, 297, 314, 315, 316, 324,
    338, 340

Cooper, Gnr. Ralph, 281, 393, 393*n.*
Copeland Hotel, 4, 9, 10, 11, 16, 64, 189
Copp, Terry, 31
Coppinger, Lieut. Tommy, 197*n.*
Corbett, Gnr. Jim, 290
Corinstine, Major R. W., 340*n.*
Cornwall, 376
Corps (British): 1st, 388*n.*; 12th, 123*n.*; 30th, 265*n.*, 388*n.*
Corps (Canadian): 1st, 233; 2nd, 388*n.*
Corps (U.S.A.): 1st, 388*n.*; 5th, 388*n.*; 7th, 388*n.*
corrections of the moment (*see* gunnery)
corvettes, 191, 192
Cotton, Robert, 259, 386
Couch, Lieut. C. W., 109*n.*
Courageous, HMS, 49
Courseulles, 390*n.*
Cowan, Major G. A., 270, 338, 340*n.*
CRA (commander royal artillery), 122, 160
Crackers club, 366
crash action (*see* gunnery)
Crerar, Lt.-Gen. Harry, 233
Crimea, 201
Crinnians Grove, 37
Crosby, Bing, 270
Crosier, Gnr. Ed, 83
cross-country (motorcycling), 239
Crossett, Sgt. Stan, 290
Crown and Thistle, 138*n.*
"crystal night" (*see* Kristallnacht)
curfew, 127
CWACs, 93*n.*-94*n.*
Czechoslovakia, 5, 22, 197*n.*
Czechs, 7; RAF squadrons, 363*n.*

Daladier, Edouard, 22
Danzig, 7, 8

D'Arcu, Sgt. Leonard Joseph, 207*n.*
Darling, Lieut. Sidney, 305, 311, 312
Davis, H/Capt. Eldon, 344
Dawson, Lieut. Howard T., 218
D-Day, 42*n.*, 375, 389; stats, 376*n.*, 388*n.*
Deacon, Lieut. Don, 197*n.*
Deal, 375
Dean, Lieut. "Dizzy," 152, 197*n.*
De Gaulle, General Charles, 389
de Havilland Aircraft, Canada, 272
Demeray, L/Bdr. Morris Allen, 207*n.*
Denmark, 24*n.*, 27, 51
Dennis, Sgt-Major Glen F., 272, 287, 289, 305, 306, 314, 315, 337
Depression, Great, 3, 13, 31*n.*, 58
Desert Rats, 370
Devil's Punchbowl, 239
Dieppe, 205, 206, 218, 219, 225, 301, 317, 361, 370, 371, 381, 394
Dill, Field Marshal Sir John, 101
Distinguished Service Order (DSO), 131*n.*
divisions, British: 50th (Northumbrian), 388*n.*; 51st Highland, 268, 269
divisions, Canadian: 1st, 28, 36, 121, 277, 293, 312, 312, 313, 322, 331, 357; 2nd, 59, 108, 120, 121, 122, 124, 225, 233, 300, 301, 302, 313, 322, 348, 351, 357, 371, 375, 381, 388*n.*, 401; 3rd, 283, 312, 338, 339, 357, 388*n.*; 4th Armoured, 77*n.*, 357, 388*n.*; 5th Armoured, 77*n.*, 340*n.*, 357, 388*n.*
divisions, New Zealand, 268
divisions, U.S.A.: 1st, 322*n.*, 388*n.*; 4th, 388*n.*; 29th, 388*n.*
dog-tags, 373
Dome Dancehall, 291
Dominion of Canada, 14, 145
Don 5 telephones, 105
Doncaster Racetrack, 350

Douglas, Lieut. Robert, 317, 348
Dover, 121, 374, 375, 391
Downs (hills), 235
Drewry, Capt. John L., 343*n.*
Driemel, Gnr. Wally, 393, 398
Drury, Major (Lt.-Col.) C. M.
    "Bud," 338, 340*n.*, 353, 379
DSO (*see* Distinguished Service Order)
Dudley, Sgt. John W., 207
"Dumbells" (Plunketts), 40
Dunhorse pub, 348
Dunkirk (Dunkerque), 29*n.*, 55, 66,
    67, 96, 97, 109, 133, 158, 197*n.*,
    266; boats lost, 56*n.*, 191*n.*;
    personnel saved, 57; planes lost,
    56*n.*; weapons lost, 69*n.*
Dunlop, Jack, 12
Dunsmore, Gnr. (Sgt.) John, 114
Dupuis, Hervé, 40*n.*
Dutch (RAF) squadrons, 363*n.*

Eager, Gnr. Martin David Conrad,
    207*n.*
"Eagle Day" (*see* Operation Adler)
East End (London), 114
East Grinstead, 367*n.*
East India Docks, 402
Easter, 304
Eastergate, 221
Eden, Hon. Anthony, 101, 270, 271*n.*
Edgbaston, 259
Edinburgh, 357
Edinburgh Castle, 388
Edmonston, Lieut. John, 123
Egypt, 200
Eighth Army (*see* armies)
Eisenhower, General Dwight, 32*n.*,
    389
El Adem, 201
El Alamein, 267, 268, 269, 284, 370
Elizabeth II, 32*n.*
Elizabeth, the Queen Mother, 3, 101
Ely, Capt. Dave, 294

embarkation leave, 187
Embleton, C. E., 273, 377
Emden (battleship), 24*n.*
Empress of Australia, 87-92
Empress of Britain, 4
Empress of Canada, 1
Empress of Japan, 195, 196, 382
Empress of Scotland, 195, 196, 197
English Channel (*see* Channel)
Esbjerg, 24*n.*
Essen, 327*n.*
Essex Scottish, 35*n.*, 225, 235
Ethiopians, 20
Everett, Sir Percy, 7
Everett, Lieut. Russ, 173, 197*n.*
exercises: Bumper, 132; Elm, 299;
    Fox, 121; Harlequin, 338; Simmer,
    205, 209; Spartan, 299-302, 364;
    Step, 373; Victor-Blast, 357;
    Waterloo, 120; Welch, 302, 303
    (*see also* operations)
Exeter, HMS, 49

Fair, Lieut. A. W. "Al," 197*n.*, 382,
    383
Faith, Percy, 44
Farnon, Robert, 398
Farr, Tommy, 291
Findlay, Jim and Ruth, 189
Finland (Finns), 27, 50
Flanders, 53, 69, 158
Fleet Street, 118, 269
Flensburg, 110*n.*
Fleury, Major (Lt.-Col.) Wm., 131*n.*,
    141*n.*, 283, 287, 288, 291, 295,
    313, 314, 315, 316, 318, 319, 320,
    321, 323, 337, 339, 343, 353, 353*n.*
Flight 665 Air OP Sqdn., 197*n.*
Flying bombs, 401*n.*
Flying Fortresses (*see* fortress)
Flying OP, 197*n.*, 284*n.*, 294, 379
Flying Scotsman, 382
Folkestone, 375

FOO (forward observation officer), 127, 132, 133, 156, 205, 211, 215, 230, 231
food-poisoning, 303-307
Ford Airfield, 276, 364
Forgy, Lt. Howell, 200n.
foraging, 224
Fort de la Duchere, 206
Fortress (plane), 363, 364
forward observation officer (*see* FOO)
Foulkes, Maj-General Charles, 372, 373
4th Field officers, on July 7, 1944, and May 5, 1945, Appendix K
Foynes, 6
France, 5, 26, 66, 96, 109, 125, 200, 364, 389
Fraser, Brig. R. A., 121
Free French Forces, 389
French (RAF) squadrons, 363n.
Fromow, Lieut. Lloyd, 126, 133

Garnons Convalescent Centre, 326, 329, 397
Garrow, Ramsay, 16
Garth, HMS, 208, 215
gas, poison, 42n.
gas capes, 139
gas masks (*see* respirators)
General Hospital, 14th, 326, 365
Geneva, 21
Geneva Convention, 42n.
George IV, 291
George VI, 3, 8, 11, 20, 50, 87, 101, 368, 371, 372n.
George Medal, 197
Georgetown University, 271n.
German guns (Calais), 391
German tactics, 286
Germans, 284, 381, 387
Germany, 270, 327, 361, 363
Gettysburg, 192
GIs, 357
Gibraltar, 293

Gilbey's Gin, 318, 348
Ginsberg, Lieut. Hymie, 165
Glasgow, 92
Glebe Collegiate, 24, 99
Gloster Meteor (jet), 353, 353n.
Gloucester, Duke of, 101
Godlewski, Gnr. Stan, 45, 82
Goering, Field Marshal Herman, 91, 118n., 126
Goodwood Park, 296
Gordonhead Officers' Training Centre, 145, 146
Goulding, Major Frank Ernest, 337
Gow, Bdr. George Leslie, 207n.
Graham, Capt. Wm., 294, 297, 298, 312
Graham-Browne, Capt. W., 270
Grange, Lt. S. G. M. "Sammy," 146, 147, 270, 293
Gravelle, Gnr. Claff, 46
Gray, Gnr. Charles Stanley, 207n.
Great Lakes, 8
Great War (*see* World War I)
Greek (RAF) squadrons, 363n.
Green Street, 137, 140, 205
grenades, 349
Greenock, 92
Grenoble, 293
Grey, Sir Edward, 18
grid (*see* gunnery)
Grout, Lieut. Robert C., 421
Grovesnor House Hotel, 110
Guelph, 43, 45
Guilford, 110
Guildhall, 118
Gulf of St. Lawrence (*see* St. Lawrence)
Gunbuster, 265
gunnery: acks, 41, 159; airburst ranging, 138, 154; angle of sight, 247; artillery board, 40, 157, 159, 233, 287n., Appendix E; artillery director, 40; barrage, 233-34;

cardinal-point ranging, 262, 425, 427; close bracket, 230; contour lines, 246; convoy discipline, 77, 78, 81; corrections of the moment, 74, 234; crash action, 79, 127, 138; dial sight, 157; difference from Americans, 263, 263-64n.; direct fire, 260; director, survey, 157; drag ropes, 105n.; drift, 170; driving band, 170; droop, 170; fire for effect, 127, 262; Flying OP (see Flying OP); GPO, 159-61, 301; grid, 157, 159, 160; gun-drill (French 75), 105; jock column (see jock column); jump, 170; lanyard, 104; leaning into barrage, 233; lifts, 233; map reading (English roads), 236-238; meteor telegram, 74, 122, 170; Mike target, 258, 261, 265, 362; Monkey target, 362; muzzle blast, 174; muzzle velocity, 248n.; "off line" or "on line," 128; OP, 1940 style, 265; open sights, 138, 260; pivot gun, 157, 261n.; proximity fuse, 401n.; quick target, 230; ranging by FOO, 244-49; rifling, 170; right ranging (by guns), 247n., 262; salvoes, 171, 174; sight clinometer, 170; smoke screens, 138; spike guns, 97n.; survey, 265n., (surveyor) 333; troop fire, 171, 174; Uncle target, 261-264, 265; Victor target, 262, 264, 265; William target, 263, 263n., 265; zero line, 157
guns: 12-pounder, 198; 18-pounder, 40, 170; 40-mm Bofors, 400; 4.5-inch howitzer, 40, 170; 25-pounder, 29, 120, 134, 135, 170, 171, 173, 197n., 268; 269; Appendix D; 75-mm (1898) French, 104; 75-mm (German), 213; 88-mm, 212, 213;

6-inch, 198; 9.2-inch, 97, 407; 12-inch, 97; 18-inch, 97; Adolf Guns, 391n.

Halifax, 4, 87, 190, 193, 195, 186
Halifax bombers, 363
Hamburg, 327n., 363
Hancock, Bdr. Harry, 207n.
Hanks, Sgt.-Maj. A. C., 131, 374n.
Hardy, Reg, 71
Harris, Major (Lt.-Col.) W. Eric, 30n., 45, 55, 109, 110, 131n., 242, 334
Harrison, Capt. John, 131, 141, 219, 338
Harvey, Lieut. Leonard M., 119, 228, 231, 251, 267, 270, 280, 281, 296, 297
Haskins, Minnie Louise, 50
Hastings, 126, 129, 132-38, 138
Hauser, Capt. (Royal Regt.), 211
Heller, L/Sgt. Irving, 207n.
Hereford, 326, 328, 397
Highland Light Infantry of Canada, 388n.
Hillier, Gnr. George, 290
Hilton, James, 397
Hinman, Major F. K. M., 30
Hipkiss, Gordon, 384n.
Hitler, Adolf, 5, 7, 8, 9, 10, 11, 12, 17, 18, 22, 27n., 28, 42n., 67, 113, 118, 121, 122, 125, 126, 165, 329, 370, 387
Hoag, Ian V., 409
Hog's Back, 130
Holland, 24, 52, 53, 54, 389
hollow charge, 344, 349
Holmbush House, 340
Holocaust Memorial Council, 271
Home Guard, 99, 286, 350
homesickness, 341, 394-96
Hooper, Bdr. Ron, 290
Hoover, Herbert, 22
Horrocks, Lt.-Gen., Sir Brian, 265n.

Horse Palace (CNE), 37, 41
horses, 26*n*.-27*n*.
Horsham, 137, 140, 339
hospitals: 14th General (East
 Grinstead), 326, 365; Petawawa
 Camp, 178
Hotel Dieu, 216
Hotel Metropole, 393*n*.
House of Commons (British), 53, 57,
 67, 270
Howker, Sgt. Ed, 292
Hull (Que.), 43
Hunter, Gnr. "Bull," 39, 46, 352
Hurricanes, 68, 126, 206
Hussars, 1st, 391*n*.
Hutchinson, Major George, 17
Hyde Park Corner, 350

Iceland, 27, 90
IGs (Instructors in Gunnery), 52, 134,
 139, 141, 231, 241, 242, 245, 246,
 249, 261, 324, 325, 343
Imperial Airways, 6
India, 45, 155, 268
Indian (RAF) squadrons, 363*n*.
infantry training for gunners, 349
Instructors in Gunnery (*see* IGs)
International Nickel, 82
invasion barges, German (*see* barges)
invasion stand-to, 101
Ireland, 6, 71, 401
Irish Sea, 138
Irwin, Lieut. F. Ray, 197*n*.
Italy, 270, 300, 322, 331

Japan and Japanese, 17, 135, 197, 200,
 270
Jews, 17; genocide begun, 270
jock column, 77, 127, 258
Johnson, "Ching," 290
Johnson, Bdr. "Red," 272
Jorgens Hill, 74
Journal (Ottawa), 4, 9, 10, 12, 14, 16,
 38, 59, 66

Joyce, William (*see* Lord Haw Haw)
Junkers 88, 226

Kaiser Wilhelm, 24
Kaplan, Lieut. Max, 197*n*.
Karski, Jan, 271*n*.
Keefler, Brig (Maj.-Gen.) R. H., 342,
 343, 368
Kennedy, John F., 68*n*.
Kennedy, Joseph, 68
Kent, 123*n*., 375, 376, 401
Kharkov, 201
Kiely, Gnr. Leonard, 182, 184, 185,
 186
Killeen, Gnr. J. Carl, 40*n*., 207, 207*n*.
King George Officers' Club, 397
King, Wm. Lyon Mackenzie, 11, 22
King's Regulations, Canada, 168
Kingston, 51
Kitching, Maj-Gen George, 77*n*.
Knapp, Lieut. W. W., 379
Kristallnacht, 12
Krawda, Gnr. Joseph, 207*n*.
Krupp, 327*n*.

Labour in Vain pub, 221, 296
LAD (light aid detachment), 352
Lake Cabin Lodges, 37, 42
Lake Huron, 37
Lalonde, L/Bdr. F. H., 207
lamps electric, 106
Lanark and Renfrew Scottish, 12, 13
Lancaster bombers, 363
Land Army girls, 281
language learning *en masse*, 286-7
Lansdowne Park, 25, 33, 36, 38, 39
Lansing, Bdr. Deane Cummings,
 207*n*.
Larkhill and School of Artillery, 52,
 122, 130, 133, 134, 155, 231, 283,
 324, 325, 343, 357
latrine paper, 319, 320
Laurie, Lieut. E. Stuart, 220, 287, 295,
 317

Lavigne, Lloyd George "Doc,"
    32–34, 39, 45, 289, 352
Lavigne, Myrtle, 32
Lawless, Lieut. J. M., 218
Lawson, Lieut. Luke, 230
League of Nations, 42n., 329
leaning into barrage (see gunnery)
Le Cateau, 260
Leicester, 94
Leipzig Barracks, 94, 95
Le Mans, 96
Lennox, Lieut. Gordon E., 378, 390
Leonforte, 131n.
Letitia, 197, 198
Lewis, Lieut. L. W., 218
Lewis machine gun, 198
Lewis's department store, 115
Leyland trucks, 58
Liberators (planes), 363
Libya, 201
lifts (see gunnery)
Lightning (plane), 363
Littlehampton, 225
Liverpool, 91
Llandovery, 250, 251
Lloyd, Lt.-Col. Frank Percival, 55,
    77, 80, 81, 94, 98, 131, 136, 221
Lloyd, Sgt. George, 221
London, 5, 8, 11, 17, 18, 68,
    93n.–94n., 99, 106, 110, 113, 114,
    118, 121, 132, 198, 317, 350, 358,
    390, 394
London Bridge Station, 117
London Illustrated, 155
Lord Haw Haw (Wm. Joyce), 110,
    110n.
losses in material and personnel, Sept.
    1940–June 1942, Appendix G
"lost generation," 13
Louis, Joe, 9
Low Countries, 26, 52, 55, 65, 125
Luftwaffe, 27n., 92n., 113, 114, 118n.,
    200, 226, 227

Lyons, 206, 208

MacDonald, Ramsay, 21, 22
MacFarlane, Lieut. J. Douglas, 391,
    392
Mackie, Colonel, 407
Madagascar, 201
Madawaska, 9, 15, 16
Maginot Line, 28, 50, 53, 66, 76
Magna Carta, 381
Maidstone, 106, 379
Malta, 200
Manchester, 118
map-reading on English roads, 237–39
Maple Leaf Gardens, 163
Marine Court Hotel, 126
Marmon Harrington (trucks), 58
Marsgate, 375, 376
Marsh, Beryl, 384n.
Marsh, Joy, 387
Martello tower, 126
Massey Foundation, 326
Massey, Hon. Vincent, 328
McCarter, Brig. G. A. "Nick," 256
McCarthy, Fireman Tony, 198
McCarthy, Tony, 198
McCleary, H/C Raymond, 74, 112,
    275, 278, 312, 339, 360, 400
McConnell, Sgt. Keith, 39, 290, 348
McCutcheon, Capt. W. J., 205n.
McEwan, Gnr. (Sgt) Charles, 87, 88,
    115
McFetridge, Lieut. M. C., 206n.
McGill University, 326
McGillis, Gnr. "Slim," 46, 114
McIntosh, Gnr. David Brown, 207n.
McIsaac, Lieut. J. F., 197n.
McKenna, Lieut. J. J., 183
McLean, Gnr. Donald, 207
McNaughton, Lt.-Gen. "Andy," 109,
    122, 158n., 174n., 338;
    McNaughton's "travelling circus,"
    96, 110

McNaughton, Capt. E. M. D. "Teddy," 174n.
McNeil, Police Sgt. "Mac," 182, 184, 185
McParland, Gnr. Warren, 115
McPhail, Agnes, 21
Mediterranean, 331, 360
Medland, Major Tom, 30, 55, 58, 75, 109n., 110, 131n.
Megantic (Que.), 196
Merriwell, Frank, 15
Merthyr Tydfil, 252, 253
Messick, 2nd/Lieut. Joseph E., 152
meteor telegram (*see* gunnery)
Meteorological Section (Survey Regt.), 122
Metropolitan Life, 14
Metropolitan (London) Police, 350
Meyer, Capt. Kurt, 5n.
Middleton (Sussex), 225
Middleton, Drew, 69
Midlands, 281
Midway Island (battle of), 417
Mike target (*see* gunnery)
Military Police, 378
militia, 24
Miller, Sgt-Maj. "Dusty," 155, 156, 158, 160, 228, 260
Mills, Gnr. Archie, 207n.
mine-laying, 349
miniature ranges, 229-231
Minsk, 125
Mitchell, Lieut. Jack, 390
Mitchell (plane), 364
Molotov, Soviet foreign sec. Vyacheslav, 51
Molotov cocktails, 51, 100
Monks Common, 335, 337, 338, 340, 343, 348, 351
Monteigne, Sgt. Bill, 221
Montevideo, 49
Montgomery, Lt.-Gen. Bernard, 108, 123n., 126, 127, 267, 268, 284;

inspection by, 368-374; King and Churchill critical of, 372n.
Montreal, 23, 69, 326
morale, 388, 389, 335-344
Morocco, 269
Morrison, Hon. Herbert, 117
Moscow, 8, 51
Mosquito (plane), 364, 364n.
Mount Tremblant, 163
Mulberry, 401
Munich, 27n.
Munich Crisis, 4, 11
Munro, Ken and Joyce, 399
Murdoch, Lt. Wm., 270, 343, 378
Murray, RCN Rear Admiral W. E., 193
Mussolini, Benito, 22, 122n., 328
Mustang (plane), 364, 365
Mutual Network, 44n.
muzzle brake, 412
muzzle velocity (*see* gunnery)

NAAFI (Navy, Army, Airforce Institute), 251, 318, 342, 377
Nairne, Caroline, 4
Narvik, 88
National Research Council, 437
naval losses, Allied, in Atlantic, Appendix F
naval losses, Axis, Appendix F
naval losses, British and U.S., in all theatres, Appendix F
Nebraska, 207
Netherlands (*see* Holland)
Neutrality Act, U.S., 192
Newfoundland, 6, 197
New Guinea, 201
New York, 18, 207
New York Times, 56, 69
New Zealand, 268, 363n.
Newhaven, 206
Newstreet station, 384
Nichols, Beverly, 23
Nissen huts, 339

Nixon, Capt. George, 380
Non-Permanent Active Militia
   (NPAM), 30, 42
Norfolk, Duke and Duchess of, 319
Norfolk Hotel, 110
Normandy invasion, 123n., 365, 389,
   390, 402; numbers involved, 376n.
North Africa, 127, 200, 206, 268, 284
North Atlantic, 71, 137
North Bay, 59
North Camp Station (Aldershot), 94
North Nova Scotia Highlanders,
   388n.
North Shore Regiment, 388n.
Northiam, 129
Northumberland, 350
Norton (motorcycle), 239
Norway, 27, 51, 88
Norwegian (RAF) squadrons, 363n.
Notre Dame de Bon Secours, 212
Nova Scotia, 145
Novello, Ivor, 385
Number 1 CARU (see CARU, #1)
Number 14 General Hospital (see
   General Hospital)
"numbers one," 324
nuns, working as nurses, 216

observation post (see OP)
Occupied Europe, 293
Oflag 7B (prisoner-of-war camp),
   207n.
Ogilvie, Flying Officer Keith
   "Skeets," 99
Old Bailey, 117
OP, 126, 127, 174, 244, 314
operations, Allied: Bodyguard,
   377-78, 387; Fortitude South, 387;
   Fortitude North, 387
operations, German: Adler ("Eagle"),
   92n.; Sealion, 91
Oran, 269
orchestras: 4 RCA, 392n.; Geraldo's,
   393; Robert Farnon's, 398

Ordnance Corps (badges), 168
Orillia, 77
Osler, Lieut. C. R., 109n.
Ostapyk, Nicholas, 39
Ottawa, 9, 11, 156
Ottawa Citizen (see Citizen)
Ottawa Journal (see Journal)
Owen, Lt. Jack, 380
Oxford, 301
Oxford Street, 115
Oxford University, 21

Pacific, 135
Paget, General Sir Bernard, 338
Paladium, 115
Palermo, 322n.
Palestine, 18
panzers, 55, 109, 125
"paper war," 139
paratroopers scare, 103
Pare, Lieut. A. A., 162, 165
Paris, 8, 28
Park Lane Hotel, 110, 292, 383, 395
Pas de Calais, 68, 387
Patton, Lt.-Gen. George, 387
pay and allowances, 83n., 358n.
Pearkes, Maj-Gen. J. R., VC, 121
Pearl Harbor, 135, 192
Peggy's Tea Shop, 138n.
Pembroke, 4, 15, 16, 60, 61, 63, 171,
   183, 188
Pembroke Patrol, 64
Penelope, HMS, 200, 200n.
Peppal, Lieut. J. R., 109n.
permanent force, 155
Petawawa Military Camp, 4, 55, 57,
   59, 60, 61, 73, 77, 145, 146, 154,
   158, 158n., 162, 163, 181, 188,
   196, 339
Petawawa Point, 16, 73
Petawawa River, 182
Petrolia, 115
Petworth, 276-7
Philippines, 201

Phillips, Sgt. George R. "Lefty," 290, 412*n.*
Phillips, Gnr. Hordon J., 207*n.*
Phippen, Mrs. F. H., 35*n.*
phonetic alphabet, 361
"Phoney War," 27, 50, 65
PIAT (Projector Infantry Anti Tank), 349
Picadilly, 110, 350, 390
Picadilly Circus, 366
"Picadilly commandos," 359
pilotless aircraft (*see* V-I)
pistol-shooting practise, 349
Pitman, Senator Key, 68
Plate, River, 49
Plunkett, Al, 40, Appendix A
Poland, 7, 10, 18, 26, 27, 49
Polish underground, 271
Polish (RAF) squadrons, 363*n.*
Portland Road, 259
Porto Empèdocle, 322*n.*
Portsmouth, 205
Possingworth, 137, 139
Pourville, 205
Pressier, June, 277
Price, Sgt. C. B., 46
Prince of Wales, 382
prisoners of war taken at Dieppe, manacling of, 207, Appendix H
Prize Troop, 210
propaganda leaflets, 28
proximity fuse (*see* gunnery)
Prudhomme, Gnr. "Bo," 46
Puys, 206
Pyrenees, 293

quads, 58, 350
Quebec, 70, 87
Queen Elizabeth, 382
Queen Mary, 382
Queen Victoria Hospital, 367*n.*
Queen's Bar, Aldershot, 111
Queen's Bar, Hastings, 138*n.*

Queen's Own Cameron Highlanders of Canada, 206
Queen's Own Rifles of Canada, 388*n.*
queues, 384
Quisling, Vidkun, 51

"R Talk" (radio telephony), 361
radios, 52, 52*n.*, 134, 215; #11-sets, 105
RAF, 24, 50, 56, 60*n.*, 92*n.*, 99, 116, 118*n.*, 209, 214, 238, 284, 327, 363, 382, 384; flying school, 294
Railway Hotel, 221, 222, 279, 336
Ralston, Hon. Colonel J. L., 102
Ram tank, 345
Ramillies, HMS, 201
Ramsgate, 375
ranging (*see* gunnery)
rations, 98
RCHA (*see* artillery regiments)
Reader, Gnr. Cy, 274, 277
recreational trucks, 250
recruiting, 31, 65
Red Dean, 381
Red Lion, 138*n.*
Redesdale, 348, 350, 351
Reeve, Gnr. Ted, 163
refugees (children), 198
Regal Building, 31
regiments (*see* artillery regiments)
Régiment de le Chaudiere, 388*n.*
Regimental Sgt.-Major (RSM), 340
Regina Rifles, 388*n.*, 391
Reichstag, 8, 11
Remarque, Erich Maria, 21, 23
REME, 19th Light Aid Detachment, 378
Renfrew, 9
reprisals, 423
respirators, 42, 80
Revenge, HMS, 89, 90
Rhineland, 4, 8

Rhyl, 346, 347
Richardson, Sgt-Major F. H. R., 325
Richardson, Capt. Tommy, 238, 279, 341, 343*n.*, 351, 352
"Richardson's Bypass," 341
Rileys (*see* Royal Hamilton Light Infantry)
Ritt, Freddie, 12, 189
Ritz Hotel, 252, 388
road signs (lack of), 236-39
roadbuilding, 348
Roberts, Maj-Gen. J. Hamilton, 97, 233, 300, 301; getting guns back from Brest, Appendix B
Rome, 328
Rommel, Field Marshal, 201, 268, 370
Roosevelt, Franklin D., 68, 271*n.*, 417
Roskill, Capt. S. W., 193
Ross, Colin "Hefty," 24
Ross rifles, 100
Rotary Club, 7
Rouen, 216
Roy, Alice, 16, 189
Royal Airforce (*see* RAF)
Royal Artillery, 158
Royal Cdn Corps of Signals, 51
Royal Cdn Horse Artillery (*see* RCHA)
Royal Cdn Navy, 191, 192
Royal Flying Corps (WW I), 163
Royal Hamilton Light Infantry, 35*n.*, 128, 225, 235
Royal Military College, 42, 45
Royal Navy, 92, 191, 192, 205
Royal Oak, HMS, 49
Royal Pavilion, 291
Royal Regiment of Canada, 35*n.*, 205, 207, 208, 209, 225, 235
Royal School of Artillery, 52
Royal Scott (train), 93

Royal Welsh Fusiliers, Angelsey Battalion, 100
Royal Winnipeg Rifles, 388*n.*, 390
Ruhr, 363
Rumania, 17
Runfold, 133
Runneymeade, 381
Russia (Russians), 7, 27, 50, 121, 130, 133, 200, 227; territory and equipment losses, 125-6
Rye, 126
Ryerson, Lieut. (Royal Regt.), 211, 212

Saarbrücken, 50
St. Brides Church, 117
St. Lawrence: River, 8; Seaway, 32*n.*; Gulf of, 190, 195
St. Martin-in-the-Fields, 136
St. Matthew's Church, 153
St. Paul's Cathedral, 99, 115, 116, 117
Salamanca barracks, 108, 121
Salisbury Plain, 227
Sarnia, 43
"Saturday-night soldiers," 12, 42
Saunders, Lieut. Tait M. "Moose," 205, 207*n.*, 317
Saunders, Gnr. Wm, "Buck," 82, 352
Savage, Major Gordon C., 338, 340, 373
Savoy Hotel, 223, 252, 393
Scandinavia, 387
Scapa Flow, 49
Scheer (battleship), 24*n.*
Scotland, 23, 312, 350, 357
Scott, Gnr. Wm. Mortimer, 207*n.*
Seaford, 123, 134, 232
second front, 381
Secord, Gnr. Les, 89
Sedlescombe, 126
Sennybridge, 138, 139*n.*, 224, 227, 231, 233, 237, 240-58, 260, 283, 303, 311, 357, 402
Seulles River, 390

Shaw, George Bernard, 8
shell dressings, 376
Shelley, Norman, 57
Shilo, Camp, 145, 146
Shireland Pub, 259
Shrapnel, Lt.-Gen. Henry, 158
shrapnel shells, 158, 159
Sicily, 131n., 300, 322, 327
Siegfried Line, 8
Simonds, Lt.-Gen. Guy Granville,
   77n., 368
Simpson's (store), 44
Sinclair, Lieut. Wm. Reynolds, 230,
   280, 282, 290, 305
Singapore, 196
"Sitzkrieg war," 51
Six Bells, 138n.
skiing, 162-65
Slindon, 219
Smith, Major N. E., 131n.
Smith, E. Norman, 66
Smolensk, 126
Smythe, Major Connie, 163
SNAFU, 121, 122, 258
sonar, ship's, 149
songs (soldiers'), 40
South Africa, 268
South African (RAF) squadrons, 363n.
South African War, 260
South Downs, 134, 232, 233, 289, 296
South Saskatchewan Regiment, 123,
   206n.
Southeastern Command, 108, 286
Southern Railway, 221
Southover Hall, 135
Spain, 208
Spam, 223
Spaniards, 20, 293
Spanish Civil War, 9, 51
special duty, warned for, 187
Spitfire, 6, 68, 126, 206, 338, 382
Sportsmen's Battery, 163
SS, 12th, 5n.

SS-Leibstandarte, 5
Stacey, Mrs., 297
Stalag 8B, 207n.
Stalingrad, 226, 284
stand-to position, 225
Star Inn, 232, 289
Sten guns, 312
Stettin, 207n.
Steuart-Jones, Capt. (Major, Lt.-Col.)
   E. W., 82, 279, 291, 295, 313, 316,
   318, 319, 320, 338, 343, 344n.
Stevenage, 350
Stevens, Gnr. Bill, 255
Stevenson, Lieut. W. D., 197n., 218
Stewart, Lieut. (Royal Regt.), 210
"sticky-bomb," 139
Stokes, Gnr. Morley, 87-88
Stormont, Dundas and Glengarry
   Regiment, 388n.
Strand, the, 115, 117
submarines (see U-boats)
Sudenland, 5
Suez, 200, 226, 268
Supermarine (Spitfire), 382
supernumeraries, 218n.
Surrey, 123n.
surveyor (see gunnery)
Sussex, 123n, 128, 232, 243, 254, 303,
   311, 353
Sutherland flyingboat, 190
Sveinson, Gnr. Egill, 207n.
Sweden, 27
Swordfish (plane), 197
Syracuse, 322n.

Tangmere airfield, 206, 276, 364
tank shooting, 228-29
Taylor, Lieut. (Royal Regt), 211
Tees, Lt.-Col. (Brig) P. C., 121, 233,
   241, 321, 323, 343
Telescombe Cliffs and Hall, 217
Thames, 49, 55
Thompson, Dorothy, 69
Thompson, Capt. W. B., 208

"thunderflashes" (69-grenades), 124
Tin Hat Chronicle, 45
Tobruk, 199, 200, 201, 268
Todd, Lt.-Col. P. A. Stanley, 136,
  140, 219, 233, 235, 247, 256, 258,
  270, 280, 283
Toronto Telegram, 163
Toulouse, 293
Tower of London, 110n.
Trafalgar, Battle of, 192
Trafalgar Square, 115, 116, 119, 208,
  269
Trans-Canada Highway, 160
Tremaine, Col. A. V., 59
Tripartite Pact nations, 270
troop train, 82
Tunbridge Wells, 130
Tunisia, 284
Turnbull, Lieut. Ken H., 378, 401
"Twilight War" (see "Phoney War")
Typhoon fighters, 364

U-Boat, 199
ultimatum, 19
Uncle target (see gunnery)
Underground (French), 293
uniforms, shortages of, 36n.
Union Station (Ottawa), 71
United Nations, 270
United States, 18
Upper Canada College, 100
Upper Ottawa Valley, 10
Utah, 7

V-1 (vergeltungswaffe-1, flying
  bombs), 353n., 399, Appendix J
Vale of the White Horse, 111
Van Steeburgh, Lt.-Col. W. E., 171,
  172, 173
VE-Day, 198n.
Verneuil, 214
Versailles, 5
veterans (WW I), 17
Vichy France, 206, 208, 293

Victor target (see gunnery)
Victoria, B.C., 145
Victory Loan, 377
VIPs, 156, 171

WAAF (Women's Auxiliary Airforce),
  378
Walberton, 205, 219
Waldershare Park, 375, 391
Wales, 99, 227, 240, 350
Walker, Gnr. E. C., 290
Wallis, A. J., 423
Walton, Gnr. H. W., 272, 274
Wantage, 111
War Measures Act (Cdn), 7
Warsaw, 11, 26, 27
Washington, 270
Waterloo Station, 115, 116, 119
Waterloo, Battle of, 156, 192
waterproofing gunk, 402
Waters, Capt. John M., 191, 193
Watkins, Eddie, 277
Wavell, General, 267
WAVS (Women's Auxiliary Voluntary
  Service), 280, 297
Wedd, Lieut. W. G. R., 209
Welch, Capt. Malcolm "Tim," 402
Wellington bomber, 300
Welsh, Major G. A. "Tiger," 30n.,
  55, 131n.
West Downs, 303
West End, 111, 114, 358
West Wall, 357, 364, 370
Westerbork Concentration Camp,
  271n.
Westergate Wood House, 205
Western Front, 27, 54, 111n.
Westminster Abbey, 8
Weymouth, 376
White Armoured Scout Car, 378
Whitechurch, 255
Whitehall, 18
Whitelaw, Col. R. G., 147, 148-52,
  165

Whiteways Crossroads, 320
Wibe, Sgt-Major Arthur, 34, 42
Wilkinson, Gnr. M. J., 306
Wilkinson, Royal Navy Signaller, 215
Wilcox. Gnr. Tony, 45, 46, 47
Wilfrid Laurier University, 31
Wilhelmina (Queen of the
   Netherlands), 99
Wilhelmshaven, 24
William target (*see* gunnery)
Williamsburg, 165
Wilmot, Jerry, 398
Wilson, Gnr. Boba, 257
Wilson, Lieut. (Capt) (Major) Don,
   45, 46, 47, 82, 127, 135, 224, 231,
   247, 248, 272, 287, 289, 292, 293
Winchelsea, 126, 128
Windsor, 58
Women's Auxiliary Volunteer
   Service (*see* WAVS)

Woodrow, Capt. G. E., 109*n*.
World War I, 21, 42*n*., 87, 121, 159,
   162, 188, 260
Worthing, 312, 340
Worthington, Lt.-Col. (Maj-Gen)
   Frank, 76, 77, 78, 79, 80*n*., 133
Wren, Major Gordon, 338, 340*n*.,
   379
Wyght, F. C. L., 276

Yapton, 225, 275
YMCA, 117, 273, 377
York, Duke of, 158
Young, Captain McGregor, 41, 75,
   111, 113, 131*n*., 133, 338
Yugoslavian (RAF) squadrons, 363*n*.

Zeppelin, 6